CHRISTY MATHEWSON

CHRISTY MATHEWSON
A Game-by-Game Profile of a Legendary Pitcher

by
RONALD A. MAYER

McFarland & Company, Inc., Publishers
Jefferson, North Carolina, and London

ALSO BY RONALD A. MAYER

The 1937 Newark Bears

*Perfect! Biographies and Lifetime Statistics
of 14 Pitchers of "Perfect" Baseball Games,
with Summaries and Boxscores* (McFarland, 1991)

WITH GERALD TOMLINSON

The New Jersey Book of Lists

The present work is a reprint of the library bound edition of
Christy Mathewson: A Game-by-Game Profile of a Legendary Pitcher, *first published in 1993 by McFarland.*

LIBRARY OF CONGRESS CATALOGUING-IN-PUBLICATION DATA

Mayer, Ronald A., 1934–
 Christy Mathewson : a game-by-game profile of a legendary pitcher / by Ronald A. Mayer.
  p. cm.
 Includes bibliographical references and index.

 ISBN 978-0-7864-4121-1
 softcover : 50# alkaline paper ∞

 1. Mathewson, Christy, 1880–1925. 2. Baseball players—United States—Biography. I. Title.
GV865.M37M39 2008
796.357'092—dc20   92-50890

British Library cataloguing data are available

©1993. Ronald A. Mayer. All rights reserved

*No part of this book may be reproduced or transmitted in any form
or by any means, electronic or mechanical, including photocopying
or recording, or by any information storage and retrieval system,
without permission in writing from the publisher.*

Cover photograph: Christy Mathewson, pitcher for the New York Giants, ca. Dec. 14, 1910 (Library of Congress)

Manufactured in the United States of America

*McFarland & Company, Inc., Publishers
 Box 611, Jefferson, North Carolina 28640
  www.mcfarlandpub.com*

To Daniel and Stephanie
with love
from Poppy

Acknowledgments

I would like to thank the following members of the Society of American Baseball Research for their prompt and generous assistance: Arthur Ahrens, Bob Bluthardt, Pastor Leslie J. Boone, Morris Eckhouse, Myron Eisenberg, David M. Goodman, Christopher D. Green, Tom Knight, Sutton Landry, Steve Mark, John J. O'Malley, Frank Phelps, Bob Richardson, William Ruiz, John Schwartz, Jim Skipper, Mike Sparrow, Keith Sutton and my friend Gerald Tomlinson.

Frank Williams of the SABR deserves special recognition for his valuable contributions. Frank patiently answered all my "off the wall" questions and, thankfully, set me straight about the scoring peculiarities from 1901 to 1919. He indeed was a savior.

I would also like to express my appreciation to those who graciously assisted me in my research efforts: Bill Deane, senior research associate, and Pat Kelly, photo collection manager, both from the National Baseball Library in Cooperstown; Narda Tafuri, librarian at Miller Library, Keystone Junior College, LaPlume, Pennsylvania; Doris Dysinger, Special Collections/University Archives Assistant, Ellen Clarke Bertrand Library, Bucknell University; and the staffs of the East Hanover Township Public Library and the Morris County Free Library in Whippany, both located in New Jersey.

Finally, if not for the love and support of my wife, Arlene, this book would still be a dream.

Contents

	Acknowledgments	*vii*
	Preface	*xi*
1	Factoryville to New York	*1*
2	Inauspicious Start, 1900	*9*
3	Rookie Season, 1901	*18*
4	Saved by McGraw, 1902	*36*
5	First 30-Game Season, 1903	*50*
6	First Pennant!, 1904	*67*
7	World Series Hero, 1905	*86*
8	A Bout with Diphtheria, 1906	*108*
9	Most Victories in National League, 1907	*127*
10	Most Career Victories, 1908	*147*
11	Lowest Career ERA, 1909	*169*
12	Most Victories in National League, Again, 1910	*186*
13	M and M Boys, 1911	*201*
14	Tough World Series Loss, 1912	*221*
15	Masterful Control, 1913	*243*

CONTENTS

16	Last Great Season, 1914	*263*
17	The End Is Near, 1915	*281*
18	Farewell Matty, 1916	*295*

Appendices

Appendix A:	Milestones in the Career of Mathewson	*311*
Appendix B:	Mathewson's Lifetime Pitching Record	*313*
Appendix C:	Mathewson's 373 Career Victories	*314*
Appendix D:	Classic Matchups: Mathewson vs. Brown	*339*
Appendix E:	Mathewson's Career Victories vs. Opposing Teams	*340*
Appendix F:	Mathewson's 24-Game Winning Streak vs. St. Louis	*341*
Appendix G:	Mathewson's 22-Game Winning Streak vs. Cincinnati	*342*

Notes — *343*

Bibliography — *353*

Index — *359*

Preface

Christy Mathewson pitched for the New York Giants in the National League from 1900 to 1916. During this 17-year span this remarkable right-hander established himself as one of the premier pitchers of his era and of all time.

Mathewson won 373 games, third highest in baseball history (tops in the National League with Grover Cleveland Alexander) and lost 188, resulting in a .665 winning percentage, the sixth highest in the major leagues. His lifetime earned run average is a minuscule 2.13, placing him fifth among the all-time leaders. Not surprisingly, his single-season achievements are equally impressive. As a result of his pitching exploits, Mathewson has left an indelible mark on the National Pastime.

Christy Mathewson, the man, left an even larger imprint on baseball than his pitching records indicate. Tall, handsome, intelligent and soft-spoken, the fans loved him; the press adored him; his teammates idolized him. He was a devout Methodist who rarely drank, swore or smoked—an All-American boy. He was a refreshing hero in the rough, rowdy and raucous world of baseball. He was larger than life.

Said baseball historian Alexander Scourby, "All at once the game received a new respectability. Young ladies could now ask their escorts to take them to the Polo Grounds to see a college boy play."[1]

Donald Honig writes in *The Greatest Pitchers of All Time*, "He was the first American sports hero whose appeal crossed all social, economic and cultural boundaries."[2] Clearly, Christy Mathewson was a unique individual both on and off the field, publicly and privately.

The focus of this book, however, is on Matty's achievements on the mound, which have justifiably reached legendary proportions. I have also attempted to swing a wider brush to capture the charm and innocence of this fascinating period in baseball history. To a lesser degree, I touch on Mathewson's personal life and those colorful and wacky characters of the early 1900s—personalities like John McGraw, Joe McGinnity, Rube Marquard, Charlie Faust and Bugs Raymond to name a few.

What kind of a book is this? That question can best be answered by defining what it isn't. It isn't a biography and it isn't a chronology. It's something in between; a hybrid I call a chronography.

In reality, it is a thorough examination of every game pitched by the immortal Mathewson, and a nostalgic return to the wonderful and glorious early decades of the 1900s when the National League was growing, the American League was still an infant and the players were wild and unruly. I hope I have captured it all in an interesting format.

Chapter 1
Factoryville to New York

"Matty was the greatest pitcher who ever lived, in my opinion," claimed Fred Snodgrass, a teammate of Mathewson from 1908 to 1915.[1] Chief Meyers, a Cahuilla Indian, who caught almost every game Matty pitched for seven years, agreed. He was "the greatest that ever lived."[2] In *The Hurlers,* author Kevin Kerrane boldly claims, "Christy Mathewson was the greatest pitcher of the dead-ball era, if not the best pitcher in baseball history."[3] In 1955, at the age of 73, Branch Rickey, who had a keen eye for baseball talent, proclaimed in an interview with Gerald Holland, "The greatest pitchers I have ever seen were Christy Mathewson and Jerome Dean."[4] Famed sportswriter John Kieran once said, "Matty was the greatest pitcher I ever saw. He was the greatest anybody ever saw."[5] High praise like this, voiced by baseball experts and Mathewson's peers, clearly places this immortal right-hander among the greatest pitchers who ever graced a mound.

Whether Matty was *the greatest* pitcher who ever lived is moot and a subject avid baseball fans delight in arguing. Some say Cy Young was the greatest, others Walter Johnson and still others will vote for "Three Finger" Brown, Rube Waddell, Eddie Plank, Ed Walsh, Grover Cleveland Alexander and more recent heroes like Bob Feller, Warren Spahn, Sandy Koufax, Tom Seaver. The list is endless.

Obviously, they were all great. And Christy Mathewson's career and single-season records compare favorably with all of them. He was a remarkable pitcher and an extraordinary man. These two facts are indisputable.

In his 17 years in the National League, almost all of which were spent with the New York Giants,* Christy Mathewson won 373 regular season baseball games while losing 188 for a .665 winning percentage. His victory total ranks first in the National League (tied with Grover Cleveland Alexander), third in major league history and his winning percentage ranks sixth. His career ERA of 2.13 is the fifth lowest of all time. In addition, Mathewson's 79 shutouts is third best in the major leagues behind Alexander (90) and Walter Johnson (110).

---

*In 1916 Mathewson won one game pitching for Cincinnati. He also managed the Reds from 1916 to 1918.

I

The folks in Factoryville are proud of their Hall of Fame hero (photo by Arlene C. Mayer).

Matty won 20 or more games in a season 13 times (12 consecutive). He won 30 or more in a season four times and had league leading winning percentages in 1905 (.795) and 1909 (.806). In five consecutive seasons his earned run average was two or under, and in 1909 it was an incredible 1.14. He led the National League in total victories for a season four times; ERA five times; total games once, games started and completed twice; most innings pitched once; most strikeouts five times and most shutouts four times.

Mathewson's outstanding performances in four World Series did nothing to diminish his fame. He appeared in 11 games and, in spite of a deceiving 5-5 record, pitched brilliantly. For example, in 1905, in an incredible display of pitching skill, he hurled three shutouts against the Philadelphia Athletics. He also holds World Series records for most shutouts (4), complete games (10) and is second in losses (5), games started (11) and innings pitched (101.2). His composite World Series ERA is a very low 1.15.

But there was much more to Christy Mathewson than pitching statistics and records. One could argue convincingly that Mathewson, like Babe Ruth who restored faith in the game after the 1919 Black Sox scandal, brought respectability and acceptance to a popular game suffering from a severely tarnished image. Mathewson brought with him a clean-cut look, impeccable moral standards and an aloof, aristocratic reserve.

1 • *Factoryville to New York*

In the early 1900s professional baseball was still a rowdy and raucous game, played by ruffians from all walks of life who were tough talkers and hard drinkers. Umpires were treated miserably and fair game for players, managers and even spectators. They often literally risked life and limb. Heavy gambling was commonplace and eventually culminated in the 1919 Black Sox Scandal. It was not a pretty picture.

Davy Jones, who played in the major leagues from 1901 to 1915, told author Lawrence Ritter in his classic book *Glory of Their Times*, "I was going with a girl at the time and after I became a professional ball player her parents refused to let her see me anymore. In those days a lot of people looked upon ball players as bums, too lazy to work for a living."[6] In the same book, famed outfielder Sam Crawford (1899–1917) commented, "Baseball players weren't too much accepted in those days, either, you know. We were considered pretty crude."[7] The legendary Connie Mack once said that sensible people thought the game "to be only one degree above grand larceny, arson and mayhem."[8] Rube Marquard's father told him, "Ball players are no good and they never will be any good."[9] In later years, Marquard's father changed his opinion and could often be heard boasting about Rube's accomplishments on the field.

Clearly, a baseball game at the turn of the century was not the place frequented by ladies and young boys. Understating the real world of that time, it simply was not a respectable game. What it needed was a genuine hero, the kind later created in Hollywood, but believable. And that's exactly what the American public was handed.

Christy Mathewson, fresh out of Bucknell College, was a tall, nobly handsome young man who in some youthful photographs, reveals an unfailing resemblance to movie actor James Caan. Matty rarely drank, swore or smoked. The few occasions when he did it was always in moderation. He was reserved, somewhat shy, especially around people he didn't know. His aloof and aristocratic public behavior, which is well documented, added to his legend and idolatry. Product of a small, rural community, he was a devout Methodist who did not play ball on Sundays.

For the most part Mathewson was a mild tempered man. He could, however, be provoked to anger as baseball historian Harold Seymour records in his book *Baseball, the Golden Age*. Matty had slugged a lemonade boy at a game in Philadelphia and the boy came away with a split lip and several loose teeth. Seymour also points out that Matty was not loved by all. Some players felt he had a "swelled head," some fans labeled him "brusque and aloof" and on occasion he had been "ungracious" with photographers. These human traits, infrequently as they were displayed, did little to tarnish his image and legend. Christy Mathewson was indeed an anachronism in an era when baseball players were unruly and undisciplined on and off the field. Matty gave the game what it needed most, respectability.

Chief Meyers said of Mathewson, "He had the sweetest, most gentle nature. Gentle in every way."[10] In *Baseball: An Informal History,* author Douglass Wallop quotes a reporter in 1909 as follows: "Christy Mathewson talks like a Harvard graduate, looks like an actor, acts like a businessman and impresses you as an all-around gentleman."[11] Author Noel Hynd in his wonderful book *The Giants of the Polo Grounds* wrote, "In time he [Mathewson] would become exactly what the image-conscious National League most needed: a stellar athlete of impeccable personal behavior, an example to be put before the adults and children of the nation."[12] Writes Donald Honig in his book *The National League,* "Christy Mathewson became the nation's first genuinely admired sports idol."[13]

Christy Mathewson was born on August 12, 1880, in Factoryville, Pennsylvania, a small town in the heart of the state's anthracite coal region. It is slightly more than 10 miles north of Scranton, a city where Mathewson would play some early baseball.

Matty was the oldest of five children born to Gilbert and Minerva Mathewson. Both parents were born in England and were considered wealthy. Gilbert was a gentleman farmer and Matty's mother a wealthy woman in her own right.

Factoryville at the time was populated by simple, religious country folk who scorned the evils of drink. It is no surprise, then, that Matty's mother wanted him to become a preacher. In spite of his mother's wishes and the religious atmosphere in which he was raised, Matty said, "I never gave the matter serious thought."[14] He did, however, promise his mother he would never play baseball on Sundays. Mathewson was true to his word. In fairness, it must be pointed out that Sunday baseball was only legal in Chicago, Cincinnati and St. Louis during the years Matty was pitching, which made his promise much easier to keep.

According to his own admission, at an early age Mathewson wanted to be a professional baseball player. He started his path to the major leagues, after graduating from Factoryville grammar school, when he enrolled at Keystone Academy, a school founded by his great-grandmother. At Keystone he was a member of the football team and was the captain of the baseball team, where he played second and pitched. He also pitched for the YMCA in Scranton. After Keystone, Matty entered Bucknell College in Lewisburg, in 1898, on a scholarship. Lewisburg is approximately 100 miles southwest of Factoryville, a sizeable journey in the days of the horse and buggy. At Bucknell Matty was a well-rounded, popular student and athlete. In today's vernacular, he would be considered "a big man on campus."

He was class president, a member of Phi Gamma Delta fraternity, active in several literary societies, a member of the glee club and an excellent chess and checker player. In those days checkers was a very popular sport, particularly in the clubhouse.

Mathewson's checker playing is legendary. He often played more

Top: Mathewson grew up in this house in Factoryville, now occupied by Mrs. Betty Gennarelli. A new porch is under construction. Note the barn to the left. *Bottom:* Still standing today, this barn is supposedly the one Mathewson threw baseballs at as a youth in Factoryville (photos by Andy Conklin).

than one opponent at a time and would beat them all. It's been told that at the Pittsburgh Athletic Club he once played 12 opponents simultaneously in chess and beat all of them. Mathewson was also a good billiard player, fair golfer and a great poker player who was not averse to making a few dollars.

On the diamond, Mathewson was a superstar. He often hooked up in pitching duels with a great left-hander from a rival Pennsylvania school, Gettysburg. The pitcher's name was Eddie Plank. After pitching one year for Bucknell (1899), Matty played professionally for Taunton that summer. In those days collegiate rules permitted students to play professionally.

In football his powerful legs made him a strong fullback and great drop-kicker. His nickname was "Gum Boots" and he won three letters in football. Walter Camp, credited with significantly changing the game of football, thus earning the name "Father of American Football," selected Mathewson (as a kicker) for his All-American team in 1900. Commented Camp, "He's just about the greatest kicker I've ever seen in years, that Mathewson boy. Maybe the greatest kicker ever."[15]

In spite of all this activity, Mathewson still found time for romance. His campus sweetheart was Jane Stoughton and he married the young lady in 1903. They had one child, Christopher, Jr., which is a tragic story in itself. In 1933, eight years after Mathewson passed away, Christopher's young bride was killed when a plane he was piloting crashed. Young Christopher was badly hurt and had to have his leg amputated. In 1950, at the age of 43, Christopher Mathewson, Jr., was burned to death in an explosion in his home in Helotis, Texas.

Mathewson was a big lad, even as a youngster, and would eventually reach six feet one and a half inches and weigh 195 pounds. In Factoryville they called him "Husk." In the National League he was tagged with the sobriquet "Big Six." The origin of his nickname to this day is still uncertain.

McGraw, for example, said "Big Six" came from a prominent boxer in New York. Some said baseball writer Sam Crane hung the name on Mathewson after a famed New York City firehouse. Big Six was the number of the firehouse noted for its efficiency in speeding to many of the city's large conflagrations. Still others claimed it came from the Big Six Typographical Union, a powerful force at the time. The matter was thought to be settled in 1923, by Mathewson himself, in response to a letter from *The Sporting News*. Matty claimed "Big Six" simply referred to his height. When the author checked with *The Sporting News* to verify the response no reference could be found in Mathewson's voluminous file. It appears, however, there was no confusion to whom the nickname belonged and about its popularity. Whether true or not, it's been written that the nickname was so well known that Mathewson received mail addressed simply with the number 6.

Mathewson made his debut in professional baseball in the summer of 1899 with the Taunton club of the New England League. Prior to Taunton, Mathewson played semipro ball for the Honesdale Reds (Orange County League) in 1898 and 1899. In the summer of 1898 his record was 8-3, including a 5-1 victory at Port Jervis for the league championship. He played again for Honesdale in 1899 but left for Taunton, after pitching a three-hitter, on July 18.

Taunton at the time was a small industrial city about 30 miles south of Boston. The manager of Taunton was Nathaniel Kellog who is credited with bringing Mathewson into professional baseball. He spotted the youngster on the sandlots of Pennsylvania and convinced him to join the Taunton club. He played in only 17 games and posted a 5-2 record (one account had his record at 2-12). He earned $90 a month, but the team went broke and he had a difficult time collecting. On the last day of the season Mathewson beat the Portland Sea Gulls, managed by John "Phenomenal" Smith, who pitched in three professional baseball leagues during his eight-year career—Union Association, American Association and finally the National League.

After the loss Smith met up with Mathewson and told him that the New England League would not be operating the following year. Smith then told Mathewson that he would have a team somewhere and he wanted Matty to pitch for him.

That fall Mathewson returned to Bucknell to continue his studies. During the football season the team traveled to Philadelphia for a game and the trip turned out to be the most important of his life. Prior to the game Matty was visited by none other than Phenomenal Smith. The persistent Smith, no doubt recognizing Mathewson's pitching potential, made him a firm salary offer to play for his Norfolk club. According to Mathewson, the conversation went like this: "'Mathewson,' he said to me that day in Philadelphia, 'next summer I am going to manage the Norfolk team in the Virginia League, and I'll give you a steady job at eighty dollars a month. Your contract with the Taunton club called for ninety, I know, but you did not collect it, whereas you are sure of this money because the Norfolk team has substantial backing.'"

Matty immediately signed the contract and later in the afternoon kicked two field goals for Bucknell in a 20–10 loss to the University of Pennsylvania. Back at the hotel, Smith met up with Mathewson again and, obviously in a good mood, gave his newly signed right-hander a raise in salary!

"You played a great game this afternoon," he said. "Because I like the way you kicked those goals from the field, I am going to make your salary ninety dollars instead of eighty."[16]

With Mathewson's determination to become a major league pitcher, and Smith's offer in hand, he joined the Norfolk club in the Virginia League in 1900. It was to be the beginning of the legend. By the end of

July, Mathewson posted an outstanding 20-2 record for a phenomenal .909 winning percentage! It came as no surprise when the New York Giants, a struggling last-place team with numerous problems, called him in late July.

This was the beginning of Christy Mathewson's journey on the road to the Hall of Fame and baseball immortality. This long road, however, would have some potholes along the way with the first one coming in surprising and rapid fashion.

Chapter 2

Inauspicious Start, 1900

W	L	Pct	ERA
0	3	.000	5.08

Baseball in 1900, and the decades thereafter, was a marvelous game. It was a game played on natural grass with rough infields littered with stones that frequently caused erratic play. Gloves were tiny, often not much larger than a hand, and designed more for protection than for catching a ball.

It was also a game, unlike today, that thrived on strategies designed to manufacture runs. The hit and run, sacrifice bunt and steal were basic offensive weapons employed frequently by managers. The dead ball contributed to the strategy too. It virtually eliminated the home run and its dramatic and sudden influence on the outcome of a game. Assuring the ball remained dead, it was rarely replaced with a fresh, clean version during the game. And if that wasn't enough to keep the ball lifeless, the practice of the day was for spectators to return all balls hit into the stands! Sam Crawford, the great Cincinnati and Detroit outfielder, claimed, "We'd play a whole game with one ball, if it stayed in the park."[1]

These conditions made for an exciting game that allowed the pitcher to let batters swing away, not fearing the long ball, and that let the defense take over. Christy Mathewson was ideally suited for this type of pitching and he used it to perfection. He was strong, but still paced himself during the game. He was a smart hurler who knew each batter's "groove," the terminology of the day, which meant the hitter's weakness. Once Matty discovered that weakness, whether it was location or a specific pitch, that's all the batter would see.

This was how baseball was played in 1900 when Mathewson arrived at the Polo Grounds from Norfolk, his minor league club, in late July sporting an impressive 20-2 record. Obviously, the Giants were anxious to see what the kid right-hander could do in the big time.

The arrangement the Giants had with Norfolk was straightforward. The Giants would pay $1,500 (some reports were as high as $2,000) and if they liked what they saw, they would keep Mathewson. If not, they would send him back to Norfolk.

Mathewson, the devoted family man, is giving his son, Christopher, a lesson in pitching (photo courtesy Miller Library, Keystone Junior College, LaPlume, Pennsylvania).

Not yet 20, this soon-to-be baseball idol of America brought with him, if not experience, certainly a mighty pitching arsenal. Mathewson possessed a fast ball that future Giant manager John McGraw said matched Amos Rusie and Walter Johnson, a curve that rivaled Nap Rucker's, and his invincible fadeaway, a pitch destined to become famous.

Though he was not the originator of the fadeaway, Matty was the first pitcher to give it widespread popularity. The fadeaway is today's screwball, further popularized by Carl Hubbell in the 1930s and later by Tug McGraw, among others. For a right-hander, like Mathewson, the ball is thrown with a reverse twist (counter-clockwise) of the wrist so that the ball

2 • Inauspicious Start, 1900

breaks in on right-handed batters and away from left-handed batters. It had a deadly effect on hitters, but was used sparingly by Mathewson because it took a toll on his arm. As he admitted in his book, *Pitching in a Pinch*, "Pitching it 10 or 12 times a game kills my arm, so I save it for the pinches."[2]

Apparently Mathewson learned of the pitch, and first started developing it, while at Taunton in 1899. At Taunton he met up with a pitcher named Virgil Ned Garvin who was trying to make it back to the major leagues. Garvin had pitched unimpressively in two games for Philadelphia in 1896. Hoping a unique pitch would return him to the major leagues, Garvin was working on this reverse curve when Mathewson met up with him. Although by most accounts Garvin is credited with bringing the fadeaway to Mathewson's attention, others credit a left-handed pitcher by the name of Williams. Regardless of who was responsible, Matty perfected and exploited the pitch to its fullest.

When Mathewson finally arrived, the New York Giants were in last place with a dismal record of 23-43. It was clear that the root cause of all their problems was owner Andrew Freedman. As author Steven A. Riess, in *Touching Base*, claims, "He was a remarkably unpopular owner, perhaps the most hated in the sport's history."[3]

The downfall of the New York Giants began with the purchase of the club by Freedman back on January 17, 1895. An unscrupulous real estate lawyer, Freedman in the years ahead would turn the entire team upside down while making enemies faster than rabbits multiply.

Author Noel Hynd in his book, *The Giants of the Polo Grounds*, unmercifully claims, "Andrew Freedman was a man of breathtaking arrogance, appalling miserliness, and uncompromising dishonesty."[4] Hynd, however, supports his contention with overwhelming evidence, for example, Freedman's cozy connection with "The Tammany Hall ring of crooks," his "tainted" purchase of the Giants and, finally, his inept handling of a club that in 1894 won the Temple Cup Series* in four straight games.

One of Freedman's first acts as the new owner was to fire manager John Montgomery Ward and put in his place third baseman George Davis, an illogical move at best. It wouldn't be long, however, before Ward would take his revenge. With the firing of the well-respected Ward, the circus began in earnest. Next Freedman took away complimentary passes from former players and friends of the club. Then he fired a salvo at Charlie Byrne, the Brooklyn club president, suggesting he move his team out of town. Obviously, Freedman wanted no competition in the lucrative New York market.

In 1894, a Pittsburgh sportsman named William C. Temple donated an expensive trophy in his name to the winner of a playoff series (best four of seven games) between the first and second place teams in the National League. It was known as the Temple Cup Series and lasted for four years.

The destruction continued, this time with the press and, in particular, Sam Crane, a distinguished baseball writer for the *New York Commercial Advertiser*. Crane repeatedly criticized Freedman's actions and in retaliation the impulsive owner lifted Crane's Polo Grounds press credentials. But that didn't stop the tenacious Crane; he simply purchased a ticket into the game and filed his stories anyway.

Freedman then widened his attack on the press to include the *New York Sun* and the *Cincinnati Enquirer*. Finally, his irrational behavior got the best of him and he punched out *The New York Times* reporter assigned to the Giants. Freedman even had the poor taste and judgment to go after Henry Chadwick, who wrote for the *Brooklyn Eagle* and *New York Clipper*, was the originator of the baseball box score and some say the game's greatest historian. Freedman was bent on self-destruction, and eventually he would achieve his goal.

In Freedman's first season as owner, 1895, New York finished ninth in a 12-team league with a record of 66-65. This is surprising considering newly appointed manager Davis was replaced after 33 games, himself to be replaced by another player/manager, first baseman Jack Doyle. Doyle did better than Davis; he lasted for 63 games only to be replaced by Henry Watkins. It's been said of Watkins that he was the most unqualified manager in major league history. Watkins was an actor who had most recently been employed by the James A. Bailey's circus, no doubt valuable experience, at least for the direction Freedman was taking the club.

If matters could get any worse, Freedman then went after his star pitcher, Amos Rusie, who had won 23 games and led the league in strikeouts (201) and shutouts (4) for a club one game over .500. Freedman fined Rusie $100 for missing a curfew, but refuted by the star pitcher who claimed "I was in bed at 11 o'clock that night." Later in the season, in a game against Philadelphia, Freedman fined Rusie another $100, saying he wasn't trying to pitch. Angered by Freedman's moves, Rusie would not sign his 1896 contract unless the fines were rescinded. Freedman refused and Rusie sat out the entire season. In the meantime, he hired John Montgomery Ward as his attorney to file suit against Freedman for $5,000 in damages and to be released from any claims the New York club had on his services. This was the same Ward who Freedman fired as manager when he bought the club in 1895. The other owners, fearing an unfavorable ruling and, more importantly, what the consequences might bring to baseball and the reserve clause, reimbursed Rusie for $5,000 (salary, damages and interest). Years later in an interview with *The Sporting News* Rusie said, "That $5,000 I received for not playing was almost $2,000 more than I would have been paid for playing the season."[5] Rusie was now satisfied and returned to win 28 games in 1897, but he never spoke to Freedman again.

Before the 1896 season began, however, Watkins was let go and Freedman installed Arthur Irwin as his new manager. After Irwin could do no better than a 36-53 record, he was replaced by third baseman Bill Joyce who gave the by now demoralized New York fans a glimpse of hope finishing the season with a 28-14 mark and an overall seventh-place finish. Restoring some semblance of sanity on the field, while Freedman continued fighting the press and sundry personnel, Joyce guided New York to a third-place finish (83-48) in 1897 and surprisingly completed the full season.

The honeymoon, however, didn't last. After a 22-21 record in 1898 Joyce was fired and replaced by the remarkable Adrian "Cap" Anson. After 22 games, Anson had enough of Freedman and quit. Joyce returned to complete the season, and another seventh-place finish.

During the next two years Freedman continued to run the New York franchise into the ground while he changed managers as often as he changed his socks. Two new managerial names cropped up in 1899, John Day and Fred Hoey. In 1900 Buck Ewing started the season, but he only lasted 62 games before Freedman went full circle and hired George Davis, the manager he had started with in 1895. New York Yankee fans will be quick to recognize a striking resemblance between the tactics of Freedman and those of another illogical and unpopular baseball executive by the name of George Steinbrenner. The similarity is uncanny.

Noel Hynd put it best when he said, "By this time, 1900, Freedman had accomplished the mission ordained for him. The Giants were dead last. They had few quality players and no fans. In a brief but tempestuous six years, Freedman had brought the franchise to ruin."[6] Ninety years later, New York fans had to endure another demise—this time it was at Yankee Stadium, ironically not far from where the majestic Polo Grounds stood—orchestrated by Steinbrenner, albeit it took him longer to accomplish.

This was the chaotic situation, in late July 1900, that awaited a naive, 19-year-old Bucknell right-hander who was getting his first opportunity to pitch in the major leagues. No matter, in a few years he would team up with the legendary John McGraw to bring excellence and respectability back to New York.

The Season

July 17

Christy Mathewson pitched in his first major league baseball game against the Brooklyn club at Washington Park on a day when the temperature reached 94 degrees by one o'clock. Matty made his historic appearance in the fifth inning when manager George Davis removed left-hander Ed Doheny with two men on base, no outs and the score tied 5–5.

Matty faced six batters in this inning: Joe Kelley walked, loading the bases. The next batter, veteran Bill Dahlen flied to center allowing Jimmy Sheckard to tag up from third and score. But Lave Cross followed with a single, filling the bases once more. Matty bore down on Tom Daly, enticing the Brooklyn first baseman to sky to center as another run scored. Matty loaded the bases for the third time in the inning when he hit Duke Farrell with an errant pitch. Moments later Brooklyn hurler Joe McGinnity whiffed to end the inning with the score 7–5, Brooklyn leading. The Giants scored a run in the top of the sixth narrowing the gap to 7–6. Brooklyn came roaring back with five more runs in the sixth and another in the seventh off Matty. The final score was 13–7. Matty's stat line in four relief innings read: three hits, six runs, two walks and three hit batters.

It was an inauspicious start at best, but at least he did escape the loss. He was vindicated somewhat by this comment in *The New York Times:* "Mathewson has lots of speed and gives promise of making his way."[7] *Sporting Life* was more circumspect. "He showed up well enough to receive a further trial."[8]

July 25

Mathewson received his second pitching opportunity, again in relief, this time against the strong Pittsburgh club, featuring Honus Wagner at second base. This was the year the Flying Dutchman would lead the league in batting with a lofty .381 average, including 45 doubles and 22 triples. This was another tough assignment for the youngster as he replaced George Mercer in the third inning with the Giants trailing 3–1. Matty pitched poorly again. By the time he got out of the third inning six runs had crossed the plate and Pittsburgh led 9–1. In all, Matty gave up eight runs in seven innings as he was batted freely by hard-hitting Pittsburgh. Matty escaped the loss, but did little to ingratiate himself with his manager or for that matter the New York fans who were by now accustomed to being buried in the cellar.

August 4

Mathewson pitched his third straight game in relief, this time against St. Louis, replacing Bill Carrick after three innings. The Cardinals pounded Carrick for eight hits and four runs and led 4–1 when Matty took over. The young right-hander checked the Cardinals with one run in his first three innings of pitching and when the Giants scored four runs in the top of the seventh they led 7–5. Unfortunately, Matty couldn't hold it, giving up three runs in the Cardinal's half of the seventh. But the Giants came right back in the eighth to tie the game at 8–8, all to no avail as St. Louis broke the tie in their half of the inning when Matty gave up a walk and two hits. The final score was 9–8. It was Mathewson's first loss of his major league career.

Trivia buffs will delight in knowing that the man who scored the winning run for St. Louis was none other than the great John J. McGraw. Little Napoleon accounted for two hits and three runs in the game against his future star pitcher and close friend. Although McGraw only played in 99 games for St. Louis, he did bat a nifty .344.

September 6

The way Mathewson pitched in his first three relief appearances, it was not surprising that he didn't get his next chance until a month later. It was against the same St. Louis club that took credit for his first major league loss. This time the game was played at the Polo Grounds, which made very little difference. New York lost by a score of 11–4.

Matty came on in relief of Ed Doheny who gave up eight runs in the first three innings and was tagged with the loss. The left-hander would wind up losing 14 games in 1900 and was traded in June of the following year to Pittsburgh for Heinie Smith. Matty allowed three runs, seven hits, two walks in five innings, an improvement over his previous outings, albeit only slightly.

After four relief appearances totaling 21 innings, Mathewson had given up 28 hits and 22 runs! Not very impressive and at this point, at least from the stats, few baseball experts would have ever predicted that this young, raw and unproven right-hander would become one of the greatest pitchers of all time.

September 13

Seven days later Mathewson got the call from manager George Davis to start his first major league game. It was against Chicago at the Polo Grounds. Matty pitched nine innings, allowed seven hits, six runs, walked three and struck out five. It was a fine pitching performance as the press pointed out. "Mathewson pitched his first full game ... and while he lost to Chicago the result was thus because of costly errors behind him. He should have won, as Loftus' men could find him but for six hits."[9]

The final score was 6–5 and some of the blame for the defeat was hoisted on Dirty Jack Doyle. The first baseman committed an error in the first inning which was responsible for at least two of the four runs Chicago scored.

In addition, Mathewson could have just as easily won the game since there were several opportunities with men on base where a hit would have been decisive. With a little luck Matty might have picked up his first major league victory instead of his second loss of the season.

September 26

Christy Mathewson ended his short major league season at Boston's South End Grounds on a sour note. Manager Davis called for him in the fifth inning with what he thought was a comfortable 7–4 lead. Once again Matty had trouble holding the lead as a combination of wildness and Boston batting drove him from the mound.

George Mercer came on in relief but it was too late as New York lost 8–7. Mathewson allowed four runs, two hits, but walked six and failed to strike out a batter in three and two-thirds innings. It was Matty's third loss in six appearances.

Back to Norfolk

Christy Mathewson's short trial with New York was less than impressive. He pitched in six games, five in relief, and one in which he started. His total pitching line looked like this: 33⅔ innings, 37 hits, 32 runs, 20 walks and 15 strikeouts. His best performance was on September 13, when he went the distance against Chicago only to lose 6–5 on some sloppy play by first baseman Dirty Jack Doyle. His record stood at 0-3 with an ERA of 5.08. It appeared that Matty was not quite ready for the big time.

Clearly New York management was not impressed with Matty's brief showing so they returned him to Norfolk rather than pay the $1,500. He was then drafted by Cincinnati for a reported $100. At the time Cincinnati was owned by John T. Brush. Months later Brush proceeded to trade Matty back to New York for a sore-armed Amos Rusie who had not pitched in two years. On the surface it appeared to be a strange deal.

The reality of the situation, however, was much different. Cincinnati owner Brush, a devious man in his own right, knew he was going, in the not too distant future, to New York to assume ownership of the Giants. He naturally seized upon the opportunity to get rid of an over-the-hill Rusie for a young pitcher with unlimited potential.

The Rusie-for-Mathewson trade turned out to be a shrewd move by Brush. Rusie's arm was finished. He pitched only 22 innings in 1901 before retiring from baseball. By 1902 Brush had purchased the New York Giants, acquiring most of Freedman's stock for $200,000. Now he could sit back and watch Mathewson pitch his way to the Hall of Fame.

The story, however, is getting ahead of itself. The fact is Freedman was still the owner of the New York Giants at the end of the 1900 season and New York's last-place finish was frustrating the impatient owner.

Actually, Freedman's frustrations went much deeper than the dismal standing of his team. The Brooklyn club, led by owner Charlie Ebbets, was enjoying unprecedented success. Ebbets' club finished first in both 1899 and 1900 as Freedman seethed. (Once again, Steinbrenner comes to mind,

2 • Inauspicious Start, 1900

with his obsessive desire for his beloved Yankees to dominate the Mets in the popularity game played in the profitable New York market.)

Brooklyn's success and popularity were only part of Freedman's worry. Rumors were rampant that the Western League, headed by president Ban Johnson, would seek major league status in 1901 as the American League. Moreover, Johnson wanted desperately to place a team in the lucrative New York market. Clearly, Andrew Freedman was faced with serious problems.

Chapter 3
Rookie Season, 1901

W	L	Pct	ERA
20	17	.541	2.41

Rumors of the imminent formation of the American League ceased to be rumors when Ban Johnson placed franchises in three National League cities: Chicago, Boston and Philadelphia. The remaining five teams were located in Detroit, Baltimore, Washington, Cleveland and Milwaukee. The new league would begin with the 1901 season and the National League, naturally, was unhappy with events. The Nationals knew that for the new upstart league to be successful they would have to obtain star ball players. And it was no secret where these players would come from and that it would require some heavy cash. Johnson, in his eagerness to obtain quality players, chose to ignore the reserve clause and the "jumping" from the National League to the American League began in earnest.

Cy Young, Joe McGinnity, John McGraw, Jimmy Collins and Nap Lajoie were some of the stars who jumped to American League teams in 1901. The following two years the American League further claimed Wee Willie Keeler, Sam Crawford, Elmer Flick, Ed Delahanty, Jesse Burkett, Bobby Wallace, Jack Chesbro and Wild Bill Donovan.

This unsettling war between the two leagues also had a significant effect on the New York Giants' 1901 roster. Three of their four front-line pitchers—Bill Carrick, Pink Hawley and George Mercer, who combined for 50 of the Giants' 60 wins in 1900—wound up in the new American League. Cynical Giants fans possibly cheered their departure since the trio also lost a total of 56 games. From a positive standpoint, it gave Mathewson and Luther Taylor, two key players of the future, the chance to pitch on a regular basis over a full season. The Giants also lost Kid Gleason to Detroit. Gleason, who was the Giants' mainstay at second base in 1900 would turn in a fine season for the Tigers—batting .274, scoring 82 runs and driving in another 75. Rounding out the more important changes, New York bought John Ganzel and Algie McBride for cash and traded Dirty Jack Doyle to Chicago for Sammy Strang.

The truth of the matter is that all the shuffling didn't amount to much. The Giants' problems were much deeper than player personnel. What they

3 • Rookie Season, 1901

Manager John McGraw and Mathewson at Spring Training. The two greats were lifelong friends (photo courtesy Miller Library, Keystone Junior College, LaPlume, Pennsylvania).

sorely needed was a strong field leader and stable ownership. They would get both in 1902. In the meantime, Giants fans would have to endure one more dismal and inept season of baseball. There would be one bright spot, however, by the name of Christy Mathewson. His pitching and star quality would give Giants fans renewed hope and sustain them until help arrived the following year.

The Season

April 26

After rain canceled New York's opening day game on April 18, the Giants lost the next day in Boston 7–0 as Luther Taylor was hit hard. Taylor was a deaf-mute and in an era less sensitive to physical handicaps was stuck with the nickname Dummy. Amusingly, legend has it that Taylor was once ejected from a game at the Polo Grounds because he insulted umpire Hank O'Day in sign language.

The 20-year-old Christy Mathewson then had to endure five consecutive rain outs before the weather cleared and he finally got his chance to face Ned Hanlon's Brooklyn Club at the Polo Grounds. Mathewson pitched a splendid game for his first major league victory. He allowed four hits and three runs while striking out eight. The final score was 5–3. Matty would record another 372 wins before retiring in 1916.

April 30

Four days later Mathewson won his second major league game trimming Philadelphia 3–2 at Baker Bowl. He allowed three hits and only one earned run, fanning four and walking three. Reported *The New York Times*: "Mathewson had the Philadelphia National League baseball team completely at his mercy today...."[1]

May 3

Christy Mathewson won his third straight game as he returned to the mound on three days' rest to beat Boston 2–1. Second baseman Bobby Lowe, who had one of the three hits off Matty, scored the unearned run for Boston in the fifth on a passed ball by Giants catcher Broadway Aleck Smith. Smith was tagged with the sobriquet Broadway because he was viewed as being streetwise, a gambler and a dapper dresser. It's been said that he even placed bets for John McGraw. New York's record was now 3-4.

May 6

A "large Monday crowd," mainly present to see the New York "pitching phenomenon," Christy Mathewson, cheered their hero as he made his grand appearance on the field. He delighted the crowd by striking out Philadelphia's first batter of the game, center fielder Roy Thomas, on three pitches. When the game ended the "bleacherites followed him down to the clubhouse to give him an extra round of cheers."[2]

Matty pitched a splendid game, blanking Philadelphia 4–0 on five hits. It was obvious he was quickly capturing the hearts of New York Giants fans.

May 11

The largest crowd of the season filled Washington Park in Brooklyn to see Christy Mathewson, the boy wonder from Bucknell College, pitch.

They weren't disappointed as Matty only allowed two hits while recording his second consecutive shutout (7–0). Curt Bernard, Kip Selbach and George Davis collected five of the nine hits for New York while driving in six of the seven runs. It was also New York's fourth victory in a row moving them into third place in the National League pennant race. Commented *The Sporting News*, "Mathewson's greatness was never so much in evidence, and he was made a popular hero by a greater part of the 8,500 present."[3]

In the early 1900s only one umpire was used to work a game,* which often caused untold grief. One ump frequently had trouble following the action, especially when the game became too fast. Calls would be missed because of poor position; rhubarbs would ensue, then get out of hand and the ump would eventually lose control of the contest. One such incident occurred two days after Matty threw his 7–0 shutout.

The story begins with Brooklyn trailing 7–6 as they came to bat in the ninth inning. Brooklyn managed to load the bases with two out. Bill Dahlen came through with a clutch single scoring two Brooklyn runners, but quick fielding enabled New York to throw out the man going from first to second. *The New York Times* wrote, "Brooklyn took the field confident in the belief that their team was one run ahead. Several of the spectators in the grandstand, however, had some doubt to this, and they asked O'Day [umpire] whether one or two runs had been scored. He replied 'one' and in a second the whole Brooklyn team surrounded him, gesticulating and throwing their gloves down upon the ground to add force to their arguments."[5] With Brooklyn continuing to rave and rant umpire Hank O'Day had no choice but to declare a forfeit. New York won 9–0. It's an amusing story and reflects the type of mischief the one-umpire system could cause. The use of two umpires would not become common practice until 1906.

May 15

"Dey can't hit de ball with a cricket bat,"[6] said one youngster to another while watching Christy Mathewson warm up in front of the grandstand. How correctly observant was the youth as Mathewson won his sixth consecutive game and third straight shutout beating Chicago 4–0 at the Polo Grounds. His scoreless streak now reached 31 innings and moved New York into first place in the National League.

Curt Bernard continued to play well in center field for the Giants replacing the injured George Van Haltren. He made several wonderful catches, particularly a line drive off the bat of Charlie Dexter in the first inning.

*Lawrence Ritter in his book, The Story of Baseball, *points out that a single umpire "would call balls and strikes behind a catcher until a man got on base, and then move out and call balls and strikes from behind the pitcher so he could be closer to the bases in case of an attempted steal."*[4]

May 21

Mathewson won his seventh straight game defeating Pittsburgh 2–1 at the Polo Grounds, but not before his scoreless streak ended at 39 in the ninth inning on an unearned run.

It was an exciting game for the nearly 7,000 spectators who came to cheer their college hero. But it was also a strange and unique game in which umpire Billy Nash was barred from the Polo Grounds by New York owner Andrew Freedman, who claimed that Nash was incompetent and that his decisions created disorder during the game. He also said he would not accept a person who boasted of not being a home umpire.* Nash's place was taken by two players—Pittsburgh's Chief Zimmer and New York's John Warner, both catchers. (Clubs would use players to officiate when an umpire became ill or was injured.) According to later accounts of the game the two fill-in umpires did a commendable job and received very little grumbling or griping from either side.

May 24

Christy Mathewson, on only three days' rest, returned to the Polo Grounds to beat Cincinnati 1–0, posting his eighth consecutive victory and fourth shutout of the early season. The masterful right-hander allowed three hits while walking one batter in the ninth inning. New York's record stood at 14-7 with Matty accounting for more than half of the victories. This fast start kept the Giants in first place, at least temporarily.

May 28

On a wet and soggy field at the Polo Grounds, Christy Mathewson lost his first game of the 1901 season. It was a heartbreaker. St. Louis, behind the fine pitching of Jack Powell, beat Mathewson and New York 1–0. Matty walked only one batter in the entire game; but the walk resulted in a St. Louis run in the second inning, enough of a margin for Powell, who checked New York with only six hits. With Matty's winning streak now at an end, *The Sporting News* took the occasion, on the front page, to praise the young pitcher. "Mathewson's name is a household word in Manhattan and he is regarded throughout the country as the game's greatest pitcher."[7]

May 30

New York split the Memorial Day doubleheader against St. Louis at the Polo Grounds, winning the first game 6–4 in the morning and losing

---

*Home umpire, or Homer, was the name given to an umpire who favored the home team on close decisions. Unheard of today, it was an accepted practice in the early years of the twentieth century.

A rare glimpse of Mathewson in a Cincinnati uniform. He pitched one game for the Reds, beating Three Finger Brown in the final major league appearance of both hurlers (photo courtesy Miller Library, Keystone Junior College, LaPlume, Pennsylvania).

in the afternoon 6–5 in ten innings. Only 2,500 fans attended the morning game due to cloudy weather. The afternoon game, however, was a different story.

A record crowd of 28,500 jammed their way into the Polo Grounds, hoping to see the young phenom from Bucknell University. There was not an empty seat available and spectators stood six and seven deep behind the roped area in the outfield. As the game progressed, a portion of the crowd was allowed on the field. Fans extended from the right field foul line to the New York bench. Those in front sat on newspaper to avoid the damp ground and enjoyed the game as best they could.

Roger Denzer started the game for New York and pitched well. Mathewson came on in the seventh, to the delight of the huge crowd, with the score tied 5–5. It was his first relief appearance of the season and it turned out badly as he gave up a run in the tenth on a passed ball by catcher Frank Bowerman, allowing the runner to advance to third, where he eventually scored on a fly ball.

June 1

Christy Mathewson was packing the Polo Grounds every time he pitched. Even against seventh-place Boston, the crowd was estimated between 17,000 and 20,000 and stood two and three deep behind the roped outfield.

Matty pitched magnificently, defeating Boston 2–1, allowing five hits and one run while fanning ten batters, his season high. His record was now 9–2.

Kip Selbach was the offensive star of the day. In the ninth inning with the score tied and two out, he doubled home George Van Haltren, who had singled and stolen second. It was a fine victory for New York and kept them in first place ahead of Cincinnati. Immediately after the game New York embarked on their first Western trip to St. Louis, Cincinnati, Pittsburgh and Chicago.

June 5

Christy Mathewson lost his third game of the season to St. Louis 4–3 at Robison Field. He pitched well for the first four innings, facing the minimum 12 batters. But in the fifth, with a 3–0 lead, he ran into trouble. The Cardinals scored two runs, capped by an exciting steal of home by Dick Padden to make the score 3–2. Padden's steal might have upset young Matty, for in the sixth inning he gave up two more runs and, with St. Louis hurler Jack Harper checking the Giants, lost the game 4–3.

Matty continued to attract large crowds even away from the Polo Grounds. It was estimated that approximately 6,000 spectators attended the game at Robison Field, one of the largest of the season.

June 8

Over 11,000 visited League Park in Cincinnati to see the great Christy Mathewson pitch. No doubt the Cincinnati fans had mixed emotions: they welcomed the victory but were disappointed in the young right-hander's performance. Mathewson took his worst beating of the season as he was hammered for nine hits and six runs in eight innings. The final score was Cincinnati 6, New York 4.

His season record now stood at 9-4 with the Giants still in first place at 18-12.

June 11

"Mathewson was the magnet that drew one of the largest crowds of the year, in spite of threatening rain,"[8] to Pittsburgh's Exposition Park, so reported *The New York Times*. Apparently the pounding Mathewson took in Cincinnati did little to dampen the enthusiasm of the local fans. They had been discussing Matty's appearance for the previous two days and were anxiously awaiting his arrival.

Unfortunately, he was not at his best. The weather was also a factor as the game was called after the Giants failed to score in the fifth inning. Pittsburgh won 4–0. It was Mathewson's third straight loss and proved that the young phenom from Factoryville was indeed human.

June 15

After leaving Pittsburgh, New York traveled to Chicago where they defeated the locals on June 13 by a score of 9–7 and the next day 4–1, putting themselves back in first place.

Mathewson was now called on to complete the three-game sweep, but the rookie was not up to the challenge. He was pounded for five runs in the first inning and with future Hall of Famer Rube Waddell on the mound, the game was over early. Waddell, the eccentric left-hander who would star for Connie Mack's Athletics for six years, scattered three hits and allowed two runs while striking out ten. It was Waddell's day as Mathewson finished the game giving up nine runs and 13 hits for his sixth loss and fourth in a row.

June 19

After a poor road trip where the Giants lost 7 of 12 games, but still remained in second place, Christy Mathewson opened the home stand at the Polo Grounds against Pittsburgh. With the score tied at 5–5 after nine innings, the game was called on account of darkness. New York led 5–3 going into the ninth, but Matty weakened, allowing Pittsburgh to score two runs and if not for a fine throw from George Van Haltren in center field to nab Ginger Beaumont at the plate, would have lost.

June 24

Christy Mathewson, who hadn't won since June 1, broke out of his slump and pitched a fine game against St. Louis, beating them 3–2 on six hits. In spite of this solid performance, it took a clutch run in the ninth to win the game. Sammy Strang singled in Piano Legs Hickman with the winning tally. Hickman was tagged with the nickname because of his unusually thick legs, supporting a 5-foot 8-inch, 190-pound frame. Matty's record now stood at 10-6.

June 26

Mathewson notched his second consecutive victory and eleventh of the season by beating Cincinnati 6–2. Except for the fifth inning, when he allowed two runs, Matty was in total command of the game. He allowed nine hits, but only walked one batter.

Mathewson's uncanny control throughout his career was as important to his success as his fast ball, sharp-breaking curve and the famous fadeaway. Including this game, Matty had pitched in 149 innings and walked a mere 32 batters, a ratio of 1.93 per nine innings. Although his lifetime ratio would be 1.58, even at this tender age Matty's control was superb.

Roger Bresnahan, who caught Matty for almost seven full seasons, said, "you could catch Matty sittin' in a chair."[9] Chief Meyers, his catcher in later years, added, "He had almost perfect control. Really, almost perfect."[10] Ring Lardner once said, "He's got ten to one better control than any guy I ever seen, and I've saw the best of them."[11]

June 29

The matchup of Christy Mathewson and Chicago's Rube Waddell had all the earmarks of a classic duel between two great pitchers. It was anything but, as New York pounded Waddell for nine runs in the first four innings. The final score was 14–1. The unpredictable Waddell had to leave the game in the fourth after being injured when a ball hit by Mathewson caromed off his hand. Matty pitched one of his best games of the year, allowing four hits, while striking out five and walking one in the second inning.

Two days later Dummy Taylor beat Chicago 6–4 at the Polo Grounds in a game where all hell broke loose. The brouhaha centered around Chicago's first baseman, Dirty Jack Doyle (a well-deserved name since he used any trick in the book to win games, many of which did not abide by the rules). Doyle was well known in New York. He had played 90 games for them in 1892 and full seasons from 1893 to 1895. He even had a stint as manager in 1895, the year Freedman purchased the club. Jack didn't like the belligerent owner (who did?) and often let him know it, which led to his firing after only five weeks. In the following two years Doyle played for Baltimore, and played a portion of 1898 with Washington before he hooked up again with New York, leaving after the 1900 season for Chicago. New York fans and Dirty Jack Doyle were no strangers.

As the story was reported, a burly, vociferous fan was heckling Doyle throughout the game. When the obnoxious fan fired some personal remarks at the Chicago first baseman and then invited him into the stands, the action began. Doyle accepted the man's invitation, entered the stands and promptly belted him on the jaw with a left, all before the police and other players could intervene. Later, Doyle had to leave the game because in the scuffle he injured the same hand he had broken weeks before.

July 4

New York's second Western trip began with a doubleheader against Pittsburgh. They split, winning the morning game 5–3 behind Christy Mathewson and then getting shellacked in the afternoon 12–0 to remain in second place.

Matty finally won a game away from the friendly confines of the Polo Grounds, but it took a three-run rally in the twelfth inning to clinch the elusive victory. Not at his best, Matty allowed 11 hits, struck out ten, and walked six, his high for the season.

One of the three opponents facing Mathewson was none other than future Hall of Famer Jack Chesbro. He would record a fine year for Pittsburgh with a 21-9 record and an ERA of 2.38.

Two days later, in the final game of the Pittsburgh series, the players had to officiate their own game. National League president, Nick Young, in answer to a protest that umpire Harry Colgan not be used granted permission to the teams. New York selected Charlie Buelow and Pittsburgh Jack O'Connor. Turn-of-the-century baseball indeed had its charm.

More importantly, New York lost the game 6–2, the series three games to four and up to this point six of seven at Exposition Park. Manager George Davis and the rest of the Giants were eager to flee the city of Pittsburgh.

July 8

Christy Mathewson won his fourteenth game of the season and fifth straight beating Cincinnati and Dick Scott for the second time, 9–3. Mathewson had trouble all afternoon with his control. He walked four batters and hit two more. One of the two players he hit almost resulted in a tragedy. He beaned Jake Beckley with a fast ball and the first baseman dropped to the ground as if shot. It took five minutes and the work of two doctors before he regained consciousness.

Batting helmets were not used in the major leagues until many years later, and only became mandatory in 1971. So Beckley took the full force of Matty's fast ball. Ironically, Jack Beckley's nickname was Eagle Eye.

The star of the day was player-manager Davis. He had four hits, two of which were home runs, drove in four and scored three times. If that wasn't enough, Davis made a sensational play at third to cap the day.

In an unrelated matter, umpire Hank O'Day was again having problems on the field, this time in St. Louis in a game against Brooklyn. Apparently, spectators were incensed at a decision he made in the eighth inning. He was literally mobbed by the fans and lucky to come away with only a split lip and some minor scratches. If it wasn't for the police, who had to draw their revolvers, and the St. Louis players O'Day might have spent the night in the hospital.

July 12

New York arrived in St. Louis, after splitting the four games with Cincinnati, and opened the series with Mathewson on the mound. Matty pitched brilliantly but lost 3–2 in 11 innings. Mathewson allowed six hits and one walk, striking out ten. The game-winning run in the eleventh was the result of an error and a collision between Algie McBride and Sammy Strang. The tough loss dropped the Giants into fourth place.

July 15

With only two days rest, the amazing Christy Mathewson pitched a brilliant no-hitter, his first in the major leagues, defeating St. Louis 5–0. It was Matty's fifth shutout of the season and salvaged the only victory for New York in the four games. His record was 15-7.

No doubt the no-hitter buoyed Mathewson's teammates as they hopped a train and headed for the bustling city of Chicago.

July 19

The euphoria over Matty's no-hitter came to a sudden halt in Chicago. New York lost the first two games by scores of 7–4 and 6–5 and were looking to Mathewson to put a halt to the slide.

On this afternoon they should have looked elsewhere. Matty was hit hard, giving up five runs on 12 hits as Jack Taylor held New York to two runs in the ninth inning. The Chicago right-hander scattered ten hits and was especially effective with men on base. Matty's record now stood at 15-8.

New York's demise was far from over. They lost the next two to Chicago by scores of 7–2 and 5–2, making it five in a row. By any standard it was a disastrous road trip. New York managed to win only four games while losing 13, with the added embarrassment of five straight to Chicago. When they began this road trip the Giants' record stood at 29-21, good enough for second place. When the trip ended they were a game under .500 at 33-34 and had tumbled to fifth place. It was a dispirited and gloomy pack of players that boarded the train in Chicago heading for New York.

July 23

Back at the Polo Grounds New York continued their losing ways. Now it was becoming contagious as the rookie Mathewson was drubbed by Brooklyn 8–3. For the first time in 24 starting assignments, Matty did not complete the game. In the second inning Brooklyn scored three runs when Matty, apparently losing his composure, walked two batters and threw two wild pitches. When Matty showed no improvement in the third inning, Davis replaced him with Roger Denzer. It was Matty's ninth loss of the season.

July 25

It was now Brooklyn's turn to cross the East River for a game at the Polo Grounds and, since Matty had pitched only two innings on July 23, Davis called on his star rookie to beat the local rivals.

Although Mathewson pitched well, scattering ten hits and giving up five runs (four of which were due to errors), on this day he was no match for the Brooklyn hurler, Frank Kitson, who pitched a splendid one hit shutout. The 28-year-old right-hander would finish the season at 19-11 with a respectable 2.98 ERA.

This was Matty's third straight defeat bringing his record to 15-10. In all three games he was pounded: on July 19 (12 hits), July 23 (six hits in two innings) and this game, ten hits. It was obvious Matty was in a pitching slump, no doubt brought on by fatigue. Up to this point he had pitched 217 innings and, unaccustomed to the heavy workload, was beginning to pay the price.

July 29

Mathewson was called on again to halt New York's dismal slide in the standings as they faced Boston at the Polo Grounds. Matty pitched considerably better than his three previous starts, but was simply not the dominant pitcher he had been early in the season. He lost to Boston 5–4 in ten innings, allowing 11 hits and walking three.

His mound opponent was Charles Augustus Nichols, more widely known as Kid Nichols. This durable right-hander was at the end of his fabulous career but still managed to win 19 games and post a fine 3.22 ERA. In 1949 he would be elected to the Hall of Fame.

Matty's record now stood at 15-11 and what he needed more than anything was a victory.

August 1

In today's parlance one would say that Christy Mathewson won ugly. Boston scored four runs in the first and one in the fourth for a 5-0 lead. Luckily for Mathewson his teammates had no trouble solving the deliveries of Bill Dineen and Kid Nichols, the latter after relieving in the seventh inning with the score tied 5-5, allowed four more runs (three in the ninth) for the loss.

The real ugly part came in the last of the ninth with New York leading 9-5. Matty was tagged for three runs and narrowly escaped a tie ball game. The final line on Matty was 12 hits, four walks and eight runs, not pretty but enough to record his sixteenth win against 11 defeats.

August 5

Mathewson lost a heartbreaker to Philadelphia, the first game of a doubleheader, in 11 innings by a score of 6-3. Trailing 3-1 entering the ninth inning, New York scored twice to tie the game. In the process, Giants' left fielder Kip Selbach was tossed out of the game by umpire John Dwyer for protesting strike calls. No one knew it at the time, but Selbach's ejection would play a key role in Philadelphia's three run outburst in the eleventh.

The inning started poorly and ended even worse. Ike Van Zandt (who played only three games during the season), Selbach's replacement, let a ball get away from him; Sammy Strang followed with an error. Mathewson, unnerved by lack of support, turned wild, in addition to allowing two hits. When the mess finally ended, Philadelphia had collected three runs and the victory.

Matty's record was now 16-12 and New York was firmly entrenched in sixth place, after losing the second game.

August 8

At the Polo Grounds New York split a doubleheader with Brooklyn, losing the first game 3-0 and winning the second behind Mathewson 4-1. Matty pitched a splendid game in spite of giving up nine hits. In the sixth inning, with New York leading 4-1, Matty conducted a clinic on clutch pitching.

With Wee Willie Keeler on second and Jimmy Sheckard on first and no outs, Mathewson fanned Cozy Dolan on three pitches. The great Joe Kelley singled, loading the bases. Matty then reared back and struck out Tom Daly and Bill Dahlen to end the inning. His record now stood at

17-12 and he was on his way to his first of 13 seasons in which he would win 20 or more games.

During the late 1800s and early 1900s it was commonplace in the National League for umpires to literally fight with belligerent managers, rowdy players and unruly fans. This problem existed when the league was formed by William A. Hulbert in 1876 and precious little was done to correct the unhealthy situation.

That is until Ban Johnson came along. Johnson, founder of the American League in 1901, was fully aware of this serious and challenging perplexity. As president of the Western League he did everything in his power to support umpires and, thus, help establish the game's respectability. Although his policies were less than successful, there were signs that baseball officials were accepting umpire support as crucial to discipline on the field.

Ban Johnson carried his policies with him into the new American League where he was much more successful. Witness this comment by author James Kahn from his book, *The Umpire Story*: "Under Johnson the many-lived umpire was to be reborn again, and this time to a position of unprecedented authority, dignity and secularity."[12]

In *Ban Johnson: Czar of Baseball* author Eugene Murdock takes this success one step further claiming, "His [Johnson] firm leadership, as reflected in his umpire policy, was responsible for the American League's successful challenge to the National League in the Great Baseball War and for its supremacy over the National League in the first two-thirds of his presidency."[13] In spite of this, 1901 was the worst year Johnson experienced for his umpires. On August 8 he suspended Baltimore first baseman Burt Hart for assaulting umpire John Haskell. Commented Johnson, "This is the first time a player of the American League has struck an umpire, and it is an offense that cannot be overlooked." He also indicated this was not the final word. "I am waiting for more complete reports from my umpires before taking final action in the matter, but it is certain that the act will be sufficiently punished."[14]

The Hart/Haskell incident was just one of many. Ironically, on the same day Johnson was discussing the Hart case, Milwaukee player and future Hall of Famer Hugh Duffy landed a right on the jaw of umpire Al Mannassau. Apparently Duffy didn't appreciate Mannassau's fair ball call which scored the winning run.

On reflection these stories seem amusing, but it's doubtful they were to the participants and personnel responsible for maintaining orderly conduct.

August 13

Christy Mathewson and Kid Nichols hooked up at the Polo Grounds in a classic matchup between two great pitchers. No one was disappointed.

In a superb exhibition of pitching both right-handers hurled scoreless baseball for nine innings. In the tenth, however, Mathewson weakened. Boston scored three runs and Nichols had his shutout.

This was Mathewson's thirteenth defeat of the season, and since July 12 his record was a disappointing 3-7. Matty pitched in over 255 innings and there was still a month and a half remaining in the season. It appeared the young right-hander was arm-weary and fatigued. In fact, it was reported the pain was so bad at times it prevented him from sleeping.

August 15

No rest for the weary. On only one day's rest Mathewson and Nichols faced each other again in the second game of a New York–Boston doubleheader. This one, however, went 11 innings and ended in a 5–5 tie, called on account of darkness.

It was becoming a long season for New York and Matty as the team was entrenched in sixth place with a miserable 38-50 record. Unfortunately, the situation would become even worse.

August 19

Believe it or not Mathewson and Nichols faced each other for the third time in seven days with Nichols emerging the victor as Boston won 11–6 and dropped the Giants into seventh place. Although New York played a poor game in the field, committing five errors, Mathewson was batted freely. He gave up three runs in the second, three more in the fourth and five in the seventh. More telling was the 13 hits he allowed. Matty struck out one batter, further evidence he was a very tired pitcher. The weary young man was struggling as his record stood at 17-14.

August 26

Christy Mathewson pitched one of his finest games in weeks by trimming Philadelphia 3–1 on three hits. Apparently the extended rest between starts was just what Matty needed. The only blemish on this fine performance was his lack of control, particularly in the ninth inning when Philadelphia scored on a hit, walk, wild pitch and finally a balk. It was Matty's eighteenth victory of the season against 14 defeats.

In the American League Ban Johnson continued to encounter problems maintaining order on the field. Umpire John Haskell was in the middle of another ugly scene at Washington in the game against Chicago. This time Frank Shugart, Chicago's shortstop, hit Haskell and, to make matters worse, teammate John Katoll tried to do the same, but failed as both players were arrested. Even a spectator got into the act, retaliating by punching Shugart. Fortunately, the police reached the disgraceful scene in time to avert a riot.

Also in the American League, John McGraw announced he had played his last game for Baltimore. But he made it clear that he would retain his ownership interest in the club and manage from the bench. At the time McGraw made the surprising announcement he was flat on his back in bed with a broken knee in a plaster cast. The feisty McGraw, however, continued to play through 1906, albeit sparingly. As the world would soon discover, his forte, beginning in 1902, would be as a managerial genius.

August 29

New York's season was unraveling. The pitching staff was in dire straits and their record had tumbled to 42-59. Manager Davis, in desperation, was using outfielders Piano Legs Hickman and George Van Haltren on the mound. Previously New York had signed Frank Murphy and in a few days would sign Al Maul, who had pitched for Philadelphia before his arm went out. Even Ike Van Zandt would get a turn to pitch. It was a patched up rotation that must have infuriated owner Andrew Freedman. Davis, in a further display of futility, even used a weary Mathewson in relief of Dummy Taylor. Matty held Philadelphia scoreless in the ninth, but New York still managed to lose 7–6.

August 30

After pitching one inning of relief the day before, Matty came back to start against the Philadelphia Phillies. He pitched well for five innings, but when fatigue set in, he lost his fast ball and was clobbered. He allowed 15 hits, his high for the season, and walked six, a far cry from the Mathewson who won his first eight games of the season and was unbeatable.

New York finally hit rock bottom when they lost to Chicago 10–4 on September 3 and tumbled into last place. If this wasn't demoralizing enough, New York would play Pittsburgh at the Polo Grounds six straight games (three doubleheaders) and lose all six! The losses were bad enough, but the scores were downright embarrassing: 12–6, 10–3, 15–1, 15–7, 15–2 and 13–4. It was a massacre of huge proportions that buried New York in last place and all but clinched the pennant for Pittsburgh.

During this massacre a more serious incident occurred. On September 6, at a public reception while attending a Pan-American Exposition in Buffalo, New York, President McKinley was shot by Leon Czolgosz, an emotionally disturbed fanatic. For eight days the country held its collective breath while the president fought for his life. Sadly, the end came on September 14 with McKinley whispering in a feeble voice, "Good-bye—good-bye, all." Moments later he continued, "It is God's way. His will, not ours, be done."[15] The president was dead.

On September 19 all games in both the National and American

leagues were canceled out of respect for President McKinley as he was laid to rest in Canton, Ohio.

Reported *The New York Times,* "It was a spectacle of mournful grandeur. Canton ceased to be a town and swelled to the proportions of a great city. From every city and hamlet in Ohio, from the remote corners of the South, and from the East and West, the human tide flowed into the town, until 100,000 people were within its gates, here to pay their last tribute to the fallen Chief."[16]

September 9

The recuperative powers of a 21-year-old are amazing. Given nine days' rest, Mathewson took the mound at the Polo Grounds and defeated St. Louis 5–1 in the first game of a doubleheader. Matty pitched an outstanding game, scattering five hits while coasting to victory number 19. Matty was strong throughout, fanning eight Cardinals and appeared to be at the top of his game. He indeed was one of the few bright spots of the Giants' season.

September 21

New York began its last Western road trip of the season in fine fashion. They beat Cincinnati 5–1 behind the three hit pitching of Mathewson. It was Matty's twentieth victory of the season and the first of many 20-plus years.

Approximately 250 miles away in Chicago's West Side Park one of the greatest baseball games in the history of the National League (up to that time) was unfolding. Chicago's Long Tom Hughes blanked Boston for 17 innings, rendering a meager eight hits over this span. His opponent, Bill Dineen, also gave up only eight hits but allowed a run in the seventeenth inning to lose this remarkable pitching extravaganza 1–0.

September 25

After winning two of three games in Cincinnati, New York traveled to Pittsburgh where the Pirates swept the three game series. Mathewson lost the final game getting battered for 14 hits and ten runs in eight innings. Right from the start Pittsburgh jumped all over Matty, scoring three runs in the first inning. They added three more in the fifth and four in the sixth. The final score was 10–5. Two days later the Pirates clinched the National League pennant when they defeated Brooklyn 5–4.

October 5

The New York Giants lost a doubleheader to their Brooklyn rivals,

8-0 and 4-2, an appropriate ending to a miserable season. In the first game Wild Bill Donovan blanked New York 8-0 on three hits for his league-leading twenty-fifth victory.

In the second game Mathewson lost 4-2 and had to be removed in the seventh inning, not surprisingly, because of a sore arm. He trailed at the time 4-0. In spite of losing his last two games of the season, Matty finished with a fine 20-17 record. Interestingly, both contests were umpired by ball players, including Mathewson in the first game. No doubt, by the end of the season umpires were either run out of town or just plain weary from the constant badgering they had had to endure. The men in blue have come a long way.

For New York Giants players the 1901 season was a grueling and frustrating struggle and for the fans another disappointment (this time seventh place). They were becoming all too accustomed to miserable seasons and a wacky owner bent on destroying the franchise while making enemies with most everyone he met.

For Christy Mathewson, what started out as a super season, 9-2 by June 1, turned into simply a good, solid effort at 20-17. After June 1 Matty's record was 11-15, a reflection of fatigue and a sore arm. Mathewson even feared he had seriously injured it. On a barnstorming tour after the season all he could do was lob the ball over the plate. In Factoryville, he was getting massage treatment and later in New York would follow up with soaking his arm in a sauna. When Matty won four of five games at the start of the 1902 season, concern about his troubled arm was quickly dispelled.

If nothing else, the 1901 season clearly demonstrated that Matty had the pitching skills and fan charisma that translates into large crowds, both young and old, male and female. Some even went so far as to claim that when Matty pitched the crowds were twice as large!

In retrospect, 1901 was the year that Christy Mathewson made the baseball world aware he was something special and destined to be the idol of America. The years ahead would solidify this image and firmly fix his place in baseball history.

Chapter 4
Saved by McGraw, 1902

W	L	Pct	ERA
14	17	.452	2.11

Frenetic New York Giants owner Andrew Freedman continued his wild antics during the winter of 1902 and right on into the new baseball season. Freedman's craziest move involved a brazen attempt to control baseball by offering a plan to operate the National League as a trust. It was called "syndicate baseball" and would work this way: "Players would be owned by a central league office and assigned to teams year by year. The owners would fix prices around the league and control all stock."[1] It sounded unbelievable but Freedman almost succeeded.

Once the plan was made public, however, the issue then focused on who would become president of the National League. The battle lines were clearly drawn. Supporting Freedman in his bid to retain incumbent president Nick Young were owners John T. Brush (Cincinnati), Arthur H. Soden (Boston) and Frank Robison (St. Louis). The antisyndicate group, who were backing Albert Spalding, consisted of owners Barney Dreyfuss (Pittsburgh), Charlie Ebbets (Brooklyn), Alfred J. Reach (Philadelphia) and Jim Hart (Chicago).

The battle eventually wound up in court and was finally settled when compromise candidate Henry Clay Pulliam was agreed upon.

Throughout the battle for the National League presidency and the war of words with Spalding, Freedman continued to assure New York baseball fans he was doing everything possible to bring a championship flag to the city.

For example, on January 8, 1902, he said to the press, "I am going to do the best I can to get a winning team." Later, he discussed his ownership status, "I hope to bring the New York team up to a high pitch of excellence, and I certainly do not intend to sell out my interest in the New York club."[2] Not unexpectedly, neither of these remarks turned out to be true.

In fairness to Freedman, a number of changes in player personnel were made during the winter, but nothing significant enough to substantially improve the club. Freedman did cause a minor flap when he announced that his new field manager would be Ned Hanlon, the current Brooklyn manager. "I made Hanlon an offer of $25,000 for a two-year contract to manage the team, and he has accepted."³ A day later Hanlon denied he agreed to the contract and Freedman backed off and admitted it was only a verbal commitment. So who did the penny-pinching owner get to manage in 1902? Who else but Horace Fogel, a former Philadelphia sportswriter who had managed the Indianapolis club in 1887.

The two most significant events for the Giants in 1902 occurred in July and September. The first and most important was the hiring of the fiery 29-year-old John J. McGraw in early July. It was Freedman's last and most meaningful act as owner of New York. But as author Noel Hynd stated, "It was doubtful that Freedman could have ever grasped the momentousness of what he was doing."⁴ McGraw would stay at the Giants' helm for the next 30 seasons and develop a close relationship with Mathewson that endured for years.

The other important event was the sale of the New York club to John T. Brush in late September for $200,000. Brush was the former majority owner of the Cincinnati ball club and the current chairman of the Executive Committee of the National League. With Cincinnati, he was also the man who engineered the Amos Rusie for Christy Mathewson trade. At the time (1900) it seemed puzzling, but now it appeared to be a cleverly planned maneuver.

At last the New York baseball fans were free of the highly controversial and quixotic Freedman. They had a new owner and manager dedicated to winning baseball. As Brush stated, "I intend to give the New York club my personal and, if necessary, undivided attention. Manager McGraw will be a fixture. He and I have got one baseball ambition, and that is to secure a first-class club of players for this city."⁵

For Christy Mathewson the future under McGraw looked even brighter. Matty would develop an almost father-son relationship with his cantankerous skipper while emerging as a true superstar and idol of America. But ... there was one more miserable season to endure.

The Season

April 17

Before an enormous Polo Grounds crowd of over 24,000, Christy Mathewson pitched the season's opening game for the New York Giants, blanking Philadelphia 7–0. The Seventh Regiment Band led the joyous pregame ceremonies playing "There'll Be a Hot Time in the Old Town Tonight." At 3:30 p.m. sharp umpire Hank O'Day tossed out a bright, shiny baseball and the 1902 season was underway.

It was all New York from start to finish. This game account sums up Matty's great performance. "The pitching of Mathewson was wonderful.

Mathewson, idolized by millions, especially kids, is probably giving this youngster tips on what it takes to become a great pitcher (photo courtesy Miller Library, Keystone Junior College, LaPlume, Pennsylvania).

He knew exactly when and where to place each ball, and he did it with a skill and judgment which, if kept up, will make him easily the champion pitcher of America."[6]

April 21

Mathewson won his second straight game defeating Boston at the Polo Grounds by a score of 6–3. Matty was in control throughout the game except for the sixth inning. Sloppy play by catcher George Yeager and left fielder Jim Jackson coupled with Matty's wildness allowed Boston to score three runs. He settled down after that as the Giants added two insurance runs in the seventh to clinch the victory. New York's record stood at 2-2 and Mathewson had both victories.

April 24

Three days later Mathewson concluded the four-game series with Boston, this time losing 8–4. Although Matty was not at his best, the right-hander could have fared much better if it were not for Jim Delahanty. In the sixth inning the right fielder allowed a single to get by him clearing the bases, giving Boston a commanding 6–1 lead. New York scored three runs in the bottom of the ninth, but still fell short as Matty gave up ten hits in the game.

May 1

With six days' rest Mathewson returned to the mound with a vengeance as he shut out Philadelphia for the second straight game. This performance even topped his first shutout. Matty gave up only two hits while fanning nine. He was in total control, not allowing a single Philadelphia player to reach third base. The star right-hander chipped in to help his cause by hitting a home run into the roped off area in right field.

The next day New York beat Philadelphia 5–1. It would put them in second place, behind mighty Pittsburgh, with a record of 9-5. This would be, however, the high point of the season. After May 2 New York headed in one direction and that was straight down until it hit rock bottom.

May 7

New York traveled to Chicago to begin its first road trip of the season. Mathewson opened against the Cubs and pitched well enough to win, allowing five hits and four runs. He had the misfortune, however, of facing Chicago's ace, Jack Taylor, who would win 22 games for a team finishing under .500 for the season. More impressively, Taylor would turn in a league-leading 1.33 ERA. In this game Taylor blanked New York 4–0 on two hits and two walks.

Later, because the pitching distance was too short, the game was ruled a "no decision" and all the records thrown out. Mathewson was not charged with a loss.

May 14

It had been a week since Mathewson last pitched, but the rest did little good; St. Louis batted him for nine hits and seven runs. Fortunately for Matty, New York had little trouble solving the delivery of Irish born Mike Joyce. The Giants pummeled Joyce for 14 hits and ten runs. It wasn't a pretty win, but it was a victory nonetheless and brought Matty's record to 4–1.

In the meantime, the team continued its downward slide and was now in sole possession of third place. Hope for a New York pennant was unrealistic even this early in the season. The major reason was Pittsburgh: after 22 games the Pirates sported a 19-3 record! Pittsburgh was on its way to an awesome season and another pennant, led by Honus Wagner, Ginger

Beaumont, Tommy Leach and a pitching staff of Jack Chesbro, Deacon Phillippe and Jesse Tannehill. In 1902 Pittsburgh would win 103 games while losing only 36 for a .741 winning percentage.

May 17

Mathewson lost his second game of the season and first of the year at Cincinnati as the Reds defeated him 6–1. Cincinnati scored two in the first, three more in the sixth and another in the eighth. In the meantime the Giants were being handcuffed by Bill Phillips who scattered six hits. New York lost the next two games to Cincinnati to bring its record to 14-12 before heading to Pittsburgh to face the club that would finish the season 27½ games in front of second-place Brooklyn.

May 21

Dummy Taylor opened the Pittsburgh series, but was replaced in the seventh inning by Mathewson with New York leading 3–2. It was Matty's first relief appearance. He allowed the tying run to score on Billy Lauder's wild throw, but held Pittsburgh hitless during his short stint. In addition to his clutch pitching, Matty scored the winning run in the eighth inning, scampering all the way from first on Jack Doyle's double. Matty's record was 5-2, including two shutouts.

Commented *The New York Times*, "Mathewson, the fading idol of the New York team, regained some of his lost laurels here today..."[7] And to think, it was on April 17, a little more than a month before, that Matty was hailed as the "champion pitcher of America." How fickle the press.

May 30

After Mathewson defeated Pittsburgh in relief, New York fell apart and lost the next six games on the road before returning home to face the Philadelphia Phillies. Over 26,000 fans turned out for the doubleheader at the Polo Grounds, but left disappointed as the Giants lost twice. Mathewson pitched well in the first game but had to leave after nine innings with the score tied 3–3, when his arm grew limp. Roy Evans replaced him but was nailed for three hits, two runs and tagged with the loss.

When New York was shut out 6–0 in the nightcap its record went to 15-20 and a drop to fifth place. It was going to be another long season for the New York faithful.

June 6

Mathewson opened the Pittsburgh series at the Polo Grounds and pitched well, allowing four runs in eight innings, and left with the score tied. The game ended after 11 innings, due to darkness, with the score still knotted at 4–4.

Earlier in the week, after nine consecutive losses, the Giants, in desperation, announced they were changing captains. Second baseman George Smith replaced Jack Doyle. When the team continued to lose, it was clear New York's problems were more serious and switching captains would do little to solve them. So Freedman fired his manager, Horace Fogel, and replaced him with his brand new captain. In a heart-to-heart talk with Smith, Freedman said, "Mr. Smith, you are now manager and captain of the team. I want you to work hard and have your men do the same and regain our lost prestige." Now here's the clincher from Freedman, "I will hold you responsible for any lack of good ball playing."[8]

June 13

Cincinnati, in its first game of the season at the Polo Grounds, defeated the Giants 7–5. Tom Sparks started the game but was relieved by Mathewson in the sixth with New York trailing 5–3. Matty allowed two runs on three hits but Sparks suffered the loss. It brought the Giants' record to a miserable 19-26 as they took direct aim at last place, reaching that unenviable position five days later.

June 16

Three days later, against the same Cincinnati club, Mathewson started and lost 6–4. It was an atypical Mathewson game. The right-hander allowed 12 hits and struck out only one batter—shortstop Tommy Corcoran. Matty's record stood at 5-3 and he was beginning to struggle.

June 25

New York and Mathewson lost to Philadelphia 3–1. It was a game Matty should have won as errors accounted for two of the Phillies' runs. He pitched splendidly, scattering six hits, and was frustrated when center fielder Steve Brodie killed an eighth-inning rally by falling victim to the embarrassing hidden ball trick. Nothing was going right for New York as Matty's record slipped to 5-4.

July 2

Mathewson lost another heartbreaker before the home-town crowd, this time to Boston by a 4–3 score. He hurled a fine game, scattering eight hits while striking out eight and walking two. It was vintage Mathewson, and if it were not for catcher Frank Bowerman's error and passed ball in the eighth, he would have been a winner.

This was Matty's first pitching assignment in a week. In the previous three games, manager Smith, in a zany move, tried Matty at first base! Not surprisingly, the press was critical. "Christy Mathewson, the former pitcher, was again tried at first base. He did nothing remarkable. Compared with Tenney of the Bostons, who played a like position, he was lacking in that quick judgment and snappy work necessary to the proper covering of the position."[9] The next day New York would head for St. Louis to begin its second western swing.

July 5

The Giants lost the July 4 doubleheader to St. Louis, 7–5 and 2–0, then called on Mathewson the next day to get them back in the win column. Mathewson pitched brilliantly but lacked offensive support from his teammates as he lost a squeaker, 1–0. It was his fourth consecutive loss. Matty allowed six hits but a wild pitch in the second inning accounted for St. Louis' lone tally. His record was now 5–6.

As poorly as the Giants were playing, it came as no surprise when rumors began circulating that New York was seeking a new player-manager to take the place of Smith. The man most often mentioned as the likely replacement was John J. McGraw, current player-manager and part owner of Baltimore in the American League. At the time, McGraw was under suspension by American League president Ban Johnson for repeated arguing with umpires. Secretary Fred Knowles flatly denied the rumor while McGraw sidestepped the issue, neither confirming nor denying he was leaving Baltimore for New York.

Two days later, on Monday night (July 7) at the Northampton Hotel, John McGraw met with the Baltimore club directors and "demanded that they either pay him the $7,000 he calculated the club owed him or give him his outright release."[10] The following morning when the directors reconvened McGraw received his release in exchange for his stock holdings which Baltimore president John K. Mahon bought for $6,500. On July 9 McGraw signed with New York at a salary rumored to be $10,000 a year for two years. "Actually his contract called for a salary of $11,000 a year for four years, which made him the highest-paid ball player or manager (on a straight salary basis) up to that time."[11]

According to McGraw, Freedman had given him complete control of the team and he would begin work immediately. Added McGraw, "I have orders to spend any amount of money I feel disposed to in order to strengthen the team, and I will set about that task at once."[12]

July 8

While McGraw was in the middle of switching baseball teams and leagues, Christy Mathewson returned to his brilliant pitching form by blanking Chicago 1–0 on six hits with near-perfect control. It was Matty's first win since May 21, one of the longest droughts between victories in his 17-year career. With the win, he evened his record at 6-6.

Interestingly, on this same day, McGraw was quoted as saying, "I wish to state that I shall not tamper with any of the Baltimore club's players."[13] McGraw should have added, that is until July 16.

July 12

New York split the first two games of the Pittsburgh series and looked to Mathewson to win the third and deciding contest. Matty gave up four runs on eight hits, but the star of the day was Hall of Famer Jack Chesbro, who flipped a five-hit shutout while fanning 11 Giants. Chesbro would lead the league in victories with 28 and tie Matty and Chicago's Jack Taylor for most shutouts with eight. The powerful Pittsburgh club was led by another Hall of Famer, Fred Clarke (.321 and 104 runs for the season), and by Ginger Beaumont (a league-leading .357 and 194 hits), who combined to score all four runs off Matty.

July 15

After Pittsburgh, the Giants were swept in Chicago so McGraw chose Mathewson to open the series at Cincinnati. Wrong choice—Matty should have stayed on the train. He ran smack into a Cincinnati buzz saw and was out of the game before breaking a sweat. He left after the second inning, trailing 6–0. Matty's record was now 6-8. The one bright moment of the day for the Giants came in the second inning when Mathewson, Smith and Hal O'Hagen pulled off a rare triple play! Small consolation.

July 17

Two days later Mathewson redeemed himself by whipping Cincinnati 6–3 for his seventh win of the season. He allowed eight hits and fanned five. If nothing else it was a confidence builder for the young man who was struggling to keep his record above .500.

A bigger boost came the day before, on July 16, when Freedman, with McGraw as his envoy, bought controlling interest in the Baltimore club. After the purchase, Freedman immediately released pitchers Joe McGinnity and Jack Cronin, first baseman Dan McGann, catcher Roger Bresnahan and outfielders Joe Kelley and Cy Seymour. Kelley and Seymour went off to Cincinnati, the other four joined New York. To make room for the new players McGraw released nine Giants! One of them, outfielder Jack Hendricks, joked about his firing. "There is a story that McGraw fired me the first day. That is a big lie. It was the second day. I hid in the clubhouse the first day."[14]

From 1902 to 1908 "Iron Man" Joe McGinnity won 151 games for the Giants and, in August 1903, he pitched both ends of three doubleheaders and won all six games (photo courtesy National Baseball Library, Cooperstown, N.Y.).

Mrs. John McGraw, in her book, *The Real McGraw,* pointed out that her husband took no chances when it came to securing the services of McGinnity, even to the point of demanding the following note on Stafford Hotel stationery:

> Baltimore, MD
> July 16, 1902
>
> I agree to play Base Ball for the New York Base Ball Club the balance of the season 1902 for the sum of Two Thousand Dollars $2,000. I also agree to sign for the season 1903 for Four Thousand Dollars $4,000. Salary above mentioned to be paid in semi monthly installments. I further agree to live up to all club rules, training dissopation [sic] etc.[15]
>
> Joe McGinnity

It's also been told that McGraw sent Frank Bowerman to Cleveland to get Dummy Taylor who had jumped New York after the disastrous 1901 season. Bowerman had caught Taylor in 1901 and was even taught sign language by the pitcher. McGraw's instructions were, "Go see him in Cleveland. Bawl the hell out of him . . . and give him what he wants. Don't come back without him."[16] Bowerman's mission was successful.

July 24

Mathewson feasted on the Brooklyn club, defeating them 2–0 at Washington Park. Matty pitched a marvelous game, giving up five hits in recording his fourth shutout. He struck out 11, including the side in the fifth. And his control was superb as he walked one batter. His record was even again at 8-8.

July 28

In a rain shortened, five-inning game Mathewson pitched his second consecutive shutout against Brooklyn by the identical score of 2–0. Matty extended his scoreless innings to 16 and probably had McGraw scratching his head at shortstop trying to figure out why in the world anyone would play his star right-hander at first base.

August 1

New York split a doubleheader with St. Louis at the Polo Grounds. McGinnity lost the first game 4–3, but Mathewson came back in the nightcap to win his tenth game of the season 4–2. Although Matty was roughed up for 11 hits, he managed to spread them out and was always tough in the clutch. The Giants' record was an appalling 28-56 as they were now firmly entrenched in last place.

August 5

On three days' rest, Mathewson returned to pitch a fine game against first-place Pittsburgh, but lost 3–0 when Jesse Tannehill tossed a nifty two-hitter. Matty gave up seven hits, walked one and struck out 11 batters but was no match for Tannehill, who would finish the season with a 20-6 mark and a minuscule 1.95 ERA. Tannehill, along with Chesbro and Deacon Phillippe, the big three of the Pittsburgh staff, would win 68 of the 103 victories (66 percent).

August 9

A sizeable crowd of 14,000 turned out at the Polo Grounds to watch New York split a doubleheader with Chicago. Mathewson lost the first game 8–2, bringing his season's mark to 10-10. Matty did not pitch well, being tagged for 12 hits but his teammates were even worse, both at the plate and in the field. Play became so erratic that the Chicago players were actually laughing at New York's clumsiness. Even the fans joined the fun with applause anytime a New York player successfully completed a routine play. It was an embarrassing loss and a horrible display of professional baseball.

August 13

Mathewson upped his record to 11-10 when he trimmed Cincinnati 4–2 at the Polo Grounds, earning New York a split of the doubleheader. Since late July, Matty had been winning more and showing signs of the consistency he displayed the previous year. This was in large part due to his new manager. McGraw, in sharp contast to his predecessors Fogel and Smith, had Mathewson pitching every four days since July 24. The regulated work schedule was now beginning to pay off.

Early on McGraw recognized Matty's superior talent and was dismayed to discover how his star was being utilized. Upon taking over the team he said, "The club at that time was in last place by 14 games — a good, safe margin. The attendance was almost nothing, and when I first walked onto the field to see my team, I found Christy Mathewson playing first base."[17]

August 18

The Giants began their final road trip on a high note by whipping the Chicago Cubs four straight. Mathewson completed the sweep when he tossed a four-hitter and blanked the Cubs 5–0. It was his sixth shutout of the season. He received a great deal of support, mainly from George Browne, Bresnahan and Steve Brodie, who collected eight of the 12 hits off Jack Taylor.

August 21

Encouraged by their fine play in Chicago, the Giants were eager to get to Pittsburgh and take on the first-place Pirates. The results were far different at Exposition Park with Pittsburgh winning two of three and tagging Mathewson with one of the losses. Matty pitched well enough to win on most occasions, allowing six hits and two runs, but had the misfortune of drawing Sam Leever as his opponent. Leever threw a three-hitter and had the Giants eating out of his hands. Matty's record was now 12-11, not all that bad for a team mired in last place with a pathetic 36-66 record.

August 26

After splitting two games in St. Louis, New York traveled to Chicago where Mathewson opened the series by hurling his seventh shutout of the season. The final score was 6-0. Matty scattered eight hits, walked three and fanned six. New York pounded Henry Thielman for 11 hits. It was the third time this season Thielman lost to Matty.

September 1

The Giants, flushed with success from their western road trip where they won seven of 11 games, opened at the Polo Grounds with a doubleheader against St. Louis. They lost both ends 6-4 and 8-2! Mathewson was the victim in the second game, giving up 12 hits and all eight runs. His record went to 13-12, while the Giants were hopelessly lost in last place with a 39-71 mark.

September 6

In one of the dullest and sloppiest games of the year, Christy Mathewson was pounded by Pittsburgh for 13 hits and nine runs. He walked five and was credited with a wild pitch. It was not one of Matty's better days. In fairness, he was given little support. Short on catchers, the Giants were forced to use Jack Robinson, who had trouble handling Matty, allowing four passed balls. Add errors by Lauder, Browne and McGraw and it's easy to see why the score ended 9-3.

The most excitement occurred in the fourth inning when a fire started under the grandstand behind the New York bench. It was quickly extinguished by buckets of water handed by the players to the spectators.

September 10

New York and Chicago split a doubleheader at the Polo Grounds. It was the Cubs' last visit to the big ballpark. The Giants lost the first 4-3 but won the second game behind the splendid pitching of Mathewson. He blanked Chicago 6–0 on seven hits, while maintaining perfect control. He didn't allow a Chicago player to get beyond second base. Matty topped off the great day by hitting an opposite field home run, scoring George Smith ahead of him. It was Matty's fourteenth win and his last of the season. The shutout was his eighth, the best in the league.

September 15

New York and Mathewson continued their inconsistent play, this time against Brooklyn at the Polo Grounds. The Superbas, as Brooklyn was called then, won 7–2. Matty gave up nine hits and three walks. Contributing to his demise were five errors by his teammates, including three by third baseman Lauder.

The lack of support Matty experienced all season was finally catching up to him. Reported *The New York Times,* "Mathewson did not appear to be in his best form, and at times acted peevishly, but this might be attributed to the weak support he received from his club mates in the field."[18] Idols are human too.

The truth is that Mathewson was unhappy with the constant turmoil on the club and when the season ended had agreed to go to St. Louis in the American League. He even accepted a $500 bonus, knowing full well he was under contract with New York for 1903. Matty's move to St. Louis never materialized. The two warring leagues made peace and, among other things, settled the thorny issue of disputed players, which resulted in Mathewson remaining Giants' property. He returned the bonus to St. Louis.

September 23

Mathewson lost his fifteenth game of the season as Boston squeezed out a 2–1 victory at the Polo Grounds. Matty's pinpoint control, of all things, failed him. Both Boston runs scored on wild pitches! The rest of Matty's game was typical. He allowed six hits and struck out eight as his record dropped to 14-15.

September 29

Mathewson lost his sixteenth game and third straight when he was hammered by Brooklyn for five hits and four runs in the second inning. The final score was 5–2. In all, Matty was roughed up for 11 hits, including a home run by Jimmy Sheckard in the fifth inning. The Giants continued their anemic batting with three hits and two unearned runs. No doubt Matty and the rest of the club were anxiously waiting for the miserable season to end.

October 4

Mercifully, the New York Giants' 1902 season came to an end when they split a doubleheader in Boston. Mathewson lost the first game 5–2, his seventeenth loss of the year. Matty allowed seven hits, but Boston was fortunate to bunch them. The first four men in the lineup did most of the damage, accounting for five hits and four runs.

New York won the second game 5–1 behind the superb pitching of "Iron Man" Joe McGinnity who narrowly missed a shutout. The righthander picked up his colorful nickname, so the story goes, while in the minor leagues. A young scribe asked him what he did for work in the off season and McGinnity replied he was an iron man—he worked in his father's foundry. The name suited him perfectly for he was a strong and durable pitcher who utilized a sidearm delivery that minimized the strain on his arm. During his career he would pitch both ends of five doubleheaders. Upon joining New York he already had pitched two in 1901 for Baltimore and in 1903, in a phenomenal display of strength and durability, would pitch three doubleheaders in the month of August, winning all six games!

As expected, Christy Mathewson, his teammates and the New York fans were disappointed and discouraged over the 1902 season. And from a personal standpoint, Matty had to be especially disheartened at his 14-17 record, even though he posted an outstanding 2.11 ERA. It was particularly discouraging after the 20-17 mark in his rookie year. His chief concern, beyond the poor support from his teammates, was his lack of pitching consistency—brilliant one day, terrible or mediocre the next time he went to the mound.

In spite of this bleak picture, the future still looked promising for New York. There was new and dedicated ownership, attendance was on the rise and now they had an aggressive field manager who, soon after taking over the helm of the demoralized club, was boasting to the fans that the team's performance would be changing dramatically, and as early as 1903! John McGraw was true to his word. He would also influence Matty's development while the two became good friends. The close relationship would help transform the young lad from an unpolished gem to a sparkling diamond.

Chapter 5
First 30-Game Season, 1903

W	L	Pct	ERA
30	13	.698	2.26

At the end of the 1902 season, when the National League looked at the attendance figures for the year, it revealed the senior circuit had been outdrawn by over 500,000 customers by the upstart American League. This revelation, which went directly to the core of the war—money—put the National League in a more conciliatory mood. They offered Ban Johnson the opportunity to merge the two leagues, but the stalwart president refused. The inevitable was soon to come.

In January 1903, with both leagues now seeking peace, a pact was reached called the National Agreement. It gave the American League major league status and permitted a franchise to be placed in New York, but not in Pittsburgh, where the National League's best team resided.

Beyond that, territorial cities were established in each league—American: Boston, New York, Philadelphia, Washington, Detroit, Cleveland, St. Louis and Chicago; National: Boston, New York, Brooklyn, Philadelphia, Pittsburgh, Cincinnati, St. Louis and Chicago. Additionally, the governing of the two leagues would be the responsibility of a three-man National Commission. The commission was composed of National League president Harry Pulliam, American League president Johnson and Cincinnati owner Garry Herrmann, elected by the other owners.

With the agreement in place, the commission then turned to the more thorny and highly emotional issue of ballplayers, especially those that jumped from one league to the other during the war. After much bickering, it was agreed that 1902 would be the base year. All players who jumped to the new American League before the 1902 season would stay with their present team; players who jumped after the start of the 1902 season would be ordered back to their original clubs. As previously discussed, Mathewson was ruled Giants' property and never made it to St. Louis in the American League.

With the baseball war essentially over, McGraw and Brush were now faced with the reality of additional competition when Johnson, as agreed, transferred the Baltimore franchise to New York.

5 • First 30-Game Season, 1903

"They were the Highlanders, so-called because their first president was Joseph Gordon and the Gordon Highlanders were then the best-known regiment in the British Army. Also, they played their games at Broadway and 165th Street, one of the highest points of land in Manhattan,"[1] pointed out author Joseph Durso. The Highlanders, although decimated by McGraw's raiding when the franchise was in Baltimore, managed with some chicanery of their own, to acquire a star pitcher, hitter and manager—Jack Chesbro of Pittsburgh, Wee Willie Keeler of Brooklyn and Clark Griffith of Chicago (AL). The Highlanders played respectable baseball in 1903, finishing fourth and in years to come would build a dynasty under a new and familiar name, the New York Yankees.

The 1903 season would be a milestone for New York Giants fans. The team was basically the same as at the end of 1902 except for outfielder Sam Mertes, signed away from the Chicago White Sox and the acquisition of Billy Gilbert, who played shortstop for Baltimore. McGraw made one other important addition, mustachioed Thomas J. Murphy, the skilled Baltimore groundskeeper. "John McGraw's baseball was based on speed and alertness," said his wife. "He needed the best-kept grounds in the league, and Murphy provided it."[2]

The big difference in 1903 would be a full season of McGraw's skillful leadership, which would gain the New York club respectability. McGraw's wife, Blanche, described her husband's fierce competitiveness in these words: "Defeat was his mortal enemy. He was a force that knew only one compromise: victory."[3]

For Mathewson personally, 1903 would be a critical year, one in which he became close friends with McGraw. In fact, the Mathewsons and McGraws shared a rented ground-floor furnished apartment at Columbus Avenue and 85th Street and traveled to the Polo Grounds together. During these early morning trips, the manager would pour out his baseball knowledge to Mathewson, especially what pitches batters could hit easiest, as they went off to the game.

After a disappointing 14-17 record the previous year, Mathewson was still a popular figure and attraction with the fans. As one baseball historian commented, "If he was already the favorite of New Yorkers, he wasn't yet the superstar and superhero he would become within a few years."[4] Mathewson would begin to blossom into a superstar and genuine American idol.

The Season

April 17

Over 20,000 enthusiastic fans came out to the Polo Grounds to watch Christy Mathewson pitch the opener against Brooklyn. To the crowd's disappointment, Matty pitched poorly right from the start. He allowed Brooklyn to score four times in the first inning. Not to be denied, New York came roaring back with four runs in the bottom of the first and another in the third to give Matty a 5–4 lead! It was not enough. Matty gave up three more runs in the fifth and single tallies in the seventh and ninth innings. It was a bad day for the young man. In addition to the eight hits, he walked five and threw two wild pitches. His teammates contributed to the defeat too with six costly errors. The final score was Brooklyn 9, New York 7.

Earlier in the week, Ban Johnson must have felt a great deal of pride and satisfaction when he read in the morning paper that National League president Harry C. Pulliam issued rigid instructions to managers, players and umpires on the rules and conduct of the game. By making the rules uniform, it was Pulliam's intent to avoid, as much as possible, different interpretations by umpires, thus reducing arguments and brawls on the field. In addition, he made it clear that rough play and misconduct on the playing field would not be tolerated.

"Rowdyism on the ball field of the National League will not prevail during the season of 1903," he said. Then he became more specific and spoke to the heart of the matter. "Managers, Captains and players are especially warned against attacking the umpire in any manner after the completion of the game or by any action, overt or secret, trying to influence the spectators against the umpire and cause him bodily harm."[5]

It was the credo Ban Johnson had been preaching for years in the Western League and, most recently, in the American League.

April 21

Mathewson pitched his second inaugural game in a week, this time at Brooklyn's Washington Park as the Twenty-Third Regiment Band regaled the fans with a choice musical program. Mrs. Charles H. Ebbets, wife of the Brooklyn owner, threw out the first ball and play began.

Unlike the Polo Grounds opener, Matty pitched brilliantly against Brooklyn, recording his first victory of the season. He allowed three hits and two walks and won by a score of 2–1. Catcher Jack Warner, a familiar face to New York fans (he played for the Giants from 1897 through 1901), drove in the winning run in the ninth inning.

April 27

It wasn't pretty, but it was a victory. In an old-fashioned slugfest Mathewson beat Boston 10–7 as New York maintained its narrow first-place lead over the reigning champs from Pittsburgh. Matty allowed six hits, one of which was a grand slam by second baseman Frank Bonner and another homer by first baseman Fred Tenney with a man on base.

5 • *First 30-Game Season, 1903*   53

May 1

Mathewson had an easy time of it at Baker Bowl, where a slim crowd of 1,391 had little to cheer about, as he held Philadelphia to three runs while New York pounded Chick Fraser for 11 hits and 11 runs. In marked contrast to previous games, New York played errorless baseball and now boasted a record of 9-3. It was Matty's third win against one defeat. He also helped his cause with a home run.

May 7

Mathewson whipped Philadelphia 8–4 for the second time in a week, this victory coming before the home crowd at the Polo Grounds. He was far from dominant but was able to pace himself and scatter nine hits. Matty often extolled the virtues of coasting during games in which he was comfortably ahead so that he could conserve his strength for that critical moment when caught in a jam. As Matty confessed in later years, "I have always been against a twirler pitching himself out, when there is no necessity for it, as so many youngsters do. They burn them through for eight innings and then, when the pinch comes, something is lacking."[6]

It is interesting to note that in the eighth inning Joe McGinnity, not even in the game, was ordered off the bench and out of the grounds by umpire August Moran. Apparently, the Iron Man was arguing too vociferously and Moran, no doubt, recalling Pulliam's strong edict to the umpires in April, tossed the pitcher.

May 12

For eight innings Christy Mathewson dominated the Cincinnati Reds at the Polo Grounds. He even had a no-hitter through seven. But in the top of the ninth, with the game still scoreless, Matty came unglued. His demise came with Kelley on second and two out. In the "pinch," as Matty liked to refer to tight situations, the young right-hander gave up a single to Jake Beckley, followed by Harry Steinfeldt's triple over George Van Haltren's head in center field. When the inning ended Cincinnati had scored four runs. New York made a good try in their half of the ninth but only managed one run for a final score of 4–1.

This was one time Matty failed to follow his own advice as he struck out a season-high 13 batters. He often said, "A pitcher must remember that there are eight other men in the game ... to stop balls hit at them, and he must have confidence in them."[7]

May 16

If there was any question of Mathewson's charisma and drawing power, this game left little doubt as an estimated crowd of 31,500 were packed into the Polo Grounds to watch their idol trim the champion Pittsburgh Pirates. The local police had their hands full as fully 500 spectators forced their way into the game after thousands were turned away. It was standing room only.

It was a typical Mathewson-pitched game: eight scattered hits, mixed with seven strikeouts and perfect control. The final score was New York 7, Pittsburgh 3, with Roger Bresnahan, Jack Warner, Billy Lauder and Billy Gilbert accounting for most of the seven runs.

The victory kept New York in first place with a 16-7 record. The new team in town, the Highlanders, were struggling with a 10-12 mark, a sixth place standing in the American League.

May 19

For the second time in four days Mathewson beat the Pirates, this time in relief of Dummy Taylor, by a score of 4–3. Matty entered the game in the eighth with Pittsburgh leading 3-2. New York scored single runs in the seventh and eighth innings while Mathewson blanked Pittsburgh on one skimpy hit. His record stood at 6-2.

May 20

After beating Pittsburgh in a two-inning relief stint, McGraw called on Mathewson to start the next day. Matty met the challenge by scattering hits and blanking the champs 2–0. New York took the series three games to one with Matty winning all three.

He was at his best in the sixth inning when Pittsburgh loaded the bases with two out. Here was the classic "pinch" Mathewson frequently talked about. "In most Big League ball games, there comes an inning on which hangs victory or defeat," he said. "Certain intellectual fans call it the crisis; college professors, interested in the sport, have named it the psychological moment; Big League managers mention it as the 'break,' and pitchers speak of the 'pinch.'"[8] Regardless of the name, Matty met the challenge. He struck out Kitty Bransfield to end the inning and went on to win his seventh game of the season.

President Pulliam, determined to maintain orderly conduct in the game and enforce his earlier edict, announced he was barring Van Haltren from the coaching lines for five days for inciting the spectators in the previous Tuesday's game.

May 26

Mathewson beat the Chicago Cubs 4–3 at the Polo Grounds for his eighth victory against only two losses. He was off to a fast start. After Chicago tied the score in the ninth, the Giants came back with a run in their half to record the victory. Matty's control was shaky; he allowed three walks and three wild pitches. New York's record stood at 22-9 and manager McGraw had his team fired up and playing winning baseball.

May 29

Christy Mathewson received a rousing ovation from the Polo Grounds spectators after he pitched his second shutout of the season, blanking Boston 3-0. Matty gave up five hits while walking three. It was his ninth win against only two losses.

Under McGraw's guidance, Mathewson's pitching was drastically different from the previous year's, as was the performance of the entire team. McGraw was applying his magic and the fans loved it, as record crowds turned out to watch the Giants.

The following day, however, New York split a doubleheader with Boston while Chicago took two from St. Louis and moved into first place, a game ahead of the Giants.

June 1

The Giants began their first western road trip with the initial stop in Pittsburgh to face the third place Pirates at Exposition Park. Mathewson trounced the struggling Pirates 10-2 for his tenth win of the season. Both teams wound up with ten hits each, but the difference was that Matty scattered his, except for the sixth inning when the Pirates bunched three hits for two runs. It was the fourth time Matty had beaten the champions in this young season.

June 4

Mathewson opened the Chicago series, under threatening skies, with another easy victory. He allowed four hits and after the second inning no Chicago player reached second. In the meantime, New York was beating up on Carl Lundgren for 11 hits and nine runs.

Matty's seventh straight victory set the tempo for the next three games at West Side Park as the Giants won by scores of 5-2, 7-4 and 9-4. The series sweep moved McGraw's men back into first place.

June 9

After the Giants were delayed a day in reaching St. Louis, Mathewson opened the series, as he did in Chicago, by trouncing the locals 11-2. Matty allowed two runs in the first, then blanked St. Louis until the seventh when McGraw, realizing the game was won, replaced him with little-used

Roscoe Miller. Matty's record was now 12-2, including a string of eight straight victories.

Two umpires were used in the game, James Holliday and August Moran, a practice that was slowly creeping into the game. It was around 1906 in the American League when two arbiters became the standard practice and in 1912 when both leagues used two umpires per game and two in reserve.

June 13

Christy Mathewson continued his marvelous pitching, this time dominating the Cincinnati Reds, tossing a nifty one-hitter, the hit coming in the first inning when Hall of Famer Joe Kelley tripled down the third-base line. After that it was all goose eggs for Cincinnati. The final score was 4–0 with Browne, Bresnahan and McGann doing most of the damage for New York off left-hander Frank "Noodles" Hahn.

In 1903 Hahn would lead the Cincinnati pitching staff with 22 victories. He obtained his nickname, so the story goes, because he was shrewd and crafty. In other words, he used his noodle.

Matty's record stood at a spectacular 13-2 with three shutouts and nine consecutive victories. The Giants' record was 34-13. They were in first place and riding the crest of an eight-game winning streak. What a difference a year makes.

June 18

After arriving back on the east coast from a highly successful western trip (9-3), the Giants journeyed to the city of brotherly love where they split two games with Philadelphia. Still in first place, Matty opened the home stand at the Polo Grounds against Chicago and lost a heartbreaker 1–0, snapping his nine-game winning streak.

The sparse crowd of 5,000, mainly due to the poor weather, were witness to a fine pitcher's duel between Mathewson and Jake Weimer. Matty allowed seven hits, but his wildness cost the game. With the bases loaded in the fifth inning, Matty walked Jimmy Slagle forcing home the only run of the game. New York had several chances to score and had a runner on third a number of times, but 20-game winner Weimer wiggled out of each jam.

The loss, coupled with a Pittsburgh victory, knocked New York out of first place. They would never get back in for the rest of the season.

Noteworthy was the recognition the press gave to the men in blue. "Two umpires—Johnstone and Moran—officiated during the game with very little friction or trouble, the double system working very satisfactorily."[9]

June 22

Over 19,000 spectators poured into the Polo Grounds to watch McGinnity and Mathewson pitch the doubleheader against Chicago. The Iron Man won the first in ten innings 5–4, but Mathewson was roughed up in the second game. He allowed 13 hits and ten runs, six coming in the ninth inning when nothing went right for Matty. Less than halfway through the season his record stood at 13-4.

June 26

More than 10,000 persons, the largest Friday crowd of the season, wildly cheered Mathewson and New York as they defeated first-place Pittsburgh 8–2. It was Matty's fifth victory of the season over the powerful Pirates and upped his record to 14-4.

The big news, however, came the day before when National League president Harry Pulliam announced that the Cincinnati peace agreement of six months had been violated when the Detroit club's (American League) management released Norman "Kid" Elberfeld to the Highlanders where he was currently playing shortstop. According to New York president John Brush, Elberfeld was under contract to the Giants for the year 1903, but at the Cincinnati conference he was awarded to Detroit at the same time Ed Delahanty was designated for Washington and George Davis to Chicago in the American League.

Detroit's action prompted Brush to request permission from Pulliam to exercise its legal rights to the services of Davis (who was under contract to New York for the 1903 and 1904 seasons at the time of the Cincinnati agreement). Brush's argument was that it was "unfair and subversive" that Elberfeld be permitted to play for the Highlanders, strengthening the rival club. Pulliam agreed and another major league baseball war began heating up.

With Pulliam's permission McGraw inserted Davis into the lineup at short. He did not, however, figure in the outcome of the game. New York left fielder Sam Mertes was the batting star. In the fifth inning he doubled with the bases loaded driving in three runs. Mertes would lead the league in doubles (32) and RBIs (104) for the season.

June 30

The St. Louis Cardinals visited New York and the Polo Grounds for the second time this season and promptly trounced the Giants 4–2 before a small but enthusiastic crowd of 4,500. Mathewson's downfall came in the sixth inning when St. Louis bunched three hits along with Davis' error, which accounted for three runs.

Davis would appear in only four games at the Polo Grounds because

Chicago White Sox owner Charles Comiskey "secured an injunction in federal court in New York City to keep him off the field."[10]

July 6

On July 2 New York left for Chicago to begin its second western swing. The first two games were split and now Mathewson faced Chicago for the third and final game of the series. Matty won easily by a score of 5–1. It was his fifteenth victory of the season and helped New York stay close to first-place Pittsburgh.

The efforts of presidents Johnson and Pulliam to maintain peace and order on the field between players and umpires was beginning to show results. Every so often, however, an incident would erupt to remind baseball magnates there was still a long way to go. Such an incident occurred on July 7 at the American League park during the game between the New York Highlanders and Chicago White Sox. According to *The New York Times*, in the seventh inning, "umpire John F. Sheridan rushed over toward the visiting players' bench and struck right fielder Green of the Chicago team across the head with his mask. Green retaliated by striking Sheridan with his fist, and a rough and tumble fight ensued."[11]

The fight was the result of Sheridan calling Green out on a close play at first. The Chicago outfielder continued to argue vociferously until Sheridan had heard enough and rushed Green. The umpire was taken from the grounds to the thirty-third precinct station house and locked up on a charge of disorderly conduct. An hour later, he was released on bail posted by President Joseph Gordon of the Highlanders. In *The Umpire Story*, author James Kahn saw a different side to Sheridan. "He had a positive manner, calling his plays decisively and clearly, but he had a deep understanding of his job, and was a master of restraint as well..."[12]

July 9

Mathewson got lucky in St. Louis. The Giants scored three runs in the ninth to overcome a 2–1 deficit and hand Matty a 4–2 victory. McGinnity blanked St. Louis in the bottom of the ninth to preserve the victory.

The pitcher who took the loss for the Cardinals was rookie Mordecai Peter Centennial Brown, more commonly known as Three Finger. At age seven Brown, visiting his uncle's farm, got his hand caught in a corn shredder. He lost most of his index finger and injured his pinky and thumb.

Brown never was blazing fast, but as he claimed, "that stub helped my curves. It really made 'em break off sharp."[13]

This game was the first of their head-to-head matchups, classic confrontations of two great pitchers who never failed to excite and thrill baseball fans over the years.

July 11

Two days later, in Cincinnati, Mathewson returned the favor for McGinnity, relieving him in the seventh inning when the Reds scored five runs, which could have been even more were it not for catcher Jack Warner who picked off Harry Steinfeldt napping on third base. The final score ended 8–6, New York. McGraw's men were still in second place, behind Pittsburgh, with a 43–24 record.

July 15

It took Mathewson 14 innings but he still managed to beat Pittsburgh 6–3 for his seventeenth win of the season and sixth against the Pirates. It was an exciting game. New York trailed 2–0 in the ninth but then erupted for three runs to take the lead. In the bottom half of the ninth Pittsburgh tied the game and it remained that way until the fourteenth inning, when New York scored three more runs.

Adding to the excitement of the game was the ugly mood of the Pittsburgh fans, which resulted in additional police being assigned to the game to protect Giants catcher Frank Bowerman from possible harm. The reason stemmed from an incident that occurred on June 26 at the Polo Grounds prior to the game. Apparently Bowerman slugged Pittsburgh manager Fred Clarke in, of all places, the ticket office, in a dispute over the catching abilities of the Giants' Jack Warner. The next day Pittsburgh owner Barney Dreyfuss complained to New York management for not reprimanding Bowerman. The *New York Daily Tribune,* however, pointed out that Dreyfuss' men were guilty of rowdyism too. The newspaper went on to point out in a game in May Doheny threw a bat in the way of Bowerman and McGinnity who were trying to catch a pop fly, later Wagner interfered with the Iron Man at second base and, finally, Clarke interfered with Bowerman. It was all part of the long-standing hatred these two teams had for each other. It would eventually escalate into the "Hey, Barney!" incident the following year.

July 21

New York's 15-game western road trip turned out to be more disappointing than the 8–7 mark would indicate. They lost their last three games to Pittsburgh, which marked a turning point in their drive for the pennant. Prior to the three losses, New York was playing at a .648 clip; after the losses they played at a .507 pace.

The Giants continued their losing ways in their first game back east. Mathewson lost to Brooklyn at Washington Park 4–1. Matty pitched well enough to win, but Ned Garvin was simply outstanding, allowing five hits, walking none and blanking New York for eight innings. In the ninth the

Giants managed to eke out one run to avoid the shutout. Matty's record now stood at 17-6.

July 24

Mathewson suffered his second defeat in four days, this time at the hands of Philadelphia, 3-0 at Baker Bowl. Bill Duggleby held New York to five hits, as they had difficulty figuring out the right-hander's deceptive curve ball. Matty's record was now 17-7 with 62 games remaining.

July 28

Matty lost his third straight game, as Boston trimmed the Giants 5-3 at the Polo Grounds. Ed Gremminger, Boston's third baseman, was the hitting star of the day. In four trips to the plate, he sacrificed, singled, doubled and drove the ball over Bresnahan's head (playing center field) to the ropes for a home run. In the meantime, New York was totally baffled by Vic Willis, who over a fine 13-year career would win 248 baseball games. Mathewson's record now stood at 17-8.

July 31

Mathewson lost his fourth straight game and second in four days to Boston. The game was at South End Grounds and the score 4-1. Matty pitched reasonably well, giving up six hits and four walks, but his teammates failed to hit Boston's newly acquired pitcher Walter "Pops" Williams. The southpaw allowed only three hits, walked four and struck out as many. Williams had pitched for Chicago and Philadelphia before arriving in Boston and this would be his last year in the major leagues. Matty's record was now 17-9 and he was showing signs of tiring. Since June 18 his record was 4-7.

August 3

The New York Giants were in a bona fide slump, losing 11 of 13 games and tumbling into third place. McGinnity, in an unusual request, asked McGraw if he could pitch both games of the doubleheader against Boston on August 1. McGraw, no doubt trying to shake up his players, readily agreed. The Iron Man stunned the large crowd by pitching magnificently, winning 4-1 and 5-2. In the first game he allowed six hits and walked only one batter. In the second game he showed signs of tiring when Boston scored two runs. McGinnity would pitch two more doubleheaders during August.

"Mathewson proved himself to be a true Giant here today, for although the home team made as many hits as the visitors, his coolness at trying times enabled his team to defeat Boston in an eleven inning game by a score of 4–1,"[14] so began the *New York Daily Tribune* account of Matty's eighteenth victory. But it wasn't easy. New York had to score three times in the top of the eleventh and then nervously watch Matty, with two men on in the bottom of the eleventh, fan the next three batters. In all, Mathewson struck out 11 and walked two.

August 7

After three days of steady rain New York finally got a chance to play Philadelphia as over 10,000 enthusiastic Giants fans delighted in the doubleheader victory. Mathewson won the opener 7–5, but was far from baffling. He allowed nine hits, five walks and struck out ten. Mathewson, Browne, Bresnahan and McGraw accounted for eight of New York's ten hits and four of the seven runs. Matty's record was 19–9. Dummy Taylor won the second game 6–2 as the Giants moved back into second place by percentage points.

August 10

In an interborough pitchers duel at Washington Park, Mathewson bested Brooklyn's Henry Schmidt (21–13 in 1903) by a score of 3–1. Matty pitched splendidly, allowing five singles and two walks. If it were not for Warner's passed ball in the ninth, Matty would have had a shutout. As it was, he reached a personal milestone—his twentieth victory—and was headed for his best season in a Giants uniform.

Two days earlier (August 8), McGinnity did the double dandy again, this time beating Brooklyn 6–1 and 4–3 at the Polo Grounds before a sellout gathering of 31,647. McGinnity, repeating his splendid doubleheader victory of a week ago at Boston, kept New York securely in second place. More importantly, McGraw's men were still within hailing distance of first-place Pittsburgh.

In the opener, New York scored four runs in the first inning, Brooklyn scored one and after that it was all McGinnity. He scattered six hits over the next eight innings, walked none and won easily in one hour and forty-five minutes.

The second game was entirely different. Greeted by thunderous applause from the partisan crowd, McGinnity pitched well, but found himself trailing 3–2 when New York came to bat for the last time. It was an exciting finish. Jack Dunn and Billy Gilbert singled, Warner bunted toward third and was safe on third baseman Dutch Jordan's errant throw, Dunn scoring. McGraw sent Van Haltren to bat for McGinnity and the pinch hitter came through with a single inside the first-base line scoring Gilbert for the victory.

As soon as Gilbert crossed the plate, thousands of excited spectators jumped from the stands and rushed to New York's bench and hoisted McGraw on their shoulders in joyful celebration. Noted the *New York Tribune,* "It was suggested after the game that the name of the grounds should be changed from the Polo Grounds to 'McGinnityville!'"[15]

Ninety miles south at Baker Bowl in Philadelphia 16 people died and another 125 were injured when a walkway between the grandstand and the left field bleachers, which overhung the street, collapsed. The tragedy occurred at 5:40 in the afternoon with Boston at bat in the fourth inning of the second game of the doubleheader. Apparently, two drunken men were quarreling in the street outside the park. As more and more spectators left their seats and gathered to watch the two drunks, the walkway couldn't hold the weight and collapsed. Later it was discovered that the wooden supports holding the walkway were rotted.

Outside the grounds was a horror scene with bodies strewn all over the street and others buried under the wreckage. Some victims were unconscious and those injured and awake were moaning with pain. It was a horrifying disaster that reverberated throughout the city of Philadelphia for months to come.

August 13

New York won its third doubleheader in a week, this time against St. Louis by scores of 6–2 and 9–7. Mathewson won the opener, his twenty-first victory of the season. It was another fine performance by the right-hander. He allowed seven hits and only one walk while fanning ten. It was Three Finger Brown's second loss to Mathewson, a pitching rivalry that would continue through 1916.

August 17

New York's luck ran out, at least in doubleheaders, as they split with Cincinnati, winning the first 7–4 behind Mathewson and losing the nightcap 9–5. Over 13,000 came to watch the two games at the Polo Grounds as Matty chalked up his twenty-second win against nine losses. It was a typical Mathewson-pitched contest—seven hits, one walk.

August 20

New York split another doubleheader, this time with Pittsburgh, 13–7 and 4–1. New York scored seven runs in the first inning of the opener on sloppy play by the Pirates and Mathewson pitched six innings (relieved by Miller) for his twenty-third victory. It was the seventh time Matty had beaten first-place Pittsburgh. In the second game Pittsburgh scored three runs off Taylor in the fifth inning to clinch the victory and keep the Giants five games in back of them.

5 • First 30-Game Season, 1903

August 21

Scheduling demands and rainouts resulted in yet another doubleheader at the Polo Grounds. Pittsburgh's Sam Leever shut out New York 3–0 in the opener, highlighted by shortstop Honus Wagner's marvelous fielding. The Flying Dutchman also incurred the displeasure of the more than 16,000 spectators when he hooked first baseman Dan McGann's neck while running out a grounder. Some thought it a "playful" action, but the majority did not as they "hissed" Wagner when he came to the plate in the fourth inning. The hisses quickly turned to cheers when he lined a double into the left field gap, scoring Tommy Leach.

Mathewson won the nightcap 9–5, the eighth time he had beaten Pittsburgh. Although he gave up 11 hits, only one was for extra bases, Ginger Beaumont's double (he would lead the league with 209 hits). Matty's record was now a princely 24-9 and he was working on a streak of seven straight.

August 24

The McGinnity and Mathewson pitching combination for the doubleheader against Chicago at the Polo Grounds drew more than 10,000 fans. Most were disappointed with the first game as Chicago won 7–3, due to eight errors, five by shortstop Charlie Babb. McGinnity suffered the loss.

In the nightcap, umpire Hank O'Day called the game due to darkness after Chicago made out in the seventh with the score 8–1 in favor of New York. This was Mathewson's eighth win in a row and twenty-fifth of the season. He did it in customary fashion—six hits, one walk.

August 26

Boston snapped Mathewson's eight-game winning streak at South End Grounds by a score of 6–5. Matty, with a comfortable 5–1 lead in the sixth, faltered and was pounded for five runs by the Beaneaters. He was replaced by Taylor. The game was also marred by a wild ninth inning when umpire August Moran called Bresnahan out at the plate; if allowed, it would have been the tying run. The entire New York team surrounded Moran arguing and threatening with McGraw and Gilbert the most demonstrative. Moran quelled the disturbance when he ordered McGraw and Gilbert off the field. New York won the second game 3–2 in ten innings.

August 28

Mathewson beat Boston 12–6 in a slugfest at the South End Grounds. Matty allowed three runs in the first and ninth innings to capture his twenty-sixth victory against ten losses. New York was in high spirits as they headed home, still in second place, with an excellent chance of overcoming the Pirates in the pennant race.

Three days later the Iron Man did it again! For the third time in August McGinnity pitched both ends of a doubleheader and won both. In doubleheader games in 1903 McGinnity was perfect with six victories. This time the victim was Philadelphia by scores of 4–1 and 9–2. The double marathon lasted three hours and three minutes and at the end the Iron Man showed no signs of fatigue. In fact one observer believed McGinnity looked fresh enough to pitch a third game.

September 2

In a rare display of wildness Mathewson lost to Brooklyn 4–1 at the Polo Grounds. In the first inning Matty walked three batters, which led to three Brooklyn runs. The Superbas added another run in the fourth while Bill Reidy was holding New York scoreless until the ninth. Matty allowed only six hits, but walked a total of seven, which was his downfall. His record was now 26-11.

September 5

In a rain shortened five-inning game, Mathewson one-hit Brooklyn 3–1 at Washington Park. (*The New York Times* declared the game a no-hitter, but the official scorer saw it differently.) Brooklyn scored in the fourth as the result of two errors by right fielder George Browne. Even in this shortened game, Matty managed to strike out five batters and now owned a record of 27-11. The Giants were running out of time though as the Pirates kept winning and now enjoyed a nine and one-half-game lead.

September 8

Mathewson and Brooklyn's Reidy met for the third time in a week. Reidy won the first, Mathewson the second and this time the game ended after eight innings, due to darkness, in a 4–4 tie. It also closed out New York's season at the Polo Grounds as they headed for Philadelphia and then on to their last western swing.

The umpire who called the game on account of darkness was Tim Hurst, one of the all time great arbiters. The story most often told about Hurst, whether authentic or not, goes like this, "When umpiring in Philadelphia he used to call games on account of darkness, though the sun would still be shining, so he could get the six o'clock train back to New York."[16] Although this game was in New York, one wonders if Tim had an appointment in Philadelphia.

September 12

After sweeping the doubleheader in Philadelphia, New York moved west for the last time with the first stop St. Louis. Matty won a close game in extra innings 4–3. In the top of the tenth, with the game tied at 3–3, Jack Warner reached first safely when second baseman John Farrell booted a grounder. Matty sacrificed him to second and when George Browne beat out another bunt Warner went to third. Roger Bresnahan flied to Jack Dunleavy in right, scoring Warner. Matty retired the Cardinals in the tenth for the victory, his twenty-eighth against 11 losses.

September 15

After taking three out of five from St. Louis, New York moved on to Cincinnati where they lost the opener 8–0 as Mathewson was touched for four runs in five innings. Bill Bartley, a new pitcher McGraw obtained from the Texas State League, replaced Matty in the sixth. The rookie gave up four runs but settled down the next two innings. Mathewson's record was now 28-12.

September 18

Three days later Mathewson returned to League Park to beat Cincinnati 7–5 in relief of Dummy Taylor. Entering the bottom of the sixth, Taylor had a 4–2 lead but couldn't hold it as Cincinnati scored three runs. The Giants tied the game in their half of the seventh before Matty got the call from McGraw to replace Taylor. New York went on to score single tallies in the eighth and ninth innings to win the game for Mathewson, his twenty-ninth of the season.

September 19

In spite of Mathewson pitching two innings of relief the day before, McGraw chose his star hurler to open the Chicago series at West Side Park. Matty pitched well but lost to the four-hit pitching of 21-game winner Jack Weimer, 3–0. The victory moved Chicago within one game of the second-place Giants. Mathewson only allowed four hits, but his four walks, coupled with two New York errors accounted for all three Chicago runs. It was Matty's thirteenth and last loss of the season.

September 21

Manager John McGraw, determined to hold on to second place, called on his ace for the third times in four days to face the surging Chicago Cubs. Matty answered the call by beating Chicago 8–3 for his thirtieth victory of the season. He would win 30 or more games three more times before his career ended.

By the fourth inning, Matty had a 6-0 lead and coasted the rest of the way. Not surprisingly, he tired late in the game, giving up a run in the eighth and two more in the ninth. This was Mathewson's last game of the season, finishing it with a marvelous 30-13 mark. Led by McGraw, New York wrapped up the season five days later with an 84-55 record and a creditable second-place finish.

The 1903 season for the New York Giants, by any standard of measurement, was a wonderful success. McGraw, at the helm for a full season, brought his rejuvenated players into second place, six and one-half games behind pennant-winning Pittsburgh. This performance was a major improvement over 1902 when New York finished last, 53½ games in back of the same Pittsburgh club!

The team batting average leaped from .238 to .272; runs rose from 401 to 729; and stolen bases increased from 187 to 264. Bresnahan (.350 average), Mertes (league-leading 104 RBIs) and Browne (.313 average) had outstanding seasons along with the pitching duo of Mathewson and McGinnity who accounted for 61 of the 84 New York victories.

As Mrs. McGraw stated, "Overnight this most ridiculous club in baseball had restored public confidence in New York."[17]

Mathewson had a magnificent season with a 30-13 mark and a 2.26 ERA. He led the National League with 267 strikeouts, while issuing 100 walks in over 366 innings, the most in his career. Noted for his pinpoint control, Matty would lower his bases on balls dramatically in the seasons to come.

McGraw, who cultivated Mathewson's friendship and trust, contributed greatly to the pitcher's outstanding performance. It was a marked departure from the previous year when Matty was pitching on an irregular basis and even used sparingly at first base and in the outfield. McGraw's unwavering confidence and controlled leadership were exactly what Mathewson needed at this critical juncture in his career. The stage was now set for these two giants of the game to control the destiny of the New York club in the years ahead.

Chapter 6
First Pennant!, 1904

W	L	Pct	ERA
33	12	.733	2.03

Taking a last-place club, 53½ games in back, to second place, six and one-half behind the leader, in one season would be reward enough for most major league managers. Not John McGraw. To him winning was what the game of baseball was all about and he was determined to win the National League pennant in 1904.

McGraw, a shrewd planner and quick to recognize deficiencies in his club, began preparing for the new season well before the 1903 campaign was over. First, he picked up right-handed pitcher Leon "Red" Ames late in the 1903 season. Ames came directly from the Ilio, New York, town team. It was a solid acquisition that would begin paying dividends in 1905 when he became a dependable starter for New York. He also signed George "Hooks" Wiltse, a young left-hander with no major league experience, who would win 136 games over a span of 11 years for the Giants. It's been said the nickname Hooks was derived either from his curve ball or nose, or both. He bought Art Devlin, a 25-year-old third baseman from Newark, who would remain a fixture at that position for eight years. From Jersey City in the Eastern League McGraw bought their leading hitter, Harry "Moose" McCormick.

Lastly, over the winter McGraw struck a deal with Brooklyn for a player he had been eager to obtain for years. He sent Charlie Babb, a mediocre infielder, and pitcher Jack Cronin, who had a poor season, to Brooklyn for scrappy veteran Bill Dahlen. Commented McGraw, "Now I have the man I wanted ever since I have had charge of this team. There is no better shortstop in baseball."[1]

The Giants of 1904 were comprised mostly of veteran ball players. The infield, now anchored at shortstop by Dahlen, placed McGann at first base, Gilbert at second and Devlin at third. In the outfield, from left to right, were Mertes, Bresnahan and Browne. Mathewson, McGinnity and Taylor did most of the pitching with the 24-year-old rookie Wiltse making an impressive showing. Bowerman and Warner would share the catching duties.

This photo was taken in 1904, one of the earliest of Mathewson in a New York Giants uniform (photo courtesy Miller Library, Keystone Junior College, LaPlume, Pennsylvania).

Mathewson was now entering his fifth season in the National League and his first on a club that possessed veteran talent at every position. It was destined to be an exciting year for Matty, who would experience the satisfaction of being a key member of a pennant winner with national attention focused on him.

The Season

April 14

On the eve of the opening game McGraw, never one to mince words, staked his claim to the 1904 pennant. "I have the strongest team I've ever led into a pennant race. I ought to come in first."[2]

An early morning snowstorm did not dampen the enthusiasm for the opener at Brooklyn's Washington Park. A record crowd of over 15,000 gathered to greet the four large automobiles carrying members of the two teams. The excitement mounted when the players marched across the field, led by the Twenty-third Regiment Band, for the hoisting of the American flag. Welcoming speeches and ceremonial hoopla delayed the game until after 4:00 p.m.

At that time the New York Giants and Christy Mathewson took control of the game. After four innings with the score 5–1 in favor of New York and Mathewson pitching superbly there was little doubt of the eventual outcome. Matty gave up three hits and one run coasting to an easy 7–1 victory. Browne, McGann and Bowerman had seven of New York's ten hits.

April 18

Mathewson needed relief help in the bottom of the ninth from McGinnity for New York to hold on to a come-from-behind 7–6 victory over Philadelphia at Baker Bowl. Matty was far from puzzling as he was touched for ten hits and six runs in eight innings. The official scorer awarded this game to the Iron Man. It was New York's fourth win in a row as the team was off to a fast start. Devlin and McGann were the hitting heroes.

The previous day, baseball was played on Sunday for the first time in the history of the National League in Brooklyn. The locals beat Boston 9–0 behind the splendid pitching of Oscar Jones. "Twelve thousand persons were present, and notwithstanding the law prohibiting baseball playing on Sunday no effort was made to stop the contest."[3]

April 21

From 1:00 p.m. to 4:00 p.m. the Polo Grounds was awash in gorgeous decorations of flags and bunting while the Seventh Regiment Band entertained the lively crowd with popular music. Although no official figures were announced, New York management claimed it was a record-breaking crowd of well over 32,000 with rows of onlookers standing behind the roped area in center field. Over the winter, John T. Brush had increased the seating capacity in center and right fields and erected a new, handsome clubhouse. He even offered 12 entrances to facilitate large crowds entering the ballpark. It was a magnificent three hours that had the large crowd, including many women, primed for a New York victory with Christy Mathewson on the mound.

It turned out to be, however, one of the most humiliating opening day defeats in New York Giants history. The final score was 12-1 and Matty didn't get past the fifth inning in which he gave up six hits and had the fans calling for his removal! Wiltse entered the game at that point and when the inning was over Philadelphia had scored seven runs. It was a frustrating day for McGraw and his men and a letdown for the enthusiastic spectators.

April 25

New York, behind the solid pitching of Mathewson, walloped Brooklyn 9-2 at the Polo Grounds. The Giants pounded out 16 hits with six players getting at least two each. Matty coasted to his second victory giving up six hits as New York was already entrenched in first place with a 7-1 record. Amusingly, someone in St. Louis suggested that the error column be eliminated in baseball scores because it would help build confidence in the ball players. The radical suggestion was not met with wide approval.

April 30

Mathewson ran his record to 3-1 as he turned in another easy victory, this time over Boston by a score of 10-1. Wiltse replaced Matty in the seventh inning with the score 8-0 and allowed Boston's only run. In his previous victory, on April 25, Matty was replaced by Billy Milligan after seven innings when he had another big lead. It appeared McGraw's strategy was to give his star pitcher as much rest as possible, especially when the game was lopsided. McGraw remembered the previous year when Matty faltered at the end of the season due to overwork.

In an interesting aside, the Sunday baseball issue was beginning to heat up in earnest when some players were arrested at Washington Park for playing on the Sabbath. The Brooklyn Supreme Court was involved along with the police commissioner and the American Sabbath Committee. Rumors began to surface that the Giants might play baseball on Sunday and Brush did nothing to dispel them, saying he would abide by the law and the will of the people.

May 5

New York scored five runs in the top of the ninth off Boston to break a 5-5 deadlock and clinch a 10-5 victory for Mathewson. Devlin, McGann, McCormick and Dahlen supplied the offense as Matty scattered 11 hits for his fourth victory. New York's record was now 12-3 and McGraw was thoroughly enjoying the fast start. His team hitting was solid and capable of exploding for lots of runs, while his pitching staff of Mathewson (4-1), McGinnity (5-0) and Taylor (3-1) had accounted for all 12 victories.

May 10

The Giants continued their winning ways on their first western road trip of the season by beating St. Louis 2–1 on May 7 and 5–1 on May 9 behind the outstanding pitching of McGinnity. The Iron Man was now 7-0.

Mathewson, trying to make it three in a row and a sweep of the series, failed miserably. Matty lasted only one inning as he was pounded for five runs. Milligan came on in relief but fared no better. In all St. Louis collected 17 hits and won easily 14–1. Matty's record was 4-2 and the two defeats were shellackings.

May 12

Mathewson was clobbered for the second straight game. Cincinnati scored four runs in the first inning but New York bounced back with four of their own in the third. It was to no avail as Matty was not himself. He gave up 13 hits and as many runs, losing his third game of the season 13–7. Although his teammates gave him solid offensive support, which would have been good enough to win on most days, their defensive game was questionable as they committed six errors, one of which was by Mathewson.

While Cincinnati was exploding for their four runs in the first inning McGraw was doing some exploding himself ... at umpire Bob Emslie. Apparently Emslie had enough of McGraw's lip and tossed him out of the game. There's a famous story told about Emslie and McGraw in which the manager irritated the umpire by calling him a "blind robber." As the story goes, Emslie "showed up at a Giants' practice with a rifle, placed a dime on the pitching mound, and then with a shot fired from behind home plate sent the coin spinning into the outfield. Reportedly, McGraw never again challenged his eyesight."[4]

May 16

Mathewson had a 5–0 lead in the fifth inning with two out when Pittsburgh scored its first run on two singles sandwiched between a balk. The next inning, Pittsburgh jumped all over Matty for five more runs and won the game 6–5. It was the first time Mathewson had lost to Pittsburgh since 1902. His record was now even up at 4-4.

May 20

Mathewson lost his fifth game of the season and fourth straight when Chicago, trailing 2–1 going into the bottom of the ninth, scored twice to win the game. It was a heartbreaking loss for Matty but what made it even more bitter was that the defeat knocked New York out of first place. For the next month the Giants would be in and out of the lead.

May 23

Christy Mathewson and Chicago's lefty, Jake Weimer, hooked up in a magnificent pitching duel which was finally called at the end of 11 innings with the score 1–1. Umpire Bob Emslie called the game, which was played at West Side Park in order that the Giants could catch a train for New York. Both pitchers matched each other: Matty allowed six hits, Weimer seven; Matty walked one, Weimer none.

Riding the train back to New York McGraw was unhappy with the 7–7 road trip. He left the Polo Grounds in first place and returned in third. But there was one bright spot, Joe McGinnity. The durable right-hander was pitching brilliantly and sported a perfect 10–0 record.

May 27

Back home, the Giants immediately began feasting on Brooklyn with McGinnity and Taylor taking the first two games of the series. It was McGinnity's eleventh straight. Mathewson won the third game 3–1, his first victory since May 5. The win put New York in a tie with Chicago for first place. Matty allowed six hits and four walks and his wildness in the third inning cost him a shutout. Dan McGann stole five bases in the game, the first player to do so since 1900. Four other players would duplicate the accomplishment in later years: Dave Lopes (1974), Lonnie Smith (1982), Alan Wiggins (1984) and Tony Gwynn (1986). The American League record is six, held by Eddie Collins, who did it twice in 1912.

New York took the next two games from Brooklyn; one at the Polo Grounds and one at Washington Park, making it a five-game sweep. In the process McGinnity ran his winning streak to 12 straight.

May 30

New York split a doubleheader with Philadelphia at Baker Bowl winning the morning game 15–4 and losing in the afternoon 5–4. Matty was the beneficiary of the hard-hitting New York attack in the first game while Taylor took the 5–4 loss. The next day McGinnity shut out Philadelphia at Baker Bowl, improving his winning streak to 13 straight.

The Sunday baseball controversy continued as American League president Ban Johnson announced that his New York club would not play on the Sabbath even if the National League were successful in their efforts. His reasoning was that the property was too valuable to jeopardize the club's future rights.

June 2

Threatening weather kept the attendance at the Polo Grounds to less than 4,000 as Mathewson pitched a splendid four-hitter, beating Cincinnati 2–1. Matty walked one and struck out six, improving his record to 7-5. Although he pitched well it still took sloppy play by Cincinnati in the bottom of the eighth for New York to score two runs and snatch the victory. The two runs came about on a missed pop-up by first baseman Mike Donlin, a single by Art Devlin and a wild throw by catcher Heinie Peitz, which hit the second base bag and caromed into left field.

June 6

The Giants clobbered Pittsburgh's Roscoe Miller who left the game after three innings trailing 11–0. His counterpart Mathewson, the recipient of the Giants' power hitting, departed in the fifth inning as McGraw, confident that the victory was secure, took advantage of the opportunity to rest him. The batting heroes were Gilbert, who collected three hits including a home run and double; Bresnahan, with three hits including a homer; Mertes, with a triple and double; and Browne, with four hits, two of which were doubles. Matty's record stood at 8-5.

Two days before, a record crowd of 37,223 jammed into the Polo Grounds to watch McGinnity go after his fourteenth consecutive victory. The Iron Man pitched brilliantly for 11 innings but was matched pitch for pitch by Cincinnati's Jack Harper as the game ended deadlocked at 2–2. It was the largest crowd to witness a baseball game in the Polo Grounds and, for that matter, in the United States.

June 10

With McGinnity's winning streak reaching 14 when he shut out Pittsburgh 2–0 on June 8, New York moved into first place by a narrow margin over Chicago which arrived at the Polo Grounds for the first of three games.

Mathewson won the opener 5–0 on a brilliant one-hitter, increasing New York's first-place lead over Chicago. The game was marred by a feisty group of Giants players, led by McGraw. It began when Mertes was ejected from the game by umpire Charlie Zimmer over a disputed strike call. Next, McGraw was sent from the third base coaching box to the bench and incredible as it may seem, Taylor, the deaf-mute, was sent from the first base coaching box to the clubhouse. Later some jokester offered an explanation saying it was for making too much noise. It was quite evident from these actions and others during the season that McGraw's spirited leadership was becoming contagious among his players. This kind of wild exuberance would be commonplace throughout the season. It's not surprising since McGraw was a hellcat in the third base coaching box. "He insulted rivals, baited umpires and stoked up the fans," claimed author Durso.[5]

The following day, June 11, the Iron Man's 14-game consecutive winning streak came to an end. He lost to Chicago 1–0 in 13 innings when the opposing pitcher Bob Wicker threw a nifty one-hitter. Is it any wonder Tom Meany, noted sportswriter and author, said about McGinnity, "he certainly was made to be a pitcher, one of the best and one of the most durable."[6]

June 13

In a surprise move McGraw sent Mathewson to the mound to face Chicago in the deciding game instead of Taylor, who had been scheduled to start. McGraw was determined to take the series and remain in first place. Mathewson pitched a fine game and if it wasn't for a base on balls and Devlin's error in the first inning the outcome might have been different. The final score was 3–2 with Three Finger Brown besting Matty for the first time in three matchups. The loss dropped New York back into second place while Matty's record stood at 9-6.

A close check of the box score revealed three famous names: Tinker, Evans, Chance, as in the double play combination. Commented author Benton Stark in *The Year They Called Off the World Series*, "Although Tinker and Evers did not speak to each other through most of their careers, due originally to a fight over a carriage to the ballpark, their fame, along with Chance's was linked and immortalized by Franklin P. Adams in a poem appearing in the *New York Globe*:

> These are the saddest of possible words,
> Tinker-to-Evers-to-Chance.
> Trio of Bear Cubs fleeter than birds,
> Tinker-to-Evers-to-Chance.
> Ruthlessly prickling our gonfalon bubble,
> Making a Giant hit into a double,
> Words that are weighty with nothing but trouble.
> Tinker-to-Evans-to-Chance."[7]

June 16

After New York and St. Louis split the first two games of the series at the Polo Grounds, game three went into the bottom half of the ninth with the score 2–2. Mathewson had allowed seven hits and now the game rested squarely with his teammates to either clinch the victory or go to extra innings. It looked like the latter when, with Bill Dahlen on third and Jack Dunn on first, Roger Bresnahan hit a sharp grounder to shortstop Danny Shay who tossed to Dave Brain at second for the inning-ending force. Brain, however, dropped the ball! Dahlen crossed the plate and New York won 4–3. It was Matty's tenth win but more importantly, it was the beginning of New York's 18-game winning streak, one of the longest in baseball history.

June 20

The Sunday baseball controversy came to a head, or so it seemed, on June 18 when William J. Gaynor of the Brooklyn Supreme Court prohibited the playing of baseball on Sunday. This declaration was made on a Saturday. The next day, in spite of Gaynor's ruling, New York whipped Brooklyn 11–0 at Washington Park as George Wiltse pitched a three-hitter. Oddly, there wasn't a policeman on the grounds and no arrests were made or the slightest attempt to stop the game. The controversy, however, was far from over.

In one of the sloppiest games of the year New York beat Brooklyn 12–4 as Mathewson coasted to his eleventh win. New York pounded out 13 hits and Brooklyn chipped in with nine errors, five by Charlie Babb, the shortstop McGraw traded away over the winter. It was the Giants' fifth consecutive victory.

June 23

Mathewson beat Boston 6–2 at South End Grounds, increasing New York's winning streak to eight straight and widening their first-place lead over Chicago. Matty scattered nine hits, walked three and fanned nine. He helped his own cause by driving in two of the four runs in the damaging sixth inning. Mathewson's record was now 12–6.

Three days later the Sunday baseball controversy raised its ugly head once more when Brooklyn's battery, pitcher Oscar Jones and catcher Frank Jackitsch, were arrested along with a program seller and charged with a misdemeanor. They were taken to the local station house and eventually released after a $200 bond was posted for each.

June 30

Mathewson went to the mound after a week's idleness and apparently the rest was helpful as he blanked Boston 3–0. He allowed eight hits but was tough with men on base, in several instances stranding Boston runners at third. Bresnahan had a fine day at the plate collecting two hits, driving in a run in the sixth inning and scoring another in the bottom of the eighth.

This outstanding and versatile athlete, who was voted into the Hall of Fame in 1945, played every position during his 17-year career. He and Mathewson would form one of the best batteries in the National League, but that wouldn't happen until 1905.

With Matty's thirteenth victory, New York ran its winning streak to 14 in a row. The Giants were red hot and hadn't lost a game since June 15.

July 4

New York won both ends of the holiday doubleheader with Philadelphia at the Polo Grounds. In the morning game, which drew a slim 9,624, Taylor beat Tully Sparks 4–1. In the afternoon game 22,000 spectators witnessed Mathewson register one of his easiest victories of the season. Matty left after seven innings leading 11–1. Ames came on in relief and gave up two meaningless runs in the ninth.

New York's winning streak now stood at 18 in a row and put a virtual lock on the National League pennant. The next day, however, the streak ended when Philadelphia edged New York 6–5.

July 6

Mathewson coasted to another easy victory as New York clobbered Philadelphia 12–3. Matty pitched six innings, giving up five hits and no runs. Bresnahan, Dahlen, Gilbert and Bowerman accounted for ten of the 13 hits. Ames relieved in the seventh and gave up three runs.

The big news locally came the next day when pitcher Jack Chesbro of the Greater New York club (the name commonly used by the press) of the American League lost to Boston 4–1. It ended a 14-game winning streak for the right-hander who would win 41 games during the season, the most in the game's history.

July 9

The Giants started their second western road trip on a positive note, whipping St. Louis twice, 5–3 and 5–2. McGinnity relieved in both games. In the first he took over for Mathewson in the eighth but gave up a run to tie the score at 2–2. New York scored three in the ninth to win the game for McGinnity, his twenty-first against two losses.

In the nightcap the Iron Man registered his twenty-second victory, this time spelling Wiltse. New York scored two runs in the ninth while McGinnity held St. Louis scoreless.

July 12

Mathewson won his seventh consecutive game defeating Cincinnati at League Park by a score of 7–4 in ten innings. It was Matty's sixteenth win of the season and he helped his own cause in the seventh when he tripled home Bowerman with two out and scored later on McCormick's single. Cincinnati tied the game in the ninth, sending it into extra innings. But New York scored three runs in the tenth on a triple, double, two singles and a Cincinnati error. Matty's record stood at 16-6.

July 15

New York defeated Cincinnati 5-2 at League Park behind the solid pitching of Mathewson who gave way to McGinnity in the eighth. The Iron Man allowed one hit over the last two innings preserving Matty's seventeenth win and eighth in a row. Sam Mertes was the offensive star of the game. The left fielder had a big day with four hits, including a home run, and drove in four runs.

July 19

Mathewson blanked Pittsburgh for eight innings but gave up two runs in the ninth to sustain a bitter 2-1 loss, his first defeat since June 13. Both teams played flawless baseball and Mertes in left field was sensational, making several acrobatic catches and saving a possible four runs for Pittsburgh. On one of the catches Mertes leaped fully two feet in the air, against the bleachers, to pull down Tommy Leach's drive which would have gone for a home run. It was a tough loss for New York and Matty while over 5,000 Pittsburgh fans were frantic in the ninth and left the game feeling wonderfully satisfied.

July 21

Mathewson won his first game of the season in relief by defeating Chicago 4-3. McGinnity started the game at West Side Park but needed help in the sixth inning from Matty as Chicago scored twice. In the seventh Matty gave up a home run to Frank Chance to tie the score at 3-3. In the ninth Bresnahan drilled a Jake Weimer fast ball into left field. It went for a home run when Jim Slagle slipped going after the ball.

July 23

The first two games of the New York-Chicago series were split, setting the stage for another classic matchup between Christy Mathewson and Three Finger Brown. Matty won this contest handily 5-1, blanking Chicago for the first eight innings. The press claimed a crowd of over 25,000, the largest ever to see a Saturday game in Chicago. This was the fourth confrontation between the two, dating back to July 9, 1903. Mathewson won three of the four games.

New York would beat Chicago the next day 6–4 and take the series three games to one. The Giants ended their western swing with a 10-6 record and were now solidly entrenched in first place.

July 29

The Giants lost a squeaker, 1–0, when Brooklyn hurler John Cronin outdueled Mathewson in a well-pitched game. Matty's momentary loss of control in the first inning, however, was the real culprit and, in fact, was the cause of his defeat. In the first inning with men on first and second and two out he walked the next two batters to force in the only run of the game. Matty's prior three losses, also heartbreakers, were by narrow margins of 2–1, 3–2 and 3–2.

Although it was a frustrating loss for New York and Matty, McGinnity salvaged the day by blanking Brooklyn 2–0 in the second game of the doubleheader.

August 3

It appeared to most spectators that Mathewson had a cinch victory over Chicago when he entered the ninth inning with a 4–0 lead. Up to that point he had allowed four hits and did not walk a batter. In fact, many of the over 6,000 fans began to leave the Polo Grounds when Matty retired first baseman Frank Chance for the first out. Four hits and an error later halted many of the departing fans in their tracks as the score went to 4–3 with Shad Barry on first with two out.

To the relief of many, the game ended shortly thereafter when Bowerman threw a perfect strike to Gilbert at second to nab Barry trying to steal. It was victory number 20 for Mathewson and put New York's first-place mark at 63-24, a .724 winning percentage. In spite of this outstanding record McGraw still found something to gripe about and was banished from the third base coaches box to the bench by umpire Charlie Zimmer for the umpteenth time this season.

August 6

It was pretty clear among savvy baseball fans who would win the National League pennant in 1904. McGraw had his men on the move and no team could stop the juggernaut. In the American League, however, it was an entirely different story. The day before the Greater New York club beat Cleveland 5–0 to create a three-way battle for the pennant. Excited American League fans were fully enjoying the 1904 season and a look at the standings showed why: New York in first (.614), Chicago second (.613) and Boston third (.611). This battle continued until the last day of the season when Boston would emerge as the American League pennant winner.

Even though the Giants were making a shambles of the National League race it did not hurt the attendance as 20,488 spectators came out to the Polo Grounds to watch Mathewson whip fifth place St. Louis 8–1. Matty left after six innings with a comfortable 7–1 lead and was replaced by Ames. His record was now 21–8.

August 8

Mathewson beat St. Louis for the second time in three days, this one in relief by a margin of 4–3. McGinnity started the game and, after holding St. Louis to two hits over the first four innings, began to weaken, leading McGraw to yank him for pinch hitter Mike Donlin who had just arrived from Cincinnati. He was part of a three-way trade of outfielders that sent Harry McCormick to Pittsburgh who in turn sent Harry Sebring to Cincinnati. "Turkey" Mike, who got his nickname because of his strut, was a heavy drinker and an all-around wacky character. When McGraw approved the trade Donlin had been sitting out a month suspension enforced by Cincinnati manager Joe Kelley for drunken behavior in Chicago. Years later, when he was out of the game and night baseball was flourishing in the minors, the thought of playing at night was shocking to him. He said, "Jesus! Think of taking a ball player's nights away from him!"[8]

McGraw was well aware of Donlin's penchant for prowling, but he also knew he could hit. Over a 12-year major league career Donlin's batting average was a solid .334.

Back to the game, Mathewson entered in the ninth with the score knotted at 3–3. Matty fanned the first two hitters and got the next one on a fly to left where Mertes made a fine catch after a long run. New York scored a run in the bottom of the ninth for Matty's twenty-second win of the season against eight losses.

August 11

New York beat Cincinnati 5–2 at the Polo Grounds before a modest crowd of 7,876. Mathewson was superb. Reported *The New York Times*, "Much of the success of the local team was due to the skillful pitching of Mathewson, who not only kept the Cincinnati hits down to six, but struck out eleven men."[9] The victory upped his record to 23–8.

August 16

New York lost its first doubleheader of the season as Pittsburgh outplayed them by scores of 7–2 and 4–1 to the disappointment of the over 23,000 spectators at the Polo Grounds. In the first game Mathewson was gone after two innings as Pittsburgh roughed him up for five hits and five runs. Wiltse took over in the third but New York never could catch up. It was Matty's ninth loss.

It is interesting to note that in spite of the fact that two umpires were being used more frequently in the National League, this doubleheader was officiated by one. Jim Johnstone umpired both games alone, a total of almost four hours.

August 17

After being hit hard by Pittsburgh the previous day, McGraw decided to give Mathewson another shot at the Pirates. As Yogi Berra once said, it was déjà vu all over again. Matty was pounded for 13 hits and six runs but was lucky enough to pick up the victory when his teammates retaliated. Browne, Donlin, Mertes and Dahlen had hot bats, accounting for eight of the 11 hits and five of the nine runs. The final score was New York 9, Pittsburgh 6. It was Mathewson's twenty-fourth win of the year.

August 20

After New York and Pittsburgh split six games at the Polo Grounds, the same two teams were at it again with the venue shifting to Exposition Park. It was the Giants' last western swing of the season. By now Mathewson had figured out why Pittsburgh hit him so hard at the Polo Grounds and the results were dramatically different. In a rain shortened six-inning game he blanked the Pirates 5–0 on three hits. It was a quality outing and upped his record to 25-9.

August 24

After the Pittsburgh series in which New York took two out of three games, McGraw's men hopped a train and headed for Chicago for a series opening doubleheader. Mathewson pitched a masterful first game, blanking Chicago on three hits. He walked one, struck out three and paced himself beautifully. It was a perfect example of fully utilizing the players behind him, a tactic he advocated in his book *Pitching in a Pinch*.

The second game was halted after ten innings, deadlocked at 2–2. The entire doubleheader was marred by rowdy behavior between the players and umpires. The on-field shenanigans stirred up the fans and they began throwing bottles at the umpires, which nearly resulted in a forfeit to New York.

August 27

As he did in Chicago, Mathewson opened the St. Louis series, defeating them 9–3. Bresnahan, Browne and Dahlen led the New York offense as the team scored seven runs in three innings to clinch the victory. Matty's record was now 27-9. New York would win the next three games against Chicago, sweeping the series, before moving on to Cincinnati.

August 30

It was the fourth consecutive series opener for Mathewson and as he did in the prior three he pitched excellent baseball, trimming Cincinnati 3–1 at League Park. Matty scattered eight hits and at the plate he contributed mightily; with two hits, an RBI and a run scored. Bresnahan and McGann picked up the other two RBIs. Matty improved his mark to 28-9.

The next day New York took both ends of a doubleheader from Cincinnati to close out their final western swing. And what a road trip it was. McGraw must have been ecstatic on the train from Cincinnati to New York reliving the phenomenal 12-2 record and the last seven in a row.

September 5

In spite of the Giants' total dominance over Boston and a pennant race that was virtually locked up, one of the largest crowds of the year turned out at the Polo Grounds for the doubleheader. Over 37,000 screaming fans watched New York beat Boston twice, 6–1 and 4–3.

In the first game Mathewson had the Beaneaters shut out until the ninth inning when Jim Delahanty and Tom Needham both tripled to register their only run. Matty's record now stood at 29-9. Red Ames won the nightcap 4–3.

September 8

New York ended its winning streak at 12 when Dummy Taylor lost the first game of a doubleheader 9–8 to Philadelphia at the Polo Grounds. Mathewson wasted no time starting a new streak when he beat Philadelphia 4–1 in the second game which was halted after six and a half innings due to darkness. It was victory number 30 for the 24-year-old who was experiencing a marvelous year.

Another member of the pitching staff, George Wiltse, was quietly turning in a fine season himself. While the three main hurlers, Mathewson, McGinnity and Taylor, were receiving most of the attention from the fans and press, Wiltse was hurling magnificent baseball. Just the day before the rookie beat Philadelphia 6–3 for his tenth consecutive victory. He would win two more games before Cincinnati would snap his streak on September 22, and he would finish the season with a 13-3 mark and 2.84 ERA.

September 12

New York and Mathewson lost to Boston 3–1 at South End Grounds. It was only the second time Boston beat New York in 19 games. In fact, with a little more offensive clout from his teammates, Mathewson could have won the game since he only gave up three runs. His record was now 30-10.

September 16

Four days later Mathewson was back to his winning ways when he defeated Brooklyn 2–1 on a dandy four-hitter in the first game of a doubleheader. Two of the hits, a home run and triple, were by rookie Emil Batch. Apparently Matty hadn't figured out Batch's hitting flaws being so new to the league. Mathewson, by his own admission, studied the opposing hitters from the time he entered the National League in hopes of discovering their weakness or in the vernacular of the day, their hitting "groove."

In fact, Matty recalled the first time he faced the great Honus Wagner. Jack Warner was catching and walked out to the box to confer with his pitcher. Matty asked Warner, "What's his groove, Jack?" Warner replied without cracking a smile, "A base on balls."[10]

New York won the second game 5–3 behind the pitching of McGinnity.

September 21

New York lost both ends of the doubleheader to Cincinnati 6–4 and 2–0 bringing its record to 99-37 and stalling the bid for victory number 100. Mathewson was hit hard in the first game giving up nine hits, six for extra bases. It was his eleventh loss of the season as Jack Harper spun a five-hit shutout.

New York's 100th victory came the next day when McGinnity beat Cincinnati 7–5 to clinch the National League pennant. His battery mate was 52-year-old Orator Jim O'Rourke, who had played years before with New York and had let it be known he wanted one last fling with his old club. McGraw, in a rare act of kindness, signed O'Rourke and had him catch the first game. The successful attorney and minor league baseball executive picked up a single in four trips to the plate and scored a run, but more importantly could tell his grandchildren he caught the game that clinched the National League flag in 1904.

September 24

New York trimmed Pittsburgh 3–1 behind Mathewson's strong pitching at the Polo grounds. He allowed four hits, two each by Ginger Beaumont and Tommy Leach as he controlled the game right from the start. It was Matty's thirty-second win of the season and the fourth time he defeated Pittsburgh.

The game was momentarily interrupted in the second inning so that Harry Stevens, the famous concessionaire who hawked scorecards for a nickel, could present a loving cup to president John T. Brush. The gift was from members of the team and was inscribed with a message of appreciation for the 1904 season. The names of the players and manager were also engraved on the cup, including the secretary Fred M. Knowles and Stevens. It was a fitting celebration for a wonderful season.

September 29

Chicago scored five unearned runs in the second inning and trounced New York 7–3. Mathewson was roughed up for 13 hits and it appeared the entire team was simply going through the motions now that they had won the National League pennant.

The Giants would continue to sleepwalk through the rest of the 1904 schedule, dropping the next four games, to run their losing streak to six straight. Their indifferent play did not go unnoticed and was criticized by the press. In fact, Matty was singled out for his indifference and lack of hustle. The fans, who paid their hard-earned cash to see professional baseball, were not too thrilled with the Giants either.

October 3

Before an almost nonexistent crowd of 300, Christy Mathewson struck out 16 batters and beat St. Louis 3–1 for his thirty-third and final victory against 12 defeats. Matty's 16 strikeouts established a new season record surpassing the 15 set on June 15 by Fred Clade of the St. Louis Browns in the American League. It was a fitting and proper season-ending performance for a man who would lead the National League in strikeouts with 212.

A week later New York baseball fans were still cheering, only this time it was for the Highlanders in their showdown against Boston for the American League pennant. With Boston sporting a game and a half lead it meant New York would have to win both games of the doubleheader. More than 28,000 spectators jammed into American League Park to see New York's ace Jack Chesbro (going for win number 42) square off against Boston's Bill Dineen. It was a pitcher's duel from the start as the game entered the top of the ninth tied at 2–2. With two out and Lou Criger on third, Freddy Parent worked the count to 2-1, then Chesbro reared back and fired. The pitch slipped from Chesbro's hand, sailed over catcher Red Kleinow's glove and banged against the back wall. It became one of the most famous wild pitches in baseball history. Criger scored and Boston led 3–2. New York mounted a threat in the last half of the ninth but it ended when Patsy Dougherty struck out and Boston became the 1904 American League champs.

By any standard, rising from last place to a National League pennant in two and a half years was a marvelous achievement. It was accomplished with excellent pitching, solid hitting and aggressive running on the bases.

New York won 106 and lost 47, feasting on Brooklyn, Boston and Philadelphia. They dominated these three clubs with a mark of 56-9. Against Brooklyn they were 19-3, Boston 20-2 and Philadelphia 17-4. The 106 victories set a new National League record. Of course much credit had to be heaped on the genius of John J. McGraw. Building a winning club from the ashes of defeat and leading them in his aggressive and rowdy fashion, McGraw had no equal.

Credit must also be generously spread among the talented ball players McGraw assembled. McGinnity (35-8), Mathewson (33-12) and Taylor (21-15) won 89 of 106 games (.839) while rookie Wiltse finished with a 13-3 record. Surprisingly, New York lacked a .300 hitter (except Donlin who was acquired late in the season), but what they did have was several solid and consistent clutch hitters who compiled a team .262 batting average, good enough to lead the league. Individually, Dahlen (2.68) led the league with 80 runs batted in and Mertes (.276) was right behind him with 78. Browne (.284) led the league in runs scored with 99. McGann (.286) led the team with six home runs while Bresnahan's (.284) versatility and consistent play contributed to the fine season.

The other very important factor and the hallmark of a McGraw team was base stealing. Dahlen (47), Mertes (47) and McGann (42) ranked in the top five in the league. The team's total of 283 was by far the best and rivaled only by Chicago with a distant 227.

The 1904 season, however, was marred by one incident that did not occur on the field but in the minds and hearts of Brush and McGraw. As early as July they said their club would not play a postseason game with the American League representative. Officially though, and true to their word, it was announced to the public on October 6. The Giants would not play Boston for the world's championship.

McGraw's reasoning, at least on the surface, was "if we didn't sacrifice our race in our own league to the box office we certainly are not going to put in jeopardy the highest honor in baseball simply for the box office inducements."[11]

The real reason was more complex and had to do with personalities and egos. McGraw had an unforgiving hatred for Ban Johnson and Brush was still peeved over the Highlanders cracking the New York market and offering additional competition to the Giants. "The truth is that for both Brush and McGraw, disdain for the American League upstarts was mixed with fear of losing to them, as Pittsburgh had done in 1903. Those feelings outweighed the opportunity for big profits in a New York–Boston matchup,"[12] wrote author Charles Alexander.

The real losers in the battle over the World Series were the fans and ball players. The fans lost a wonderful opportunity to see professional baseball at its best and most competitive. The ball players lost money, pure and simple. McGinnity and Donlin were both outspoken in their criticism of Brush and McGraw.

6 • *First Pennant!, 1904*

There was little question that Christy Mathewson turned in his finest season to this point in his career. His 33 victories were a personal high while the 46 starts and 212 strikeouts led the National League. No doubt Mathewson was disappointed not to be participating in a World Series, but his demeanor and personality prevented him from voicing any criticism of McGraw (his friend), or the owner. It was not Matty's style; he kept his thoughts to himself.

But it wouldn't be long, however, before Mathewson would get a chance to pitch in his first World Series. And what a memorable moment it would be.

Chapter 7
World Series Hero, 1905

W	L	Pct	ERA
31	9	.775	1.27

In spite of the flap over the lack of a World Series in 1904, John McGraw and the New York Giants were riding the crest of a popularity wave. New York was back on top of the baseball world after a long hiatus. And the New York fans loved every minute of it.

Unlike the previous year when McGraw was still building his club and making dramatic changes, the 1905 team remained basically the same as that of the championship club. There were some minor differences, however. Mike Donlin, acquired late in the 1904 season, would be around for the full year to play center field. Roger Bresnahan, who was used in five different positions the previous year, would do the catching most of the time. One important addition was the purchase of Sammy Strang from Brooklyn in February. In effect, Strang would take over Bresnahan's role, filling in capably in the infield or outfield. According to author Charles Alexander, "McGraw's willingness to use him fourteen times to bat for somebody else 'in a pinch' prompted the baseball writers to coin the term 'pinch hitter.'"[1] Finally, Red Ames would turn in a career year for a team already rich in pitching.

The 1905 season would turn out to be a tumultuous one with the fury beginning early in a game at Philadelphia and climaxing with the "Hey, Barney" incident in Pittsburgh. It appeared to be a deliberate campaign by New York to harass and intimidate umpires, opposing managers, players and even rival owners; no one was spared. It incited the fans too. Led by McGraw and eagerly followed by his players, the Giants were greeted by angry fans and a harsh press and both were often justified. "Always they were on a hair edge," McGraw recalled about his 1905 players, "ready to get into a row if anybody pulled the trigger."[2] This kind of rowdyism and excitement accomplished one other important thing; it brought out spectators and in large numbers. It was a wild and frenetic season with the New York Giants running roughshod through the league.

Even Christy Mathewson, soft spoken, reserved, dignified, slow to anger, the quintessential family man, got caught up in the frenzy. The

7 • World Series Hero, 1905

Top: First Presbyterian Church, still functioning today in Lewisburg, where Mathewson married Jane Stoughton and later attended (photo by Arlene C. Mayer). *Bottom:* The Memorial Gateway, leading to the Bucknell University football stadium, is dedicated to Mathewson (photo by Arlene C. Mayer).

incident occurred at Baker Bowl when he slugged a lemonade boy. That episode, and the constant turmoil that followed New York throughout the season, however, did little to detract from Mathewson's on-field performance. He continued his mound mastery from the previous season, and after an incredible display of pitching excellence in the World Series, would shed the mantle of local hero and claim his role as the nation's number-one idol.

The Season

April 15

On April 14, Joe McGinnity opened the season for New York at the Polo Grounds and waltzed to a 10–1 victory over Boston. The baseball game and the win were the least spectacular events of this grand day. The ball players of both teams were driven through the streets of New York to the Polo Grounds as thousands cheered. It was estimated that 40,000 people (with thousands turned away) were at the park waiting. The true count was more like 24,000. "They filled every nick and crevice that a human body could squeeze into," noted *The New York Times*. "All the stands about the grounds were packed. The fences behind them were lined and even the flagpoles and stanchions that offered a chance for hand to cling to or foot to rest on was eagerly seized."[3]

The Polo Grounds was decked out in its finest with flags and bunting liberally draped throughout the park. Dignitaries from all walks of life gathered to greet John McGraw and his champion Giants. The mayor, surrounded by the fire, police and street commissioners, represented the local government while Harry Pulliam, president of the National League was the official baseball majordomo. Among the famous were John Montgomery Ward, former Giants shortstop, pitcher, manager, nemesis of Andrew Freedman and organizer of the Brotherhood of National League Players; and Adrian "Cap" Anson, one of the all-time great players and a true pioneer of the early game. But it was heavyweight boxing champion Jim Jeffries who the spectators fawned over and tried to shake his hand. It was truly a magnificent day.

On April 15 Christy Mathewson, like McGinnity in the opener, waltzed to an easy victory. New York lambasted Boston's Dick Harley for 16 hits while Matty allowed only two and was replaced by Hooks Wiltse after six innings. Dan McGann, Sam Mertes, Bill Dahlen, Art Devlin and Billy Gilbert all had at least two hits each.

April 24

At Philadelphia's Baker Bowl Mathewson was the hero of the day, both on the mound and at the plate. With New York trailing 4–3 in the top

7 • World Series Hero, 1905

of the ninth, McGraw let Matty hit and he promptly singled to left, scoring Gilbert and Frank Bowerman to take a 5–4 lead. Then Matty checked the Phillies in their half of the ninth for his second win of the young season.

First baseman McGann was absent from the lineup having been fined and suspended by Pulliam for fighting with Philadelphia catcher Fred Abbott in the series opener the day before. It was the first of many fights during this wild season. It was also the game in which Mathewson, caught up in the frenzy, stepped out of character and "knocked down a boy selling lemonade who happened by the Giants' bench, splitting the youth's lip and loosening several teeth."[4]

April 23 was an eventful day for another reason. Brooklyn, in its game against Boston, tested Justice Gaynor's ruling (in 1904) prohibiting baseball on Sunday. Although police were present throughout Washington Park, no arrests were made. Apparently club officials decided the way to get around the violation was to not charge admission but to collect anywhere from 25 cents to a dollar for a scorecard—depending on the seat.

May 1

On a cold day at South End Grounds in Boston, Mathewson won his third game of the season 8–2. Matty was in command from the start and at times appeared to be simply toying with the Boston batters. The cold weather, which forced the players to don their sweaters, kept the crowd to a mere 1,500 shivering fans. New York's early record reached 9-3, good enough for first place. This was Matty's one hundredth career victory, one of many milestones he would accomplish in the years ahead.

May 6

In a well played game at the Polo Grounds Boston defeated New York 2–1. Matty scattered ten hits but had the misfortune of facing left-hander Irv Young, who pitched a wonderful game in which he allowed seven hits and did not walk a batter. Interestingly, Young had two nicknames; Young Cy and Cy the Second, both of which distinguished him from the elder and legendary Cy Young who was pitching for Boston in the American League. The nicknames were not the only thing that separated the two pitchers; there was a matter of 448 victories! Cy Young finished his career with 511 wins and Irv with 63.

In spite of this loss New York (13-4, .765) remained in first place ahead of Pittsburgh (10-7, .588) and Chicago (11-8, .579).

May 11

Mathewson gave the small crowd of 4,000 at the Polo Grounds something to cheer about in the first inning when he struck out the first three St. Louis batters. He continued his mastery giving up five hits, two of the infield variety, while turning in his first complete game shutout of the season. Only six balls were hit to the outfield as Matty notched his fourth win and New York's first-place record improved to 16-5.

To this point McGraw's pitching staff was superb. Ames led the contingent with a 5-0 record followed by Dummy Taylor (2-0), Matty (4-1), McGinnity (4-2) and Wiltse (1-2). Hooks would eventually find himself and finish the season with a fine 15-6 mark and 2.47 ERA.

May 18

In their first visit of the season to the Polo Grounds the rival Pittsburgh Pirates beat New York and Mathewson 7–2. Pittsburgh, featuring a star-studded lineup of Hans Wagner, Ginger Beaumont, Fred Clarke and Tommy Leach, bunched their nine hits and tagged Matty with his second loss of the season. The next day (May 19), with Taylor on the mound for New York and Mike Lynch for Pittsburgh the intense hatred between the two teams ignited into an ugly incident that eventually involved the Pirates' owner. It started when McGraw had words with umpire Jim Johnstone. McGraw, in a loud voice, implied that the umpire was influenced by Barney Dreyfuss, the Pittsburgh owner. Dreyfuss, who was seated in the stands, overheard McGraw's remarks.

The incident intensified the following day (May 20) when McGraw called Pittsburgh pitcher Lynch a quitter. Manager Fred Clarke took offense and complained to Johnstone, who ordered McGraw out of the game. Later, Mathewson was also thrown out of the game from the coaching box.

On his way to the clubhouse McGraw spotted Dreyfuss and began shouting "Hey, Barney!" accusing him of welching on gambling debts and controlling umpires through his protégé Pulliam (who was Dreyfuss' team secretary in Louisville and Pittsburgh). McGraw was a master at stirring up trouble and was at his best on this day. According to author Frank Graham it was McGraw's strategy to upset the Pittsburgh club enough to rattle them. "His plan," commented Graham, "was to ride them hard, soften them up, get them off balance and, having thus reduced their effectiveness, to slay them."[5]

A few days later Dreyfuss lodged a formal complaint to Pulliam who submitted the matter to the league's board of directors who were to meet June 1 in Boston to pass judgment. In the meantime, McGraw called Pulliam on the phone and lashed out at him. Pulliam reacted by fining McGraw $150 and suspending him for 15 days.

The board was composed of Dreyfuss, Brush, Boston's Arthur Soden (who owned part of the Giants) and Jim Hart from Chicago, the only unbiased member. Not suprisingly, Brush, Soden and Hart voted against Dreyfuss and exonerated McGraw. In what appeared to be a bone for

Dreyfuss, Soden and Hart voted with him to commend Pulliam's punishment of McGraw.

McGraw and Brush were not satisfied, however. Lawyers for the Giants received a restraining order from the superior court of Boston. Frustrated and powerless, Pulliam told the press he would return all fines to McGraw. "Not surprisingly, the New York Giants became the most hated and reviled baseball team in the country. All over the league they were the targets of street thugs and ballpark hoodlums."[6]

May 23

Mathewson pitched his second shutout when he blanked Cincinnati 7–0 at the Polo Grounds. Matty allowed three singles, walked one and fanned eight. In four of the nine innings he set the Cincinnati club down in order. Dahlen and McGann were the hitting heroes; the former belted two home runs and scored twice, while the latter had a double, single and scored two runs.

The losing Cincinnati pitcher was Orval Overall who was known as the "Mathewson of the Pacific Coast." A check of the records show that Overall was 106-71 lifetime (3-1 in World Series play) with a 2.24 ERA. It was a fine seven-year career, but with due respect to Overall, there was only one Christy Mathewson.

May 27

New York beat Brooklyn 4–1 at the Polo Grounds behind another fine pitching job by Mathewson. In fact, if it wasn't for Bresnahan's poor throw in the seventh inning Matty would have had his third shutout. As it was he upped his record to 6-2. Red Ames at 7-0 and Taylor at 5-0 were still undefeated as New York was enjoying an excellent start.

The next day the brouhaha over playing baseball on Sunday, which had begun anew in late April, came to a head. The New York police commissioner instructed his inspectors and captains to stop all Sunday baseball. His edict affected the game between the Giants and Brooklyn at Washington Park. The commissioner wanted no further invasion of the law until it was settled in the courts, claiming the selling of programs in lieu of admission was simply a subterfuge. The edict also affected semiprofessional games in the New York area and almost resulted in the arrest of the Iron Man. It happened like this: McGinnity was asked to pitch for the Visitation club, which played on a field at Forty-sixth Street and Second Avenue. When he arrived at the grounds McGinnity got into an argument over the amount of money he was to get paid so he refused to put on a uniform which turned out to be a blessing. While everyone was standing around the police moved in and arrested all the players except the Iron Man, who had not yet donned his uniform.

June 1

Mathewson won his seventh game, defeating Boston for the third time this season. The score was New York 8, Boston 2. Matty was hit freely but with a 5–0 lead after three innings he paced himself letting his teammates do most of the work. Donlin, George Browne and Devlin collected eight of New York's 12 hits as the Giants' record reached 31-9 and gave them a seven and one-half-game lead over Pittsburgh. The next day Ames would be the beneficiary of five runs in the top of the thirteenth to improve his record to 9-0. The rest of the staff wasn't too shabby either: Taylor 6-0, Matty 7-2, McGinnity 7-3.

June 7

The Giants began their first western road trip with the initial stop in Pittsburgh. Mathewson opened the series with a 5–3 victory, helping his own cause with two hits and an RBI. It was a 1–1 game until the eighth when, with the bases loaded, Bresnahan delivered a clutch single scoring Donlin and Browne. Mertes followed with another hit on Patsy Flaherty's first pitch scoring McGraw for the third run of the inning. Pittsburgh managed two runs in their half of the eighth to close the gap to 4–3. Matty drove in Devlin in the top of the ninth with an insurance run and the game ended 5–3. His record was now 8–2.

June 9

Two days later, in a wild game at Exposition Park, McGinnity and Mathewson were battered by Pittsburgh, losing 12–6. New York scored five runs off Sam Leever in the first inning but a combination of poor pitching by starter McGinnity and Matty in relief, plus sloppy infield play gave the Pirates six runs in their half of the first. Pittsburgh came back with three more off Matty in the second and the rout was on. In all, the Giants committed six errors and Mathewson suffered his third loss of the season.

McGraw, no doubt, was embarrassed at the performance of his two ace pitchers, not to mention what he thought of the six errors and all-around uninspired infield play. As author Alexander pointed out, "Baseball was never a game to McGraw, never just practice, never without meaning."[7]

June 13

The fifth career matchup between Mathewson and Three Finger Brown was a dandy. New York beat Chicago 1–0 at West Side Park as Matty hurled a brilliant no-hitter, narrowly missing a perfect game. Dahlen and Gilbert each made an error. It was the second no-hitter of

7 • *World Series Hero, 1905*

Roger Bresnahan, a versatile player, caught Mathewson from 1905 to 1908. In the 1905 World Series he caught Matty's three shutouts and Joe McGinnity's one against Philadelphia (photo courtesy National Baseball Library, Cooperstown, N.Y.)

Matty's career. He faced only 28 men as a double play erased one of the errors. Brown pitched a marvelous game too, allowing five singles and one run. He often lamented the fact that this was Matty's second no-hitter and he, Brown, had never pitched one.

Years later, McGraw had this to say about his star pitcher. "He was pretty much the prefect type of pitching machine. He had the stature and strength, and he had tremendous speed. There was never another pitcher like Mathewson."[8]

June 17

New York defeated St. Louis 7–2 at Robison Field, behind the fine pitching of Mathewson and Wiltse. It was a brutally hot day in St. Louis, which eventually caught up to Matty but not before he completed six innings. Wiltse finished in fine form by blanking the Cardinals over the last three innings. It was Mathewson's tenth win of the season.

June 21

Four days later Mathewson whipped Cincinnati 6–3 at League Park; it was his eleventh win. New York struck early, scoring four runs in the first and two more in the third. Handing Mathewson six runs early in a game spelled trouble for any club. Matty paced himself, scattered seven hits and recorded another relaxed victory. The next day New York beat Cincinnati 2–1, improving its record to 42-18 and a comfortable eight and one-half-game lead for first place. After the game the Giants hopped a train to New York ending their first western swing with an unimpressive 8-8 mark. In fact, the Giants had to win the last three games against Cincinnati to salvage the .500 record. Matty was outstanding, however, winning four of their eight victories.

June 24

New York celebrated its return home by defeating Boston 2–1 in an exciting 12-inning game at the Polo Grounds. Bowerman was on first with two out in the bottom of the twelfth when Mathewson lofted a fly ball to center field. At this point, it looked like the game was headed for the thirteenth inning. Rip Cannell, however, dropped the ball! He retrieved it quickly, threw to shortstop Ed Abbaticchio who fired to the plate as Bowerman, chugging all the way from first, slid safely under the tag. Abbaticchio, catcher Tom Needham and a host of Boston players objected vigorously to umpire Jim Johnstone's safe call. As the argument progressed, the fans from the grandstand and open seats came on the field and began to crowd around Abbaticchio and Johnstone, who almost came to blows. Fortunately, a squad of policeman prevented what could have easily turned into an ugly scene. Wisely, Johnstone was escorted from the field.

Lost in the exciting ending of the game was the outstanding pitching of Taylor and Mathewson. Taylor started and went nine innings, allowing one run and four hits. Matty took over in the tenth and blanked Boston the rest of the way on one hit. It was his twelfth win of the season.

June 29

Mathewson enjoyed another easy victory as New York scored seven runs in the first three innings off Brooklyn's Mal Eason at Washington Park. The final score was 11–1 with Matty leaving after pitching five innings of shutout baseball. Claude Elliot pitched the last four, giving up one run. Donlin, McGann, Dahlen and Gilbert accounted for nine of the 13 hits and more than half the runs. McGann's two hits were for extra bases, a home run and a triple. The steady first baseman would turn in a fine year for McGraw, batting .299 while driving in 75 runs.

July 4

New York split the holiday doubleheader with Philadelphia at Baker Bowl. They lost the first game 2–0 and won the second 6–3. Mathewson pitched well in defeat, scattering eight hits and only walking one batter. But he was no match for Jack Sutthoff who pitched a magnificent three-hit shutout. It was Matty's fourth loss of the season. New York took the second game behind McGinnity who was headed for another fine year. The Giants' first place margin over the Pirates was now seven games.

July 12

With Chicago visiting the Polo Grounds, the local fans were treated to another Mathewson–Three Finger Brown confrontation. This time Brown was invincible, allowing two hits as Chicago easily beat New York 8–1. Brown would have had a shutout if it wasn't for Billy Maloney who dropped a fly ball off the bat of McGann and subsequently scored on Mertes' hit. Matty, on the other hand, gave up 12 hits while his teammates committed five errors. It was a bad day for New York and its star pitcher.

July 15

At the Polo Grounds over 25,000 Giants fans screamed with joy when Browne hit a home run in the bottom of the ninth with Bresnahan on first to defeat Pittsburgh 8–7. As soon as Browne crossed the plate a mob of enthusiastic fans surrounded their hero, hoisted him onto the shoulders of two brawny men and carried him off the field. It was a thrilling victory for the Giants, all the more so because it came at the expense of Pittsburgh, their hated rivals.

It was an exciting game right from the start with New York commanding a comfortable 6–0 lead with McGinnity on the mound. Pittsburgh, however, woke up in the sixth scoring two runs and then in the seventh scored five more on two walks, a single, triple and home run before McGraw could yank the Iron Man and replace him with Mathewson. Matty shut the door on the Pirates, allowing no hits in two and two-thirds innings for his fourteenth victory. It also increased the Giants' first-place lead over Pittsburgh to eight games.

July 18

Three days later the undaunted Pirates bounced back and beat New York and Mathewson 2–1. Matty gave up eight hits, including a home run, in seven innings but was fortunate to escape with only two runs scored against him as New York played errorless ball and made some clutch defensive plays with men on base.

There was never a dull moment when New York and Pittsburgh faced each other and this game was no exception. In the seventh inning a rambunctious Giants fan threw a bottle at Pittsburgh's right fielder Otis Clymer when he was chasing Strang's single. Luckily the fan's toss was off the mark. The incident caused umpire Johnstone to halt the game until order was restored.

Johnstone's partner in this game was a young man by the name of Bill Klem. It was his rookie year in a big league career that would stretch through 1940. He was regarded as the greatest umpire of all time. Klem was autocratic, scrupulously honest, had a thorough knowledge of the rules and demanded discipline during a game. Is it any wonder that he and McGraw would possess one of the strangest relationships ever. "At times it reached degrees of unbelievable bitterness — a relentless conflict between two tenacious and obstinate men, each determined to break the other's will. At times they were friendly; they took trips together, dined together, and with their wives had family parties together."[9] Fortunately for baseball their odd relationship did not detract from their superior abilities as arbiter and manager.

July 21

In a poorly played and boring game New York buried St. Louis 14–2 at the Polo Grounds. Mathewson left after five innings with a 10–2 lead and was replaced by Elliott. Mertes was the offensive hero of the day when he smacked a grand slam home run into the right field bleachers in New York's six-run second inning. It was Matty's fifteenth victory against six losses and kept the Giants six games ahead of Pittsburgh.

About mid-week rumors began to fly that a movement had been launched by several club owners to merge the two leagues into one 12-club league and dump both Harry Pulliam and Ban Johnson. The new league would include the most profitable clubs from both the American and National Leagues with only one club permitted in each city. Pulliam, as expected, said he would fight the proposal. "Baseball is thriving at present as it never did before," he added. "The National League, when it was comprised of twelve clubs, nearly died. Since the formation of an eight-club circuit the game has prospered. Larger crowds are being attracted than ever before. The game is conducted fairly and squarely, and the lovers of the sport know it and appreciate it."[10]

The 12-club league never materialized and the American and National leagues stayed with eight teams until 1962 when two clubs were added to each league.

July 25

New York beat Cincinnati 7–2 as Mathewson registered his sixteenth win of the season. The Giants staked him to a 3–0 lead in the first inning but Matty's erratic pitching (five walks) allowed Cincinnati to close the gap to 4–2 until the eighth inning when Bowerman homered with two men on making the final score 7–2.

The local fans got a scare in the first inning when Reds' catcher Ed Phelps was knocked unconscious by the backswing of Sam Mertes. Physicians at the game came to his aid as blood flowed from a gash on the head. He was rushed by ambulance to the hospital, treated and eventually released.

July 29

Mathewson successfully opened New York's second swing into western cities by defeating Cincinnati 3–0. He scattered nine hits and walked only one batter. He had trouble in the first inning with men on second and third and no out but bore down by fanning Joe Kelley and Cy Seymour and retiring Tommy Corcoran at first. After that narrow escape Matty dominated the rest of the game, notching his seventeenth win. The Giants' first-place lead over the Pirates was now seven and one-half games.

August 2

After sweeping all four games at Cincinnati, New York moved on to Exposition Park to meet Pittsburgh. It was a typical Mathewson-pitched game. He scattered seven hits, walked one and struck out five as New York squeaked by the Pirates 3–1, increasing its lead to 10½ games. The most excitement came in the fourth inning when the great Honus Wagner was called out at first base on a close play. Wagner became so enraged he fired the ball at umpire George Bausewine, who had no alternative but to eject the star shortstop. This incident, and numerous others throughout the season, clearly signaled it would be a long time before umpires would be able to maintain discipline on the field and gain the respect they needed to control the game.

Not all the excitement, however, was on the field. The next day

Barney Dreyfuss, fresh from his fiasco with McGraw, was assaulted at Exposition Park, his own home grounds. Thomas J. Ward, said to be a student of the priesthood from Minneapolis, attacked Dreyfuss who was seated in his box seat. Cooler heads prevailed and Dreyfuss was persuaded to withdraw assault and battery charges. No doubt McGraw had a real chuckle when informed of the Dreyfuss attack.

August 5

The fourth and last game of the Pittsburgh series saw umpire Bausewine entangled in another brouhaha. It was only three days before when Wagner, in an emotional frenzy, threw a ball at him, now he was pitted against the master umpire baiter, John McGraw. The incident occurred in the last half of the ninth with the score tied 5-5. Mathewson gave up a double to the first batter Claude Ritchey. The next hitter, George Gibson, bounced back to Matty who threw to Devlin at third trying to get Ritchey. Bausewine called the play safe and the argument began. McGraw raced onto the field and refused to leave after repeated warnings by Bausewine. After New York's appeal to the second umpire, Bob Emslie, was turned down, the Giants still refused to play ball. Bausewine, after timing the delay forfeited the game to Pittsburgh 9-0, delighting the 18,383 spectators, a record crowd at Exposition Park. New York immediately appealed the game to President Pulliam and on August 26, he announced his decision to uphold the umpire. The rule at the time was such that a win or loss was charged to the pitcher in the game; therefore, Mathewson was charged with the loss. By today's rules, he would not be. By taking the last three games of the series, the Pirates cut the Giants' lead to seven and a half games.

August 8

In Chicago, Taylor started the second game of the series and after three innings New York led 4-3. But in the bottom of the fourth inning, after Taylor had given up six hits and three runs, McGraw had seen enough and replaced him with Mathewson. Matty blanked Chicago the rest of the way and Taylor was credited with the victory since today's five-inning requirement was not in effect in 1905.

In an interesting bit of baseball history, the next day in Pittsburgh rookie umpire Klem had to hide in the ladies' room of the grandstand at Exposition Park while several gamblers went looking for him. A half an hour later Klem made his escape from the grounds through a side gate. The reason for Klem's hiding happened this way: before the game there was some heavy betting on Pittsburgh with the odds in their favor 10-3. So in the ninth inning with Boston leading 5-2, the gamblers were looking for a scapegoat. When eight Pittsburgh players became abusive Klem chased them all from the field and fined each ten dollars. This angered the gamblers and the chase for Klem was on. More importantly, this incident illustrates the open and widespread gambling that existed in the early years of baseball and clearly shows why Klem built a reputation on fair and impartial umpiring.

August 10

Two days later, in a magnificent pitcher's duel, Mathewson bested Chicago's Big Ed Reulbach, a marvelous hurler with a lifetime 181-105 (.633) mark, by a score of 1–0. Matty allowed three hits, walked one and struck out six. Reulbach allowed four hits, walked none and struck out six. New York scored its lone unearned run in the sixth when Strang was safe on an error, stole second and scored on McGann's single. Matty's record was now 19-7.

In a totally unrelated matter, a 38-year-old Chicago lawyer was fulfilling his duties as judge in the United States District Court for the Northern District of Illinois, an appointment he received in March from President Theodore Roosevelt. The judge, with the colorful name of Kenesaw Mountain Landis, would eventually become the first commissioner of the game and would, along with Babe Ruth, rescue professional baseball after the Black Sox scandal of 1919. Landis was named after Kennesaw (he used only one "n") Mountain where his physician father was wounded during the Civil War.

August 17

Mathewson didn't pitch again until New York opened at the Polo Grounds after a successful western road trip. The Giants won 10 of 16 games and felt secure with their eight-game lead. Matty accounted for four of the wins. From a financial standpoint, it was one of the best road trips in the club's history, drawing 116,000 spectators or more than 7,000 per game.

The seven days between starts obviously agreed with the ex–Bucknell star as he pitched his second consecutive three-hit shutout, defeating Chicago 3–0 for his twentieth win. His control was perfect, rarely going as high as three balls on a batter. In his last four victories, covering 36 innings, Matty issued a mere three bases on balls, a phenomenal display of control.

August 21

Before one of the largest Monday crowds at the Polo Grounds (14,000) New York easily defeated Pittsburgh 10–2. It was a dull game compared to the previous contests between these two clubs with the only semblance of fireworks coming in the eighth inning when umpire Johnstone tossed out McGraw for questioning one of his decisions.

Behind Mathewson's fine pitching New York played errorless ball and took advantage of every Deacon Phillippe lapse on the mound. The Giants stole five bases including Devlin's swipe of home in the sixth.

August 24

In a doubleheader with Cincinnati the Giants won the first game 8-0, behind Mathewson's masterful pitching, and tied the second game 6-6, called after nine innings due to darkness. *The New York Times* described Mathewson as invincible. He allowed two scratch hits and walked one batter. The first game victory marked New York's twelfth consecutive win against Cincinnati. Matty's record was 22-7.

Both managers, Kelly and McGraw, were put off the grounds by umpire Bausewine, keeping McGraw's streak alive. It was the third successive day in which the Giants manager had been fined ten dollars and ejected from a game.

August 26

In the second straight doubleheader, New York beat Cincinnati 2-0 and 6-5 extending its winning streak over the Reds to 14 straight. In the first game McGinnity hurled a nifty five-hit shutout as the Giants played errorless baseball. The second game, however, was a wretchedly played contest in which New York was lucky to win. Four of the Giants' six runs were due to wild pitches by Orval Overall. In the ninth with the score 6-4 and the bases loaded, McGraw yanked Taylor and brought in Mathewson who slammed the door shut on Cincinnati. Matty struck out Tommy Corcoran, got Harry Steinfeldt to fly out, Shad Barry scoring on the play and then induced Fred Odwell to ground out.

Interestingly, the Cincinnati center fielder in the second game was a rookie by the name of Al Bridwell who in 1908 would be New York's regular shortstop. In *The Glory of Their Times*, he told author Lawrence Ritter what the relationship was like between rookie and veteran at that time. "They'd try to keep you away from the plate during your turn in batting practice, and sometimes you had to pick up a bat and drive them away."[11]

August 28

In one of the most poorly played games of the year New York easily defeated St. Louis 8-1 as Mathewson scattered nine hits for his twenty-third win and fifth straight. St. Louis committed only three miscues but their errors of omission and general all-around lackluster play turned the game into a travesty. There were two consoling factors, however. Only 2,200 fans witnessed the farce and it only lasted one hour and thirty-five minutes. The Giants' first place lead over the Pirates was eight and a half games as the season was drawing to a close.

September 1

Mathewson was in rare form as he defeated Philadelphia 4–1 at the Polo Grounds. He allowed three hits and walked only one batter and that came in the eighth inning. He fanned nine. Dahlen's costly error in the first inning prevented Mathewson from gaining another shutout. Matty's record was now 24-7.

September 4

On a rain-drenched, soggy field at the Polo Grounds, New York swept a doubleheader from Philadelphia 7–1 and 11–6. The first game, in which McGinnity won easily, didn't start until three o'clock. The second game was called after eight innings due to darkness with Mathewson still on the mound after spotting Philadelphia five runs in the second. The Giants gave Matty plenty of support as they assaulted pitchers Bill Duggleby and Togie Pittinger for five runs in each of the fifth and seventh innings. It wasn't pretty but it was win number 25 and seventh straight.

September 7

Three days later the combination of McGinnity and Mathewson faced Boston in another doubleheader at the Polo Grounds. This time the Giants split, the Iron Man losing a heartbreaker 1–0 while Matty pitched a splendid three-hit shutout in the nightcap, winning 3–0. It was a scoreless game for six innings but New York broke through on Vic Willis for a run in the seventh and two more in the eighth. It was Mathewson's twenty-sixth win; his last loss was recorded on August 5 and it was the forfeited game. The Giants' lead, however, was down to five games as the Pirates kept battling.

September 12

New York split another doubleheader at the Polo Grounds, this time with Brooklyn as the twin bills began to pile up late in the season. Mathewson won the first game 3–2 for his twenty-seventh victory (ninth straight) but he had to wait until the bottom of the ninth. Donlin led off with a double to right, was sacrificed to third by McGann and scored on Dahlen's single to right center.

The second game was called after seven innings as the threatening weather darkened the skies making it difficult to see. Umpire Hank O'Day halted the contest with New York trailing 8-5.

September 16

At Boston's South End Grounds Mathewson won the second game of the twin bill 3-1 after New York took the first game 7-1. It was not an easy victory for Matty as Boston's Irv Young pitched a wonderful game, allowing five hits and walking one batter. It was Mathewson's twenty-eighth victory and tenth consecutive, which the press failed to mention.

September 19

Doubleheaders continued to pile up as New York traveled to Philadelphia for two games. They lost the first 3-2 but came back in the second game to win 2-1 as Mathewson flipped a two-hitter and didn't walk a single batter for his eleventh consecutive victory. All season, with few exceptions, Matty dominated batters game after game. This victory upped his record to 29-7.

It is interesting to note that if today's rules had been in effect, Mathewson would have registered a 16-game winning streak. Here's how: from July 21 to August 2, Mathewson won four consecutive games; from August 10 to September 19 he won another 11 straight; on August 5 (forfeit game) he was charged with a loss, today he would not be; on August 8 he relieved Taylor after three innings with New York leading 4-3; the game ended that way with Taylor getting credit for the victory while today's rules would have made Matty the winner.

September 23

New York began its third and final western swing by losing three straight to the Cubs at West Side Park. Mathewson was outpitched by Carl Lundgren in the second game of the series. It was Matty's first loss since August 5 and ended his consecutive game winning streak at 11. It was a brilliant pitcher's battle with the winner being determined by Dahlen's mental lapse. It happened in the fifth inning with two out and Johnny Evers and Jimmy Slagle on first and second. Doc Casey hit to Dahlen who, after bobbling the ball, dashed to second in an attempt to force Slagle. Umpire Emslie called the play safe while Dahlen, thinking he had a force out, rolled the ball to the mound. On third an alert Evers realized Dahlen's blunder, dashed home with the only run of the game. It was a tough loss, Matty's eighth of the season.

September 25

New York, happy to get out of Chicago, moved on to Pittsburgh to face their second place challengers, now trailing by only five and a half games, in a crucial three-game set. Mathewson opened the series and won easily by a score of 10-4, his thirtieth. Apparently Pittsburgh felt intimidated by New York's presence and the importance of the three games as they gave up five runs in the first on only one hit. Deacon Phillippi, usually a steady pitcher, hit three batters in that fatal inning and Honus Wagner chipped in with a throwing error, which cleared the bases. It was a poor start for Pittsburgh, which could ill afford to lose many more games to the Giants.

September 26

New York won again the next day, this time 9-5, as Pittsburgh continued to play poorly under pressure. Lynch started for the Pirates and gave up eight walks and hit a batter, all in six innings. When he left the Giants led 8-5. Ames started for New York and was pitching well but in the late afternoon, when the sky began to darken, making it difficult to see the ball, McGraw inserted Mathewson. The shrewd move paid off as Pittsburgh had difficulty seeing Matty's fast ball compared to Ames' slower deliveries. Mathewson blanked the Pirates over the last three innings. When New York won the following day, completing the sweep, its lead bulged to eight and a half games and dashed any hope of a Pittsburgh pennant.

September 29

In St. Louis the Giants lost the first game of the series the previous day but bounced back to win a doubleheader, 6-5 and 5-1. Mathewson won the 6-5 game but he did it the hard way and with a lot of help from his teammates. Leading 4-1 in the bottom of the ninth Matty gave up a bases-loaded triple to Danny Shay which tied the score and sent the game into extra innings. New York scored two runs in the eleventh to go ahead 6-4 but Matty almost let it get away again by allowing St. Louis to score a run in the eleventh. It was his thirty-first and last victory of the regular season. Two days later, on October 1, New York beat Cincinnati 5-4 in the first game of a doubleheader to clinch the National League pennant for the second consecutive year.

October 5

The Giants arrived home from their final western road trip in which they won seven, lost six and clinched the National League flag. The welcome home celebration was dampened somewhat as Philadelphia beat the Giants and Mathewson 4–1 in the first game of a twin bill. They managed to salvage the day with a 5–3 triumph in the second game. It was Matty's last appearance of the regular season (it ended two days later) in which he compiled a marvelous 31-9 record.

The World Series

New York ran rampant through the National League in 1905, winning 105 games and losing 48 for its second straight pennant. The team batting average was .273, best in the league as was the 291 stolen bases, a phenomenal record. On an individual basis, Mathewson led the pitching staff with a 31-9 mark and a league-leading 1.27 ERA; McGinnity won 21 and led the league in games pitched with 46; Ames had a fine season (22-8) while Taylor and Wiltse added 15 wins each. Turkey Mike Donlin led the Giants with a solid .356 batting average and Sam Mertes was the top RBI man with 108. It was a marvelous team effort. Years later in his book McGraw said, "The one big factor in that 1905 team, which in many ways I consider my greatest ball club, was team spirit—that indomitable determination to win games regardless of who got the individual credit."[12]

Now it was McGraw's job to make certain that his champion Giants carried that "team spirit" into postseason play. Yes, there would be a World Series in 1905. After receiving so much public criticism for refusing to participate in 1904 Brush relented and agreed to the match with the American League champs. In fact, Brush went one step further. He submitted a set of suggestions for the conduct and operations of the World Series to the three-man National Commission which, after some refinement, they adopted. The so-called "Brush rules" have remained the core of World Series' conduct ever since.

The anticipation of the 1905 World Series was sky high among Giants fans. Those loyal to the club, who had been faithfully following the Giants since April and boosting attendance to record heights, were hungry for a World Championship, all the more so after their frustration the previous year. On top of fan enthusiasm, the ball players were eager to earn additional money that they missed out on in 1904; McGraw was determined to prove he was the best manager and his club the best in baseball; and Brush was delighted to add more money to already overflowing coffers.

The Giants' opponent was the Philadelphia Athletics, who had barely beaten out the Chicago White Sox for the American League pennant. Their manager, the venerable Connie Mack, was the antithesis of McGraw. Tall, stately, virtually unemotional, Mack was easygoing with his players who preferred private lectures as opposed to McGraw who didn't hesitate to chastise and scold openly. Their managing styles were far apart too. Once the game began Mack would rely on his players to know what to do; McGraw dictated every move.

7 • World Series Hero, 1905

As the opening game approached both managers appeared confident in their team's abilities and the outcome of the series. "Waddell and Plank will mow down those National League fellows as sure as you live and as for the rest of the team I am not a bit doubtful," said Mack. Commented McGraw, "We can beat the Philadelphians in batting and furthermore we can beat them running the bases. The only question left open for argument, then, is the pitching."[13] It was an interesting comment which revealed McGraw's respect for Mack's pitching staff.

Regardless of what each manager voiced, Mack entered the series at a distinct disadvantage. His eccentric and unpredictable star, Rube Waddell, would not be available for the series. The official explanation for his absence was that he was injured horsing around with a teammate a month earlier and his condition had worsened. Widely circulated rumors claimed big-time gamblers had gotten to Waddell. The rumors, however, were never substantiated and the pitcher indignantly denied them. (McGraw, Donlin and Dahlen, not averse to a wager or two, all managed to place bets with Philadelphia followers.) Whatever the true reason, Mack was still without his ace and would have to rely on right-handers Charles "Chief" Bender and Andy Coakley and lefty Eddie Plank.

October 9

The opening game of the World Series was played at Baker Bowl because Philadelphia owner Ben Shibe won the coin toss, so the Giants had to travel to the City of Brotherly Love and they did it in grand style, riding in a special car attached to the regular train. Accompanying McGraw and the team were several notables, headed by boxer James J. Corbett and Louis Mann, a vaudeville comedian. From the hotel the Giants drove to the grounds led by a band of music and greeted by cheering crowds along the way.

Almost 18,000 partisan fans packed Baker Bowl and it was estimated another 10,000 were turned away. The Giants made their royal entrance onto the field in brand new stark black flannels with white piping, white belts, white caps and hose. Across the front of the shirt was an immense "NY" in white. It was an impressive and intimidating uniform.

On the mound for New York was the incomparable Christy Mathewson and for Philadelphia future Hall of Famer Eddie Plank with a 25-12 record, 2.26 ERA and a league-leading 36 complete games in 41 starts. As great ones often do, Mathewson reached new heights of brilliance in this pressure-packed World Series. He went the distance blanking Philadelphia 3–0 on four hits and his control was perfect. Although the Athletics had scoring opportunities in the third, sixth, eighth and ninth innings, Matty stiffened his resolve and pitched out of each jam. Lefty Plank hurled a fine game himself, scattering ten hits and giving up two runs in the fifth and one in the ninth.

The scene for the second game shifted 90 miles north to the Polo Grounds where 24,992 saw Philadelphia's answer to Mathewson, Chief Bender, hurl a four-hitter beating New York by the same 3–0 score. It evened the series at one game apiece.

October 12

The third game of the series was scheduled for October 11 in Philadelphia but was canceled because of wet grounds. At least that was the official ruling by umpires Hank O'Day and John Sheridan. The press, however, reported that the real reason was the lack of gate receipts. At game time only about 4,000 spectators had passed through the turnstiles, largely due to the ominous sky and threat of rain. After getting the word from McGraw and Philadelphia captain Lave Cross, the umpires made it official.

The third game finally got underway at Baker Bowl where the temperature hovered around 65 degrees. Mathewson, with two days' rest, continued his pitching mastery by tossing his second consecutive shutout beating Philadelphia 9–0. Matty allowed only four hits but this time walked one batter. He was tough in the clutch again as no runner advanced beyond second.

In contrast, Andy Coakley was assaulted by New York. He allowed nine runs on eight hits and walked five. The Giants also ran wild swiping five bases. In fairness to Coakley his support was questionable as the Athletics committed four errors, three by second baseman Danny Murphy.

Due to the "rain out" on October 11, games four and five would be played at the Polo Grounds. New York's pitching dominance continued in game four as McGinnity beat Plank 1–0 in a marvelous pitching duel. An unearned run in the fourth inning accounted for all the scoring. The Giants now led the series three games to one and the future looked bleak for Mack and his Athletics.

October 14

Truth is stranger than fiction, an old adage that must have originated after Mathewson beat Philadelphia 2–0 before 24,000 spectators for his third consecutive shutout and New York's right to claim the World Championship. In yet another splendid pitching exhibition, Matty allowed six hits and did not walk a batter in defeating his mound rival, Chief Bender. In 27 innings of World Series pitching (seven days) Mathewson allowed no runs, 14 hits, one walk and struck out 18 batters—a phenomenal achievement that added lustre to an already radiant reputation. Christy Mathewson was indeed a pitching machine. Many years later, *The Sporting News* put out a list of the greatest achievements in the history of baseball. Matty's three World Series shutouts ranked ninth.

The 1905 New York Giants were the World Champions of baseball

7 • World Series Hero, 1905

and they were richly rewarded for their efforts. Blanche McGraw noted in her book that, "Each Giant received $1,142 and a diamond-studded gold button, emblematic of their World's Championship. John McGraw received a new three-year contract, with no extra clauses this time, calling for a salary of $24,000 per year!"[14] The salary claimed by Mrs. McGraw might have been wishful thinking or the result of a fading memory since other reports list McGraw's salary at $15,000 per year. Whatever the true figure, McGraw was well rewarded and deservedly so. He was on top of the baseball world and the toast of New York.

Mathewson, almost from the beginning of his big league career, was the star attraction who was worshipped by the New York fans. His classic good looks, college background and impeccable lifestyle coupled with a pitching mastery that dominated hitters spread his reputation throughout the country, making him the idol of all America. Now his legendary feats in the World Series elevated Mathewson to the ultimate pinnacle as a national hero larger than life.

Chapter 8
A Bout with Diphtheria, 1906

W	L	Pct	ERA
22	12	.647	2.97

John McGraw, elated over his great success the previous year and soaking up the adoration heaped upon him, boldly predicted another World Championship for the New York Giants in 1906. Based on the club's performance, especially the way they handled Philadelphia in the World Series, few people doubted him. McGraw and the Giants were on top of the baseball world and enjoying every minute of it. Never one to miss an opportunity for showmanship, often to the point of arrogance, McGraw dressed his club for the upcoming season in *new* black uniforms. And to remind everyone who the best team in baseball was, he had the white "NY" removed from the front shirt and replaced with a white "World's Champions." He also had the horses that drew the Giants' carriages to and from enemy ballparks, draped with big yellow blankets bearing the same words—World Champions.* This bit of haughtiness did little to ingratiate him or his club with crowds in opposing cities.

McGraw, no doubt a disciple of the "if it ain't broke, don't fix it" school, returned from spring training in Memphis with virtually the same personnel he employed to win in 1905. His club was set and ready to repeat as World Champions. Baseball fortunes, however, can change overnight. That's exactly what happened to McGraw and his club. Even before the new season began the Giants were in trouble and headed for misfortunes that were impossible to overcome. It all began when Christy Mathewson was laid up with a serious illness and didn't pitch his first game until May 5! On May 15 Mike Donlin, after getting three hits, broke his leg on a hard slide into second base against Cincinnati. Roger Bresnahan, who had a

---

This idea, however, was first used in 1886 by Chris Von der Ahe, owner of the St. Louis Browns, the best team in the American Association. His club defeated the heavily favored Chicago White Stockings of the National League in postseason championship play. As a result, Von der Ahe drove around St. Louis "for months in a carriage with horses draped with blankets adorned with the inscription St. Louis Browns, Champions of the World."

8 • A Bout with Diphtheria, 1906

Left: This large bronze plaque to the left of the Memorial Gateway at Bucknell University was given by professional baseball in honor of Mathewson and in part reads: "He was one of the greatest figures in competitive sport of all time." *Right:* To the right of the Memorial Gateway the inscription on this bronze plaque traces Mathewson's career as an athlete, soldier and gentleman (photos by Arlene C. Mayer).

fine year in 1905, was beaned by a pitch and never fully recovered. Finally, there were some early signs that shortstop Bill Dahlen (now 36) was slowing down.

Years later in his book *My Thirty Years in Baseball,* McGraw said about the 1906 season, "our loss in that particular year was due to a series of accidents that practically put us out of the race."[2] The biggest reason the Giants would finish second in 1906, with a hefty 96 victories, was the Chicago Cubs. The Cubs won 116 games, a record that still stands today. This powerhouse was led by the celebrated double play combination of Joe Tinker, Johnny Evers and Frank Chance, third baseman Harry Steinfeldt (.327 average, 83 RBIs), right fielder Frank Schulte (.281 average, 60 RBIs) and the awesome pitching of Three Finger Brown (26-6, 1.04 ERA), Jack Pfiester (20-8, 1.56 ERA) and Ed Reulbach (19-4, 1.65 ERA).

Despite the rash of injuries to his club and Chicago's outstanding team, McGraw never gave up. In mid–July he made two moves which turned out to be a case of too little too late. He traded Sam Mertes, who claimed to be unpopular with the Catholics on the team because he was a Mason, and Doc Marshall for William "Spike" Shannon, a switch-hitting outfielder. Author Frank Graham in his book *The New York Giants,* claimed "Shannon ... [was] one of the first, if not the first, outfielders ever to wear sun glasses."[3]

McGraw also convinced Brush to purchase outfielder Cy Seymour from Cincinnati, which he did for $12,000 (some reports listed the amount at $10,000). Seymour was a familiar face at the Polo Grounds having played with the Giants from 1896 until 1900, mainly as a pitcher and outfielder before he stopped pitching in 1901. Seymour led the league in hitting with a .377 average in 1905 with Cincinnati but never came close to duplicating that season with the Giants.

The 1906 baseball season, in spite of McGraw's efforts and the Giants' valiant play, belonged to the Chicago Cubs. They were almost invincible. They were also in for a big surprise when they met the White Sox, their crosstown rivals, in the World Series.

Christy Mathewson was now entering his sixth full season with the Giants and, after his fabulous year in 1905, the young man from Factoryville was a national idol. Whatever he did from this point on only added to the legend. Although Matty would record another fine season, it turned out to be a struggle and a disappointment compared to the excitement and glory of 1905.

The Season

May 5

More than three weeks into the season Christy Mathewson finally felt well enough to take his turn in the pitching rotation for the New York Giants. Prior to the beginning of the season Matty had contracted diphtheria (first thought to be a cold) and had to be separated from his wife, who was pregnant, and the players on the team. It was a dreaded disease in those days and one in which McGraw had a personal interest. At the age of 12, five members of his family, including his mother, died of diphtheria.

Matty eventually fought off the illness and in a weakened condition returned to the Polo Grounds to face Boston. It was a warm and enthusiastic crowd that gathered to greet their World Series hero and Matty didn't disappoint them. He pitched a fine game. His fast ball lacked its usual zip, however, as he gave up seven hits, including two doubles and two triples but he left the game after seven innings leading 4–3. Joe McGinnity came on in relief and after an easy eighth inning, gave up three runs in the ninth as Boston won 6–4. The Giants remained in first place with a 15–5 record with the second place Cubs close behind.

A lot happened in the three weeks that Mathewson was laid up with diphtheria. For openers, San Francisco was jolted by a severe earthquake which left thousands dead and many more injured. Initial estimates of the damage were as high as $200 million in a time when you could buy a good cigar for two cents. Baseball was doing its part to help the earthquake victims. On April 29, in a benefit game between the New York Highlanders and the Philadelphia Athletics over $5,600 was raised for the San Francisco Relief Fund.

On a much lighter note, the Giants won two opening day games, with Red Ames on the mound in both. He beat Philadelphia 3–2 at Baker Bowl on April 12 and Brooklyn 8–2 at the Polo Grounds on April 20.

In what seemed like a never-ending battle, Sunday baseball made the news again as the law was challenged or more appropriately sidestepped by Brooklyn. Instead of the program-selling ploy tried in 1905, this time president Charles H. Ebbets' scheme was free admission with the hope patrons would voluntarily donate money. Deputy Commissioner Arthur J. O'Keefe in charge of the Brooklyn Police Department said, "If the Sunday games at Washington Park are to be free games, in the literal sense of that term, Mr. Ebbets may be right in assuming that they will not constitute a violation of the law. If, on the other hand, an admission fee is exacted in any manner we will consider the law violated, and will act accordingly."[4] The game was played and Brooklyn lost to Boston 5–3. No arrests were reported, but voluntary contributions were not the answer nor would this be the last time Sunday baseball in New York would be an issue.

The coup de grace came on April 26 after the Giants had beaten Philadelphia 4–3 and McGraw was leaving the playing field. Overhearing some uncomplimentary remarks by a spectator, the feisty manager hauled off and slugged the agitator and then calmly proceeded to the clubhouse. A policeman was summoned but refused to arrest McGraw claiming he did not witness the assault and, furthermore, could not make the arrest without a warrant.

May 14

Nine days passed before a physically weakened Mathewson pitched again. During this time New York and Chicago swapped first place several times and it appeared that an exciting pennant race was building between the two clubs. Mathewson beat Cincinnati 6–3 in a game which saw New York record its second victory of the season's first western road trip. Matty gave up nine hits and issued an unheard of seven walks. In spite of this weak performance, Cincinnati could only manage one run as the Giants came to bat in the top of the ninth with the score deadlocked at 1–1. Invincible for eight innings, Cincinnati pitcher Orval Overall came unglued in the ninth, allowing four hits and as many walks as the Giants scored five runs. Cincinnati scored two runs in the bottom half of the ninth but Matty held on for his first victory of the season.

In an unrelated matter, it was interesting to note that the Standard Oil Company raised its price of gasoline to dealers from 15 to 18 cents a gallon. The dealers in turn raised their price to 25 cents. Several automobile owners were outraged and claimed Standard Oil with having a monopoly and being able to charge whatever they wanted. Shakespeare said it a long time ago: "What's past is prologue."

May 18

After taking three out of four in Cincinnati, New York lost the first two games in Pittsburgh and called on Mathewson to put a halt to the losing streak, but to no avail: Matty lost 7–6 as he gave up 14 hits. It wasn't all his fault, however. With Pittsburgh ahead 7–6 in the top of the ninth and Dahlen on second with the tying run, Honus Wagner saved the day for Pittsburgh. As Dahlen took his lead off second, carefully watching Al Leifield coming to a stretch on the mound, Wagner moved toward Dahlen and gently touched him with the ball for the third out. As if the hidden ball trick wasn't embarrassing enough for Dahlen, an angered McGraw slapped him with a heavy fine.

May 21

By losing three of four games to Pittsburgh, the Giants dropped out of first place and now headed for the Windy City to face front-running Chicago in an important series. The Cubs walked away with the first game 10–4 extending their lead over New York to three full games. McGraw called on Wiltse to stop the red hot Cubs and the left-hander pitched well, allowing six hits and three runs in five innings. Mathewson took over for Wiltse with a 5–3 lead and blanked the Cubs until the ninth. The final score was New York 6, Chicago 4. The Giants won the next day 8–2 and were only one game behind Chicago.

May 24

After a miserable day of rain, Mathewson started the final game of the Chicago series. Still in a weakened condition from the diphtheria, he lasted only two and a third innings, giving up two runs on three hits and two walks. He left leading 5–2 but George Wiltse let Chicago tie the game in the fifth. In the eighth inning Tinker, the Cubs' shortstop, made an error allowing New York to win 6–5. Matty was credited with the victory, which under the rules of the day was determined by the official scorer who felt Matty pitched better than Wiltse. By taking three of four from Chicago the Giants moved back into first place by percentage points.

May 26

Mathewson pitched the second game of the St. Louis series and won 5–4 when George Browne singled in two runs in the ninth. McGinnity finished the game as Matty picked up his third win of the season. One of the two umpires for this game was Hank O'Day, a man, according to Mathewson, who seldom smiled and was stubborn and bullheaded. Claimed Matty, "If a manager gets after him for a decision, he is likely to go up in the air and, not meaning to do it, call close ones against the club that has made the kick, for it must be remembered that umpires are only 'poor weak mortals after all.'"[5]

New York split the next two games at St. Louis and ended the road trip 9-7. They began their western swing on May 12 in second place, one game back of Chicago. They returned home still in second, one and a half games behind the Cubs. McGraw had to be pleased that his chargers were still in the pennant race in spite of setbacks to Mathewson and Donlin.

May 30

Back east, New York split a doubleheader with Brooklyn at Washington Park by scores of 2-0 and 5-2. Dummy Taylor took the loss in the first game as Harry McIntire hurled a nifty four-hit shutout. In the second game Mathewson allowed eight hits and two runs picking up his fourth win against one loss.

Over in the American League, Connie Mack's Athletics were in first place while the Chicago White Sox, the ultimate pennant winners, were languishing in sixth place struggling to play .500 baseball. But that would change in a hurry.

June 4

New York scored four runs off Philadelphia hurler John Lush in the first inning, spotting Mathewson a comfortable lead before he even threw his first pitch. Matty, still recovering from his bout with diphtheria, gave back all four runs and never finished the first inning as Wiltse relieved with two out. The Giants, however, came back with three runs in the seventh and another in the ninth to win for Wiltse 9-6 at Baker Bowl. Frank Bowerman, Art Devlin and Dan McGann were the hitting stars as New York was desperately trying to keep pace with the high flying Cubs.

The day before, Brooklyn beat Boston 3-1 at Washington Park and successfully challenged the Sunday law under their voluntary contributions scheme. The plan, however, was modified slightly since some fans who were dropping 25 cents in the box were sitting in the grandstands and not where they belonged in the bleachers. The new scheme called for the fan to hand the money to an attendant, who then made sure spectators sat in the proper section.

In an amusing twist, Deputy Police Commissioner O'Keefe, a constant attendant at Sunday games, helped break up a crowd crunch at the entrance to the park by letting fans in the front go into the game without paying. He was loudly cheered by the spectators for his efforts.

June 7

On June 5 the first-place Chicago Cubs began a four-game series with New York at the Polo Grounds. The Giants were in second place trailing the Cubs by one game so the series was important and offered them an opportunity to get back into first place. Although the stage was set for a happy ending the script must have been written by a loyal Chicago fan. The Cubs won the first two games by scores of 6–0 and 11–3, dropping New York into third place (Pittsburgh moved into second), three games behind Chicago.

McGraw called on Mathewson to stem the Chicago tide. For the second straight game Matty never got out of the first inning! He allowed four hits and five runs. McGinnity finished the first and before the Giants even came to the plate they trailed 11–0. McGinnity left after the second inning with George Ferguson completing the fiasco as Chicago, on 22 hits, beat New York 19–0. It was one of the worst defeats in Giants history.

The next day New York redeemed itself somewhat by beating Chicago 7–3, but it was clear to everyone that this Giants club was not the same as in 1905 and, equally important, the Cubs were a superior team.

June 15

Mathewson didn't return to the mound until June 15, which meant he pitched a total of one inning (two-thirds on June 4 and a third on June 7) in 16 days since May 30.

In the meantime, the Sunday baseball dilemma made the news again. Police Commissioner Bingham ordered no playing of Sunday baseball for admission whether directly or by subterfuge, no doubt referring to the voluntary contributions scheme. Brooklyn president Ebbets decided to obey Bingham's order, but then had a change of heart when a Brooklyn magistrate discharged two men who had been arrested for displaying contribution boxes at a semipro game.

With renewed hope the wily Ebbets devised yet another plan to circumvent the no-baseball-on-Sunday law. Contribution boxes would still be in vogue but now patrons would be asked to contribute *after* the contest ended. Since this was the method used when the Brooklyn magistrate made his favorable ruling, Ebbets decided to give it a try. It didn't work! Ebbets, his manager Patsy Donovan, Cincinnati manager Ned Hanlon, Brooklyn pitcher Mal Eason and Cincinnati pitcher Chick Fraser were all arrested. They were taken to the Berger Street Police Station and released on bail. Adding to Ebbets' demise, Brooklyn lost 3–0. It wasn't easy being a trailblazer.

Back at the Polo Grounds, Mathewson pitched a quality game by beating St. Louis 2–1. Still weak from his illness, but beginning to show signs of his 1905 form, Matty scattered eight hits for his fifth victory against two losses. He was particularly tough with men on base as St. Louis stranded 11 runners. Bresnahan scored the winning run in the eighth when the usually sure-handed second baseman, Pug Bennett, juggled Sam Mertes' ground ball with the bases loaded.

June 21

Mathewson picked up his sixth win in a wild game against Pittsburgh at the Polo Grounds that saw three Giants ejected, a makeshift lineup and an exciting finish. It started when McGraw was tossed out of the game by his old nemesis Bob Emslie. It intensified an inning later when Hank O'Day heaved starter McGinnity and first baseman McGann. O'Day's action was more serious since it necessitated a juggling of the lineup: Mathewson taking the place of McGinnity; Bowerman going to first; Marshall catching and seldom-used Alec Smith in right.

With New York trailing 4–2 after five, Matty blanked Pittsburgh over the next four innings, keeping his club in the game and setting the stage for the exciting finish. Sam Leever began the fatal ninth by walking Dahlen. Devlin followed with a single to left and, when Wagner booted Billy Gilbert's grounder, the bases were loaded. Sensing Leever was tiring, manager Fred Clarke yanked him in favor of Chappie McFarland. Bowerman greeted the new hurler by singling to left, scoring Dahlen. Strang batted for Matty but fanned. As the crowd cheered Bresnahan, the best he could do was pop to Jim Nealon at first. The bases were still loaded with two out and New York trailing 4–3 as Doc Marshall, part-time catcher and outfielder, strolled to the platee. A lifetime .210 hitter, Marshall ran the count to 3-2 before he singled to center, driving in two runs to win the game for Mathewson 5–4. Marshall was hoisted on the shoulders of some exuberant fans and carried off the field in tribute to their hero.

Earlier in the week, the National League of Professional Baseball Clubs met and decided in quick fashion to donate $500 to help the Pacific Coast League which was suffering due to the damage caused by the 1906 earthquake and subsequent fires. Closer to home, in their own league, two resolutions were passed. The first was for home teams to provide proper dressing rooms on the grounds, including lockers and hot and cold water, for visiting teams. Lack of facilities was causing serious problems. Many of the visiting teams were forced to dress at their hotel, even putting on their spike shoes, which hotel managers found objectionable, causing them, in several instances, to refuse to grant accommodations. It was agreed this resolution would be studied further and reported on in December.

The other resolution, which would cost nothing, was passed immediately. It involved moving batting practice from in front of the grandstand, where it was dangerous to spectators, to the diamond. The resolution also changed the time, making it begin one hour before the game.

Dummy Taylor, a deaf-mute, pitched with Mathewson from 1900 to 1908. In 1904 Taylor won 21 games (photo courtesy National Baseball Library, Cooperstown, N.Y.).

June 23

In a fast-paced one hour and twenty minute game Mathewson tossed a six-hit shutout against Philadelphia, by far his finest performance of the season. It appeared Matty was finally shaking off the last remnants of his debilitating disease. In nine innings he walked two batters and only once did a Philadelphia player reach as far as third base. His record was 7-2. It was performances like this that molded McGraw's opinion of the great pitcher. "There has never been a pitcher like Mathewson in the past and I do not expect to see another like him for the next quarter of a century," claimed McGraw.[6]

The Sunday baseball challenge added yet another chapter to the saga when it was announced that Police Commissioner Bingham was not satisfied with the decision by the magistrate and would stop future Sunday games and arrest the managers regardless of what method was used to collect money. He continued to insist the issue must be settled by the courts. So the battle to play ball in New York on Sunday would continue for another 13 years, until 1919 when it was finally legalized. On May 4 recordbreaking crowds jammed into the Polo Grounds and Ebbets Field to witness National League baseball for the first time ever (legally) on the Sabbath. The Giants lost to the Phillies while the Dodgers beat Boston. These historic games put an end to the long and controversial struggle.

June 27

Mathewson registered his eighth win when he defeated Boston 6–4 at South End Grounds. This was Matty's third consecutive complete game start, attesting to his improved health. He scattered six hits, walked three and struck out five. This was the first of four games with last-place Boston and McGraw saw an opportunity to sweep the series, thus putting more pressure on first-place Chicago. When New York took the second game 4–2 it moved ahead of Pittsburgh into second place and trailed the Cubs by only two games.

In the American League the pennant race was even tighter. There was a three-way tie for first place among Philadelphia, the 1905 champs, Cleveland and the New York Highlanders: all had identical 36-24 records. It was an exciting time for baseball fans throughout the nation, but particularly in New York where the Giants and Highlanders were in tight pennant races that kept fan interest at a high level.

June 30

Three days later Mathewson lost to Boston 4–3 at the Polo Grounds. Mathewson lasted only seven innings, giving up all four runs on six hits. Wiltse came on in relief and did a fine job, blanking Boston in the eighth and ninth. New York made a valiant effort in the bottom of the seventh, scoring three runs on two key hits, a double by Devlin and a single by Bowerman, but fell short of tying the game when Bowerman was caught trying to steal second. It was Mathewson's third loss of the season, dropping the Giants three and a half games behind Chicago and one and a half in back of second-place Pittsburgh.

July 5

In an exciting duel at the Polo Grounds, Mathewson outpitched Boston's Jeff Pfeffer, moving New York ahead of Pittsburgh into second place. It was a scoreless tie as the Giants entered the ninth. Gilbert led off by beating out a slow bounder to Allie Stroebel. Bowerman sacrificed him to second but Matty skied to Cozy Dolan in right field. Pfeffer, not anxious to face Bresnahan, gave him a base on balls. Strang finally put an end to the suspense by singling to center, scoring Gilbert. In the meantime, Chicago was beating Pittsburgh for the second day in a row.

When attendance figures were released on July 4 they showed baseball's popularity was skyrocketing. The total attendance was 143,000 (American League 75,000; National League 68,000) and many of the clubs experienced record crowds at their parks. The National Pastime was clearly capturing the imagination of the country.

July 10

The day before New York defeated Cincinnati 5–3 at League Park to begin its second trip to western cities. Mathewson couldn't maintain the momentum as Cincinnati touched him for single runs in the first and second innings and three in the fourth for an early 5–0 lead. Red Ames came on in relief and checked the Reds, but the best the Giants could manage off Bob Wicker was two runs. The final score was 6–2 as Matty's record went to 9-4.

Rumors continued to circulate that New York would soon be making a major overhaul in personnel in order to strengthen their team. Prominent among the names headed for New York were left fielder Joe Kelley of Cincinnati; infielder Dan Shay, catcher Mike Grady and left fielder Spike Shannon, all of St. Louis. It was a sure sign McGraw and Brush were not content with second place as the season approached the halfway mark.

July 14

In a doubleheader at Robison Field, which was characterized by the press as "dull," New York defeated St. Louis 5–1 and 4–0. Two fresh faces appeared in the lineup for the Giants, satisfying the shake-up rumors, and both made immediate contributions to the victories. Ex–St. Louis captain Shannon, who was traded for Mertes and Marshall, had three hits in the first game and scored two runs. Cy Seymour, who was purchased from Cincinnati for a reported $12,000, played center field and collected four hits and scored a run in the two games.

Mathewson was the beneficiary of New York's ten-hit attack off Buster Brown. Matty spread six hits and two walks over nine innings, recording his tenth win against four losses.

July 17

After feasting on St. Louis in a four-game sweep, the Giants still trailed Chicago by five games as they moved into the Windy City for a crucial series. The opening game pitted Mathewson against his tough rival Three Finger Brown in their first meeting of the year. Neither pitcher was overpowering, but Brown came out on top 6–2. He gave up seven hits and five walks but was tough in the clutch. Matty was touched for nine hits and walked five.

8 • A Bout with Diphtheria, 1906

The difference in the game was Joe Tinker, Matty's nemesis, who collected two hits and snapped the 1–1 tie in the sixth with a two-run homer. Mathewson always considered Tinker a dangerous hitter and rightly so: "he has been a thorn in my side and has broken up many a game," he admitted. "The only thing to do is to ... try to outguess him, but Tinker is a hard man to beat at the game of wits."[7]

July 20

In the last game of the Chicago series (which now stood at 1-1 and a tie), McGraw called on Mathewson looking for a clutch victory. It appeared, at least through seven innings, that he would get his wish. Matty had the game under control, leading Chicago 3–2, as he entered the bottom of the eighth. With runners on first and second and two out Steinfeldt walked to the plate. Matty fell behind in the count and on the 3-1 pitch the Chicago third baseman drove the ball between Bresnahan and Seymour into right center driving in two runs with a ringing triple as the Cubs fans went wild. When the inning ended, Chicago had pushed across four runs and the final score was 6–3. Chicago had taken two of the three games (Matty suffering both losses) and New York moved on to Pittsburgh, six games behind the league leaders and rapidly headed for third place.

July 25

The inevitable finally occurred. New York fell into third place when Pittsburgh drubbed the Giants in the first three games of the series. McGraw gave the ball to his ace in the final game, surprising the Pittsburgh fans, who thought Matty still weak from his bout with diphtheria and unable to pitch.

Mathewson was magnificent as he scattered eight hits and blanked Pittsburgh 3–0, sidestepping an embarrassing sweep while recording his eleventh win. New York completed its second western swing with an 8-7 record, on the surface not a bad performance. A closer look, however, revealed that the Giants left for the road trip in second place four games behind Chicago and returned in third place, six games in back of the league leaders. Although there were two full months of baseball remaining, still plenty of time to catch Chicago, it was not to be. The Cubs would continue to win at a torrid pace, 50-8 from August 1 to the end of the season, so no matter how well the Giants played it was in vain.

July 30

Back at the Polo Grounds Mathewson breezed to his twelfth victory by defeating Cincinnati 9–1 in a game that was called after eight innings due to darkness. At least that was the official reason offered by the umpires. But one could make a strong argument that Jim Johnstone and Bob Emslie took pity on Cincinnati hurler Bob Wicker, who was battered for 17 hits, including three each by Matty and Seymour.

McGraw replaced Mathewson after six innings with the score 6–0, giving his star pitcher a well-deserved rest. In this short stint Matty gave up four hits, no runs and didn't walk a batter. The victory put New York one game back of Pittsburgh and, when the Giants won again the following day and Pittsburgh lost, both teams were tied for second place with identical records of 58-32. With Chicago continuing to win at an incredible pace, virtually locking up the pennant, fan attention would soon shift to the race for second place.

August 4

New York, behind the hard-nosed pitching of Mathewson and Wiltse, defeated the high-flying Chicago Cubs 7–4 before an unofficial record crowd of 24,000. Matty gave up eight hits and four runs but walked only one batter as his teammates supplied plenty of support. It was his thirteenth win against six losses.

The victory moved New York to within four and a half games of Chicago and offered Giants fans a glimmer of hope. But when Chicago took the next three games, including a hotly contested forfeit, New York trailed by seven and a half and its hopes of back-to-back pennants were all but destroyed.

The forfeit of August 7 had its origin the day before when McGraw and Devlin were ejected from the game by Johnstone, a game New York lost 3-1. On top of this, Pulliam notified McGraw and Devlin they were suspended. This set the stage for a brazen move by McGraw.

Events happened in rapid fashion. Giants officials refused to admit Johnstone to the Polo Grounds. Shortly after four o'clock McGraw designated Giants player Sammy Strang to officiate. That's when the Chicago players left the field for the clubhouse. In a counter move, Joe Humphries, the Giants' public address announcer, strolled to home plate and said that Police Inspector Sweeney had requested the Giants not to permit Johnstone on the grounds for fear of a riot. The plot thickened as Sweeney adamantly denied Humphries' statement. Johnstone, still outside the grounds, declared the game a forfeit with Chicago the winner 9–0. The incident now escalated to a war of words. McGraw claimed that according to his interpretation of the rules New York should be the winner 9–0, not Chicago. Brush, in a lengthy statement, supported his manager's position, claiming umpire Emslie could have conducted the game but when he left, and there were no substitute umpires, the rules (article 4, section 39) called for each team to select a player to umpire. Strang was New York's choice.

President Pulliam entered the crossfire when he issued a stern statement giving his full support to the forfeit in favor of Chicago citing the constitution of the National League which clearly compels every club to accept the umpires assigned by the president.

The next day (August 8) Pulliam heightened his resolve in a highly emotional statement to the press. "I uphold the action of the umpires absolutely, and if I am not sustained by the National League Board of Directors I will not only resign my position as President of the National League, but I will quit professional baseball forever."[8]

A week later the forfeit was upheld and Chicago officially declared the winner of the game 9-0. Shortly after, Pulliam announced the reinstatement of McGraw effective August 25. Although the fiery manager lost this battle of intimidation, he did not lose graciously as he severely criticized Pulliam for displaying favoritism and threatening to take his case to court. It was vintage McGraw, a rough and tumble competitor who hated to lose more than anything else in the world.

August 9

With the disastrous Chicago series over, New York began the first of five games against Pittsburgh in the battle for second place. The Giants won 6-0, scoring five runs in the first two innings, providing Mathewson with an early cushion. Matty pitched splendidly and was replaced after seven innings by George Ferguson, who blanked the Pirates the rest of the way to preserve the shutout. Matty's record now stood at 14-6.

August 13

New York took both ends of a doubleheader against Pittsburgh, completing the five-game sweep to the delight of the 23,000 fans. The Giants won the first game 6-1 behind the strong pitching of Wiltse. Mathewson dominated the second game, scattering six hits, half by Wagner (who Matty admitted was a tough out) and allowed one run. It was an exciting game, entering the bottom half of the ninth, tied at 1-1. With Strang on second and one out Spike Shannon, who was playing superbly for New York since being acquired in a trade the previous month, singled to center scoring Strang with the winning run. It was Mathewson's second victory of the series and put New York three and a half games ahead of the Pirates.

August 18

After winning two games in St. Louis (beginning the final western swing) and extending their streak to eight straight, the Giants entered Chicago looking to cut the Cubs' seven-game lead. Before a boisterous crowd of 18,000 at West Side Park Mathewson was tapped for the opening game assignment and to no one's surprise faced Three Finger Brown. The controversial forfeit game was still fresh in the minds of the Chicago faithful as yellow and black banners, bearing McGraw's nickname, "Muggsy," bedecked the ground level box seats. "Over the years he [McGraw] developed a burning hatred for the nickname and anybody who used it, however innocently or goodnaturedly. He never explained why he felt so strong about 'Muggsy,'"[9] wrote author Charles C. Alexander.

Brown, rising to the occasion, was near invincible. He gave up seven singles and two runs. In contrast, Matty had an off day giving up 12 hits and six runs, four of which came in the disastrous sixth inning. The game ended with Chicago 6, New York 2. Tinker, who always had a great deal of success facing Mathewson, collected three hits, scored two runs and was outstanding in the field. It was a discouraging day for the Giants as they slipped back another game in their futile quest to pull ahead of Chicago.

Days later, an interesting reminder of our country's struggle for race equality appeared, oddly enough, on the sports page of *The New York Times*. The story emanated from Harper's Ferry in West Virginia where an address was read at the conclusion of the second annual meeting of the Niagara Movement, a black human rights organization. Among the demands outlined were: the right to vote and the ending of discrimination in public accommodations.

August 22

After losing two of three games to Chicago, New York traveled to Pittsburgh where Mathewson pitched the series opener and lost 2–1. It was the dreaded base on balls that caused the demise of Matty, who was noted for his pinpoint control. He issued five walks, two of which resulted in runs. Matty's record was now 15-8.

August 25

The New York Giants arrived in Cincinnati barely clinging to second place after losing two of three to Pittsburgh. The Giants now trailed Chicago by 11½ games and by the season's end this deficit would look close. Mathewson won the first game of the series but was far from overpowering, and after six innings trailed 3–2. The score could have been much worse since Matty was batted freely. But in the top of the seventh New York attacked lefty Bob Wicker with a vengeance, scoring six runs on six hits, capped by Mathewson's double. The game was called due to darkness after eight, with the final score 8–3.

Over in the American League the Chicago White Sox lost a doubleheader to Washington after reeling off 19 straight victories! The team dubbed the "Hitless Wonders" went from fourth place to first as a result of this streak. Exciting things were happening in the Junior Circuit.

August 30

Returning east, after a 7-6 road trip and trailing the Cubs by 12 games, New York split a doubleheader with Philadelphia on a sloppy rain-drenched diamond at Baker Bowl. Despite the poor field conditions it turned out to be an afternoon of exciting baseball which featured exceptional pitching by all four starters.

In the first game Tom Sparks tossed a three-hit shutout, tagging Mathewson with his ninth loss. Matty pitched well enough to win on most occasions, giving up seven hits and two runs, but Sparks was near invincible as he walked only two Giants while fanning seven. In the nightcap McGinnity blanked the Phillies 1–0 with Bill Duggleby the hard-luck loser.

The only excitement remaining in the National League was the race for second place. In the American League, however, it was a different story, with three clubs battling for the pennant. With a month remaining in the season the Chicago White Sox held a slim three and one-half–game lead over the Highlanders and a four and one-half–game lead over Philadelphia, the defending champs. The ingredients were present for an exciting pennant race, especially for Chicago fans from the south side who were eager for a pennant and confrontation with the rival Cubs.

September 3

Prior to the Monday doubleheader, New York catcher Frank Bowerman, who had been sidelined for a week with an injured thumb, was in an accident involving an automobile and a horse-drawn "runabout." It was a scene right out of a Keystone Kops comedy. Apparently the touring car and the runabout collided with the latter overturning and dumping its occupants on the ground. Bowerman claimed the wheels of the car ran over him and the horse trampled him. When the policeman arrived at the scene both Bowerman and the owner of the car were blaming each other. No one was seriously injured and, in fact, shortly after the comic incident Bowerman was back in the Giants' lineup.

New York won both ends of the doubleheader against Boston at the Polo Grounds, 4–0 and 3–2. Mathewson dominated the first game, tossing a three-hit shutout (his fifth) for his seventeenth win against nine losses. Jeff Pfeffer's wildness in the second inning resulted in two runs for the Giants and more than enough for the victory. They added one more in the fourth and another in the eighth on a home run by Seymour. In the nightcap, Wiltse picked up the win in relief of Ames.

September 6

Mathewson was in rare form as he struck out 14 Brooklyn batters at Washington Park, a major league high for the season, as New York won

6–2. In fact the game was over after the first inning when the Giants scored four runs aided by two walks and two errors by Brooklyn. Matty upped his record to 18-9.

In other contests, Chicago beat Pittsburgh in the first game of a four-game sweep, locking New York in second place, a position they would hold for the rest of the season.

September 8

Two days after registering his eighteenth win, Mathewson relieved Ames in the eighth inning of the second game of the doubleheader against Brooklyn. (New York lost the first game 6–0.) When Matty entered the score was 1–0 and he retired the side in order. The Giants failed to score in the top of the ninth and lost both games, but were still in second place as Pittsburgh was being swept by the Cubs.

September 11

New York strengthened its grip on second place when Mathewson blanked Boston 3–0 at South End Grounds. Matty scattered six hits, walked three and fanned nine. It was his sixth and final shutout of the season. This fine outing improved his record to 19-9 and it appeared he was fully recovered from his bout with diphtheria early in the season.

September 14

New York lost both ends of a doubleheader to Brooklyn, the second time within a week, but still held on to second place as Pittsburgh continued to lose. Ames lost the first game 5–3, and Mathewson the seven-inning second game by a score of 1–0. It was a painful loss for Matty as he struck out seven men in seven innings but gave up a double and single in the fifth for the only run of the game. Harry McIntire checked the Giants with four hits. Matty's record was now 19-10.

September 17

Mathewson recorded his twentieth victory in easy fashion when New York assaulted Philadelphia pitcher Walter Moser. Matty was replaced after seven innings by Ferguson, with the Giants leading 10–2. It was Matty's fourth consecutive 20-plus season. Donlin entered the game in the seventh inning and played center field for the first time since he broke his leg in May. Still rusty from the inactivity, the man who batted .356 in 1905, fanned in his only time at bat. The final score was New York 13, Philadelphia 2.

September 20

New York split a doubleheader with Pittsburgh at the Polo Grounds, winning the first game 10–4 and losing the five-inning (called because of darkness) nightcap 3–2, maintaining its three and one-half–game second-place lead. It was the last time these two clubs met, and the game all but dashed any hopes Pittsburgh had of dislodging the Giants from second place.

McGinnity won the first game easily by a lopsided score of 10–4, while Mathewson was defeated in the shortened game 3–2. Matty was not at his best as he gave up seven hits and two walks in only four innings. His record was now 20-11.

September 24

The mighty Chicago Cubs, playing at the Polo Grounds for the last time, trounced New York twice 6–2 and 10–5 to sweep the three-game series. Chicago, having clinched the pennant, apparently had more to prove as it went after Mathewson with a vengeance in the nightcap. The Cubs piled up 16 hits off Matty, four by Jimmy Sheckard, a lifetime .274 hitter, which accounted for ten runs. It ranked as one of the worst shellackings in Mathewson's career. In spite of the double defeat New York remained in second place.

September 28

The Mathewson brothers teamed up to whip St. Louis 8–2 at the Polo Grounds. Matty pitched superbly for eight innings, allowing six hits and no walks. With a safe 8–1 lead the celebrated pitcher turned the game over to his younger brother, Henry, who was making his major league debut. The youngster would have had a one, two, three inning but for some sloppy defense by the Giants, allowing St. Louis to score a harmless run. It was the senior Mathewson's twenty-first win against 12 losses.

October 4

Before one of the smallest crowds ever at the Polo Grounds, New York edged Philadelphia 7–6 in the last home game of the season. The Giants scored six runs in the first inning and Mathewson coasted the rest of the way, which was his practice when sporting a big lead. Many years later Larry Doyle, who would play with Mathewson beginning in 1907, claimed, "Matty was a great one for loafing when the pressure was off, when we were way ahead. He was only great when he had to be. In tight ball games, he was darn near impossible to hit. But when the score was lopsided, Matty didn't seem to care a whit about his reputation and he'd toss in plenty of fat ones."[10] Mathewson ended the season with a 22-12 record.

The following day brother Henry made his first major league start at South End Grounds and was the victim of extreme wildness. He walked a grand total of 14 Boston batters, hit another and allowed five hits. Needless to say Boston won the game 7–1. Not suprisingly, McGraw never thought much of Henry's pitching ability and after hurling one inning in 1907, the 21-year-old sibling of a legend would end his career with an 0-1 record, 4.91 ERA in 11 innings. Clearly Matty had a monopoly on the family pitching genes.

The New York Giants of 1906 won 96 games and lost 56. In spite of this respectable performance, they finished a distant second, 20 games behind the record-breaking Chicago Cubs. There were three important reasons for their second-place finish: first, their offense slipped from a league-leading .273 batting average in 1905 to .255; second, the absence of injured Donlin for most of the season, a weakened Mathewson as the result of diphtheria and Ames' disappointing season of 12-10 compared to 22-8 in 1905; third, and most important, was the superb playing of the Chicago Cubs, who amassed 116 victories, a record that still stands today.

To some, Mathewson's 22-12 regular season record, compared to the 31-9 the year before, plus three World Series shutouts, was a letdown. But considering the nagging illness he suffered most of the season, Matty did an outstanding job. Also, a 22-12 mark for most other pitchers would be cause for celebration. Unfortunately, Christy Mathewson's ability and performance were measured by a more demanding yardstick. It is one of the burdens of a superstar.

With the 1906 season tucked neatly away in the record books, the New York fans would have to be content for a while with reading about the all-Chicago World Series between the Cubs and the White Sox. Dubbed the Hitless Wonders, the Sox won the series in six games, banging out a total of 26 hits in the last two. With the World Series completed, New York Giants fans would wait patiently over the long winter for spring and the new baseball season, hoping McGraw could wave his magic wand and return the Giants to their 1905 form.

Chapter 9
Most Victories in National League, 1907

W	L	Pct	ERA
24	12	.667	2.00

If the New York fans thought the 1906 season was a disappointment, then 1907 would turn out to be a disaster for them. The debacle began long before opening day, when Turkey Mike Donlin jumped the club to pursue a career in acting! His decision was the result of his marriage the previous year to actress Mabel Hite, who turned Donlin's head towards the stage. At one point, however, it looked like Donlin might still play for the Giants. McGraw had agreed to pay him a $600 raise out of his own pocket. But all hope ended when McGraw and Donlin quarreled over whether the money was to be paid at the beginning or end of the season. McGraw was no dummy and wasn't about to let Turkey Mike skip halfway through the season (if it took that long) with his 600 bucks.

Newly acquired Tommy Corcoran, long-time Cincinnati shortstop, was at second base on opening day. However, it would be the 38-year-old veteran's last year in the major leagues. He began his career in 1890 with the Player's League as a barehanded fielder. When the Giants signed the youngster Larry Doyle in July it spelled the end for Corcoran. Later in the season New York would pick up another young talent, 18-year-old Fred Merkle.

Three other key players of past seasons hurt the Giants' performance in 1907. Aging shortstop Bill Dahlen, whose range in the field had narrowed considerably, barely hit .200 and first baseman Dan McGann broke his arm when he was hit by a pitch in mid–June and was out of action until July 25. Joe McGinnity, who led the league in games pitched, turned in the poorest season of his Hall of Fame career. It appeared the Iron Man was nearing the end of his days in the major leagues.

Beside the absence of Donlin and the addition of Corcoran, opening day at the Polo Grounds was historic as well as a harbinger of the season's outcome. Roger Bresnahan donned shin guards, the first time a catcher wore the protection in the National League. Noted by the press, the shin guards were a modified version of those worn by cricket players. "When a sharp foul tip rapped off of the guards in the fifth inning, sparing the Duke of Tralee [Bresnahan's nickname] from injury, the guards had officially arrived."[1] No doubt this historic event was lost in the bizarre conclusion of the game, which Philadelphia won by a forfeit 9-0. Trouble began in the eighth when a number of spectators, among the 17,000 on hand, attempted to cut across the field to avoid the crush of departing fans. After much difficulty umpire Bill Klem finally cleared all the spectators from within the roped areas. In the ninth, with Philadelphia leading 3-0, trouble began again. Noted *The New York Times*, "The instant the Giants took the field for the last time at least 1,000 men and boys leaped over the fences surrounding the playing enclosure and rushed into right field. There they surrounded George Browne and refused to heed the demands of Klem that they move back within the ropes."[2]

Hundreds more joined the melee, which prompted fans in the grandstand to begin tossing cushions. Police were nowhere to be found because earlier in the day commissioner Theodore H. Bingham had ordered his officers not to go within the Polo Grounds to enforce the law, which forbid the policing of private grounds with the city force. The fiasco ended when Klem, who had no other choice, declared a forfeit to the Phillies. Where was McGraw during this farce? Home in bed recuperating from numerous attacks of sinusitis encountered during spring training.

In spite of this troublesome start, the Giants played exceptionally fine baseball early in the season, resulting in a 17-game winning streak. Chicago, however, almost matched the Giants victory for victory. Two days after the streak ended, Chicago tied New York for first place, a discouraging development for McGraw and his men.

In early June New York lost three straight games to Chicago at West Side Park. By mid-July the Giants were 15 games behind the Cubs and an eyelash ahead of Pittsburgh. By season's end New York would be mired in fourth place with an aging and mediocre team.

One bright spot that continued to shine despite the miserable team showing was the great Christy Mathewson. Fully recovered from diphtheria, Matty would lead the league in victories (24), strikeouts (178) and shutouts (8). The right-hander's superior ability and consistency were skills not dependent on his club's performance or league standing. Mathewson was a winner with great teams or poor teams. Over the years he pitched with his head as much as his arm, which prompted poet Ogden Nash, years later, to pen this ditty which was part of a longer piece, entitled "ABC of Baseball Immortals":

> M is for Matty,
> Who carried a charm
> In the form of an extra
> Brain in his arm.[3]

9 • Most Victories in the National League, 1907

On September 30, 1989, in memory of the great pitcher, the Bucknell University football stadium was named the Christy Mathewson Memorial Stadium (photo by Arlene C. Mayer).

These four lines describe the reason for Mathewson's success better than all the words ever written about the immortal.

The Season

April 22

Mathewson pitched his first game of the season, a fine eight-hit shutout, defeating Boston 1–0 at South End Grounds. It was a scoreless

tie entering the top half of the ninth. Bresnahan walked to lead off the inning. McGann was hit by a pitch and then Dahlen singled to left, scoring Bresnahan for the only run Matty needed. It was the first of his league-leading eight shutouts.

April 26

Mathewson won his second game of the season defeating Philadelphia 5–4 at Baker Bowl in a game called after eight innings. Actually New York batted in the ninth, didn't score but played through a heavy downpour of rain. It stopped long enough for Philadelphia to put the tying run at second with one out and the heart of the order coming to bat when the skies opened pouring buckets of rain on the field. After waiting the obligatory 30 minutes umpire Charlie Rigler called the game with the score reverting back to the eighth inning.

Although Matty gave up nine hits, he was tough in the clutch, stranding nine runners. The Giants gave him plenty of support, collecting 14 hits with Spike Shannon (4), Sammy Strang (3) and Dahlen (3) accounting for ten of them. The day before New York began its 17-game winning streak.

May 3

Mathewson pitched masterfully in his first appearance at the Polo Grounds, beating Brooklyn 1–0 and extending New York's winning streak to seven in a row. Matty was in total command throughout as he allowed two hits while walking only one batter for his second shutout of the year. Equally impressive was Brooklyn's Elmer Stricklett, who gave up three hits and two walks, one of which resulted in the only run of the game.

The next day, when Hooks Wiltse shut out Brooklyn 10–0 on a brilliant one-hitter, New York moved into first place with a 15-3 mark. In this game Hank Mathewson pitched the ninth inning, allowing one hit in a mop-up appearance. It turned out to be the last time he would ever pitch in the major leagues, ending an abbreviated career which had begun disastrously the year before.

May 8

Mathewson pitched his second consecutive shutout, this time beating Pittsburgh 4–0 before 12,000 enthusiastic fans at the Polo Grounds. Matty's fourth victory extended the Giants' winning streak to ten in a row

Opposite: **Mathewson (second from right, back row) often faced left-hander Eddie Plank when Bucknell played rival Gettysburg (photo courtesy Bucknell University Archives).**

and enabled them to hold on to first place by a slim margin as the Cubs continued to match their performance by playing splendid baseball. Mathewson was off to a fast start recording four victories without a defeat, three of which were shutouts.

May 11

Before 15,000 fans, it took the combined efforts of McGinnity, Wiltse and Mathewson to defeat Pittsburgh 9–6 and up the Giants' winning streak to 11. The Iron Man lasted only one inning, giving up two hits and two runs. Wiltse came on in relief and pitched well until the seventh when McGraw yanked him with the bases loaded and no outs. Matty retired the side but not before allowing a run to tie the game. When New York scored four runs in the bottom of the seventh Mathewson walked away with an easy win, his fifth of the season.

May 17

The New York Giants defeated St. Louis in a doubleheader by scores of 2–1 and 4–0 at the Polo Grounds. The double victory extended the Giants' streak to 16 and would top out the next day at 17.

Mathewson notched his sixth victory in the first game, giving up three measly hits (two by Red Murray), one run and fanning 11 in a nerve-racking 12-inning contest. With the score tied 1–1 after five innings, the game became one of endurance as St. Louis pitcher Fred Beebe matched Matty pitch for pitch. In the bottom of the twelfth, however, Mathewson took things in his own hands by singling to right field, scoring Corcoran with the winning tally. McGinnity tossed the shutout in the nightcap, pitching one of his best games of the season.

May 21

The Chicago Cubs arrived at the Polo Grounds for the beginning of an important three-game series. New York fans were delirious with anticipation and the advanced ticket sale indicated record crowds could be expected. The first game, which pitted the two legends—Christy Mathewson and Three Finger Brown—drew 22,000 and was described by one local newspaper as a "monster crowd."

Chicago won 3–2, bunching its hits and taking advantage of two errors by Bresnahan. In spite of his first loss of the season, Matty pitched a fine game. He gave up seven hits, two walks and fanned four. The loss gave New York and Chicago identical records of 24-5. The next day, before another large crowd, the Giants moved back into first place when they trounced the Cubs 7–1.

May 23

With the Chicago series now even, McGraw was determined to win the final game at any cost. Before another packed house (23,000) he used his entire pitching staff—Wiltse, Red Ames, Mathewson, Dummy Taylor, George Ferguson and McGinnity—but to no avail as Chicago won 5–2.

Wiltse started and gave up two runs in the first inning. Ames came on in the second, was hit hard but still managed to blank Chicago through the fourth. With Chicago holding on to a slim 2–0 lead McGraw called on Matty with only a day's rest to keep the Cubs checked while New York tried to score runs. Mathewson failed miserably. Two errors and a single put runners on second and third with one out. Jimmy Sheckard then promptly smacked a three-run homer to right field widening the deficit to 5–0 and chasing Matty in favor of Taylor, who retired the side. New York did manage to score two runs in the sixth but fell short as Chicago won the game 5–2 and tied the Giants for first place.

May 25

It was a skillfully played baseball game through seven innings; New York clinging to a 3–1 lead over Boston at the Polo Grounds. Mathewson had been replaced in the seventh by McGinnity when he collided with Del Howard, who was trying to reach first on his hit to McGann. In the eighth, ten men came to bat for New York against southpaw Irv Young and when the onslaught ended the Giants had pushed across six runs and the game was out of reach for Boston. The final score was 9–1. It was Matty's seventh victory against one defeat.

Frank Bowerman was behind the plate for the second game in a row, the result of a three-day suspension of Bresnahan by McGraw. The reason given was insubordination, which was not fully explained to the press. This minor confrontation, and others they may have had over the years, did not influence McGraw's opinion of Bresnahan as a ball player. "To my way of thinking," stated McGraw, "Bresnahan was about the best catcher of all times."[4]

May 30

New York split a doubleheader with the Philadelphia Phillies at the Polo Grounds. In the morning game Lew Moren bested Wiltse by a score of 5–2. The afternoon game, which began 30 minutes late due to the enormous crowd of 25,000, was won by the Giants 6–1 behind the fine pitching of Mathewson. The overflow crowd, which taxed the Giants officials and Pinkerton guards, was six to eight persons deep around the entire field and even prevented a passageway from the players' bench to the field. To rectify the situation, the two teams positioned themselves on the grass, a mere 15 feet from the diamond.

In recording his eighth win, Matty allowed eight hits, walked two and struck out seven. In the meantime Chicago took two games from Pittsburgh and moved into first place where it would remain the rest of the season!

June 5

The Giants began their first four-city road trip with an important three-game series with the first-place Chicago Cubs. As expected, a large crowd turned out at West Side Park and gave the 50 or so policemen fits when they began heaving lemons and verbally berating the visiting Giants. For the second time in a little more than two weeks Mathewson and Brown faced each other to the delight of the Windy City spectators. Chicago fans were even more delighted at the outcome of the game as the Cubs pounded out 16 hits against Matty, crushing the Giants 8–2. It was Matty's second loss of the season, both at the hands of Chicago and Brown. It was also the fifth consecutive time Brown defeated Mathewson dating back to July 12, 1905. When Chicago beat New York the next two games to sweep the series, all hopes for a Giants pennant were dashed.

June 11

McGraw and his men were glad to escape Chicago and head for friendly St. Louis where they would sweep the three-game series. It would bolster the Giants' confidence but in reality it wasn't much of an achievement, coming at the expense of a miserable Cardinals club that would lose 101 games and finish 55½ games behind the Cubs.

The Giants completed the sweep, 8–7, in a long and hard-fought struggle. It took three pitchers to beat back the Cardinals—Taylor, Wiltse and Mathewson—with the latter picking up the victory in two and two-thirds innings of outstanding relief. Spike Shannon and Cy Seymour, each with key triples, led the New York offense. Ulysses Simpson Grant McGlynn (nicknamed Stoney) took the loss, one of a league-leading 25 for the season.

June 14

Mathewson lost a heartbreaker, in 12 innings, to the Pittsburgh Pirates at Exposition Park by a score of 2–1. Matty was pitching a splendid game, locked in a 1–1 tie with Lefty Leifield, when in the ninth he was hit in the stomach by a pitched ball. Weakened by the incident, Mathewson struggled gamely until the fatal twelfth. In that inning he gave up a double, two walks and a single for his third defeat of the season. Leifield gained the victory in his successful quest for a 20-game season, the only one in a 12-year major league career.

June 19

After losing both games, the Giants left Pittsburgh and moved on to Cincinnati where they won the first two at League Park, although the second victory on June 18 was costly. In that game Bresnahan was beaned by an Andy Coakley pitch and knocked unconscious. Although McGraw claimed the injury to be exaggerated, Bresnahan remained in the hospital for ten days before he left for his home in Toledo, Ohio, for further recuperation. In the fourth inning of the same game, McGann sustained a broken arm when he was hit on the wrist by a pitch.

Mathewson failed to make it three straight over the Reds when he lost a come-from-behind heartbreaker. Matty entered the bottom of the ninth with a slim 2–1 lead. With one out the local fans began to leave League Park fully expecting the Reds to lose, but when Lefty Davis singled, the departing spectators slowed their pace. And when John Ganzel doubled the fans stopped dead in their tracks. Moments later Larry McLean singled, driving in Davis and Ganzel for a dramatic 3–2 Cincinnati victory.

The other run scored off Mathewson was in the first inning, a home run by the Mighty Mite, little Miller Huggins. Years later the diminutive second baseman would become famous as the manager of the powerhouse New York Yankees from 1918 to 1929 when he led them to six pennants and three World Championships, including the great 1927 club.

June 22

After a miserable 5-8 road trip, the Giants were glad to get back to the Polo Grounds to face Boston. Mathewson, in a wild game, escaped the loss but not the embarrassment of being clobbered. In four innings Matty was rocked for ten hits and eight runs but New York fought back gallantly and in 12 innings won the game 11–10. Amusingly, *The New York Times* took mercy on the Giants' star pitcher in their description of the brutal second inning. "What the Bostons did to 'Matty' in the second is too painful to record in detail, but to make it short, seven hits one a double, and a pass, netted six runs."[5] Matty's record remained at 9-4.

June 27

After the short series with the Beaneaters at the Polo Grounds, the Giants traveled to Philadelphia where Mathewson and Wiltse combined to shut out the Phillies 2–0 at Baker Bowl. Matty gave up four hits in five and two-thirds innings and Wiltse, in a fine relief performance, one hit in three and one-third innings. It was Mathewson's tenth victory, but the Giants still trailed Chicago by ten games while playing .625 baseball.

The life of umpires in the early 1900s was a difficult one to say the least.

Verbal and physical abuse from managers, players and fans were commonplace in spite of efforts to improve their lot. And sometimes when the pendulum swings to correct injustices it often swings too far. Such was the case of Timothy Flood, second baseman for Toronto in the Eastern League whose short major league career was already behind him. On the surface the incident appeared to be nothing unusual in 1907. Flood was ejected from a game by umpire John Conway for disputing two called strikes. The opposing pitcher, not realizing Flood had been ejected, threw the next pitch to the plate. Flood swung and grounded to second with Conway yelling no play because he had tossed out Flood on the previous pitch. And that's when the altercation began in earnest with Flood taking a flying leap into Conway's stomach with his spikes and the umpire throwing his mask at the player. The fight was broken up quickly, Flood arrested and brought before a magistrate. He pleaded guilty and was sentenced to jail for 15 days of hard labor! Flood's troubles, however, were only beginning; the next day the president of the Eastern League suspended him indefinitely.

"Sympathizers immediately appealed to the government for a pardon, which came forward after a few days. During those few days, however, Toronto lost first place to their arch rival, Buffalo."[6]

Two days after Flood's release from jail, Eastern League president, P. T. Powers, refused to lift the suspension of Flood, thus barring him from playing in the league. Flood was sold to St. Paul in the American Association for $750 putting an end to the bizarre incident which had begun with a disputed strike call.

July 9

It was almost two weeks before Mathewson returned to the mound for New York and apparently the rest did wonders for his stamina. Matty won the first game of a doubleheader against St. Louis 5–3 at the Polo Grounds. He allowed six hits and walked only one batter. When McGinnity won the second game 6–5 with the Giants scoring two in the ninth, the team moved back into second place where it would remain for close to two weeks before Pittsburgh took over again. Matty's record was now 11-4.

July 13

Mathewson made it three straight over the Reds when he tossed a 4–0 shutout. It was Matty's twelfth win of the season and a most rewarding one since he wasn't at peak form, giving up 11 hits, but was tough in the clutch. At moments during the game it appeared Mathewson was actually toying with his opponents and then just when they were ready to strike, he reared back for something extra. The strategy never failed.

Witnessing Matty's performance at the Polo Grounds was the well-known Lillian Russell. The reigning queen of the musical stage was acclaimed by many at the time as the most desirable woman in America. Accompanying Miss Russell was her constant companion, Jesse Lewishon, copper heir and all-around playboy. It was the young man's first appearance in public since his gallstone operation in June.

The day before, New York management received good news and bad news. The good news was the return of Roger Bresnahan to the lineup. And the pitcher he faced was Andy Coakley, the man who beaned him on June 18. Showing no signs of timidity at the plate, the Duke of Tralee chipped in with two hits and scored a run to help New York defeat Cincinnati. The bad news was that zealous fans were taking it upon themselves to keep baseballs that were batted or thrown into the stands, instead of returning them, which was the practice of the day. Giants Secretary Knowles, in an attempt to crack down on the culprits, warned that in the future any person caught trying to steal a ball would be arrested.

July 17

In the battle for second place, Pittsburgh defeated the Giants 2–0 for the second day in a row at the Polo Grounds. Mathewson was the loser and the victim of poor support, both in the field and at bat. Matty deserved a much better fare since he only gave up four hits and didn't walk a batter. But the combination of three errors and two hits by the Giants was too much for even Matty to overcome.

Secretary Knowles, in a surprise move, announced that the aging veteran second baseman Tommy Corcoran, whose batting had fallen off, was given his unconditional release. It was one of the first signals from McGraw that he was not pleased with the club makeup and drastic changes would be in the offing.

July 20

On July 19 the first-place Chicago Cubs, with an 11-game lead over the Giants, showed up at the Polo Grounds to start a four-game series and walloped the locals 12–3. It increased the Cubs' lead and added to the ho-hum attitude among Giants fans.

The second game of the series, however, was an entirely different story. Mathewson and Chicago's Carl Lundgren put on a show for the 18,000 fans that they would remember for a long time. Matty was brilliant, working his fadeaway to perfection. He allowed no runs, three hits, two of which were of the scratch variety, and did not walk a batter for the second straight game. At times he was overpowering. For example, he fanned Jimmy Slagle three times.

Lundgren pitched a wonderful game also, allowing four hits and four walks. He tired in the fourth when, with two men on and a scoreless tie, Cy Seymour blasted a home run into the bleachers. Rules of the day counted the poke only a single with one run scoring, enough to win the game. The contest was played in one hour and twenty-four minutes, attesting to the excellent pitching and crisp play by both clubs.

After the Sunday day off, Chicago bounced back to trim New York 2-0 on a five-hitter by Ed Reulbach who would finish the year with an outstanding 17-4 record. The game marked the first appearance of 21-year-old Larry Doyle, the highly touted second baseman acquired from the minor leagues. It was an inauspicious start for the young man. In the field he handled one chance cleanly but on another allowed a run to score. Frank Chance was on third and when a grounder was hit to him he hesitated to throw to home just long enough for Chance to cross the plate. At bat he managed to pick up a scratch hit, but struck out twice. Over the years Doyle would prove to be a natural hitter, a marvelous acquisition, and be remembered for a line he innocently made famous, "It's great to be young and a Giant."[7]

July 25

The Giants began their second western road trip with the first stop in Cincinnati. Mathewson pitched the opening game of the series and won 4-3. Not as dominant as the previous outing against the Cubs, Matty still hurled a fine game, scattering five hits. His record was now 14-5.

Cincinnati took the next three straight and McGraw was steaming. After the final loss his frustration came to a boiling point when he got into an argument with the park security man who took none of McGraw's guff and wound up belting him. Fortunately, before the incident became ugly local police intervened.

July 29

Mathewson opened the St. Louis series by trimming the Cardinals 4-3 but made the victory much tougher than it should have been. Matty entered the bottom of the ninth with a 2-0 lead but a single, a walk and his own wild throw to first, scored two runs and sent the game into extra innings. The Giants came back with two in the eleventh on a single by Art Devlin, a triple by Seymour and another hit by Bowerman. The Cardinals nicked Matty for another run in their half of the eleventh but fell short as the Giants ace held on for his fifteenth win against five losses.

By the end of the series Dan McGann returned to the New York lineup fully recovered from the broken arm he suffered when hit by an Andy Coakley pitch on June 18. The return of the star first baseman was good news, especially with the Giants in third and seemingly headed even lower.

August 2

For the third time this season Mathewson lost to Three Finger Brown, as Chicago beat New York 5–0. Brown pitched a marvelous game blanking the Giants on four singles. Matty was no mystery in this game as he was tagged for nine hits. Al Bridwell, who would play for the Giants from 1908 to 1911, compared the two greats in an interview with author Lawrence Ritter. "Three Finger Brown, gee, he was one of the wonders of baseball. What a tremendous pitcher he was. Just as good as Matty, in my book. Better, maybe. The two of them used to hook up all the time...."[8]

During the rest of the series, New York managed to salvage one game out of five and that one was even tough with the Giants scoring a run in the ninth for the win. It was a costly victory; McGann left the game with a sprained ankle; and McGraw, Danny Shay and Dahlen were ejected by Klem with the manager being slapped with a three-day suspension.

Not all the action in Chicago was occurring at West Side Park. On August 3, a young judge in the United States Court at Chicago by the name of Landis was catapulted into national limelight when he fined the Standard Oil Company a whopping $29,240,000, in an era when a million dollars meant something. Only three years in office, Landis compelled oil baron John D. Rockefeller, Sr., to come to Chicago and testify in the case against Standard Oil, which allegedly had accepted rebates from the Chicago and Alton Railroad on shipments of oil from Whiting, Indiana, to East St. Louis, Illinois. It was a direct violation of the Elkins law. Although the harsh decision by Landis helped build his reputation, few remember that the United States Supreme Court overruled him and threw out his verdict.

On the lighter side, at least to everyone but Connie Mack, it was reported that Rube Waddell, the enormously talented but flaky left-hander, had been missing for a week. Mack, noncommital about Waddell, no doubt was privately steaming since he was in a four-way pennant race with Detroit, Chicago and Cleveland.

August 8

Glad to depart the Windy City, New York arrived in Pittsburgh and opened the series with a doubleheader victory. Mathewson won the first game 4–3 (with relief help from McGinnity), scattering nine hits for victory number 16. Wiltse blanked the Pirates in the nightcap 7–0. The double win put the Giants a half game in back of second-place Pittsburgh, where they remained after splitting the next two games with the Pirates.

August 12

McGraw called on Mathewson with three days' rest to pitch the final and pivotal game of the series. A victory would move the Giants back in second by a half game. Like a true superstar Matty beat Pittsburgh 5–3. It was vintage Mathewson; he walked two, scattered eight hits and was tough with men on base. He also upped his record to 17-6 as the Giants headed home after a 9-9 road trip.

August 15

Back at the Polo Grounds New York edged Cincinnati 4–3 behind the fine hurling of Wiltse and the relief pitching of Mathewson. The Giants were holding on to a slim 2–1 lead entering the eighth when Cincinnati nicked Wiltse for two runs.

The Giants bounced back in the bottom of the eighth with two runs of their own on key hits by Bresnahan and Bowerman to regain the lead 4–3. Matty replaced Wiltse and retired the side in order in the ninth in what would be considered today a closing role. Imagine Matty as the club's closer with his unhittable fadeaway and pinpoint control. No telling how many saves he could have recorded in an era when the term was as foreign as the designated hitter and artificial turf.

August 17

With the high-flying Chicago Cubs invading the Polo Grounds for a four-game series, the opening contest pitted Mathewson and Three Finger Brown against each other for the fourth time this season. For eight and two-thirds innings Matty pitched brilliantly before more than 20,000 jubilant fans, giving up one puny hit, a bunt single by Sheckard in the first inning. But in the ninth Mathewson's fadeaway deserted him and the Cubs pushed across two runs to tie the game at 2–2. During the rally Brown was taken out of the game for a pinch hitter with Jack Pfiester taking his place on the mound. Matty settled down and blanked Chicago until the twelfth when Johnny Kling drove a Matty delivery deep into the left field bleachers amidst a deathly silence. Pfiester retired the Giants in their half of the inning without a threat for the victory as the stunned crowd left the Polo Grounds shaking their heads. Matty's record stood at 17-7.

August 22

After New York split the series with Chicago, Pittsburgh arrived to do battle with the Giants for second place. The opening game was an embarrassment. The Pirates demolished the Giants 20–5 even though umpire Jimmy Johnstone mercifully ended the game after eight innings!

Mathewson started but lasted only three innings, giving up five runs. He was followed by Ferguson and Taylor who were just as ineffective. It appeared nothing could stop the relentless Pirates as they garnered 20 hits and nine walks for the day. To complete the demise the Giants chipped in with four errors.

There were no formal scoring rules governing pitchers' wins and losses before 1950; it was the scorer's decision. Apparently the official scorer felt that Ferguson pitched the poorest of the three—11 runs, six hits, six walks in two innings—and tagged him with the loss so Matty's record remained at 17-7.

August 23

The next day Pittsburgh continued its fine play by beating New York twice, 4-2 in ten innings and 1-0 in five innings. Matty relieved Mike Lynch in the second game, pitching one inning without allowing a hit. The double defeat dropped the Giants into third place and on top of that they lost the services of Frank Bowerman, who was hit in the head by a "fast inshoot" thrown by Jack Camnitz. Bowerman was rendered unconscious and immediately attended to by a Dr. M. W. Wolff. After regaining consciousness, he was taken to Washington Heights Hospital where he was examined by a surgeon who said the catcher was suffering from a concussion and possible fracture of the skull. The prognosis was that Bowerman would be out for the rest of the season. Either the physician was overly pessimistic or Bowerman's recuperative powers were unusual because three days later he was at the Polo Grounds visiting and claiming he would return in a week or so, which he did.

August 24

For the third day in a row Mathewson was on the mound for New York, this time with much better success as he beat the Pirates 7-4 for the Giants' first victory of the series. Matty struggled the first three innings, giving up seven hits and four runs, but as the great ones often do, he settled down and checked the Pirates with only one hit over the last six innings. Mathewson's record was now 18-7.

August 27

Like a skilled surgeon operating with exacting precision, Christy Mathewson, in one hour and twenty-six minutes, tossed a wonderful three-hit shutout over the St. Louis Cardinals. The score was 1-0. The only run of the game came in the third on back-to-back doubles by Doyle and Matty. Although the game was played before a mere 2,000 spectators and characterized by the press as "dull," it was nonetheless a pitching masterpiece. Lost in the glitter of Matty's nineteenth victory, however, was the fine pitching of left-hander Ed Karger who scattered seven hits and allowed one base on balls.

August 31

New York won two games from Boston, 3–2 and 9–6, at South End Grounds. The first game went 12 innings with Mathewson recording his twentieth victory of the season and the fifth consecutive year he reached the 20-plus plateau. Matty scattered ten hits, walked one and fanned five Bostonians.

Two days later the Giants dropped into third place. They remained there until the final week of play when the Phillies swept a three-game series and they ended the season in fourth place.

September 3

The Giants split a twin bill with Brooklyn at the Polo Grounds as the doubleheaders began to mount late in the season. Taylor shut out the Superbas in the first game 2–0 with Mathewson losing the nightcap, a seven-inning heartbreaker. Brooklyn scored the only run of the game in the first inning as Matty was uncharacteristically wild. A single and two walks loaded the bases for Brooklyn with two out. Matty heaved the next pitch over Bresnahan's head and Brooklyn scored. Left-hander Jim Pastorius scattered eight hits, was tough in the clutch and received solid support from his teammates. Mathewson's record was now 20–8.

September 6

New York defeated Philadelphia in both ends of the doubleheader by scores of 6–5 and 2–0. In the first game McGinnity was overpowering as he entered the ninth inning in relief of Taylor with men on second and third, no out and the score 6–5. The Iron Man slammed the door shut as he retired the next three Phillies to preserve the victory.

In the second game, which lasted only seven innings, Mathewson defeated Lew Moran in a tightly pitched game. Matty was a bit unsteady at times, but when he had to make the perfect pitch to get out of a jam, he did. Conversely, Moran's wild throw after allowing two singles netted New York their two runs in the third. It was all the celebrated pitcher needed to register his twenty-first win.

September 9

New York played its fifth doubleheader in seven days and, considering this demanding schedule, were happy to come away with a split. It was an unusual afternoon which saw the Giants crush Boston 10–0 in the first contest and then go down to defeat 1–0 in a shortened seven-inning game, with Mathewson taking the loss.

In this game Matty met his match in lefty Irv Young who tossed a four-hitter, a mite better than his opponent. Mathewson's record went to 21-9. The next day New York lost to Boston 3-2 to close out the season at the Polo Grounds on a sour note. If New York had any hope of challenging Pittsburgh for second place, the schedule-maker made their task more difficult. The Giants would have to finish the long and tiring season on the road.

September 13

Mathewson baffled Brooklyn all afternoon with an assortment of fast balls, curves and fadeaways to notch his twenty-second win as New York defeated the Superbas 2-1. Matty fanned 11 as he bested Brooklyn hurler Jim Pastorius, avenging his loss to the left-hander on September 3. Jack Hannifin and Dan McGann were the hitting stars for the Giants; Hannifin collecting a single, double, triple and two walks in five trips to the plate; and McGann ripping three singles and a double in four at bats.

An indignant National League president Harry Pulliam announced an all-out war on the "pop" bottle. His edict was prompted by an American League incident in St. Louis in a game against Detroit. Umpire Billy Evans was struck on the head with a soda water bottle and was seriously injured. Evans' physician said he would recover but would not be able to participate in any games for the remainder of the season. Pulliam declared that he would ban all pop bottles in National League grounds, if it were in his power to do so. He didn't have the power and throwing bottles continued into the summer of 1944. But when umpire Jocko Conlin tossed Leo Durocher out of a game in Ebbets Field, the bottle barrage from the fans was so bad that eventually bottled drinks were banned from ballparks.

September 17

The Giants, behind a weak outing by Mathewson, dropped their third straight game to Boston 6-3 at South End Grounds. The loss increased Pittsburgh's second-place lead to four and one-half games while New York found itself in a struggle to hold third place.

Mathewson pitched well for six innings; in fact he led 3-1 entering the Boston seventh when all hell broke loose. In this fatal frame Matty gave up five hits, including a Fred Tenney triple, as Boston scored five runs and all but clinched the victory. Mathewson's record now stood at 22-10.

September 21

New York won its second straight game from Cincinnati 6-2 at League Park, beginning its last western swing on a positive note. The Giants jumped all over Charlie Smith, scoring six runs in the first four innings as the right-hander's wildness (five walks) got him into deep trouble. Spotted the 6–0 lead, Mathewson blanked Cincinnati until the eighth when the Reds scored two runs to spoil his shutout bid. Matty's record was now 23-10.

The game marked the first appearance of rookie Fred Merkle, a name that would live forever in Giants infamy, right or wrong. The 18-year-old was sent to New York as a second baseman by Giants superscout Dick Kinsella. But with Doyle seemingly entrenched at second and the aging McGann suffering through an injury-plagued season, McGraw had a different notion. Noted author Hynd, "McGraw tried him [Merkle] at second, then turned him over to Dan McGann, the veteran who held down first. McGann would be in charge of tutoring his own eventual replacement."[9]

September 24

New York arrived in Pittsburgh on September 23 to begin its final showdown for second place, five and one-half games behind the Pirates. The Giants lost the opener 2–1 but the exciting game was lost in the bizarre antics of McGraw. It started when umpire Klem went to get the lineup card from McGraw and Bresnahan's name appeared. Klem claimed Bresnahan could not play without the consent of President Pulliam. He had been ejected from a game the day before in Cincinnati. McGraw argued for quite a while, finally agreeing to list Bowerman as the catcher. Just as Klem turned to leave the bench someone threw a cup of water in his face. No official action was taken by Klem since it was impossible for him to identify the culprit because several Giants were clustered around McGraw at the time of the tossing. Later, several spectators said they witnessed McGraw throwing the water.

Whether McGraw was the culprit or not, Klem had the last word. In the sixth inning McGraw was tossed out of the game, and subsequently escorted off the grounds by police for arguing a fair call. After the inning Klem heaved Devlin for arguing McGraw's case.

No question, Bill Klem was a fair-minded but tough arbiter who was quickly building a reputation that eventually would earn him accolades by some as the best umpire ever to grace the game. Not all the umpires that ran up against McGraw were as tenacious. As author Graham pointed out, "He [McGraw] had terrorized most of the umpires so they feared to offend him and quailed from the task of ordering him from the field on many occasions when he so richly had deserved banishment."[10]

It's a wonder Mathewson could maintain his concentration on the mound when he faced Pittsburgh on September 24 given the circus atmosphere conducted by ringmaster McGraw the previous day. Apparently Matty was accustomed to McGraw's tactics, especially in Pittsburgh, and so went about his business as usual. He tossed a 2–0 shutout, his eighth of the season, and improved his record to 24-10. Klem, showing no signs of being intimidated, tossed out four more Giants for arguing—Strang, Devlin, Ferguson and McGraw. It was a rough and rowdy game indeed.

October 1

Mathewson rested for a week before he faced the pennant-winning Chicago Cubs for the last time in 1907. The Giants were now mathematically eliminated from second place and, more importantly, in danger of being overtaken by Philadelphia.

Matty pitched an excellent game, taking a 1–0 lead into the bottom of the ninth but gave up the tying run with two out and then lost in the eleventh as he ran out of steam. After scoring a run in the first inning, the Giants failed to muster any semblance of an offense, nicking Chick Fraser and Carl Lundgren for two puny hits in 11 innings. It was another tough loss for Mathewson and moved the Giants closer to fourth place.

October 5

After a miserable 4-9 road trip, New York traveled to the City of Brotherly Love for a do-or-die three-game series that would determine the third-place team. Philadelphia, with a season-ending flourish, won all three games, 2–1, 7–3 and 3–2, dropping New York into fourth place. Matty was tagged with the 3–2 loss in the final game, called after the Giants batted in the seventh. It was a disappointing end to a long season for the Giants in spite of Mathewson's wonderful 24-12 record.

New York finished the season in fourth place with an 82-71 record, 25½ games behind the Chicago Cubs, pennant winners for the second straight year with a 107-45 mark. Pinpointing the cause of the Giants' poor showing was not easy. Team batting, slugging and fielding averages in 1907 showed little difference from the previous year. The category that was revealing, however, was stolen bases. The Giants swiped 83 fewer in 1907, a statistic that confirmed McGraw's impression that the team was getting old and slowing down. Of course, losing McGann and Bresnahan for a good portion of the season did not help.

The entire pitching staff, except for Mathewson, was a disappointment. For example, McGinnity went from a 27-12 record to 18-18. Conversely, Mathewson was a model of consistency with a 22-12 record in 1906 and 24-12 in 1907. In fact, Matty's record could have been significantly better were it not for poor offensive support on the part of his teammates. In Matty's 12 losses the Giants averaged a mere 1.25 runs per game. In addition, from September 3 on Mathewson won four and lost five, possibly the result of fatigue or lack of interest in a pennant race that had been over months before.

But 1908 would be a new season for the New York Giants and their star pitcher; a season in which the team would be entangled in controversy and, ultimately, in disappointment. It would also be a season in which Mathewson would stump the press in their search for superlatives to describe his masterful pitching.

Chapter 10
Most Career Victories, 1908

W	L	Pct	ERA
37	11	.771	1.43

After the Giants' dismal performance in 1907, McGraw realized the team had deteriorated, especially certain players, and drastic changes had to be made. His single-minded mission was to rebuild the team into championship caliber. Blessed with a keen eye for talent and the courage to implement bold changes, McGraw moved swiftly. "I noticed in 1907 that several of my players were slipping," he admitted. "So I stepped out and made a trade that at the time was a sensation."[1]

And what a blockbuster trade it was. In early December, McGraw sent Dan McGann, Frank Bowerman, Bill Dahlen, George Browne and George Ferguson to Boston for manager–first baseman Fred Tenney, shortstop Al Bridwell and utility catcher Tom Needham.

The press and fans were stunned and both severely criticized the trade. On the surface it appeared the impatient McGraw had made a hasty decision and traded away half the team. According to the manager's wife, however, that was not the case. "The trade of five Giants for two from the league's weakest club was deplored by fans and writers. But behind the trade were many weeks of study, floor-pacing, and speculation. John was completely rebuilding the Giants."[2]

Mrs. McGraw's slight lapse in memory after 46 years is easily understood. For the sake of accuracy, however, it must be pointed out that the Giants received three ball players, not two, and Boston was not the weakest club in the league; that ignoble distinction went to St. Louis.

Although the stats of the newly acquired players were less than impressive, McGraw knew what he was doing. The trade fulfilled his plan perfectly. He wanted Tenney at first to take over the leadership role vacated by Dahlen and he viewed the 23-year-old Bridwell as a rising star. Needham would take the place of Bowerman and spell Roger Bresnahan behind the plate.

Beside the big trade McGraw added several key players to the 1908 roster who would significantly help during the race for the pennant. He drafted two kids from the minors: infielder Charles Buck Herzog out of the

Walter Camp, known as the "Father of American Football," claimed Mathewson (first from left, first row standing) "the greatest kicker I've ever seen..." (photo courtesy Bucknell University Archives).

Pennsylvania League and right-handed pitcher Otis Doc Crandall from Grand Rapids. He also added two veterans who could hit, both former Giants: the unpredictable Turkey Mike Donlin and the well-traveled Moose McCormick.

With McGraw's new, rebuilt club in place, the 1908 season would turn out to be a wild and memorable one with the young kid Fred Merkle playing a major role. Justified or not, his name would forever be linked to the Giants' loss of the 1908 pennant. It was also a year in which Christy Mathewson would win 37 baseball games but lose one of the most critical he would ever pitch in his 17-year career.

The Season

April 14

Days before the New York Giants opened their season *The New York Times* reviewed the makeup of the new club and its chances of beating the

Chicago Cubs for the pennant. The conclusion was that the Cubs were too tough and the Giants' weak link was their pitching staff, including Mathewson! It was amusing to note this comment in the paper: "Mathewson has seen his best days on the mound." Except for Joe McGinnity's performance, the sportswriter (no byline) missed the mark by the proverbial mile.

New York opened the 1908 season in Philadelphia before a packed crowd of almost 17,000 enthusiastic spectators. The elaborate pregame festivities, in which city officials took part, ended with an imaginative flag ceremony. After Old Glory was hoisted and unfurled, thousands of diminutive stars and stripes fluttered to the ground. And the game that followed was equally impressive.

Mathewson, drawing the opening day assignment from McGraw, was the hero of the game. He pitched a splendid four-hitter and drove in two of the three Giants runs with a single in the sixth inning. Spike Shannon, Tenney and Cy Seymour had two hits each. The final score was New York 3, Philadelphia 1.

April 18

Four days later Mathewson pitched his second opening-day game, this time at Brooklyn's Washington Park, with a crowd estimated at 20,000. The result was the same, in fact even better as Matty was invincible, blanking Brooklyn 4–0 on six well-scattered hits. He fanned 12 batters. Considering the miserable weather—cold showers all afternoon—Mathewson's performance was even more impressive. The acquisition of Tenney was paying early dividends. The first baseman collected two more hits, scored a run and drove in one.

Two days later the baseball world was saddened when Henry Chadwick died at his home in Brooklyn. Known as the "Father of Baseball," Chadwick was born in England on October 5, 1824, and moved to Brooklyn in 1837. He wrote for *The New York Times,* the *Brooklyn Eagle,* the *New York Herald,* the *New York World* and the *New York Sun.* For 27 years he edited the *Spalding Baseball Guide* and in 1896 the National League voted him a pension for life as the "Father of Baseball." He was enshrined in the Hall of Fame in 1938.

April 22

The Giants played their first game of the season at the Polo Grounds before more than 25,000 cheering spectators who were stuffed into every available space. The game was halted at one point when McGraw and Brooklyn manager Patsy Donovan had a meeting to discuss what to do about the overflow crowd, which was moving methodically inch by inch closer to the playing field. Nothing was resolved and the game continued.

Mathewson, on the mound for his third consecutive opening-day assignment, hooked up with Harry McIntire in a pitcher's duel and found himself on the losing end of a 2–1 score when the Giants came to bat in the bottom of the ninth. Two outs later with Tenney on first, Donlin drove a McIntire fastball clear over the bleacher fence in right field for a 3–2 Giants victory. *The New York Times* writer W. J. Lampton captured the thoughts of the Giants' fans when he penned this cute little ditty.

> Donlin, Donlin, he is IT:
> Donlin, Donlin, made THE hit:
> Though some others made a run,
> Donlin's was the only one.[3]

New York and Mathewson were off to a fast start. Matty's record was 3-0 and the Giants were tied for first place with Chicago with identical 6-1 marks.

April 27

New York beat Boston 2–0 at South End Grounds with Mathewson pitching a jewel — a one-hitter, upping his record to 4-0. For the second straight game Matty did not give up a base on balls as he recorded his second shutout of the season. Prior to the game Tenney, the former Boston player-manager, was presented with a traveling bag from his friends.

April 29

Two days later New York lost to Boston 7–6 in 11 innings when Tenney, of all people, dropped a perfect throw from Bresnahan on Johnny Bates' attempt to beat out a bunt single, allowing Irv Young to score. Bill Malarkey took the tough loss, but Mathewson played a key role in the defeat. He allowed Boston to score two runs in the fifth, after relieving Hooks Wiltse, to tie the game. Later he was replaced by Malarkey who gave up single runs in the tenth and eleventh. After 13 games the Giants' record stood at 8-5 with Matty claiming half the victories.

May 4

Mathewson won his fifth game of the season in easy fashion as New York clobbered Philadelphia 12–2. The Giants jumped all over Tully Sparks scoring five runs in the first and at the end of six innings had built a 9–0 lead for Matty. At that point McGraw figured the game was won and decided to give his battery a rest, replacing Mathewson with Roy Beecher and Bresnahan with Needham. The 16-hit assault on Sparks was led by Tenney, Bresnahan, Art Devlin and Larry Doyle, all of whom had two or more hits.

Over in the American League, the New York Highlanders defeated the Washington Nationals 11–5 and found themselves in first place, but not for long. By season's end the Highlanders would be at the bottom of the heap, managing to lose over 100 games.

May 9

It was Boston's first appearance at the Polo Grounds and New York was anything but a friendly host. After Mathewson spotted Boston two runs in the first, New York came back with five runs in their half, highlighted by Devlin's base-clearing double. They added two more in the second and with a 7–2 lead Matty coasted the rest of the way. The final score was New York 7, Boston 3. Mathewson was perfect at 6-0.

May 13

Earlier in the week New York arrived in Pittsburgh to begin its first road trip to Western cities. After splitting the first two games, McGraw called on his ace for the final contest. Mathewson blanked the Pirates for the first three innings but was touched for a run in the fourth and roughed up for four runs the next inning. Late in the game he was replaced by the rookie Crandall but it was too late as the Giants were handcuffed by Howie Camnitz who scattered six hits for the 5–1 victory. Mathewson's record was 6-1 as the Giants headed for Cincinnati.

May 16

For the second straight game Mathewson was knocked out of the box, this time by Cincinnati, after only two innings. It was such an unusual occurrence that the next day it garnered headlines in the morning papers. Matty gave up an unearned run in the first, when Seymour botched a fly and Tenney went to sleep on first. In the second inning, however, he was tagged for three hits and two runs. McGraw pinch-hit for him in the third as the Giants were puzzled by Andy Coakley who scattered six hits for the 3–1 victory.

May 18

Two days later Mathewson was back on the mound against the Cincinnati Reds. He had asked McGraw to let him pitch again in order to redeem himself for the 3–1 loss in which he only lasted two innings. McGraw consented and probably was sorry he did. Matty was pounded for 15 hits and nine runs in seven innings, the third consecutive time he was knocked out of the box. New York wound up on the short end of a 9–5 score. It's proof, once again, the mighty are mortal too.

The Giants were happy to leave Cincinnati, after losing three of four games, and head for St. Louis to meet their accommodating cousins. Not so this trip. St. Louis took three of four and dropped the Giants into sixth place as they staggered into Chicago to meet the first-place Cubs.

May 25

For the fourth straight game Mathewson was rocked. This time, in game two of the series, Chicago blasted him for seven hits and five runs in two innings. Over his last four games Matty had pitched in 16 innings, giving up 33 hits and 22 runs! It was clearly the worst slump of his career and the fickle press was quick to take potshots at him.

Experiencing serious adversity for the first time in his career, Mathewson had no one to turn to for help; no pitching coach; no game films. He had to straighten himself out. Not an easy task for a young superstar (still only 28), who was unaccustomed to poor performances and defeat.

It was small consolation to Matty when he did not get credit for the loss. That distinction went to Wiltse who allowed the Cubs to score in the tenth inning for an 8-7 victory.

May 29

"Matty Comes to Life in Brooklyn" was the headline on the sports page of *The New York Times* on May 30. And the great right-hander came to life with a vengeance, tossing a four-hit, 1-0 gem against Brooklyn at Washington Park. After four embarrassing pitching performances, it appeared Matty had solved his problem and was back on his winning ways. It was his third shutout and, no doubt, the most satisfying of the early season as his record was now 7-3.

June 3

With the Giants bogged down in fifth place after losing two games to Boston at South End Grounds, rumors began to circulate that McGraw was planning a general shake-up of the club with particular focus on the pitching staff. Three well-known players were on the chopping block: McGinnity, Red Ames and Shannon. Prominent among these was the Iron Man who, it was reported, got wind of the changes and left the team. The gossip went so far as to claim McGinnity would be grabbed on waivers by Cincinnati and possibly pitch for the Reds the following week at the Polo Grounds. This rumor went the way of most rumors; it fizzed. In fact, McGinnity pitched for the Giants on June 8 and it was a dandy, a 4-0 six-hitter over the St. Louis Cardinals.

Back in the real world, Mathewson defeated Boston 3-0 while

fanning 11 to salvage one game out of the three-game series. It was Matty's second straight whitewash since the end of his pitching slump. His record was now 8-3 but the Giants were still mired in fifth place.

June 6

New York defeated St. Louis 3–2 at the Polo Grounds as Mathewson notched his ninth win of the season (42 percent of the team's victories). He was in command from the start, scattering four hits and striking out eight batters. He fanned Joe Delahanty, one of five brothers to play in the major leagues, three times. Amazingly, it also extended Mathewson's winning streak to 20 consecutive victories over the hapless Cardinals! The last time Matty lost to St. Louis was back on May 10, 1904.

June 11

Mathewson lost his fourth game of the season as Pittsburgh defeated New York 5–2. With better defensive support Matty could have been a winner. Bridwell, Doyle and Devlin made crucial errors which accounted for most of the Pirates runs, while Vic Willis pitched a steady game, limiting the Giants to seven hits. Matty's record was now 9-4.

A few days later rookie Fred Snodgrass logged some playing time in a game against Cincinnati in which the Giants won 3–2. Although he did little to distinguish himself, young Snodgrass would be heard of in the future, especially in the 1912 World Series. But this is getting ahead of the story. Here's what Snodgrass said about his first season with the Giants. "I was a headstrong, quick-tempered, twenty-year-old kid when I joined the Giants in 1908. And sometimes Mr. McGraw would bawl the dickens out of me, as he did everybody else. Any mental error, any failure to think, and McGraw would be all over you." Besides playing for a tough manager Snodgrass noted the attitude of veteran ball players in those days. "It was practically impossible for a youngster, a rookie, to get up to the plate in batting practice. A youngster was an outsider, and those old veterans weren't about to make it easy for him to take away one of their jobs."

However, this was not true of all players. Some veterans had a soft spot as Snodgrass was quick to point out when discussing Spike Shannon, his roommate. "He took me under his wing, helped me, encouraged me and told me what to do and what not to do. I doubt if I'd have made the club that year if it hadn't been for Shannon."[4]

June 17

After losing the series to Pittsburgh three games to one, New York played host to third-place Cincinnati with hopes of narrowing the gap between them. And that they did, sweeping all three games, including a doubleheader in which Mathewson won the first game 2–1. Matty was in a groove again almost as if he were programmed. He allowed one run on seven scattered hits, fanned seven and didn't walk a batter—vintage Mathewson. His record was now 10-4.

June 20

It was standing room only an hour and a half before game time when more than 25,000 spectators crammed into the Polo Grounds to witness Mathewson work his mound magic on the mighty Chicago Cubs. It was a jewel of a performance as Matty dazzled the Cubs all afternoon, spinning a nifty three-hitter. The final score was 4–0; it was Mathewson's fifth shutout and eleventh victory of the season as the Giants remained in fourth place.

June 23

New York split a doubleheader with Boston at the Polo Grounds, winning the first 6–3 and losing the second 9–7. Mathewson appeared in relief in both games with mixed results. In the first game he relieved McGinnity in the ninth with two men on and retired the side without allowing a run to preserve the victory for the Iron Man. In the second game Matty did not fare as well. After relieving Taylor (who went in for Crandall) with the score knotted at 7–7, Mathewson was roughed up for two runs in the ninth. It was his fifth loss against 11 wins.

Although the rookie Crandall had a bad outing in the second game, lasting only one and two-thirds of an inning, his career with the Giants would be a good one, especially from 1910 until 1912. Over that three-year span he would win 45 games while losing only 16. Mathewson thought highly of the kid from Indiana. "He has turned out to be one of the most valuable men on the club, because he is there in a pinch." Added Matty, "He is the sort of pitcher who is best when things look darkest."[5] In a ten-year major league career Crandall would register a 102-62 (.622) mark plus appearances in three World Series.

June 24

The Giants played Boston another doubleheader; this time the results were more to their liking; they won both by scores of 4–0 and 7–1. As a result the Giants moved into third place, the beginning of their drive for the pennant. Wiltse won the first game on a splendid two-hit shutout. Mathewson won the second game easily when the Giants built a five-run lead after five innings, while he was blanking Boston. After the seventh, with the score 7–0 and the brutal heat exacting its toll, McGraw sent Malarkey to the mound and he gave up a harmless run in the ninth, preserving the 7–1 victory for Matty. This was the fourth time this season Mathewson had defeated Irv Young and it was only June 24.

In the American League, Clark Griffith resigned as the manager of the New York Highlanders, claiming that hoodoo was following him. Kid Elberfeld replaced him and the club dropped from sixth place to last. With a team batting average of .236, the highest ERA and the worst fielding in the league, the diplomatic Griffith was magnanimous in blaming lady luck.

June 27

Three days later at Brooklyn's Washington Park, the Giants took another doubleheader, 4–3 and 5–2. Mathewson relieved Wiltse in the ninth inning of the first game with the Giants leading 4–3. Wasting no time, he fanned Billy Maloney, Al Burch and Harry Pattee in succession to end the game. Sufficiently tuned up, Matty started the second game before a crowd of 18,000, which could have been a lot more were it not for Brooklyn president Charlie Ebbets who closed all entrances to the grounds to prevent an overflow of spectators onto the field. By the fourth inning Mathewson was staked to a 5–0 lead and coasted the rest of the way for his thirteenth victory against five losses.

July 2

New York defeated the Philadelphia Phillies 4–3 at the Polo Grounds in spite of committing five errors. Mathewson continued his steady pitching but found himself trailing 3–1 (two runs were unearned) entering the bottom of the seventh. The Giants scored three times off left-hander Bill Foxen, then Matty blanked the Phillies the last two innings for his fourteenth win.

Wiltse celebrated the Fourth of July by pitching a ten-inning no-hitter against the same Phillies and came within a whisker of a perfect game. It happened this way: in the top of the ninth, in a scoreless game, Wiltse thought he caught the opposing pitcher, George McQuillan, looking at a third strike. Umpire Charlie Rigler saw it differently and called the pitch a ball. On his next delivery Wiltse hit McQuillan for the only Phillies base runner in ten innings. Later, McQuillan admitted the pitch Rigler called a ball was really a strike.

July 6

While Brush and McGraw were in Columbus, Ohio, looking at a 19-year-old left-hander by the name of Richard William Marquard, later to be known as Rube, Mathewson was getting revenge in Cincinnati as the Giants began another road trip. Still fresh in his mind were the two drubbings he absorbed in May by the Reds. This time Matty was determined to get even, which he did quite handily, spinning a four-hitter and defeating Cincinnati 2-1. The victory moved the Giants to within one and one-half games of first-place Pittsburgh and percentage points behind second-place Chicago.

Moose McCormick joined the Giants in Cincinnati. The outfielder had a brief stint with New York in 1904. McCormick's appearance in a Giants' uniform spelled the end for Spike Shannon who was slumping badly at the plate. Shortly after, McGraw asked waivers on Shannon.

July 9

Déjà vu; Mathewson defeated Cincinnati for the second time in four days. The score (2-1), hits (four) and walks (none) were identical as in the July 6 victory. The only difference in this game was that Matty struck out one less batter, five versus six. Revenge is sweet and no doubt Matty had evened the score with the Cincinnati Reds. His record now stood at 16-5.

July 13

Mathewson and McGinnity teamed up to defeat Pittsburgh in a doubleheader at Exposition Park. In the first game Matty continued his pitching mastery, which he began in Cincinnati, when he hurled a three-hit shutout. It was the third straight game in which he did not issue a base on balls and his sixth shutout. Mathewson's record went to 17-5.

McGinnity won the second game 7-4 but needed relief help from Wiltse. The double win put the Giants a half game back of Pittsburgh and a full game behind league-leading Chicago, their next stop.

July 16

New York defeated Chicago 4-3 at West Side Park for the second day in a row. Crandall pitched a fine game until the ninth when he needed help from Mathewson to close out the inning and the game. The two victories moved New York into second place behind the Pirates as the National League pennant race continued to tighten.

July 17

After New York won the first two games of the series, the Cubs were determined to halt their slide and sent Three Finger Brown back to the mound (he was hit hard in game one of the series) to face Matty. It was the first meeting in 1908 between the two and, as in the previous encounters, turned out to be a marvelous game. Brown won 1-0. The old adage of each pitcher matching the other pitch for pitch was never more true. Brown allowed six hits, Matty seven; Brown walked one, Matty none; Brown fanned one, Matty four. The difference between victory and defeat occurred in the third and fourth innings. In the third, Mathewson's old nemesis, Joe Tinker, smacked a home run into the bleachers for the only run of the game. In the fifth, New York loaded the bases with none out and had a marvelous opportunity to break the game open. But Brown settled down and retired the side without allowing New York to score. Up to this point, Brown had won eight of their 12 matchups.

It's not surprising then that Mathewson had high praise for his rival. "Brown is my idea of the almost perfect pitcher. He is always ready to work. [He] is a finished pitcher in all departments of the game." Added Matty, "Besides being a great worker, he is a wonderful fielder and sure death on bunts."[6]

July 21

In St. Louis, New York split a doubleheader with the Cardinals. Mathewson won the first in 12 innings 4-2 and Dummy Taylor lost a well-pitched game in the nightcap 3-1. Actually, Harry Sallee outpitched Matty but New York made the most of its eight hits managing to score two runs in the sixth and two more in the twelfth. Once Mathewson had the lead, he slammed the door shut on St. Louis, retiring the side in one-two-three order in the twelfth. It was Matty's twenty-first consecutive victory over the Cardinals as his record reached 18-6.

July 25

Back at the Polo Grounds, after completing a mediocre 8-7 road trip the Giants lost to Pittsburgh 7-2, dropping them into third place in a dandy three-way pennant race.

Over 30,000 spectators jammed the Polo Grounds to watch their beloved Matty pitch against first-place Pittsburgh. The overflow crowd settled onto the field and it took the efforts of McGraw, secretary Fred Knowles and the public address announcer Joe Humphries to contain the fans and keep them from spreading onto the playing field, which could have resulted in a forfeit.

With the crowd under control the game developed into a close contest until the top of the seventh when Pittsburgh scored five runs and chased Matty from the mound. Actually, it wasn't all Mathewson's fault. He had a lot of help from second baseman Doyle who made three errors, two in the fatal fifth. The final score was 7-2. Matty's record was 18-7 and the Giants were in third place, two games behind the Pirates and percentage points behind Chicago.

July 27

Pittsburgh took the third game of the series 4–3 with a three-run outburst in the fourth inning off Crandall. New York scored two in the eighth to pull within one run and that's the way the game remained with Mathewson coming in for one inning of relief.

The next day Wiltse and Vic Willis battled each other for 16 innings with the score ending in a 2–2 tie. Neither team scored after the sixth in this ferocious pitcher's duel.

July 29

Mathewson opened the series against his cousins from St. Louis and, in what was getting to be a habit, defeated them 1–0. He gave up two singles and a double while walking one batter. The Cards' Harry Sallee pitched a wonderful game limiting New York to four hits, but an error by Raymond Charles and a passed ball accounted for the only run of the game. It was a tough loss for the rookie left-hander, his second to Matty in a week.

For the veteran Mathewson, whose record now reached 19-7, it was his seventh shutout of the year and the twenty-second consecutive game in which he had beaten St. Louis, an incredible achievement.

August 4

New York moved into second place when it defeated Cincinnati 4–3 and 4–1 in a doubleheader at the Polo Grounds. Mathewson entered the first game in the top of the ninth in relief of McGinnity. He pitched three and two-thirds innings of near-perfect baseball and when the Giants scored in the twelfth, he picked up his twentieth win of the season. In spite of pounding out 14 hits, New York could manage only four runs which turned out to be enough anyway. It was Matty's sixth consecutive 20-plus season.

McGraw, seeing a golden opportunity to move up in the standings, called on Mathewson to start the second game and his ace responded with a magnificent performance. He allowed four hits and walked one batter in eight innings as the game was called due to darkness. With the doubleheader victories Matty's record improved to 21-7, and the Giants were in second place a half game behind Pittsburgh.

In a sincere, but feeble, attempt to stamp out gambling on the baseball grounds, Ban Johnson, president of the American League, issued a bulletin to all clubs instructing them to enforce the provisions in the league constitution prohibiting betting. "It has become an evil which must be nipped now, if the game is to be kept clean,"[7] said Johnson. Of course gambling would continue unabated for the next 11 years, until the 1919 Black Sox Scandal focused attention on the problem and threatened the integrity of the game.

August 10

Mathewson continued his pitching mastery as New York defeated Chicago for the second day in a row, remaining in second place a half game back of Pittsburgh. Two hits and an error in the first netted the Giants three runs, enough of a bulge for Matty, who gave up single runs in the last two innings. The final score was New York 3, Chicago 2. Matty's record was 22-7.

August 13

New York, still trying to catch the Pirates, defeated Brooklyn 5-3 as Mathewson pitched magnificently in relief. He took over for Ames after two innings trailing 3-2. Over the next seven innings Matty blanked Brooklyn on four hits as his teammates scored three times on timely hitting by Donlin and Seymour. Mathewson upped his record to 23-7 as the Giants headed west for their final road trip of the season.

August 17

Mathewson closed out the four-game St. Louis series with a six-inning, rain-shortened 3-0 shutout, his eighth of the season. Matty scattered four hits in registering his twenty-fourth win against seven losses. It was also the twenty-third consecutive victory against St. Louis, dating back to June 16, 1904, when he beat the Cardinals 4-3 and started New York on its way to an 18-game winning streak.

August 20

The Giants finally caught Pittsburgh and moved into a first-place tie behind the splendid pitching of Mathewson who scattered eight hits and shut out Cincinnati 2-0 at League Park. Cincinnati had several chances to score but Matty was at his best with men on base. New York managed only four hits but coupled with key walks off Andy Coakley, scored single runs in the fourth and ninth. It was Matty's twenty-fifth win and ninth shutout.

While the Giants were on the road, renovation began at the Polo Grounds to enlarge the seating capacity in the bleachers and grandstand. Plans called for an additional 5,000 seats to accommodate the increasingly large crowds that were coming to see the Giants, especially when Pittsburgh and Chicago were the opponents. Helping to attract those large crowds was the hot batting race that was shaping up between Pittsburgh's Honus Wagner and the Giants' Turkey Mike Donlin. The great Wagner was sporting a .335 average while Donlin was hitting .321. And this was just a warmup as both would improve down the stretch with Wagner eventually leading the league with a .354 average and Donlin finishing second at .334.

August 24

After sweeping the three-game series in Cincinnati, the red-hot Giants came roaring into Pittsburgh, trailing the Pirates by a half game. Huge crowds were expected at Exposition Park, while back in New York thousands were watching the games on a miniature electric diamond at Madison Square Garden and the Gotham Theatre on 125th Street. Every play was reproduced with the players' positions shown by small incandescent lights. Those watching in New York were not disappointed as the Giants took both ends of a doubleheader, 4–1 in the first game with Wiltse on the mound and 5–1 behind Mathewson in the second game. Matty scattered six hits, fanned seven and his control was perfect. His record was now 26-7 and the Giants were in first place with a one and one-half–game lead. They made it two and a half games the next day when they beat the Pirates again, 5–3.

August 26

The pitching trio of Taylor, McGinnity and Mathewson made it a clean sweep in Pittsburgh when they combined to defeat the Pirates 4–3 in a game that had everyone on the edge of their seats. Trailing 3–2 in their last at bat, the Giants scored twice when Donlin and Seymour each drove in a run. Matty pitched the ninth in relief of the Iron Man and faced only three batters but was given credit for the victory by the official scorer. According to today's scoring rules McGinnity would have been the winner. No matter, Mathewson was 27-7 and it looked like the Giants were headed for another pennant. They led both Pittsburgh and Chicago by three and a half games.

August 29

In all probability the train ride from Pittsburgh to Chicago was a joyous one. A clean sweep of the Pirates, a three and one-half–game lead, an almost unbeatable Mathewson and, except for Snodgrass, who broke his right thumb in Cincinnati, the team was healthy and on the move. But the Chicago Cubs were not to be denied. They swept New York three games with Matty losing the middle game 3–2 to Three Finger Brown. The matchup drew 27,000 spectators and at one point the field was so dense with people the police had to clear an open lane for Matty and Brown to warm up. Except for the fourth inning, when Chicago bunched five hits and scored three runs, Mathewson pitched well. Brown was better but not exceptional. He gave up five hits and walked six batters but in the tight spots he was nasty. This was Mathewson's first loss since July 25 and, when New York dropped the last game of the series to Chicago, the pennant race was destined to go down to the wire.

September 1

In spite of the three losses to Chicago, it was a good road trip for the Giants. They finished with a 9-5 record and were coming home in first place. The Giants continued their winning ways at Boston's South End Grounds with 4-1 and 8-0 victories. Wiltse won the first game by pitching out of tight spots and Mathewson coasted in the nightcap for his twenty-eighth win. With a comfortable 8-0 lead going into the bottom of the ninth, McGraw gave Matty a rest and called on Taylor to finish the game.

September 3

After a day of rain the Giants came back and trounced Boston in another doubleheader, this time by scores of 3-0 and 8-5. McGinnity took the first in easy fashion while Ames, Mathewson and Taylor combined their efforts in the second game. Ames picked up the victory with Matty pitching in the eighth and fanning two of three batters. Taylor mopped up in the ninth. In spite of the two victories the Giants led the Pirates by only a half game.

September 5

The New York Giants, behind the sharp pitching of Mathewson, defeated Philadelphia 5-1 for their sixth straight win and second over the Phillies in the current series. It was an easy victory for Matty, his twenty-ninth against eight losses. He allowed six hits and didn't walk a batter. On the mound Mathewson was the epitome of efficiency. Claimed McGraw, "Another thing that he [Mathewson] figured out was the saving of strength by pitching as few balls as possible. That meant a necessity of perfect control. In time, he got it. Never did he waste a ball without a purpose. If I remember aright he went through one whole season, averaging but one base on balls per game."[8] Actually, Mathewson had four years in which he averaged one walk or less per game in seasons in which he pitched 300 or more innings, a phenomenal display of control.

September 8

Mathewson opened the series with Brooklyn and before 10,000 screaming fans he hurled a masterful five-hit shutout (his tenth), defeating the Superbas 1-0 in 11 innings. There was little room for mistakes in this game as Brooklyn's left-hander Nap Rucker pitched splendidly. What finally did him in was a leadoff walk to Seymour who eventually scored on a clutch single by Bridwell. Matty registered his thirtieth victory, the fourth time in his career he recorded 30 or more in a season. The Giants maintained their half-game lead over the Pirates.

The pressure of a tight pennant race didn't effect McGraw's outside interests in the least. The following evening, after the Giants walloped Brooklyn 7-3 during the day, McGraw made his stage debut in a new spectacular show at the famous Hippodrome called "Sporting Days." McGraw was in charge of staging one inning of a baseball game, which included, to no one's surprise, a donnybrook with an umpire. His segment was a small part of the overall show, which received rave reviews.

September 12

New York beat Brooklyn 6-3, sweeping the five-game series and maintaining its narrow one and one-half-game first-place lead over Pittsburgh. Mathewson was the hero again, a figure bigger than life. Matty was not at his best but through eight innings he valiantly kept the Giants in the game. When they came to bat in the eighth they trailed 3-2. That's when the Giants erupted for four runs, two of which Mathewson drove in with a long triple to center field. He tried to stretch it into a home run but was thrown out at the plate. Matty's record was 31-8.

September 15

In the opening game of the St. Louis series, it appeared Red Ames was on his way to a cinch victory when he entered the eighth inning leading 4-1. When he retired the first Cardinal some Giants fans began to think about leaving early for their evening dinner. But then all hell broke loose—five hits in a row, a tie game, Ames out and Mathewson in—just like that. Actually, it provided Matty with another opportunity for more heroics, this time as relief specialist. Mathewson retired the side without further damage; Bridwell scored in the eighth on a double by Tenney and Matty whiffed two of three Cardinals in the ninth to record his thirty-second win against eight losses. Oh yes, it was his twenty-fourth consecutive victory over the St. Louis Cardinals!

September 18

Police Commissioner Bingham, upon a request from Giants' president Brush, sent 200 extra policemen to the Polo Grounds to help maintain order for the New York-Pittsburgh series. Large crowds, with some unruly characters, were expected at the four games. As anticipated, more than 35,000 squeezed into the Polo Grounds, with thousands more turned away, to witness the Giants take on the Pirates in a doubleheader. It was the largest crowd to attend a baseball game in the history of the National League and few were disappointed as the Giants trounced the Pirates 7-0 and 12-7.

In the first game Mathewson tossed his eleventh (tops in the league) shutout of the season and registered his thirty-third victory. He baffled the Pirates right from the start and his uncanny control was perfect. Wiltse won the nightcap, but needed help from McGinnity late in the game.

The extra policemen assigned to the games paid off as the record-breaking crowd was kept under control all afternoon. One disturbance did occur, however, in the first game when Turkey Mike Donlin, who was being razzed by fans, lost his temper and poked a spectator in the eye, opening a bloody gash. Security quickly stopped the fight, which could have erupted into a nasty melee involving hundreds. It's an incident the type of which was not unusual in baseball during the first decade of the new century.

September 21

With the double win over Pittsburgh, some of the more optimistic scribes were claiming another pennant for the Giants. Their optimism was quickly dashed when the Pirates won the final two games of the series, especially the 2–1 victory over Mathewson. It was a hard-luck loss for Matty as he pitched extremely well, allowing only three hits, but had the misfortune of letting Pittsburgh bunch them all in the second inning, which resulted in two runs. This was enough for Vic Willis as he had the Giants at his mercy all afternoon, giving up two hits and walking only one batter. Matty's record was now 33-9.

September 23

The red-hot Chicago Cubs came to New York for a four-game series and after winning a doubleheader by scores of 4–3 and 3–1, trailed the Giants by percentage points, which set the scene for one of the most controversial, celebrated and widely discussed games in baseball history. Mathewson and Jack Pfiester, both pitching magnificently, were locked in a 1–1 tie entering the bottom of the ninth inning, as 20,000 excited Giants fans were praying for a run. But with two out and McCormick on first it looked like the game would go into extra innings. That is until Fred Merkle singled, keeping hopes alive and sending McCormick racing to third. When the next batter, Bridwell, slapped a single to right center scoring McCormick to end the game, Giants fans went wild. Final score: New York 2, Chicago 1. Right? Wrong! What ensued is one of the most bizarre and now historic mixups in baseball history. With thousands of spectators pouring onto the field and the two umpires, Hank O'Day and Bob Emslie, running off the field, Chicago second baseman Johnny Evers, seeing that Merkle went halfway to second (never touching the bag) and then headed for the clubhouse, called for the ball from center fielder Solly Hofman. Although there have been several versions of what followed, according to author Noel Hynd, this one was given the greatest credibility: "Center fielder Hofman chased it down and threw it back, but the ball overshot Evers and bounded toward first base. Enter the Iron Man—Joe McGinnity, coaching at third that day—who saw what Evers was up to. As the ball bounded loose, and as the infield area was overrun by jubilant New York fans, the pugilistic six-foot Iron Man out wrestled five-foot-nine-inch Joe Tinker for the ball. Then McGinnity, with Tinker hanging on his back, threw the ball toward the left field grandstand, hopefully into oblivion."[9]

At this point, however, the charade was only half completed. Mysteriously, a ball appeared on the playing field, eventually getting into the hands of Evers who touched second for the force-out of Merkle. Later, when Evers demanded a call by Emslie the umpire claimed he hadn't seen the play at second. Finally, Emslie asked O'Day whether Merkle had touched second and O'Day confided he had not. Merkle was out, the run did not count and theoretically the game was still in progress. When O'Day checked the field and saw all the spectators he called the game on account of darkness.

Eventually, Pulliam got into the act and after much heated discussion, attacks and counterattacks, ruled the game was officially a 1–1 tie and a replay necessary if it had a bearing on the pennant race.

Once all the confusion, war of words, technicalities, assertions and counter-assertions were filtered out what remained from this bizarre baseball game were two things: a lost pennant for the New York Giants and poor Merkle forever saddled with the nickname "Bonehead."

McGraw was hurt deeply by the ruling, but even more so when the Giants lost the playoff game. He always believed he should have won the 1908 pennant. "I never weakened in my opinion that the awarding of the pennant to the Cubs on a technicality was unjust," he said. "Bridwell's hit really won the championship."[10]

His comments on Merkle were equally forceful. "It is criminal to say that Merkle is stupid and to blame the loss of the pennant on him. In the first place, he is one of the smartest and best players on this ball club. In the second place, he didn't cost us the pennant. We lost a dozen games we should have won."[11]

Always the consummate professional, Mathewson accepted the Merkle incident, O'Day's ruling and the lost victory in stride. "It could happen to anyone," he said. "We'll just have to beat them again. There's no sense eating our hearts out."[12]

September 24

The next day a poised and confident Mathewson, before 25,000 noisy fans, beat Chicago 5–4 in a magnificent relief role. New York staked Wiltse to a 5–0 lead as it roughed up Three Finger Brown. But in the seventh Wiltse wilted and Chicago scored three runs without making an out. McGraw, taking no chances, rushed a tired Matty to the mound to

10 • Most Career Victories, 1908

Giants first baseman Fred Merkle, right or wrong, was blamed for losing the 1908 pennant when he failed to touch second base in the September 23 game against Chicago. It forever saddled him with the nickname "Bonehead" (photo courtesy National Baseball Library, Cooperstown, N.Y.).

save the day. He retired the side, but not before the Cubs scored another run. Matty blanked Chicago the next two innings to pick up the win (another instance of the official scorer deciding the winner). It was the first time Matty had beaten Brown since his no-hitter on June 13, 1905. His record now stood at 34-9 as New York moved ahead of Chicago by a slim one-game margin.

The following day (September 25) 18-year-old Rube Marquard, who was purchased for $11,000, a sizeable piece of change in those days, made his major league debut against Cincinnati in the first game of the doubleheader. It was an inauspicious beginning for the highly touted youngster as the Reds banged him around for seven hits and five runs in five innings. Later, in discussing his debut with Mathewson he freely admitted that he was nervous and doubted his abilities. "When I saw that crowd, Matty," he said, "I didn't know where I was. It looked so big to me, and they were all wondering what I was going to do, and all thinking that McGraw had paid $11,000 for me, and now they were to find out whether he had gotten stuck, whether he had picked up a gold brick with the plating on it very thin. I was wondering, myself, whether I would make good."[13]

It would take Marquard two more years of struggling before he made "good" but when he did it entitled him to a one-way ticket to the Hall of Fame.

September 26

The Giants bounced back from their doubleheader loss to Cincinnati the day before, turning the tables by taking both games of another twin bill, 6–2 and 3–1. When the Giants scored four runs in the third inning of the first game, Matty sensed victory and cruised the rest of the way, giving up two runs on six hits, supported by perfect control. It was his thirty-fifth win of the season. To this point he had thrown over 365 innings so McGraw had to be concerned about Matty's arm. Would it hold up over the next two weeks when the pennant race would be at fever pitch and his presence needed?

September 29

Still clinging to first place, the Giants split a doubleheader with the fourth-place Phillies at the Polo Grounds. Mathewson won the first game 6–2, but was far from sharp. He was touched for nine hits, five for extra bases, but always had enough in reserve to extricate himself from dangerous situations. Matty's record was an incredible 36-9. Crandall lost the second game 7–0 and with Chicago winning the Giants now trailed the Cubs by a half game.

October 1

New York played its fourth doubleheader in a week, which gave McGraw little choice but to call on Mathewson with only one day's rest to face the Phillies again. Matty won the game 4–3 but was "hammered hard," reported one newspaper. Although Matty surrendered ten hits during the game, from the fifth inning on the Phillies did not score. It was an outstanding performance especially when you consider this was his fifth appearance in nine days and only one of which was a relief appearance. Equally important, all the games were pressure packed, which assuredly took its toll on his physical and mental stamina. It was Matty's thirty-seventh and last victory of the season. New York lost the second game 6–2 but still held on to first place by percentage points.

October 3

New York lost a hard-fought game to Philadelphia 3–2 as Mathewson, with one day's rest, pitched gallantly for seven innings before he was yanked for a pinch hitter in the eighth. In the ninth the Giants almost pulled the game out when they scored a run and had a man on third with one out. The rally fell short when Harry Coveleski retired the side without another run scoring. It was Covelski's third win over New York in five days and earned him the nickname "The Giant Killer."

The next day, before a record-breaking crowd of 30,247 at West Side Park, Chicago trimmed Pittsburgh 5–2 behind the dependable hurling of Three Finger Brown. This ended the season for both teams and placed Chicago in first with a 98-55 mark and eliminated Pittsburgh, who finished 98-56. The Giants with a record of 95-55 and three games remaining with Boston still had a glimmer of hope, but barely. They would have to win all three to tie Chicago and force a one-game playoff.

A determined and aroused New York Giants team swept Boston behind the clutch pitching of Ames (two victories) and Wiltse to tie Chicago for the National League pennant! A playoff game to determine the winner was scheduled for October 8.

October 8

Truth is often stranger than fiction and the 1908 playoff game, the result of the bizarre 1–1 tie on September 23, certainly proved the point. Clearly, if the story was written as fiction, it would be met with unanimous disbelief. Reality, however, jammed into the Polo Grounds in the form of 40,000 spectators anxious to witness the game of the century. There never was an accurate count of the crowd size since thousands entered the grounds by breaking down a section of the fence. Mathewson took the mound for New York and Jack Pfeister for Chicago. When the Giants scored a run in the first, to the delight of their screaming fans, Chicago manager Frank Chance wasted no time and yanked his starter, replacing him with his ace, Three Finger Brown. The slim 1–0 lead lasted only to the third when the Cubs pounded New York's beloved Matty for four runs on a triple, two doubles and a single! Like a true champion, Matty recovered and blanked the Cubs for the next four innings before giving way to Wiltse but it was too late. Matty's demise might have been surprising to the many Giants fans but not to his wife. "I'm not fit to pitch today," Matty said to Mrs. Mathewson before he set out for the ballpark. "I'm dog tired."[14]

Years later he admitted, "The Cubs beat me because I never had less on the ball in my life. What I can't understand to this day is why it took them so long to hit me."[15]

In the meantime, Brown was remarkable, mowing down the Giants hitters with his twisting curves and high-speed fast ball. The final score was Chicago 4, New York 2. It was a cruel ending to an exciting pennant race and saddened the throngs that made their way out of the Polo Grounds for the last time this season.

As fate would have it, the final chapter was yet to be closed on this zany season. An unidentified man, who could not get into the Polo Grounds, was killed when he fell from an elevated train rail trying to get a good view of the game. It was observed that his vacant place was quickly filled! (It was also reported that a second man died similarly.)

In spite of the second-place finish, especially the manner in which it occurred, the 1908 season was a marvelous one filled with excitement and wonderful memories that New York fans would cherish over the winter, albeit with a twisted knot in their stomachs.

For Brush, McGraw and the players it was a frustrating season and one that would be difficult to forget for a long time. To help ease the pain of defeat, Brush gave the entire proceeds of the playoff game, about $10,000, to the players while McGraw was given a new automobile estimated at a cost of $5,000. The season was not without some redeeming value. The club set a new attendance record of some 764,000 and Brush reaped in a nice profit of about $200,000.

To attempt to create new superlatives to describe Mathewson's season is foolhardy. It is more meaningful to let Matty's numbers speak for themselves. He led the league in wins (37), ERA (1.43), games (56), games started (44), games completed (34), innings pitched (390.2), strikeouts (259) and shutouts (11). Christy Mathewson was at the peak of his profession and would remain there for another six years.

Chapter 11
Lowest Career ERA, 1909

W	L	Pct	ERA
25	6	.806	1.14

Late in 1908 John McGraw began formulating plans to improve his club for the new season with the hope of finally beating the invincible Chicago Cubs. Although the Giants would still continue to struggle in their quest to win the National League pennant in 1909, the Cubs wouldn't be the obstacle. It would be the Pittsburgh Pirates, their bitter rivals. Owner Barney Dreyfuss' club would turn in a superb season with a 110-42 mark while second place Chicago won 104 and lost 49. Once again, the Giants' competition was too much and McGraw found himself a few ball players shy of a pennant winner for the fourth straight year.

The third-place finish, however, was not because of McGraw's lack of effort to field the best possible club. In fact, McGraw spared no one in his trade plans late in 1908 when he got wind that the hapless last-place St. Louis Cardinals were looking for a new manager. When McGraw offered 29-year-old Roger Bresnahan, Cardinals owner Stanley Robison quickly calculated he could eliminate one salary by putting Bresnahan behind the plate as well as have him manage the club. Robison, envisioning the Duke of Tralee still in the prime of his career in a Cardinals uniform, thought he had died and gone to heaven.

There was one catch to the deal, however. Besides wanting pitcher Arthur "Bugs" Raymond and outfielder Jack "Red" Murray, McGraw needed a catcher to take Bresnahan's place and George Schlei was his man. The problem was that Schlei played for Cincinnati! Still not unreasonable, thought Robison, who was anxious to get rid of Raymond, an incurable drinker. So on December 12, 1908, Robison sent Ed Karger and Art Fromme, two young pitchers, to Cincinnati for Schlei; then he consummated the prearranged deal with McGraw—Murray, Schlei and Raymond for Bresnahan. This trade, which resulted in breaking up an outstanding battery of Bresnahan and Mathewson, was strong evidence that McGraw would spare no one in his quest to strengthen his club and win the pennant.

Tall for his age, Mathewson (first row left, sitting) was a key member of the Bucknell University basketball team (photo courtesy Bucknell University Archives).

McGraw wasn't finished by a long shot. He signed John "Chief" Meyers, a Cahuilla Indian who spent a year at Dartmouth before playing in the minor leagues, to share the catching duties with Schlei. New York also added another outfielder to the roster, Bill O'Hara, a 26-year-old rookie who would play 115 games for McGraw, nine more the following year in St. Louis, including an inning on the mound, before vanishing from the major leagues.

Never one to let sentiment stand in the way of improving a team, McGraw released two New York favorites—Joe McGinnity and Luther Taylor. The other departure from the 1908 club, which was voluntary, was Mike Donlin who decided, for the second time, his future was on the vaudeville circuit with his wife, Mabel Hite. In fact, when Donlin demanded his baseball salary be doubled, Brush decided he could get along without him. Donlin would surface again with the Giants but not until 1911.

Christy Mathewson, coming off the finest season of his nine-year career was clearly the premier pitcher and class of the National League, if not all baseball. The years ahead, including the 1909 season, would only add to his legendary feats on the mound and cast his image in bronze as a baseball immortal.

The Season

May 4

The New York Giants opened the season on April 15 before 30,000 fans without the services of McGraw and Mathewson. The manager was nursing a severely infected finger, which for a time physicians thought might have to be amputated. Mathewson's problem was not as serious, a bruised hand caused by a line drive off the bat of Moose McCormick. But it prevented him from pitching opening day and for a total of almost three weeks. Red Ames took his place on the mound and faced Brooklyn at the newly renovated Polo Grounds. Box seats had been suspended from the upper deck and the bleachers now enclosed the outfield, raising the capacity to 30,000. Even the grandstand was painted a bright yellow. In spite of the new look, the Giants were shut out 3–0.

By the time Matty made his first appearance on the mound in Philadelphia on May 4, New York was 4-7 and resting uncomfortably in last place along with Brooklyn. The winner of 37 games the previous year did little to ingratiate himself with fans back in New York. He was tagged for nine hits and three runs in seven innings. He also walked four batters. Philadelphia won the game 5–2, completing the three-game sweep and dumping the reeling Giants into the National League basement.

For the New York faithful, however, there was a bright side to the Giants' slow start. Earlier, the New York Central Railroad announced that final scores of all baseball games would be posted in smoking cars of selective trains en route between New York and Chicago. Now baseball enthusiasts who were riding the train could keep up to date on baseball happenings in both leagues.

May 13

The season was almost a month old before the hometown fans had a chance to see Mathewson at work. In a bitter piece of irony, his first appearance at the Polo Grounds was against Chicago. The last time he faced the Cubs was on October 8, 1908, a date he and all New Yorkers wanted to erase from their memories.

The results of this game, however, were entirely different. Matty whipped the Cubs 4–1 as he tossed a neat four-hitter, bringing the Giants' record to 9-11.

It wasn't bad enough that New York was floundering early in the season; now management was faced with another dilemma. A city Alderman by the name of John Mulcahy was in the middle of preparing a bill which, if passed by the Board of Aldermen, would open a street through the center of the Polo Grounds!

Commented Mulcahy, "I have recently been requested by a number of property owners in the neighborhood of the Polo Grounds to have the street opened. I have investigated their complaints and find them well founded. The opening of the street would make the property much more valuable than at present and I am satisfied that the street for business purposes should be opened."[1] Politics as it is, nothing ever happened and the Polo Grounds remained intact.

May 17

The Cincinnati Reds made their first trip of the year to the Polo Grounds and after defeating New York in the first game of the series faced Mathewson in game two. Before a skimpy crowd of 4,000 Matty tossed a six-hit shutout, his first of the year. The final score was 6–0.

At the outset, however, it looked like it was going to be a long day for the Giants' ace. Cincinnati's first batter Dick Egan tripled to left but Matty pitched out of the jam and the Reds failed to score. Mathewson was in command the rest of the way as he registered his second win of the season.

The day before, John Heydler, acting president of the National League, held a conference with umpires to discuss the rules and to make sure the best results would be gained under the new two-umpire system. He also wanted to make sure all efforts were made to stamp out player rowdyism on the field. The rash of fights cropping up throughout the league, especially the incident with umpire Steve Cusack several days earlier, prompted his concern. The Cusack melee happened in Boston when Cincinnati catcher Frank Roth attacked the umpire after being called out on a close play at home. Several Cincinnati players, with bats in hand, also threatened Cusack. It was an ugly scene and had no place in the game's future.

May 24

Under new manager Bresnahan the St. Louis Cardinals beat New York and Mathewson 3-1 in the first game of a three-game series. Bresnahan, who was royally feted by Giants' management and fans prior to the game, accomplished something his new club couldn't do since May 10, 1904—beat Mathewson! During that long stretch Matty won 24 consecutive games against St. Louis: five in 1904, five in 1905, four in 1906, five in 1907, five in 1908. It was an unprecedented accomplishment. Few people knew at the time, but Matty was working on another streak, this one against Cincinnati, which would end at 22 straight in 1911.

Mathewson pitched a fine game against the Cards, allowing three runs on six hits, but lost because the Giants could not figure out how to score against John Lush. He scattered seven hits, walked five but the Giants managed only one run and found themselves in seventh place with a 12-15 record.

May 28

New York split a doubleheader against Philadelphia at the Polo Grounds, getting trounced in the first game 11–1 and then blanking the Phillies 3–0 in a rain-shortened six-inning contest. Matty's second whitewash of the year raised his record to 3-2 and helped keep the Giants in fifth place with a 15-16 mark.

The reason for the Giants' slow start was obvious. They weren't hitting. The team batting average was around .210, which placed them in the unenviable position of last in the league. In addition, pitchers Otis Crandall and Rube Marquard were big disappointments, especially Marquard, who along with catcher Meyers was routinely referred to in the press, replete with sarcastic overtones, as the highest priced battery ($17,500) in baseball. Later, when Marquard failed to live up to expectations the press would refer to him as the "$11,000 lemon."

Mathewson blamed Marquard's poor start with the Giants on his 1908 debut and credits coach Wilbert Robinson as the man responsible for instilling confidence in the young pitcher. It was "at just about the time the papers were mentioning him as the '$11,000 lemon,' and imploring McGraw to let him go to some club in exchange for a good capable bat boy," commented Matty. "One of Marquard's worst faults, when he first broke into the league, was that he did not know the batters and their grooves, and these weaknesses Robinson drilled into his head—not that a drill was required to insert the information. Robinson was the coacher, umpire, catcher and batter rolled into one...."[2]

May 31

New York completed its five-game series with Philadelphia by taking both ends of a doubleheader. Hooks Wiltse won the morning game 3–2 before a mere 5,000 spectators. In the afternoon game 35,000 squeezed into the Polo Grounds to see their idol, Mathewson. In Frank Merriwell tradition, Matty defeated the Phillies 5–4, capping his six-hit performance with a tie-breaking home run into the left field bleachers in the eighth inning. As Mathewson broke into his home run trot, the band struck up "Dixie" and "Marching Through Georgia." Matty's early season record stood at 4–2 as the Giants pulled even at 17-17.

June 5

While New York was opening its first western swing of the season in St. Louis, the press was hailing the imminent return of National League president Harry Pulliam. Due to the pressures of the job which had caused, on occasion, irrational behavior by the president, Pulliam had been given a leave of absence since February with John Heydler, his assistant, filling in. It appeared Pulliam had regained his health and would be ready to perform his duties within a week or two.

At Robison Field, it took Raymond, Crandall and finally Mathewson to stop the St. Louis onslaught and win the opening game of the series, 8–7. McGraw and Larry Doyle were tossed out of the game by umpire Charlie Rigler with Matty pitching the last three inings.

June 8

After winning twice in St. Louis, New York moved into Chicago with Mathewson and Three Finger Brown squared off to face each other in the first game of the series. Matty was the better pitcher on this day as he hurled a masterful two-hitter, defeating the second place Cubs 3–2. Two errors, a sacrifice and a single off Matty netted Chicago two runs in the first inning. Over the next eight innings Matty gave up only one hit while his teammates scored three runs. His record was now 5-2.

June 12

After splitting two games in Chicago, New York traveled to Ohio to meet Cincinnati in a four-game series. New York lost the first game (June 11), but Mathewson came back the next day to blank the Reds 2–0 on four hits and one walk. Matty dominated the game and was in trouble only once when Tom Downey doubled with no out. But Matty fanned the next three Reds to record the shutout, his third of the season. The victory brought the Giants' record to 22-19, putting them in fourth place nine full games behind the league-leading Pittsburgh Pirates.

It was somewhat sad to note that in a minor league game in Newark, New Jersey, the local club, behind the pitching of McGinnity, defeated Buffalo 5–4. McGinnity's mound opponent? None other than Dummy Taylor. Adding to the sorrowful scene the game was played in rain from start to finish.

June 16

Mathewson opened the series in Pittsburgh with an easy 8–2 victory, snapping the Pirates' 14-game winning streak. The Giants broke the game wide open in the sixth when they scored four runs to pad their 4–2 lead. Matty scattered ten hits to record his seventh win against two losses.

The night before, on the sleeper coming from Cincinnati, Raymond and McGraw battled over the former's misbehavior. Although it wasn't specifically stated in the press, a safe guess is that Raymond was drinking in excess, much to McGraw's chagrin. This was only the beginning; McGraw would have to endure much more aggravation before he lowered the boom on Bugs.

June 23

New York completed its road trip with a mediocre 6–5 record after losing two of three to Pittsburgh, and they were now firmly entrenched in third place. On June 22 all games in the National League were postponed and flags at ballparks flown at half-mast in tribute to George Dovey, president of the Boston club, whose funeral was being held in Philadelphia. Dovey died suddenly the previous week on a train.

On the same day in Lewisburg, Pennsylvania, Mathewson pitched four innings for the Bucknell University Alumni as they lost to the varsity squad 13–12. Matty was touched for four hits and two runs. He also played third base and contributed to the offense with three hits, including a triple.

The four-inning stint at Lewisburg was a tune-up for Mathewson when he returned to the Polo Grounds to face Boston in a doubleheader. Matty picked up a gift victory in the first game when he relieved Marquard in the ninth inning with the score tied at 4–4. Mathewson fanned two of three batters in the top of the ninth, the Giants scored in their half and Matty had his eighth win while barely breaking a sweat.

The Giants won the second game 11–1, with Mathewson handed another easy win. Matty started the game and after two innings, with a 4–1 lead, McGraw rested his star, replacing him with Crandall, who blanked Boston the rest of the way on three hits. The official scorer awarded the victory to Matty, his ninth of the season.

June 25

New York won its third doubleheader in a row by beating Brooklyn 4–2 and 9–1. Wiltse won the first game. Mathewson started the second and left after five innings with a 7–0 lead. Crandall came on in relief and gave up a run in the ninth. The victory was Matty's eighth straight as he improved his record to 10–2. After six consecutive wins the Giants still trailed Pittsburgh by nine and a half games.

Three days later a healthy Harry Pulliam was back at work and ready to resume his duties as president of the National League. During the day he held an impromptu reception and was greeted and welcomed by many of his friends. It appeared to be business as usual for the league president.

June 30

The Giants split a doubleheader with Brooklyn at Washington Park, losing the first game 7–2 as Wiltse was clobbered but winning the second game behind Mathewson's fourth shutout of the season, 3–0. Matty was stingy with the hits; he gave up four, didn't issue a pass and fanned nine. It was a quality outing and raised his record to 11–2.

In Pittsburgh, the Pirates played their first game in Forbes Field, their new million-dollar home. It was "named for General John Forbes, a British general in the French and Indian War who captured Fort Duquesne and renamed it Fort Pitt in 1758." Now erected on the grounds are the "University of Pittsburgh library and dormitories called Forbes Quadrangle. The center field and right center brick walls still stand, along with the base of the flag pole."[3]

The inaugural was somewhat tarnished, however, when the Cubs trimmed the Pirates 3–2 before more than 30,000 spectators. Ironically, 20 years earlier when Exposition Park was dedicated, the Cubs spoiled that day also by beating the Pirates.

July 3

The Giants won both ends of another doubleheader with Brooklyn, 5–3 and 2–1, but it wasn't easy. The two games took four and a half hours and 23 innings to play before a crowd of 25,000 persons (the playing field was completely surrounded), estimated to be the largest crowd ever at Washington Park. The long day was marred by the unruly behavior of fans in the front grandstand closest to the catcher. They repeatedly threw bottles, glasses and other missiles onto the field. Luckily no fights broke out.

Mathewson entered the first game in the ninth inning replacing Raymond with the score tied 3–3 and turned in a sparkling relief performance. He blanked Brooklyn over the remaining six innings on two hits and no walks. When the Giants scored two runs in the fourteenth inning, Matty had his tenth straight victory and his won-lost record went to 12-2.

July 5

The Giants played their second marathon doubleheader in a row, this one with Philadelphia lasting 24 innings, one better than the Brooklyn twin bill. The Giants won both games by scores of 3–0 and 3–2 in 15 innings, the longest game of the season in the National League. Mathewson started the afternoon game and left after nine innings with the score knotted at 2–2. Raymond picked up the victory when he blanked Philadelphia the rest of the way and his teammates scored in the fifteenth. The victory put the Giants a half game back of second-place Chicago and seven behind Pittsburgh.

July 12

New York split a doubleheader with Pittsburgh, winning the first 3–2 behind a weary Mathewson and getting shellacked in the second game 9–0. Mathewson, showing signs of fatigue, still managed to trim the first-place Pirates on four hits. It was his eleventh consecutive victory and improved his record to 13-2.

Rumors were circulating that McGraw was in hot pursuit of a young pitching phenom in the minors, but McGraw would not divulge who he was or even where he played. It was learned, however, that he was not an Amos Rusie nor a Mathewson but equal to Raymond; actually more a McGinnity type. It was all mysteriously presented, but clearly indicated McGraw's concern for his pitching staff. Without Mathewson's 13-2 record, the Giants were only two games over .500. And Matty's health was now being questioned. Some felt he was suffering from something worse than a stiff arm, claiming he was not the same man since his attack of diphtheria. He simply lacked stamina. With the benefit of hindsight, the pessimistic reports of Mathewson's demise were obviously ill founded.

July 16

New York feasted on visiting Cincinnati like a piranha in a tank of minnows. The Giants swept the four-game series with Mathewson winning the finale 2–1. Matty spread five hits and gave up one run for his fourteenth win and twelfth straight. Years later, close victories like this would prompt Larry Doyle to praise Matty for his grace under pressure. "When he was one run behind or one run ahead, Christy Mathewson was at his most glorious. It was then he would decide the time had arrived to put his arm and his brain to work and he would shoot the works at batters—slow ones, speed balls, drops, tantalizing curves and the back-breaking fadeaway. The tighter the ball game, the cooler he became."[4]

July 20

The Giants lost a heartbreaker to St. Louis 4–3 in 11 innings. They had the bases loaded, no outs in the tenth and failed to score. On top of that, Mathewson suffered a broken finger on his left hand when he was struck by a line drive off the bat of Joe Delahanty in the seventh inning. Matty was removed from the game and was expected to be out for at least two weeks. Crandall took his place with the score tied 3–3 but gave up a run in the eleventh for the loss. McGraw breathed a sigh of relief when the initial report of Matty's broken finger was changed to "mashed," the description offered by *The New York Times*.

July 27

At South End Grounds in Boston, New York split a doubleheader with the Doves, the Boston club's official nickname until 1911 when they would be called the Rustlers. The Giants lost the first 7–4 but won the second 6–2 behind the solid pitching of Mathewson. He surrendered seven hits, walked two and struck out seven for his fifteenth win of the season and thirteenth straight. The Giants were still mired in third place.

The next day, the baseball world was shocked when Harry Pulliam, who a month ago had returned to the task of running the National League, committed suicide in his room at the New York Athletic Club, where he had lived for several years. A "hall boy" found Pulliam lying on the floor in a pool of blood from a gunshot wound that traveled through his brain blowing out both his eyes. Incredibly, he was still alive, but too badly wounded to be taken to a hospital. The following morning, the 40-year-old bachelor passed away.

It appeared Pulliam had not fully recovered from his nervous breakdown, as many had believed he had. He was a man who disliked confrontations and the petty disputes of baseball. The Fred Merkle affair in which Pulliam ruled the controversial game was a 1–1 tie and would have to be replayed, if necessary, and the subsequent protests weighed heavily on him; plus the fanfare and controversy surrounding the Dr. Joseph Creamer episode (an employee of the Giants) in which Pulliam banned the physician from every major league ballpark for the rest of his life for attempting to bribe umpire Bill Klem to give close calls to the Giants. These two incidents, it appears, were too much for the idealistic and romantic Pulliam to cope with, apparently contributing to his suicide.

July 30

After taking four of five games from Boston, the Giants headed for Pittsburgh and new Forbes Field to begin their second western road trip with the hopes of chipping away at the Pirates' formidable 11½-game lead.

In his poorest performance of the season, Mathewson was shelled in the first inning with the Pirates scoring three runs on four hits. Ames relieved in the second and pitched brilliantly, allowing one hit in seven innings, but the effort was wasted as New York had trouble scoring against Vic Willis. The final score was 3–1 and the first loss for Matty since St. Louis beat him back on May 24. It also stopped his winning streak at 13. His record was now 15-3.

August 3

On August 2, Harry Clay Pulliam was buried in Louisville, Kentucky, and all games in both the National and American leagues were postponed out of respect for this baseball magnate. It marked the first time in the game's history that all scheduled contests in both leagues were postponed on the same day. After the funeral, at a special meeting of the Board of Directors, Heydler was named to succeed Pulliam.

The next day it was business as usual with both leagues offering a full schedule of games. Mathewson took the mound for New York in the opening game of the Cincinnati series and was hammered for 15 hits (his season high), and six runs. Fortunately for Matty Cincinnati hurlers Bob Spade and Billy Campbell were a tad worse and the Giants won 7–6 in ten innings. It was Matty's sixteenth win—not a particularly well deserved one, but nonetheless a win.

Lack of respect for umpires by players, managers and fans was still plaguing the presidents of both leagues, especially Ban Johnson. Tim Hurst, working an American League game in Philadelphia, did little to ingratiate himself to umpire baters or Johnson when he spat in the face of the Athletics second baseman, Eddie Collins, when Collins objected to a call. Hurst, who began his umpiring career in the National League, was a free spirit. "He loved the bright lights and in the gas-lit era was a familiar and welcome figure on Broadway. He suffered from none of the inhibitions which have frequently affected the umpires and moved easily in theatrical and sporting circles where he pleased, and with whom he pleased,"[5] commented author James Kahn. Hurst was also a feisty individual who was involved in numerous scuffles in both leagues. For the man who coined the phrase, "You can't beat the hours," the Collins incident was his last confrontation. He was bounced from baseball over it.

August 7

After losing two of three games in Cincinnati, the Giants headed for St. Louis for five games. Matty opened the series and waltzed to an easy 7–1 win. The game was over after the first inning when New York whacked Fred Beebe for four runs on six hits. Mathewson's record was 17-3 and the Giants were still bogged down in third place.

New York won the next four games from the Cardinals, for a sweep of the series, but couldn't get any closer to the Cubs than eight games. Pittsburgh was out of sight as the Giants trailed them by 14 games.

August 12

Buoyed by their sweep of St. Louis, the Giants came roaring into the Windy City and won the series-opening doubleheader 5–2 and 3–0, cutting Chicago's second-place lead to six games. Mathewson was outstanding in the second game, hurling his fifth shutout of the season for his eighteenth victory. He scattered four hits and didn't walk a batter. Fred Merkle was the batting hero in both games but also the recipient of a sarcastic press, reminding readers of the faux pas he committed in 1908 that necessitated the playoff game.

The Giants cut Chicago's second-place lead to four when they won the next two games, one of the victories stopped Ed Reulbach's winning streak at 14. He tied Pittsburgh's Jack Chesbro (1902) for the most consecutive victories in the National League, pitching from a distance of 60 feet 6 inches. The Giants lost the final game of the Chicago series, ending a nine-game winning streak, as they headed for Pittsburgh.

August 16

New York and Pittsburgh played to a 2–2 tie in a game that was stopped after eight innings when a downpour drenched Forbes Field. It was an exciting game for the 11,000 who attended even though the outcome would have little bearing on the pennant race. Pittsburgh tied the game in the bottom of the eighth off Mathewson and had men on second and third when John Miller lined a shot to right center which looked like a sure triple and a possible home run. But Giants' right fielder Red Murray was off like a bolt of lightning at the crack of the bat and caught up with the ball in deep right center, saving at least two runs and helping Mathewson sidestep a defeat. Then came the rain and the game was called. The Giants remained 10½ games behind the league-leading Pirates.

August 19

New York split a doubleheader in Philadelphia by scores of 6–4 and 1–0. Crandall won the first game for the Giants and Mathewson lost the tough second game as Earl Moore blanked New York on five hits. Sherry Magee scored the winning and only run of the game in the bottom of the ninth, tagging Matty with only his fourth loss of the season.

American League president Ban Johnson made it official when he announced that the services of the fun-loving and pugnacious umpire Tim Hurst were no longer needed. No doubt it was a painful decision for Johnson, who was a champion and protector of umpire rights, but he had clearly showed fairness in his attempt to bring peace and calm to ballparks that were at times akin to battlefields.

August 21

Two days after losing to Philadelphia 1–0, Mathewson was involved in another 1–0 game, this time on the winning side as he blanked Chicago on five hits. Matty didn't walk a batter, whiffed nine (six over the last four innings) and upped his record to 19-4.

Larry Doyle was the hero of the day, scoring the only run of the game and exciting the 17,000 fans with daring base running. In the first inning, Doyle walked and then, on a grounder back to the box, sprinted all the way to third and subsequently scored on a fielder's choice.

Doyle, who shared a room with Matty, had great respect for and was in awe of Bix Six, as were many of his teammates. Having the distinction of batting against all the greats in those days (including Matty), Doyle confessed in an interview in 1949 that Mathewson was the best, "And not because he was a Giant and my friend, but he really was the best. Marquard had speed, but he was often wild as a hawk. I'm not taking anything away from either him or Grover [Alexander], but Matty had everything they had in speed and more stuff than any five pitchers I've ever faced."[6]

August 24

The next nine games—four with Pittsburgh and five with Chicago— would represent the Giants' last chance to challenge the front-runners for the pennant. Time was running out and the Giants could not afford to slip further behind in the race. When New York lost six of the nine games and went from 11½ back of the first place Pirates to 15½ back, the season was over for the Giants.

The Giants split the opening series doubleheader with Pittsburgh, 4–3 and 11–3. Wiltse won the first game with relief help from Mathewson when he came on in the ninth with no out, two men on and the score 4–3. Matty put on his closer's cap and induced George Gibson to hit into a double play, then fanned Ham Hyatt to end the game and save the victory for Wiltse.

Bugs Raymond was clobbered in the second game and from the fifth inning on begged McGraw to take him out. Realizing the game was lost, the stubborn manager refused and took the opportunity to teach his heavy-drinking pitcher an important lesson in the value of clean living.

August 25

Christy Mathewson won his twentieth game of the season defeating Pittsburgh 3–2 on five hits. It was the seventh consecutive season in which the right-hander won 20 or more games. His appearance on the mound attracted 12,000 fans, a respectable crowd considering the outcome of the game was of little consequence.

Besides Matty's fine pitching performance, the fans were treated to an exchange of words and near fistfight between Hans Wagner and Giants coach Arlie Latham. After Wagner was robbed of a hit by Doyle in the fourth, Latham began needling him, which eventually got to the shortstop. Heated words almost ignited into a fistfight but Latham backed off and the incident vanished as quickly as it had begun.

August 28

Christy Mathewson versus Three Finger Brown, a pairing made in heaven that often meant pitching excellence and a tight game, was a huge disappointment to the locals when Matty left after two innings trailing 4–0. Actually, he had no one to blame but himself when his errant throw in the second inning opened the gates for a big Chicago rally, which, with Brown in top form, virtually iced the victory. It was Matty's shortest stint of the season. The final score was Chicago 6, New York 1. His won-lost mark was now 20–5.

August 30

Since Mathewson pitched only two innings on Saturday (August 28) and rested on Sunday, McGraw called on his star to pitch the second game of the Chicago doubleheader. The Giants had lost the first game 2–0, so McGraw was desperate for a victory. As bad as Matty was on Saturday, that's how good he was in this game. He bested Ed Reulbach by blanking the Cubs 5–0 on five hits. It was his seventh shutout and twenty-first victory of the season. He pitched superbly throughout, did not issue a walk and relied heavily on the defensive support behind him. It was Mathewson at the top of his game.

Chief Meyers, who was in his rookie year with the Giants, would catch Matty for a total of seven years before he moved on to Brooklyn, coined one of the most memorable lines in baseball. "Anybody can catch Matty," he said. "You could catch him sitting in a rocking chair."[7]

September 6

New York split a doubleheader with Boston 2–0 and 5–4 in ten innings before a big holiday crowd of 18,000 at the Polo Grounds. After the Giants were shut out in the first game, Mathewson found himself in a 4–4 tie when the Giants came to bat in the bottom half of the tenth. Matty had pitched well and deserved the win so at this point took matters into his own hands. Borrowing a page from one of Burt L. Standish's (pseudonym for Gilbert Patten) books on Frank Merriwell, he tripled to deep left center scoring George Schlei from first to win the game. His record now stood at 22-5.

September 11

The New York battery of Mathewson and Meyers teamed up to whitewash Brooklyn 4–0 in the first game of a doubleheader at the Polo Grounds. The Giants were shellacked in the second game 10–1. The split dropped the Giants to 10½ games back of the second-place Cubs with hope of catching them vanishing quickly.

Matty pitched splendidly, allowing three hits, walking one while fanning six. It was his twenty-third victory and eighth shutout. Meyers, a Cahuilla Indian, provided all the offense his pitcher needed. With the bases loaded in the second, the Chief blasted a fast ball to deep left center and lumbered all the way home for a grand slam.

September 16

The Giants began their last western road trip with a lock on third place and a chance to act in the spoilers' role when they faced Chicago and Pittsburgh for the last time this season. Appropriately, the opening game of the Chicago series pitted Mathewson against Three Finger Brown before more than 30,000 wildly enthusiastic fans, including the president of the United States, William H. Taft.

As anticipated, it was a pitcher's battle all the way with little to distinguish between the two stars. They each allowed seven hits and walked none, while Matty fanned four and Brown two. The difference in the game came in the very first inning when the Giants bunched three hits and scored two runs. The final score was New York 2, Chicago 1. This victory gave Matty the edge (two of three) over Brown in their matchups for the season. More important, the loss dropped Chicago six and a half games behind Pittsburgh and, when the Cubs lost the next two games, any hope of overtaking Pittsburgh was forever dashed.

September 22

In a game of little significance, New York and Mathewson were lucky to beat St. Louis 4–3 at Robison Field. Matty surrendered 12 hits and his teammates committed four errors, but the hapless Cardinals could only manage to score three runs. It wasn't pretty but it still counted as a victory, Matty's twenty-fifth and last of the season.

New York Giants fans, after reading about their team's victory in St. Louis over morning coffee, were shocked to discover their beloved hero, Christy Mathewson, was planning on quitting baseball after the season! The rumor, which emanated from St. Louis, claimed Matty would retire from the Giants at the end of the season in order to enter a manufacturing business with a former college mate. He was going to operate a plant for the production of railroad ties in Nova Scotia. According to the account, Mathewson admitted the business opportunity was too good to pass up. Fortunately for baseball, there was little truth to the rumor and it died a quick death.

September 25

After winning three straight from St. Louis, the Giants moved into Cincinnati and split five games, one of which ended in a 1–1 tie. This was the game Mathewson pitched and probably should have won if it were not for poor base running by Schlei and Doyle, which took the Giants out of a big inning. Taking nothing away from Bob Spade, who pitched a fine game for Cincinnati, Matty hurled a tad better and should have had the victory.

Unlike the senior circuit, the American League had a dandy pennant race going. Detroit was holding on to a slim two and one-half–game lead over Connie Mack's Athletics as the season was quickly drawing to a close.

October 2

By the time Mathewson pitched his last game of the 1909 season, a 2-1 loss to Philadelphia at the Polo Grounds, both pennant races were officially decided. Pittsburgh clinched on September 28 when the Phillies beat Chicago 3-2 and Detroit won its third straight pennant two days later when the Athletics lost a doubleheader to Chicago.

Mathewson pitched the second game of the doubleheader after Marquard was clobbered by Philadelphia for 16 hits and nine runs in the first game. Matty was also hit freely but only allowed two runs. The key to the game was the Giants' failure to solve the hurling of George McQuillan, who scattered five hits. Mathewson finished the season with a magnificent 25-6 mark.

In spite of the record attendance (783,700) at the Polo Grounds, it clearly was a disappointing season for the New York Giants players and their fans. Although they won 92 games, the Giants finished 18½ back of pennant-winning Pittsburgh and were never a serious threat from as early as mid–May. Moreover, the postseason best-of-seven series with the Boston Red Sox, third-place winners in the American League, did little to ameliorate the disheartened fans and New York management. The Giants lost four of five games; Matty won the opener 4-2 but lost the fourth game 2-0. Financially, it was also a disappointment, attracting few fans and bringing each Giants player a mere $133.

To pinpoint why the Giants could do no better than third place is not easy. There appear to be no obvious reasons. For example, the team batting average in 1909 was .255 compared to .267 the year before; the defense was off also, .954 versus .962. Conversely, the Giants stole 49 more bases in 1909 and led the league in home runs. The ERA of the pitching staff increased slightly from .214 in 1908 to .227. The excellent play of Pittsburgh (110-42) and Chicago (104-49) all season probably was the most compelling reason New York finished a dismal third.

On an individual basis, several Giants turned in fine seasons. Doyle and Murray were among the leaders in a number of offensive categories. Doyle batted .301 and led the league with 172 hits. Murray batted only .263 but had 91 RBIs and led the league with seven home runs. He also stole 48 bases, second best in the league.

For the third straight year Mathewson led the pitching staff with a 25-6 mark and a league-leading 1.14 ERA. Raymond (18-12, 2.47), Wiltse (20-11, 2.00) and Ames (15-10, 2.70) had solid seasons. The two big disappointments were Marquard (5-13, 2.60) and Crandall (6-4, 2.88), particularly Rube. McGraw explained it this way: "In the American Association he was almost unbeatable. It was on that record that we paid $11,000 for him. I still think that the immense amount of publicity following that deal in which Rube got the sobriquet of the 'eleven thousand dollar beauty' interfered a lot with his progress. I don't mean to say that Marquard was swell-headed. He was anything but that. It was nervousness over living up to a great reputation that seemed to upset him."[8]

In fairness to Marquard, the youngster certainly wasn't the sole reason for the 18½-game deficit. It was a team effort and as mentioned earlier had more to do with the excellent play of Pittsburgh and Chicago than with New York's weaknesses.

Once again, Mathewson was the class of the league and a model of consistency. In 275⅓ innings he allowed 192 hits, fanned 149 and walked a mere 36 batters. He started 33 games, completed 26 and turned in an incredible league-leading 1.14 ERA to go along with his eight shutouts. His .806 winning percentage was tops in the league and the highest he would ever record in a 17-year career. Nine full seasons in the National League, not counting 1900, and he already had recorded 236 victories. Is it any wonder he's been called by many the greatest pitcher ever?

Chapter 12
Most Victories in National League, Again, 1910

W	L	Pct	ERA
27	9	.750	1.89

The 1910 spring training camp of the New York Giants was held at Marlin, Texas, as it had been since 1908 and would continue to be through 1918. The camp, a mixture of veterans and rookies, was run by McGraw in a very disciplined fashion. Each morning the manager and his players would walk to the field where McGraw would pitch batting practice. At 11 a.m. he would lead the squad in a jog around the field and to the hotel for lunch. In the afternoon it was back to the field for intrasquad games. McGraw and the players would also travel to places like Waco, Austin, San Antonio, Fort Worth and Dallas for exhibition games.

In her book, *The Real McGraw*, Mrs. McGraw credits her husband with being the first manager to utilize split squads. "It was at Marlin, also in 1910, that John first split his team into A and B squads and played simultaneous exhibition games, an innovation at the time." Added the manager's wife, "Regular rosters were limited to eighteen and rookies, to be cut loose later, made the two teams possible."[1]

It was a typical spring training camp in 1910 except for the antics of Bugs Raymond, which would haunt McGraw all season long. Surprisingly, it started on a positive note when Raymond showed up in Marlin in February and proudly claimed he hadn't had a drink in a week. To keep Raymond on the wagon McGraw decided not to give him any spending money aside from small change for soda and candy. It worked for a while, until Raymond got smashed at a banquet in the team's honor in Dallas. As McGraw would discover during the season, this episode was simply a harbinger of future events.

The roster changes for the Giants in 1910, unlike previous seasons, were minimal. McGraw counted heavily on his youngsters coming of age. Two 23-year-olds, Fred Snodgrass and Josh Devore, who played sparingly in 1909, took over for outfielders Cy Seymour and Moose McCormick. The other kid, Fred Merkle (age 22) was installed permanently at first with

12 • Most Victories in National League, Again, 1910

Captain Mathewson was a member of the Army's Chemical Warfare Division stationed in France during World War I. He accidentally inhaled gas fumes, weakening his lungs, which eventually led to tuberculosis (photo courtesy National Baseball Library, Coperstown, N.Y.).

the release of veteran Fred Tenney. Chief Meyers would do most of the catching and, at age 30, was still relatively young. The rest of the club remained intact with Larry Doyle at second, Art Devlin at third, Al Bridwell at short and Red Murray solidly entrenched in right field.

The pitching staff remained the same except for the addition of Louis Drucke to the regular rotation. The 22-year-old right-hander, who had a 2–1 record in 24 innings in 1909, would see a lot more action in 1910.

Although McGraw put together a solid team, mixing veterans and youngsters, it was no match for the Chicago Cubs with their rebuilt pitching staff. New York would finish in second place, 13 games behind the Cubs in a dull and lackluster season. In fact, the most excitement was provided by Raymond and his drunken shenanigans.

The New York Giants, to some degree, salvaged the boring season for their fans with exciting (and lucrative for the owners and players) postseason play against their city rival, the New York Yankees. The crowds were large and the interest high as the Giants won the series four games to two. Mathewson was brilliant, winning three games and saving one. More importantly, the club finally jelled and this series was merely a dress rehearsal for the years ahead.

The Season

April 16

After losing the first two games of the new season, at Boston's South End Grounds, Mathewson went to the hill to put an end to the Giants' poor start. Matty, without skipping a beat, picked up where he had left off the previous year by hurling a six-hitter, fanning nine and icing the game in the sixth inning with a home run over the left field fence for a 3–1 victory.

Four days later New York opened its season at the Polo Grounds before 25,000 excited spectators. Hooks Wiltse made it a joyous occasion by blanking Boston 4–0 on three hits. The victory evened the Giants' early season record at 2-2.

April 27

After more than a week of idleness Mathewson returned to the mound to face the Philadelphia Phillies at Baker Bowl. In a well played and close contest Matty defeated the Phillies 3–2, snapping their seven-game winning streak, but he needed plenty of help from his teammates. In both the second and third innings Philadelphia loaded the bases but failed to score when the Giants turned snappy double plays.

Matty came close to blowing up in the fifth when the Phillies scored two runs and had a runner thrown out at the plate. Center fielder Sherwood Magee, always a tough out for Matty, was responsible for both runs when he doubled one in and scored another. Commented Matty, "Sherwood Magee of the Philadelphia National League team is one of the hardest batters that I ever have had to face, because he has a great eye, and is of the type of free swingers who take a mad wallop at the ball, and are always liable to break up a game with a long drive."[2] New York's record improved to 7-3, which placed them fourth in the early standings.

May 2

Mathewson pitched a magnificent one-hit shutout at Washington Park, defeating Brooklyn 6–0 for his third win of the season. Matty faced only 29 batters, two over the minimum. He retired the first 20 hitters before future Hall of Famer Zack Wheat topped a slow bounder to Merkle at first; Merkle couldn't find the handle and was charged with an error. But in the eighth Brooklyn picked up its first hit. Pryor McElveen grounded to short, third baseman Devlin cut in front of Fletcher, fielded the ball and threw low and wide to Merkle. *The New York Times* declared it an error and, when Mathewson went on to retire the remaining batters, credited him with a no-hitter. The *Times*' headline read: "Brooklyn Gets No-Hit Off Mathewson." The official scorer, however, saw it differently. He awarded McElveen with a hit and the game went down in the record books as a one-hitter, the fourth of Matty's career. Regardless of how the McElveen play was scored, it was a brilliantly pitched game.

Later in the week in St. Louis, President William H. Taft gave baseball's rough and rowdy image a welcome shot in the arm. "The game of baseball," he said, "is a clean, straight game, and it summons to its presence everybody who enjoys clean, straight athletics. It furnishes amusement to thousands and thousands. I like to go for two reasons: first, because I enjoy myself and, second, because if by the presence of the Chief Magistrate such a healthy amusement can be encouraged, I want to encourage it."[3]

May 6

Mathewson registered his fourth win of the season when he beat Philadelphia 3–2 at the Polo Grounds. Matty gave up nine hits but, in the clutch, he was his usual crafty self. Unlike the Phillies, New York bunched its hits in the sixth inning, scoring all three runs.

The great Wee Willie Keeler, who was at the end of his career, was released by the Yankees and picked up by McGraw to be used as a pinch hitter. Keeler batted only ten times during the season but managed three hits and ended his career with a lifetime average of .343, ninth best in baseball. Keeler's advice for hitting was simple. "Keep your eye on the ball and hit 'em where they ain't." The five foot, four and one-half inch, 140-pound hitting machine would be elected to the Hall of Fame in 1939.

May 10

Mathewson, in his first appearance of the season against the Cubs at West Side Park lasted only five innings. He was rapped for eight hits and left with the score tied 4–4. Red Ames relieved in the bottom of the sixth and was rocked for five hits and five runs in one inning. Otis Crandall mopped up and the game ended with Chicago winning 9–5. It was the Giants' second loss in a row to the Cubs as their first western road trip of the season was off to a poor start. Regardless, the Giants were in second place behind Pittsburgh with a 13-7 record.

May 13

After losing three of four to Chicago, the Giants traveled to St. Louis hoping to get themselves back on track against a weak Cardinals club. Instead Mathewson opened the series and was clobbered for seven hits and eight runs in two innings! It was an off day for the great right-hander, but in all fairness he received little support from his infield during the Cards' eight-run second inning outburst. Actually, with better defense six of the runs would not have scored. It was Matty's first loss of the season.

It's been claimed many times that errors never upset Mathewson nor interfered with his ability to pitch. True or not, this clearly was the perception of his teammates. Chief Meyers said, "How we loved to play for that guy. We'd break our backs for him. If you made an error behind him, he'd never sulk. He'd come over and pat you on the back ... he had the sweetest, most gentle nature I have ever seen."[4] Larry Doyle concurred with Meyers. "And in all the years I played with Matty, I never once heard him beef about an error made by another player while he was pitching."[5]

May 18

New York lost all four games to St. Louis, seven of its last eight and tumbled into fifth place as the train rumbled into Cincinnati. So McGraw was eager for Mathewson to open the series at League Park. He had won 12 straight from the Reds, dating back to June 17, 1908. And McGraw was hoping Matty could continue his magic and lift the Giants out of their doldrums. He did! Matty made it 13 in a row in a 10–6 slugfest but he wasn't much of a puzzle as Cincinnati pounded out 11 hits. The Giants, however, treated the previously undefeated (5-0) George Suggs harshly, scoring four runs in the fourth, four more in the seventh and two in the eighth. Matty's record was now 5-1.

May 23

Mathewson won his first game of the year in relief, defeating Pittsburgh 7–1 at Forbes Field. Wiltse was struck by a pitched ball in the fourth inning and had to leave the game with a 3–1 lead. Matty blanked the Pirates the remaining six innings to earn his sixth win against only one loss.

After a day of rain, New York edged Pittsburgh 4–3 and concluded the road trip with an awful 5-9 record. The Giants were lucky to be in third place as they headed back east.

May 28

Fred Snodgrass' double in the fifth inning drove in two runs and was the winning margin as New York defeated Philadelphia 3-2 for Mathewson's seventh win of the season. Matty gave up ten hits but was tough in the clutch.

The day before, Bugs Raymond pitched one of his best games of the season. He easily defeated Brooklyn 8-2 at Washington Park, scattering seven hits and striking out eight. No doubt Raymond's spitball had McGraw smiling for a change. It was such an effective pitch that years later McGraw still remembered it clearly and had nothing but praise for it. "I shall never forget Bugs Raymond. There, by the way, was one of the greatest natural pitchers that ever lived. Raymond's long suit, of course, was his spitball. He could make the ball do the queerest of stunts and never did he hesitate to pull one of these tricks when the team was in a hole."[6] Interestingly, McGraw claimed his star pitcher also had a spitball. "Mathewson could pitch the spitter, but rarely used it in a game. He never considered it part of his equipment."[7]

June 1

Cincinnati, the first of the western clubs to invade the Polo Grounds, had to face Mathewson and his special pitching magic in the first game of the series. Matty continued his dominance over the Reds, limiting them to four hits and winning 5-2. The victory upped his record to 8-1, increased the Giants' current winning streak to eight and his personal dominance over Cincinnati to 14 straight. New York was once again playing solid ball, in second place and trailed Chicago by a narrow margin.

June 6

Mathewson opened the series against St. Louis as he did against Cincinnati and the results were the same — New York won 5-1. Matty, in a fine outing baffled the Cardinals, giving up three hits and gaining a bit of revenge for the four-game sweep the Giants suffered in mid-May. Mathewson's record was now 9-1 and few would argue that he was the premier pitcher in baseball.

It was interesting to note that in the American League president Ban Johnson had entered into an agreement with officials representing the American Federation of Labor. The agreement, in part, provided that no cigars were to be sold without the union label in any American League park and that all printing by the league clubs must be given to union labor. It appears the treatment of umpires wasn't Johnson's only cause.

June 10

Mathewson opened his third consecutive series against an invading western club, this time first place Chicago (percentage points ahead of the Giants), but the results were different; New York lost 6–5. Entering the eighth inning, Matty had a comfortable 5–2 lead and with two out and one on Giants fans began heading for the exits. However, a walk and an error loaded the bases, bringing the dangerous Frank Chance to bat. Chance wasted no time and lined a single to right field and when Murray let the ball skip through his legs, Chance circled the bases. It was one of the few times in Matty's long career in which he blew a lead late in the game, although he did have plenty of help from Murray. His record was 9-2.

June 15

After losing all three games to Chicago and dropping three games behind the league leaders, Mathewson faced Pittsburgh in an effort to get New York back on its winning ways. Matty pitched a solid game, turning back the Pirates 5–1 on six hits. His control was perfect and he didn't allow a run until the seventh, upping his record to 10-2.

The next day it rained, postponing the second game with the Pirates and that evening Raymond, ever the free spirit, decided to referee boxing matches at the Long Acre Athletic Association. The fight fans enjoyed his performance as much as they did the fighters. It also afforded Raymond some breathing room from the private detective hired by McGraw to shadow him with the intent of keeping him out of as many bars as possible.

The following day, June 17, Raymond managed to slip everyone, including McGraw, when he was given a ball during the game and told to warm up behind the right-field bleachers. In the top of the ninth, with New York holding on to a slim 3–2 lead over Pittsburgh, starter Drucke gave up a single and a walk to the first two batters. McGraw wasted little time in calling for Raymond, which turned out to be a big mistake. Bugs hit two batters, allowed two hits and a wild pitch. When the inning finally ended, the Pirates had scored four runs and the Giants lost 6–3.

"As McGraw learned afterwards, when Raymond had gone to warm up behind the right-field bleachers (out of the manager's sight), he'd headed for an all-too-familiar saloon across Eighth Avenue and traded the warm-up ball for several shots of cheap whiskey. Then he returned to the ballpark just in time but in no condition to take the mound."[8] The furious McGraw suspended Raymond indefinitely while rumors circled that the pitcher's days as a player for the New York Giants were numbered.

June 21

Staked to an early 6–0 lead, Mathewson coasted to his eleventh win of the season defeating Brooklyn 12–1 at Washington Park. Matty was replaced in the ninth by Crandall as the New York Giants were settling comfortably into second place, four and a half games behind the Chicago Cubs.

June 25

Larry Doyle's three-run homer in the seventh inning defeated Philadelphia 4–1 at the Polo Grounds and raised Mathewson's record to 12-2 (36 percent of the Giants' wins). Matty, who was making winning look easy, hurled another fine game allowing five hits and one run. The victory cut the Cubs' lead to three games.

June 29

It appeared to the slim Polo Grounds' crowd of 3,500 to be a guaranteed victory for New York as Mathewson entered the top of the ninth leading Philadelphia 2–0. Suddenly Matty's stuff deserted him and he allowed four hits and two runs as the Phillies tied the game 2–2. When the Giants failed to score in their half of the ninth and Matty checked Philadelphia in the tenth, the stage was set for a heroic finish. In the bottom of the tenth with one out and Merkle on second, Big Six slapped a single to center to drive in the winning run and chalk up his thirteenth win. Indeed truth is stranger than fiction.

July 4

New York won both ends of the holiday doubleheader at the Polo Grounds, defeating Brooklyn 6–5 in 13 innings in the morning and clobbering them in the afternoon 12–1. Mathewson came on in relief of Drucke in the first game with the score knotted at 5–5. He checked Brooklyn the rest of the way on three hits and when Merkle singled after Bridwell doubled in the thirteenth, Matty recorded his fourteenth win of the season and his two hundred fiftieth of his career.

The double victory narrowed the gap between the Giants and Cubs to one and a half games. As a point of interest, the following day McGraw lifted his suspension of Raymond and used him against Boston in a short relief stint, this time without incident.

July 6

In a weird scoring game, New York defeated Boston 8–3 in 14 innings at South End Grounds with Mathewson besting Buster Brown in a test of endurance. Boston scored three runs off Matty in the third inning. New York was blanked until the top of the ninth when it tied the game on reserve outfielder Beals Becker's home run. Both hurlers threw more goose eggs until the fourteenth inning when the Giants scored five times. Matty blanked Boston in the bottom of the fourteenth and improved his record to a league-leading 15-2.

July 14

After pitching 19 innings in three days, McGraw kept Mathewson out of the Chicago series, where the Giants still managed to take two of three games, and saved him for Pittsburgh. For a time it looked like McGraw's strategy would work. Mathewson entered the ninth with a 3–0 lead, but was roughed up for three runs and still had the bases loaded with two outs. At this point, in a rare display of jitters, Matty lost his poise. His first two pitches to Tommy Leach were balls and sent McGraw racing to the mound to yank his ace. Ames unfortunately completed the walk, forcing in the winning run and tagging Matty with his third loss of the season.

The next day when the Giants lost their third straight to Pittsburgh with Raymond walking in the winning run in the ninth, McGraw bit his lip and reluctantly turned the other cheek. But when he showed up drunk in the St. Louis clubhouse, McGraw's patience reached its limit. He suspended Raymond for the rest of the season. *The Sporting News* reported that the Giants fans were delighted with the suspension. "New Yorkers have soured on the eminent spit ball expert...."[9]

July 16

New York lost its fourth straight game and Mathewson his second of the series to Pittsburgh 6–3. Starter Crandall, hanging on to a slim 3–2 lead, weakened in the seventh and was relieved by Matty who allowed a long fly to tie the score. The eighth inning, however, was his demise. With two out and the bases empty the Pirates managed to score three runs on three hits and an error to put the game away. Mathewson's record went to 15-4 and New York was happy to get out of Pittsburgh.

July 19

New York, behind the strong pitching of Mathewson, defeated Cincinnati 6–4 at League Park when Chief Meyers singled in two runs in the eleventh inning. It was Matty's sixteenth victory and his third consecutive start in which the game went into extra innings. There was little doubt that Mathewson was a tireless worker and a Cincinnati killer. This was his fifteenth straight win over the Reds spanning three seasons.

July 23

New York jumped all over rookie "phenom" Ed Zmich for five runs in the first three innings and Mathewson coasted the rest of the way, defeating St. Louis 9–2 at Robison Field. Matty improved his record to 17-4. In spite of his consistent pitching, the Giants still slipped to third place.

The following day New York defeated St. Louis 4–1, ending another lousy road trip with a 7-9 record. The Giants started the trip on July 9 in second place, trailing Chicago by one and a half games. They ended in third place, six and a half behind the Cubs. On top of this McGraw had suspended Raymond for the season, a pitcher the Giants counted on heavily to help win the pennant. It was beginning to look like a long and bleak season for McGraw and his men.

July 28

The Giants lost to Philadelphia 3–1 despite the steady pitching of Mathewson and dropped another game behind the first-place Cubs. In eight innings Matty gave up only four hits but the Phillies bunched three of them in the first inning to score two runs. George McQuillan, borrowing a page from Mathewson's book, scattered eight hits and blanked the Giants until the ninth when they scored their only run. Matty's record stood at 17-5 but the torrid pace he had set the first two and a half months of the season had slowed considerably. Since July 6 his record was 3-3.

August 2

The first-place Chicago Cubs arrived at the Polo Grounds sporting a six and one-half–game lead over the Giants. When New York hammered Orval Overall for four runs in the first inning with Mathewson on the mound, it looked like an easy victory and a chance to cut the Cubs' lead. Two innings later Chicago tied the score and added a run in the fifth to win 5–4. It was Matty's sixth loss, easily the most disappointing of the season, and dropped the Giants another game in back of the Cubs.

Meanwhile, rowdyism in baseball continued unabated. This time the player was the Phillies star outfielder Sherwood Magee — who was having an outstanding season and would lead the league in five offensive categories, including batting average (.331) and RBIs (123) — fought with a rowdy spectator. The man, who was warned by police after taunting Magee and several other players, continued his verbal attacks and, after the game, followed the Phillies' to the clubhouse. At this point Magee hauled off and belted the man several times in the face causing streams of blood to flow freely. There were no arrests or charges filed.

August 5

After losing three straight to Chicago and falling to third place, nine and a half games back, McGraw called on Mathewson to help avoid an embarrassing sweep. It also gave his star pitcher a chance to redeem himself after the 4–0 lead he blew in the series opener. Matty stopped the Cubs cold on seven hits and the Giants went on to win the game 10–1. It was his eighteenth victory of the season.

In the American League, the venerable Connie Mack, manager of the Philadelphia Athletics, upset pitchers in both leagues with a wild suggestion to alter the rules. Mack made it clear he would like to see more hitting and, in his opinion, the best way would be to give the batter four strikes! One can only speculate as to the thoughts running through the minds of Mack's own pitching staff—Jack Coombs, Harry Morgan, Eddie Plank and Chief Bender. Oh, to be a fly on the clubhouse wall.

August 11

New York defeated Cincinnati in a doubleheader, 5–4 and 3–2, at the Polo Grounds. Mathewson pitched the first game and was far from puzzling. He was touched for 11 hits and issued four walks but as he so often preached and practiced, saved his strength for the "pinch," the tight situation when the game is on the line. The pinch came in the ninth inning when Matty loaded the bases with no outs. Cool and calm, he retired the next two batters on forced outs at the plate and ended the game by fanning Dick Egan. Matty's record was now 19-6.

August 15

In the battle for second place, now that the Chicago Cubs all but mathematically clinched the pennant, New York split a doubleheader with Pittsburgh, losing the first game 2–1 in 11 innings and winning the nightcap by the identical score. Mathewson was the hard-luck loser in the first game, a scoreless tie for ten innings, before a large Monday crowd of 15,000. The victim of an anemic offense, Matty pitched an outstanding game until he weakened in the eleventh. His demise began when shortstop Bridwell committed an error on a throw to Merkle at first. That miscue gave the Pirates the opportunity they were waiting for and they capitalized quickly on a single by Tommy Leach and a double by Fred Clarke to score two runs. The Giants countered in their half of the eleventh, but fell a run short as Lefty Leifield pitched a superb game for the victory.

August 19

New York began its final western road trip with a 9–3 win over Cincinnati behind the fine hurling of Mathewson. It was a personal triumph for the great right-hander for two reasons: it was his twentieth victory and marked the eighth consecutive season in which he had won 20 or more games; it was also his seventeenth straight win over the Reds.

The skimpy crowd of 1,500 caused *The New York Times* to write: "Christy Mathewson has come to be considered so invincible against the Reds that the crowds will not go to see him work in Cincinnati anymore unless it's a legal holiday."[10] Although the logic of the Cincinnati fans could be questioned, in a strange way, it was the quintessential compliment afforded a remarkable pitcher.

August 23

The Giants, after winning the opening game of the St. Louis series, lost the second game by a score of 4–1 as Mathewson had an off day. Big Six was tagged for 11 hits, including three doubles, in eight innings as he suffered his eighth loss of the season. Right from the start Matty was not himself; he gave up two runs in the first and another in the third. Frank Corridon, in his last year in the major leagues, hurled a remarkable game allowing the Giants one run on five hits. New York, in third place, remained three and a half games behind second-place Pittsburgh.

August 27

In the third game of the Chicago series, the Giants avenged the first two losses when they clobbered the Cubs 18–9 in a slugfest at West Side Park. In two hours and 30 minutes, seven pitchers (four for Chicago, three for New York) gave up a total of 38 hits (23 for the Giants, 15 for the Cubs). When the fiasco finally ended Mathewson was the lucky benefactor, picking up an easy victory after six innings of pitching. His record was now 21-8.

In St. Louis, Cardinals president Stanley Robison, in a forthright statement to the press, called for action to be taken to improve the competency of umpires. "The umpiring in the National League this season has been the worst in years," said Robison. "The poor work of the umpires is going on all over the circuit. There isn't a city in the circuit that hasn't some protest over the work of the men who are hired to judge games fairly. I hardly believe there is any favoritism shown, but the umpires are simply incompetent."[11]

Robison's harsh words represented yet another criticism that the men in blue had to overcome during the early years of their existence. Umpires would survive this attack and many more before they would be recognized as a competent group of professionals and an integral part of the game of baseball.

August 30

New York moved to within two games of second-place Pittsburgh by defeating the Pirates 5–2 and sweeping the three-game series. Mathewson recorded his twenty-second victory but was far from being in top form. He was hit hard and often. In fact, the eighth was the only inning the Pirates failed to get a hit. It was a game in which Matty displayed his competitiveness, coupled with clutch pitching. The sweep at Forbes Field sent a clear signal to the Pirates that the Giants were determined to finish the season in second place.

The next day New York fans received some troubling news when they learned that Mathewson would be entering the hospital after the season. He would seek treatment for an unidentified stomach ailment and breathing difficulty. The latter condition, according to teammates, was responsible for Matty's poor pitching. The author found no evidence that Mathewson ever entered a hospital after the season.

September 7

Apparently Mathewson had no trouble breathing when he pitched eight days later against Boston at the Polo Grounds. He shut them out on seven scattered hits and upped his record to 23-8, the best in the league. It was vintage Mathewson as the Giants continued to pressure the Pirates in their quest for second place. Young Rube Marquard, who was struggling as a Giants' starter, over the years marveled at Matty's excellence. "He never thought he was better than anybody else. It was just the way he carried himself. It was the way we saw him. But it was okay, because, what the hell, when you come down to it, he *was* different, and on that mound he *was* better than anyone else."[12]

September 10

New York took both ends of a doubleheader against last-place Boston by scores of 6–1 and 3–1 at the Polo Grounds. Crandall won the first game and Mathewson the second. Matty hurled another strong game, scattering five hits, fanning six and improving his record to 24-8. The victory also helped the Giants to keep the pressure on Pittsburgh.

September 13

New York opened a crucial six-game series with Pittsburgh at the Polo Grounds by splitting a doubleheader, losing the first 11–1 and winning the second 15–3. Mathewson was pummeled in the first game for 11 hits, five runs and was removed after eight innings.

September 16

Three days later Mathewson returned to the mound and avenged his earlier battering at the hands of Pittsburgh by trimming them 3–1 on five hits. The victory improved his record to 25-9 while the Giants moved to within half a game of the Pirates. New York's relentless pursuit of second place was finally paying off.

September 20

New York split a doubleheader against St. Louis, losing the first game 5-1 and winning the nightcap 3-2 for Mathewson's twenty-sixth victory. Matty was hit hard, allowing ten hits but also fanned ten batters, which helped him get out of some sticky spots. The win moved the Giants into second place, percentage points ahead of the Pirates.

September 24

New York's final game of the season with Chicago pitted the two great rivals, Mathewson and Three Finger Brown, against each other for the first time all year. It was a strange game which saw Brown pounded for four runs in the first inning, eventually leaving after six trailing 5-1, and Mathewson blowing the lead by allowing Chicago to score two runs in each of the eighth and ninth innings, aided by Doyle's sloppy fielding. In the ninth, however, Doyle turned the boos into cheers when he singled home the winning run. The final score was New York 6, Chicago 5. Brown took the loss while Matty's record went to 27-9.

October 8

It was two weeks before Mathewson pitched again, his final game of the regular season, and during this period several important developments occurred. Chicago clinched the pennant, the Giants clinched second place and, to the delight of the New York fans, Giants' owner Brush agreed to meet the second-place New York Yankees in a best-of-seven playoff for the bragging rights of the city.

Matty's final regular season appearance against Brooklyn was a dandy. He allowed seven hits, struck out ten and left after nine innings with the score tied 1-1. Ames relieved in the tenth and wild-pitched the winning run home. Although Matty's fine effort was wasted, it did serve as a preview of what the New York fans could expect to see during postseason play.

On October 13, shortly after the conclusion of the 1910 season, the Giants met the Yankees in postseason play. Commented author Noel Hynd in *The Giants of the Polo Grounds,* "Often such city series go the way of All-Star Games—interesting contests, but ones in which the athletes go through the motions. This series, scheduled for the best of seven games, was something more. It was, in fact, a harbinger of other autumns later in the century when New York teams squared off against one another."[13]

Actually, the series turned out to be another in a long list of personal triumphs for Mathewson. Before large and enthusiastic crowds, Matty dominated the Yankees with ease. He won games one, four and six, all complete efforts by scores of 5–1, 5–1, 6–3, and saved game three for Drucke. In 30 innings Matty walked one batter. The Yankees managed to win two games and tie another.

It was also a whopping financial success. Total attendance for the seven games exceeded 103,000. Each Giants player received $1,110.62, and young Art Fletcher used his share to marry his childhood sweetheart, Blanche Dieu. Actually, the players' share was more than in some series between pennant-winning teams.

Playoff performance aside, Mathewson turned in another great baseball season, providing fans throughout the country with consistent pitching excellence and durability. Matty's stats in 1910 were simply awesome. He led the league with 27 wins and 27 complete games. He was fourth in ERA (1.89), second in strikeouts (184), second in fewest walks per nine innings (1.70) and second in innings pitched (318⅓).

Christy Mathewson, once the idol of America, was now elevated to a new status, that of a living legend. Wearing this mantle of adoration, Matty would lead the Giants to three consecutive National League Pennants and turn New York into a city of insatiable baseball zealots.

Chapter 13
M and M Boys, 1911

W	L	Pct	ERA
26	13	.667	1.99

The 1911 season reestablished the New York Giants as the premier baseball club in the National League. Not since 1905 had the Giants won the pennant, finding themselves frantically chasing either Chicago or Pittsburgh. But 1911 was different. It began a string of three fantastic years in which the Giants would win pennants with speed, aggressiveness and a grand style of play. It was the year McGraw's youngsters came of age and flourished. Larry Doyle, their new captain, emerged as the club's leader while pitcher Rube Marquard, under the careful instruction and guidance of coach Wilbert Robinson, blossomed into stardom. Mathewson, who had been averaging 26 victories a season since 1901, had another great year.

Speed was the name of the game for New York in 1911. The team stole 347 bases, a record which still stands today. Josh Devore led the club with 61, followed by Fred Snodgrass (51), Fred Merkle (49), Red Murray and Buck Herzog (acquired in July) with 48 each.

As McGraw confessed later, "Mighty few ball clubs ever put together were faster than that combination. That, I think, was the greatest base-running club I ever saw. We stole so many bases—led the league so far in that respect—that we were jokingly referred to as having literally stolen the pennant."[1]

It was a roller-coaster season highlighted by tragic as well as comic events. Along serious lines, New York baseball fans were shocked to read about the devastating fire which destroyed the Polo Grounds a mere two days after the season opened! It was believed the fire began after midnight, possibly due to a tossed cigarette. The blaze, which was described as one of the most spectacular in New York City history, destroyed the grandstand and everything else except a section of the left-field bleachers.

Brush, who was in exceedingly poor health and appeared in a wheelchair to assess the damage, decided to forge ahead and build a new concrete and steel structure, as did the Shibe family in Philadelphia with Shibe Park and Barney Dreyfuss in Pittsburgh with Forbes Field. Remark-

"Chief" Meyers, a Cahuilla Indian, who caught Mathewson from 1909 to 1915 claimed Matty was "the greatest that ever lived" (photo courtesy National Baseball Library, Cooperstown, N.Y.).

ably, the new Polo Grounds, which would seat 35,000, was completed in late June! In the meantime, Brush quickly accepted the gracious offer of New York Yankees owner Frank Farrell to use his grounds, Hilltop Park, on a temporary basis.

On a more tragic human note, the demon alcohol finally won the battle with Bugs Raymond. After winning six games McGraw, suspecting

Raymond of obtaining money through nefarious means and using it to imbibe, slapped him with a $200 fine and suspension. After 1911 Bugs Raymond would never pitch in the major leagues again. He died in September 1912 of a blow to the head in a barroom scuffle, probably the way Bugs would have wanted his end to come.

On a more hilarious note, McGraw added a new member to the club, supposedly a pitcher by the name of Charles "Victory" Faust. Stretching the powers of credulity, some argued that Faust was responsible for at least 20 victories as a good luck charm and morale builder. Regardless, the Faust story is a delightful one and an important addition to baseball lore. Here's what happened.

Early in the season in St. Louis, a tall lanky man in a dark suit and derby hat approached McGraw claiming a fortune teller told him that if he pitched for the New York Giants they would win the pennant. McGraw, always looking for the winning edge, gave Faust a brief tryout. Not surprisingly, McGraw immediately discovered the stranger could not pitch. Going along with the farce, however, McGraw kept the crazy guy, in uniform, on the Giants' bench throughout the four-game series (New York won three) in St. Louis. Tiring quickly of the charade, McGraw scooted out on Faust, leaving him in St. Louis when the club headed for other cities in the circuit. When the Giants arrived back in New York, the unsuspecting Faust was waiting for them. After the Giants won a few more games with Faust hanging around, McGraw relented and made him part of the club.

Coincidence or not, the Giants continued to win and many pointed to Faust as the reason. "The players believed in him," commented Mathewson, "and none would have let him go if it had been necessary to support him out of their own pockets. And we did win." Added Mathewson, "Charley, with his monologue and great good humor, kept the players in high spirits throughout the journey, and the feeling prevailed that we couldn't lose with him along."[2]

In spite of Faust, who was eventually committed to an institution in 1914, New York would never have won the National League pennant in 1911 without Mathewson and Marquard—the first M and M boys (not to be confused with Mickey Mantle and Roger Maris years later). Between them they accounted for 50 of the Giants' 99 victories. Matty led the club with 26 wins and the league in earned run average with a sparkling 1.99. He had become a virtual pitching machine, constantly fine-tuning his craft which resulted in uncanny consistency year in, year out. Marquard finally fulfilled his star potential, finishing the season with an outstanding 24-7 mark and a league-leading .774 winning percentage. He also topped the league with 237 strikeouts.

With this awesome pitching duo plus aggressive and talented everyday players, the Giants began a three-year span of baseball glory in the city of New York.

The Season

April 13

After the Giants were blanked 2-0 by Philadelphia in the season opener the day before at the Polo Grounds, Mathewson took his turn on the mound and was lambasted by the Phillies 6-1. He gave up an unheard of 14 hits in eight innings. Although Matty tried in vain, nothing in his repertoire was working, including his famed fadeaway. Conversely, the Phillies' Jack Rowan pitched a nifty three-hitter, baffling the Giants throughout the game.

The next day the baseball community was stunned when it discovered the Polo Grounds had burned down. With an 0-2 start, the Giants now found themselves desperately searching for a new ball park. The search ended as fast as it began, however, when Brush accepted Farrell's offer to play at Hilltop park. The Giants' new home had a significantly smaller seating capacity (16,000 versus 27,000) but the dimensions were longer, including the famous center field at the Polo Grounds. The measurements at Hilltop were: left field (365), center field (542), right field (400) compared to the Polo Grounds' left field (277), center field (433) and right field (256). Clearly, it was not a hitter's park.

April 25

Mathewson, in his second start of the season, defeated Boston 3-1 in typical fashion, scattering seven hits and pitching out of tight spots. The cunning veteran, after his poor opening performance, put to rest (once again) premature talk that he was beginning to slip. The victory was the Giants' fifth straight at Hilltop Park where they had yet to taste defeat.

April 29

Mathewson recorded his second win of the season before a large crowd of 15,000 at Washington Park, defeating Brooklyn 7-3. The Giants jumped to a fast four-run lead in the first inning on three hits and some sloppy play by Brooklyn, now called the Dodgers. Two more runs in the sixth iced the game and moved the Giants into second place behind the Philadelphia Phillies, who were playing exciting baseball.

Meanwhile, work at the Polo Grounds was progressing rapidly; the debris was being removed and the surveyors conducting the necessary preliminary work for the erection of the new concrete stands.

May 4

Mathewson easily defeated Boston 7-2 at South End Grounds for his third victory of the season. Spotted a 6-0 lead after six innings, Matty coasted the rest of the way. The Giants were now in second place with a record of 11-5 and throughout May would bounce between second and third place before moving into first at the end of the month.

Off the field Brush announced that he had obtained a long lease on the Polo Grounds from Mrs. Harriet G. Coogan and plans for the construction of a new steel and concrete stadium were moving rapidly. Although alternative locations were considered, Brush decided to stay at the present site mainly because he believed fans were used to traveling to the Polo Grounds and he didn't want to do anything to disrupt the habit.

"Most spectators reached the grounds by a special elevated express from Wall Street, while other fans spent eight cents for an East Side el to 125th Street and a transfer to the Eighth Avenue trolley which ran right to the park," claimed author Steven A. Riess. "Wealthier patrons came in carriages or automobiles. Some downtown businessmen might hire a carriage and split the expensive fare..."[3]

May 9

Mathewson's record climbed to 4-1 when he defeated his old rival Mordecai "Three Finger" Brown, in their first meeting of the year, 5–3. A driving rain limited the crowd at Hilltop Park to 9,000, but the game was well played considering the wet ball, slippery grounds and darkened sky. The pitching between the two greats was evenly matched until the fifth inning. In the fifth, with the score knotted at 2–2, Three Finger Brown lost his control. He walked two, hit another plus a sacrifice put the Giants in the lead 3–2. They added two more runs in the seventh to clinch the victory.

May 13

The Giants scored 13 runs in a marathon first inning and went on to beat St. Louis at Hilltop Park 19–5 before 10,000 bewildered fans. McGraw, seeing a golden opportunity to save his star right-hander for another day, yanked him after one inning. Marquard pitched eight innings and was hit freely but did manage to strike out 13 batters. The official scorer credited Mathewson with the victory, his fifth of the season and one of the easiest of his entire career.

The next day National League president Thomas J. Lynch lashed out at players who verbally abused umpires and threatened to issue suspensions and heavy fines if it continued. A former umpire, he found the language to be outrageous and intolerable and was ready to crack down. In spite of Lynch and others, it would be years before umpires gained the respect they deserved.

May 18

In the first meeting of the year, New York lost to Pittsburgh 6-1 as Mathewson was sent to the bench after allowing three runs in the seventh inning. At that point the game appeared out of reach with pitcher Babe Adams in control for the Pirates. Matty gave up ten hits in his seven innings of work and clearly was not fooling anyone. His record now stood at 5-2.

Construction at the Polo Grounds continued at a breakneck pace with crews working night and day. Completion was targeted for June 28, the day the Giants were scheduled to play their first home game after returning from their western trip. It was an ambitious goal and, amazingly, it was met.

May 23

Mathewson continued to cast his magic spell over the Cincinnati Reds when he defeated them 7-2 at Hilltop Park. Matty was in trouble only once and that came in the seventh when the Reds loaded the bases with no one out and a 3-0 count on David Altizer. Cool as ice, Big Six threw the next two pitches for strikes and then on the payoff delivery, his fadeaway, induced Altizer to hit back to the box for a quick double play, home to first. After the next batter walked, loading the bases again, Mathewson got Fred Beck to bounce weakly to Merkle at first and Cincinnati failed to score. The victory increased Matty's streak to 18 straight over the Reds!

May 26

Bugs Raymond, pitching a fine game, took a 3-1 lead into the eighth inning but in lightning fashion allowed the Phillies to tie the game and put runners on second and third with only one out. With little time to warm up, Mathewson was rushed to the mound. Mickey Doolan, the first batter Matty faced, flied to right where Devore caught the ball and with a perfect throw to Chief Meyers nipped the runner at the plate, tagging up from third. Matty finished the job in the ninth by blanking Philadelphia to gain his seventh win of the season and move the Giants past the Phillies into first place.

May 27

Mathewson came back the next day and hurled a masterful 2-0 shutout over the Philadelphia Phillies, further tightening the Giants' grip on first place. Before a standing-room-only crowd (thousands were turned away) at the Hilltop, Matty allowed eight hits, didn't walk a batter while fanning six. The Giants, led by Mathewson and Marquard and an aggressive style of play, were now beginning to jell, which was clearly reflected in the standings.

June 5

It looked like Mathewson was going to suffer his third loss of the season when the Giants entered the top of the ninth at West Side Park in Chicago, trailing the Cubs by a slim 1–0. That all changed abruptly when the Giants scored seven times, led by Merkle who tripled and doubled in the inning. Matty pitched an outstanding game, rarely using his fadeaway but relying on his fast ball and pinpoint control. It evened the series with Chicago at two apiece and kept New York in first place.

McGraw remained in New York during the Chicago series, tending to his ailing wife. He joined the club in Pittsburgh and while waiting for the players at the hotel was told that Bugs Raymond was missing! While everyone was puzzling over what to do about the missing pitcher, in walked Raymond without a care in the world. After a short meeting with McGraw, Raymond confessed he had ridden in the cab with the engineer, a friend he had worked with years earlier. Keeping tabs on Bugs was like picking up Jell-O with a fork and it appeared McGraw's patience was wearing thin.

June 9

Mathewson wrapped up the final game of the Pittsburgh series with a 6–3 victory maintaining the Giants' tenuous hold on first place. Although not at his best, Matty was steady throughout the game, relying on his exacting knowledge of each hitter. As McGraw once said, "From the first day, it seemed, Matty carefully studied all opposing batters. Once he learned what they could hit and what they couldn't, he never forgot. In a few years he had in that wonderful brain of his a chart of nearly every ball player in the National League."[4]

June 13

Mathewson was beating Cincinnati so easily and so often his victories were becoming ho-hum affairs. In this game, which Matty won 5–2, he allowed 11 hits and even walked three batters, but the Reds could not shake the jinx. It was his nineteenth straight win over Cincinnati. Matty's record went to 11-2 and the Giants continued to move in and out of first place.

June 17

Sometimes it's better to be lucky than good. This was the case when Mathewson had the misfortune of matching up with St. Louis right-hander Bob Harmon, who would pitch one of the best games of his mediocre career. The combination of Harmon tossing a three-hitter coupled with flawless fielding and outstanding plays by St. Louis was simply too much for Matty to overcome in spite of his two-hit gem. The Giants lost 2–1. Matty's won-lost mark was now 11-3.

The day before, after a miserable performance by Raymond against St. Louis (eight runs in six innings), McGraw, strongly suspecting that his pitcher was drinking again, hit him with a $200 fine and suspension. A week later, Raymond turned up in Connecticut playing ball for Winsted, but he quickly wore out his welcome there too. It happened this way: after partying all night, he pitched the next day against Torrington and was driven from the mound after seven innings. Torrington won 4–0. It was his last appearance for Winsted. It was also the beginning of the final chapter for Bugs Raymond. He never returned to major league baseball.

The amusing stories surrounding Raymond are endless. One of the funniest was told by his teammate Marquard about his spitball. "What a terrific spitball pitcher he was," commented Marquard. "Bugs drank a lot, you know, and sometimes it seemed like the more he drank the better he pitched [it's doubtful McGraw would have agreed]. They used to say he didn't spit on the ball; he blew his breath on it, and the ball would come up drunk."[5]

June 21

Four days later, after the tough loss to St. Louis, Mathewson returned to the mound to face Boston at South End Grounds and hurled a marvelous game, blanking the Rustlers on seven hits. The final score was 4–0 and Matty's record went to 12-3. The next day the Giants ended their first western road trip with a respectable 9-7 record when they defeated St. Louis 5–4. The seesaw battle with Chicago for first place now began to intensify.

June 24

Before 20,000 noisy fans at Washington Park, Mathewson defeated Brooklyn 7–4 for his thirteenth win of the season. Although Matty was hit frequently and on occason flirted with danger, his steady pitching in clutch situations paid off. He fanned seven, aiding his cause.

In Cincinnati umpire Bill Klem got himself into serious trouble when he let his emotions get the best of him and poked St. Louis manager Roger Bresnahan in the face. The incident occurred over a disputed called third strike to pinch hitter Bresnahan, which ended the game. For the punch Klem was fined $50 by embarrassed National League president Lynch who in mid–May lashed out at players for verbally abusing umpires.

June 28

As predicted, the newly constructed Polo Grounds opened for business a mere two and a half months after a fire destroyed most of the stadium. Although much work remained, the lower tier of the steel and concrete grandstand, which seated 16,000, was complete while construction continued on the upper tier. The unburned wooden bleachers in the outfield contained another 10,000 seats.

Surprisingly, with Mathewson on the mound, only 6,000 partisan fans showed up to witness the inauguration. Matty added his personal charm to the festive day by tossing a 3–0 shutout over Boston, his second of the season. Although he allowed nine hits, most came with the bases empty.

Interestingly, the Giants won 21 of the 29 games at Hilltop Park for a marvelous winning percentage of .724. Matty was 6–1 at the Yankees' home grounds.

July 3

Before 15,000 raucous fans at Philadelphia's Baker Bowl Mathewson proved he was mortal in the eighth inning when he weakened and allowed the Phillies to bunch four hits, including a double and triple, and score three runs. The outburst made the score 7–3 in favor of Philadelphia and that's how the game ended with Matty being tagged with his fourth loss of the season. In spite of the defeat the Giants held on to their slim one-game first-place lead over Chicago.

July 5

Two days later the Phillies, trying to prove the 7–3 victory over Mathewson was no fluke, did it again, this time by a score of 6–4. Matty had little on the ball as Philadelphia garnered 14 hits in eight innings with George Paskert, a lifetime .268 hitter, going four for four. In the second game of the doubleheader Marquard, who was now winning regularly, coasted to an easy 10–1 victory but the Giants still slipped to third place.

July 10

Mathewson lost his third straight game, a newsworthy event for the celebrated hurler. Unlike his two losses in Philadelphia, which he deserved, Matty pitched a fine game at the Polo Grounds but was the victim of what *The New York Times* called "tissue-paper support." Matty lost 3–2 in ten innings with all the Chicago runs resulting from errors, one each by Doyle, Art Fletcher and Al Bridwell in the second, sixth and tenth innings.

In spite of his reputation for self-control and forgiving teammate errors, Mathewson must have had, at least, a twinge of anger over the tough loss. Matty's record stood at 14-6 and the Giants found themselves in an exciting three-way pennant race with Chicago and Philadelphia.

July 15

Mathewson opened the series against Cincinnati at the Polo Grounds and eked out a victory with determined pitching in the ninth inning. Entering the last inning Matty had a comfortable 4–1 lead, but when the Reds scored two runs and had two men on, the 16,000 Giants fans began to squirm in their seats. Matty prevailed, however, by inducing Cuban-born Armendo Marsans to ground out weakly to Bridwell at short. It was his twentieth consecutive victory against the Reds and upped his record to 15-6.

Merkle was the hero of the day, driving in all four New York runs when he singled in the second inning and blasted a three-run homer in the sixth. Earlier in the week official league statistics showed the Giants were literally off and running since opening day. New York claimed five of the top ten base stealers: Murray (30), Devore (28), Merkle (24), Snodgrass (23) and Doyle (18).

July 20

The St. Louis Cardinals, who were surprising baseball experts around the country with their fourth-place showing, shocked New York fans when they knocked Mathewson out of the box in the second inning, scoring five runs on five hits. McGraw surmised his star pitcher did not have it on this day, yanked him in favor of Otis Crandall, hoping to use Matty again in the series. The final score was St. Louis 8, New York 5.

Never one to let personal feelings stand in the way of improving his club, McGraw pulled off a shrewd trade sending shortstop Bridwell and substitute first baseman Henry Gowdy to Boston for Charley Herzog, who had played with the Giants in 1908. There was little love lost between Herzog and McGraw but it didn't prevent the manager from acquiring this .302 hitter (at the time) who could run like a rabbit. McGraw was dead serious about winning and was determined to run his club right into a pennant.

July 22

Two days after being rudely chased by St. Louis in the second inning, Mathewson returned to the mound to defeat the Cardinals 10–2. McGraw's strategy worked! It was a day of triumph for Matty as a huge crowd of 28,000 witnessed their hero at his best — pinpoint control, blazing speed and a fadeaway that at times broke a foot wide. Because of the large gathering, one eager fan was perched high above the crowd on a steel girder. The precarious position restricted excessive cheering but was the best seat in the house.

July 26

"When the Redlegs saw Matty ... walk out on the field and into the box in the eighth inning today they lost all hope of a victory, for Matty has the hoodoo sign on them. As a result New York won out in the ninth inning by a score of 5 to 3," reported *The New York Times*.[6] Matty had more than a hoodoo sign on the Reds. He had perfect control of his fast ball, curve and fadeaway. With the game deadlocked in the eighth, Mathewson replaced Hooks Wiltse and prevented further scoring. Then in the ninth, the Giants scored two runs with Mathewson knocking in one. Matty finished the job by blanking Cincinnati in the bottom of the ninth. It was his seventeenth victory of the season and twenty-first straight against the Reds. The Giants split the series with the Reds, two games apiece, and continued to bounce between second and third place as they headed for St. Louis.

July 28

Mathewson opened the series in St. Louis and lost to the Cardinals 5–2, aided by five New York errors. Matty was far from puzzling. He allowed 11 hits but could have had a better fate if it was not for the ragged support by his teammates. The loss kept the Giants in third place with a record of 53-36, three and a half games back of league-leading Chicago.

New York won the next three games from St. Louis with Marquard winning two of them—a four-hit shutout on July 29 before 23,000, one of the largest crowds in St. Louis history, and a five-hitter two days later. It brought his record to 13-4 and coupled with Matty's 17-8 the M and M boys accounted for 53 percent of the Giants' victories.

August 2

New York scored five runs in the first two innings while Mathewson was peppered for 15 hits (all singles) but held on to beat Pittsburgh 8–4 before 10,000 fans at Forbes Field. Struggling most of the game, Matty was bailed out of tight spots by four double plays. His record was now 18-8.

August 7

It had the earmarks of a classic baseball game—two outstanding rivals, Mathewson and Three Finger Brown, facing each other with clubs battling for the National League pennant. It turned out to be anything but memorable. Chicago and Brown won 8–6 but it was far from pretty. Brown allowed 13 hits, Matty ten and each struggled to keep the game from getting out of control. Matty's record was now 18-9 and the Giants were back in third, trailing first-place Chicago by two.

Although Mathewson and Brown were rivals, Matty had a great deal of respect for the great pitcher, as did McGraw. In fact, one of Matty's favorite stories involved both McGraw and Brown. One day, according to Matty, McGraw was warming up with Art Wilson, his young reserve catcher, when he decided to try and throw a curve like Brown, with his first finger bent, as if missing. He tried several times and various ways to determine if Three Finger had an advantage, but without much success. "No, I guess he doesn't get anything extra with the abbreviated finger," remarked McGraw. "But that's lucky for you fellows, because, if I thought he did, I'd have a surgeon out here tomorrow operating on the first fingers of each of you pitchers."[7]

August 11

New York returned to the Polo Grounds after completing a less than exciting 7-7 road trip and opened with Mathewson who dispelled the rumors being whispered by some fickle Giants watchers that his fast ball had slowed and his fadeaway was no longer doing its crazy tricks. Given a 4–0 lead after two innings, Matty spread out 11 hits, hurled brilliantly with men on base and blanked Philadelphia 6–0. So much for rumors.

August 16

On this day in August Christy Mathewson's total domination of the Cincinnati Reds reached its zenith and stretched believability to the breaking point. Like rubbing salt in an open wound, Matty tossed a brilliant two-hitter and in the process threw only 92 balls! As far as anyone could tell it established a National League record for the least amount of pitches in a nine-inning game. The final score was New York 6, Cincinnati 1. It was Matty's twenty-second consecutive victory over Cincinnati and for the season his record was 20-9.

The next day *The New York Times*, in its account of the game, compared Mathewson's supremacy over Cincinnati to the movement of an arthropod. "It's about as hard for 'Big Six' to beat the Reds as it is for a centipede to crawl."

August 19

Mathewson's supremacy over Cincinnati finally came to an end in the second game of a doubleheader at the Polo Grounds, but not before he saved the first game in relief of Wiltse, who had replaced Marquard. Matty came away with a no-decision, preserving the Giants' 5–4 win by blanking the Reds over the last two innings.

In the second game, before a crowd of 35,000, Cincinnati caught up with Mathewson. Perhaps it would be more accurate to say the law of averages finally nailed the great pitcher. Either way, the Reds chased Matty after five innings, beating him 7–4 for the first time since May 18, 1908! It was a marvelous streak that extended from June 17, 1908, to August 16, 1911, and came two shy of Mathewson's twenty-four straight over St. Louis.

Quietly the name of Charles "Victory" Faust began to make its appearance in the press and the so-called good luck charm would be the topic of conversation throughout the remainder of the season.

August 24

The Giants moved into a first-place tie with Chicago when they split a doubleheader with Pittsburgh, and the Cubs lost to Brooklyn 6–5 in ten innings. Before a jam-packed crowd of 30,000 and a day threatened with dark clouds and an occasional sprinkle of rain, Mathewson lost a close game, 3–1. He pitched well, giving up two runs (only one earned) on six hits in eight innings. In fact, the outcome might have been different were it not for an error by Herzog and bad judgment by Doyle in the sixth.

In the nightcap, Marquard threw a masterful two-hitter. He fanned 11 in the faltering light with an invincible fast ball and was finally earning the $11,000 that Brush had shelled out in 1908.

The next day the Giants gained sole possession of first when they beat Pittsburgh 3–2. They would remain in first place for the rest of the season and, as many believed, in large part due to the ever-present Faust.

August 26

New York increased its first-place lead over Chicago behind the steady pitching of Mathewson, defeating Pittsburgh 6–2. It was Matty's twenty-first victory and without the services of Honus Wagner at short the Pirates were no match for the hustling Giants. Tommy Leach, who had not played the infield on a steady basis for several years and then at third, filled in for Wagner. He made three errors, all of which were costly.

New York management was happy to announce that for the first 11 playing days at the Polo Grounds, since returning from the western trip, the average attendance was 23,864. Some claimed it a record unequaled in the history of baseball and that attendance would continue to soar when the upper grandstand was completed. The glory days of the New York Giants were back and with a vengeance.

September 1

The M and M boys combined brilliant pitching to sweep a doubleheader from Philadelphia 3–2 and 2–0 at Baker Bowl. Mathewson won the first game, his twenty-second of the season, in typical fashion scattering ten hits and using his head as much as his arm. The days' honors, however, were captured by the young left-hander, Marquard, who narrowly missed a perfect game when he allowed a hit in the fifth inning and the only runner to reach first base. It was a magnificent display of pitching and a clear signal to Giants fans it was time to bury the "$11,000 lemon" tag.

In an amusing sidelight, in Detroit, 25-year-old Ty Cobb on his way to a career high .420 batting average was arrested for speeding and found guilty, but the sentence was suspended. The arresting officer swore Cobb was going 24 miles per hour in a 15-mile-per-hour area.

September 7

Mathewson lost his twelfth game of the season while Chicago won a doubleheader which narrowed the Giants' first-place lead to mere percentage points. It was a hard loss to sustain since the winning run was registered by Brooklyn in the top of the ninth with two out and nobody on base. Matty walked Bert Tooley and when Jake Daubert skied to Snodgrass in right center it looked like the inning was over, that is, until Snodgrass dropped the ball with Tooley scoring. The game ended Brooklyn 4, New York 3.

September 9

New York and Brooklyn played to a 4–4 tie before 8,000 fans at the Polo Grounds in a game that was hampered by a steady rain from the first inning on. The Giants used three pitchers: Crandall, Wiltse and finally Mathewson for two innings. New York tied the game in the ninth when Merkle scored from third on a fly to right. With darkness descending fast, umpire Jim Johnstone called the game.

September 12

New York beat Boston twice, a 9–6 slugfest and an 11–2 romp, at South End Grounds to increase its lead to two full games over Chicago. Mathewson won the second game but only pitched two innings when the Giants hammered the 44-year-old Cy Young (it was the incomparable Hall of Famer's last season) for eight hits and nine runs, including two home runs by Merkle and another by Doyle, in less than three innings. McGraw, realizing the victory was in the bag, yanked Matty and replaced him with Crandall. Mathewson's record now stood at 23–12.

The double victory marked the beginning of a period when the Giants would win 19 of 23 games played away from home. Mathewson recalled that wonderful time and also McGraw's efforts to keep his players focused on the game. "On the last western trip the Giants made in the season of 1911, when they won the pennant by taking eighteen games out of twenty-two games, McGraw refused to permit any of the men to play cards," said Matty. "He realized that often the stakes ran high and that the losers brooded over the money which they lost and were thinking of this rather than the game when on the ball field. It hurt their playing, so there were no cards."[8]

Although Mathewson's recollection of the games won on the road trip (18 of 22) is not accurate, his point about card playing clearly shows McGraw left no stone unturned to assure his players were focused on the game.

September 14

New York outslugged Boston 13–9 at South End Grounds to sweep the four-game series and move four games ahead of Chicago in the National League pennant race. Although Mathewson was not involved in the decision, he played an important role when he relieved Wiltse in the eighth and stopped the Rustlers' rally cold. When the Giants scored six runs in the ninth to lead 13–4, McGraw took out Matty, who had pitched to only two batters. Crandall came on to pitch the ninth and wiped the smile from McGraw's face when he allowed seven hits, five runs and nearly blew a cinch victory.

September 16

Before 20,000 partisan fans at spacious Forbes Field, New York began its final western swing by defeating Pittsburgh 6–2. Marquard started and pitched a fine game, but needed help from Mathewson in the eighth inning. Matty held the Pirates hitless over one and two-thirds innings and preserved the victory for Marquard, his twenty-first of the season.

Prior to the game the large crowd was treated to some good-natured fun when New York's good luck charm, Charlie Faust, pitched to the mighty Honus Wagner. As reported by the press, the Flying Dutchman whiffed on three pitches amid a storm of applause. A lifetime .327 hitter, it's safe to assume Wagner was playing to the crowd.

The following day (Sunday) New York and Pittsburgh were idle which gave Mathewson an opportunity to indulge in his favorite pastime, checkers. He visited the local YMCA and challenged all comers, playing eight games, winning two, tying five and losing one.

September 18

New York won its eighth game in a row, beating Pittsburgh 7-2 behind the steady hurling of Mathewson. With a four-game lead and the season quickly drawing to a close, the Giants were playing with supreme confidence, both at the plate and in the field and, equally important, as they had done all year, they were running with abandon. In this game the Giants stole eight bases while Matty was baffling Pittsburgh on four hits. The victory upped the Giants' lead to five games and Matty's record to 24-12.

September 20

New York increased its winning streak to 11 straight with a doubleheader victory over St. Louis, 4-0 and 7-4, at Robison Field. Marquard spun a masterful four-hit whitewash in the first game. The nightcap was a dandy seesaw battle. The Giants blew a 2-0 lead but came back to overcome a 4-2 deficit by scoring five runs in the last two innings. Matty pitched one-third of an inning in relief of Crandall and was ineffective, allowing a triple with two men on. The game was called after eight innings when rain and darkness settled in. Wiltse was credited with the victory.

September 21

The Giants' winning streak came to an end, but not until it had reached 12 straight, when they defeated St. Louis 3-2 in the first game of a doubleheader. Mathewson came to the rescue in the ninth inning when Wiltse, who had pitched a fine game to this point, weakened. St. Louis touched him for a run and had a man on second with one out when McGraw called on Matty. Big Six induced the first batter to ground out and then fanned pinch hitter Wally Smith on three fadeaways. The streak ended when New York lost the second game 8-7.

Earlier in the day Matty paid a quick visit to the St. Louis Stock Exchange to check some quotations. He was mobbed by a horde of messenger boys who coaxed him into rolling up a ball of paper and demonstrating how to throw the famous fadeaway. Matty's interest in stocks was no mere passing fancy. Some claimed he was a financial wizard who invested heavily in the market and quite successfully. Doyle regretted more than once that he did not take some of Matty's tips.

Mathewson's wife, Jane, had a more modest opinion of her husband's financial acumen. "It was sort of a hobby with Christy," she said. "He was wonderful at it, and he constantly read books on finance. But he never accepted financial favors from anyone. He could have made thousands of dollars. He was offered many products wholesale, but he always refused to accept anything on the basis of what he was as a ball player."[10]

September 23

Mathewson registered his twenty-fifth victory when he defeated Cincinnati 6–2 and moved New York ahead of Chicago by eight full games. The Giants' juggernaut was in high gear and nothing could stop it. It was now simply a matter of time before the National League pennant race would be officially over. The local fans continued to be frustrated in their desire to beat Mathewson at home, an event that last occurred on May 18, 1908!

September 28

On September 27 the Giants moved into Chicago's West Side Park for a four-game series sporting a comfortable seven and one-half–game lead. It was the Cubs' absolute last chance to pull off a miracle. When they won the series' opener McGraw wasted no time and called on Mathewson, the next day, to stop the Cubs. But Matty ran smack into his old nemesis Joe Tinker and wound up on the short end of a 2–1 score when the shortstop doubled home two runs in the third inning. It was Matty's thirteenth and last loss of the season. More importantly, it reduced the Giants' lead to five and a half, put a scare into McGraw and kept a glimmer of hope alive in the Chicago camp. It was short-lived, however. Red Ames hurled a 3–1 gem on September 30 and Marquard blanked Chicago 5–0 the next day. These two clutch victories all but closed out the season for the Cubs.

In the American League Connie Mack's Philadelphia Athletics clinched their fourth pennant in 11 years by defeating Detroit 11–5 behind star rightfielder Jack Coombs (28-12).

October 4

The New York Giants, behind the superb pitching of Mathewson, defeated Brooklyn 2–0 at Washington Park and mathematically clinched the National League pennant. Brooklyn threatened to score on several occasions but Matty bore down and escaped without allowing a run. It was his fifth shutout of the year and an appropriate climax to an exciting pennant race. Matty ended the season 26-13. The following week McGraw wisely rested Matty as the Giants played out the schedule and finished with a 99-54 record, seven and a half games ahead of Chicago.

Brightening the final week were two grand appearances by the enigmatic Charlie Faust. He first pitched against Boston at the Polo Grounds on October 7 before 1,000 shivering loyalists. The right-hander hurled one inning and gave up a hit and a run. He also had an opportunity to bat and was allowed to circle the diamond as the Boston infielders purposely threw wildly to each advancing base until Faust headed for home, where he was finally thrown out. The fans loved it. It was repeated again on October 12 when Faust pitched the ninth inning against Brooklyn in the second game of the season-ending doubleheader. He began warming up at noon and by the time he entered the game he was exhausted, but he allowed only one hit. Like the Boston players earlier, Brooklyn allowed Faust to steal second and third, after being hit by a pitch. He eventually scored on a ground out to the cheers of 8,000 fans. Enough fun, however. It was now time to get serious as the 1911 World Series approached.

The 1911 World Series, billed as a rematch of the 1905 classic between the Giants and Connie Mack's Philadelphia Athletics, exploded onto the scene when it received comprehensive national and significant international press coverage. Adding to the publicity were the ghostwritten daily accounts of the games in the New York press by McGraw, Meyers, Mathewson and Marquard for the Giants and in the Philadelphia papers by Mack, Collins and Bender. These so-called "firsthand" articles were well received by the fans.

McGraw, hoping for a repeat of the 1905 series, decked his club in dramatic black uniforms trimmed in white. It would take more than sinister dress, however, to defeat Philadelphia. Mack's team was substantially stronger than the 1905 club. Pitchers Jack Coombs (28-12), Eddie Plank (23-8) and Chief Bender (17-5) were outstanding. Second baseman Eddie Collins (.365) was one of the best in baseball and third baseman Frank Baker (.334) was the American League home-run king. The rest of the club was strong and it was no fluke that Philadelphia won 101 games during the season. McGraw and the Giants would have their hands full.

October 14

Before more than 38,000 howling fans at the Polo Grounds Christy Mathewson picked up where he left off in 1905, defeating the Philadelphia Athletics 2-1 in a masterfully pitched game. Like a highly skilled surgeon wielding his scalpel with exacting precision, Matty turned back Philadelphia on a mere 94 pitches. The Athletics scored their only run in the second inning on an RBI single by Harry Davis, which ended Matty's consecutive scoreless streak in World Series play at 28⅓.

Little Josh Devore was the hitting hero of the game when he singled in the seventh inning to give Matty the go-ahead run and the eventual margin of victory.

Several celebrities were on hand at the Polo Grounds, among them the immortal Ty Cobb, who was decked out in a new blue suit and plush upholstered hat. It was rumored he had a $100,000 bet on the Athletics. If this were true, it probably had little effect on McGraw. But when the Giants manager discovered his old friend George M. Cohan had bet on Philadelphia, he was quite upset.

The following day (October 15) was a Sunday and, since no game was scheduled, the Giants took the opportunity to attend a testimonial in their honor at the New York Theatre. The place was jam-packed with fans and, after being entertained for two hours by actors and actresses, the Giants were finally introduced to a patient audience. With the exception of Marquard, the ball players wore tuxedos. Mathewson, who everyone was looking forward to seeing, was too modest to show up. This was not unusual behavior for Matty, who rarely sought attention and, in fact, made efforts to avoid it. "My husband was indifferent to fame," Matty's wife said. "A trip ... exhibitions and dinners and handshaking didn't appeal to him."[10]

On October 16 the second game of the World Series shifted to Shibe Park in Philadelphia with the Athletics defeating New York and Marquard 3–1 to even the series. The hero of the game was Baker who clouted a two-run shot off Marquard in the sixth inning to break a 1–1 deadlock.

Marquard, who admittedly was nervous appearing in his first World Series game, took full blame for the errant pitch. In fact, on hindsight it was extremely poor judgment pitching to Baker's strength. Later, Marquard described the historic moment. "But after I had one strike on him and he had refused to bite on another outcurve which was a little too wide, I thought to cross him by sending in a fast high straight ball, the kind I knew he liked. Meyers had called for a curve, but I could not see it, and signalled a high fast ball."[11]

Mathewson, "writing" for the *New York Herald*, criticized Marquard for throwing the high fast ball, a pitch McGraw had cautioned him about during the clubhouse meeting prior to the game. Marquard was furious when he read Matty's comments the next morning, much to the delight of the Philadelphia players and fans. It would not be long, however, before Marquard would inflict his literary revenge.

October 17

Game three moved back to the Polo Grounds, and what a game it was. Mathewson was pitching brilliantly, blanking Philadelphia for eight innings and clinging to a 1–0 lead. With one out in the ninth, however, that man Baker came to bat and hit a tremendous home run into the right-field grandstand to tie the score and send the game into extra innings. From that moment on Baker was tabbed with the nickname Home Run. In the eleventh, the Athletics broke the game wide open, scoring two runs on two hits and poor fielding by Herzog and Fletcher. The Giants scored a run in the bottom of the eleventh but the rally fell short and they lost 3–2.

Marquard, perhaps with some sense of vindication, wrote in *The New York Times* that he had asked Mathewson what pitch he threw Baker. Matty replied, "The same thing you did, Rube. I gave Baker a high, fast one. I have been in the business for a long time and have no excuse."[12]

Interestingly, Matty's later recollections of Baker's home run differ on the count and blamed umpire Bill Brennan for missing his third pitch, which Matty felt was a strike not a ball. In one version the count was put at 2-1 and Matty in a hole; in another scenario Matty had Baker struck out. Blaming Brennan was probably the closest Matty ever came to resorting to an alibi in his career.

October 24

The fourth game of the series was finally played after being postponed for almost a week due to heavy rain in the Philadelphia area. With the rain delay McGraw passed up Wiltse and Ames and chose Mathewson to get the Giants even in the series. Spotted a 2–0 lead, Matty looked invincible for the first three innings, but when his fast ball slowed Philadelphia rapped him for four runs (three in the third, one in the fourth) and went on to win 4–2 behind Chief Bender. In seven innings Matty allowed ten hits, six for extra bases. Clearly, it was not his day as Philadelphia took the series advantage three games to one.

On October 25 the Giants got a reprieve when Marquard, Ames and Crandall combined for a 4–3, ten-inning victory. The Giants scored two runs in the ninth to tie and Merkle's sacrifice fly in the bottom of the tenth drove in the winning run.

The series ended the following day at Shibe Park when Philadelphia clobbered the Giants 13–2, in a game highlighted by a seven-run seventh inning. It was Mack's second World Championship and few would deny that he clearly deserved it. The Athletics out-hit, out-pitched and out-fielded the Giants. McGraw congratulated Mack after the final out and the Giants players, to a man, admitted Philadelphia was the better club.

From a financial standpoint it was a lucrative series, setting a new attendance record at nearly 180,000. Each Giants player received $2,436 and each Philadelphia player $3,655, both record amounts. The money would go a long way towards soothing the losers' hurt feelings over the winter.

Three weeks after the World Series ended, John and Blanche McGraw and Christy and Jane Mathewson, along with most of the Giants players, headed for Havana to play the two top Cuban baseball teams. It was a successful trip for the Giants, as well as for Matty, who pitched outstanding baseball. The Giants returned home before Christmas for a well-deserved rest and to look forward to another exciting season.

Chapter 14
Tough World Series Loss, 1912

W	L	Pct	ERA
23	12	.657	2.12

The New York Giants began the 1912 season with much the same personnel as the previous year, including Charlie Faust. When McGraw and the Giants returned from spring training in Marlin they were greeted by none other than the wacky right-hander, who claimed he was in fine condition and ready to pitch for the Giants. With the World Series loss still fresh in his mind, McGraw was no longer enamored with the so-called magical powers of Faust and, in fact, found him more annoying than amusing. He did agree, however, to allow Faust to sit with the team at the Polo Grounds in his street clothes.

But the most important addition to the club was right-handed spitballer, Jeff Tesreau, who was purchased in the off-season from Toronto. Tesreau won 17 games, most of them after July, and led the league with an ERA of 1.96 to help New York capture its fourth pennant under McGraw.

Rube Marquard, who came into his own in 1911, registered 26 wins, the most in the National League, including a magnificent run of 19 straight. If there were any remaining believers in the "$11,000 Lemon" tag, they were forever converted to Marquard rooters during the season. The great Mathewson, who was approaching his thirty-second birthday, added 23 victories while Red Ames, Otis Crandall and Hooks Wiltse all pitched well.

The Giants' offense was a carbon copy of the previous year. Perhaps McGraw went by the maxim, "if it ain't broke, don't fix it." Noted author Charles Alexander, "Again the Giants relied on the hit-and-run play and derring-do on the base paths to overwhelm the opposition. As a team they stole 319 bases, batted .286, and scored 823 runs, the most in the National League since 1899. McGraw had no outstanding everyday players, but his club, seasoned but still relatively young, had become a well-tuned machine."[1] Alexander is partially correct; the Giants were young, experienced and played well together. But there were some outstanding individual efforts in 1912. For example, Larry Doyle turned in a solid season,

Left to right: Giants coach Wilbert Robinson, manager John McGraw and Mathewson prior to the 1912 World Series between New York and Boston. It would be another year before McGraw and Robinson had their battle (photo courtesy Miller Library, Keystone Junior College, LaPlume, Pennsylvania).

batting .330 with ten home runs and 90 RBIs. Fred Merkle wasn't far behind either with a .309 average, 11 homers and 84 runs batted in. Actually, Red Murray led the club with 92 RBIs and Chief Meyers with a .358 batting average, second best in the league.

It was an exciting club that won 103 games and held first place from May 20 until the season's end, a relatively easier pennant than the previous year. The World Series, however, was an entirely different matter. Mathewson was the victim, once again, of a teammate's failure to execute.

The Season

April 15

McGraw, after witnessing the Giants lose two of three to Brooklyn at Washington Park, reluctantly chose Mathewson to pitch his first game of the 1912 season in Boston where the weather conditions were less than ideal. Matty did little to right a listing ship. He was hit hard and often on

14 • Tough World Series Loss, 1912

Catcher "Chief" Meyers (left) and pitcher Rube Marquard were battery mates for the Giants from 1909 until 1914 and for Brooklyn in 1916 and 1917 (photo courtesy National Baseball Library, Cooperstown, N.Y.).

this cold, damp day at muddy South End Grounds. The final score was Boston 3, New York 0, as right-hander Hub Perdue handcuffed the Giants on seven hits.

April 19

The New York Giants, amidst the usual fanfare, opened the season at the Polo Grounds with a resounding 6–2 victory over Brooklyn. Mathewson recorded his first win, but gave up 13 hits. He was hittable but unbeatable. Prior to the game Matty was presented with a new automobile, a gift from his thousands of admiring fans. Only 18,000 turned out to see the Giants and Matty, the result of bad weather and the somber mood of the public over the disastrous sinking of the *Titanic* on April 14.

Two days after Matty won his first game, the Giants hosted the Yankees, who were now wearing the famous pinstripes, in a charity game at the Polo Grounds for the benefit of the survivors of the "unsinkable" *Titanic*. The game, which the Giants won 11–2, netted almost $9,500 for the survivors. It was the first time two big league clubs met at the Polo Grounds on a Sunday.

April 25

Mathewson recorded his second win of the season when he defeated Philadelphia at Baker Bowl 3–1. The victory was somewhat tarnished since the Phillies had only three regulars in their lineup, the others on the bench nursing a variety of injuries. Matty gave up seven hits, walked one and fanned six, a model performance by Big Six.

The game also served to introduce the Phillies' 17-year-old infield "sensation" by the name of Gene Steinbrenner, who nicked Mathewson for two hits. Unfortunately for the kid, it would be his only claim to fame and the only hits in his abbreviated major league career. The Giants' record went to 7-3 and now appeared to be playing solid baseball.

May 3

In a wild and exciting game at the Polo Grounds, New York pulled off a triple steal but lost 8–6 in ten innings as Mathewson was blasted in relief. Matty entered the top of the tenth with the score deadlocked 6–6, the result of the Giants scraping and clawing to overcome a 5–0 deficit. To the dismay of his fans, Matty was drilled for three doubles, which iced the game for Philadelphia.

Umpire Bill Klem, who was getting heat from all sides during the game, began ejecting players with abandon. When the count reached four, Klem announced he wanted silence and if it was not forthcoming he would clear the bench. Not surprisingly, one of the men Klem tossed was McGraw. These two strong-willed personalities, in spite of continued fighting, shared a unique relationship. Claimed author Frank Graham, "They battled through all the years that McGraw remained in baseball—and off the field were friends through the years too."[2]

May 4

Mathewson, like a true professional, revenged the previous day's loss by whipping the Phillies 4–3, for his third victory of the young season.

14 • Tough World Series Loss, 1912

Matty entered the eighth inning with a comfortable 4–0 lead as the Giants, with McGraw's daring coaching at third, were running wild on catcher George Graham. They wound up stealing nine bases, but almost lost the game when Matty faltered in the eighth. In a rare loss of control, Big Six walked two men and gave up a home run to Tom Downey, but settled down to record the victory. After the game the Giants began preparing for a trip to St. Louis to begin their first western swing.

May 8

New York piled up nine runs in the second and third innings off St. Louis pitching to hand Tesreau what everyone thought was an insurmountable lead, but when the 23-year-old tired in the ninth McGraw sent in Mathewson to get the last two outs. New York won 11–8, its third straight victory over the Cardinals, moving them to within half a game of first-place Cincinnati.

May 9

Mathewson's brief relief appearance the day before turned out to be a tune-up for his starting role against St. Louis, which he won handily 8–3. The outcome was never in doubt as Matty appeared to toy with the Cardinals, easing up when the situation seemed safe and bearing down when he was in a jam. The victory, coupled with a Cincinnati loss, moved the Giants into first place where, except for one day (May 19), they would remain the rest of the season!

After sweeping St. Louis, the Giants moved on to Chicago and won three more with Marquard's winning streak now reaching six straight. Unquestionably, McGraw had his charges playing excellent baseball with everyone contributing to the effort.

May 18

Mathewson opened the important series with second-place Cincinnati before more than 20,000 fans, including an impressive array of dignitaries on hand for the elaborate dedication ceremonies of the new $400,000 Redland Field. The gala event included a band concert, fireworks, pennant hanging and an address by Pennsylvania governor John K. Tener. American League president Ban Johnson and Chicago White Sox president Charles Comiskey were also present. It was a festive afternoon for the large crowd, made even more exciting by the 4–3 Cincinnati victory over Matty who pitched well but was victimized by Doyle's poor fielding in the eighth.

Redland Field notwithstanding, the real fireworks erupted a few days earlier in the American League when Johnson suspended Ty Cobb indefinitely for going into the grandstand and striking a spectator who was using abusive language towards the ball player. In support of Cobb, the Detroit players retaliated and refused to play the Philadelphia Athletics on Saturday, May 18—in essence, staging a strike, the first ever in baseball. A furious Johnson acted swiftly and decisively. He canceled Monday's Tigers-Athletics game (no baseball on Sunday) and threatened all the Detroit players with banishment from organized baseball if they failed to play Washington the next day. The players folded and Johnson fined each $100 and set Cobb's suspension at ten days and a meager $50 fine.

During these hectic days it seemed everyone, from the average fan in the street to club presidents, had an opinion about Cobb's action and the subsequent strike. Matty was no different. "Of course, Cobb is a high-strung individual, who is more likely to resent remarks made to him from the stands than most players, but still the epithets that are applied to some of the fellows in some cities, especially those where no regular police are stationed, should be stopped." Continued Mathewson, "I personally think it rather foolish to strike a spectator; not that some of them don't have it coming to them, but the player invariably is the sufferer."[3]

May 22

Mathewson pitched a marvelous three-hitter to beat Cincinnati 6–1 in the final game of the series, which New York won three games to two. After Cincinnati collected three hits over the first three innings, Matty was in total command, retiring the next 18 straight with only seven balls reaching the outfield. It was an awesome performance and raised his record to 5-3.

Appearing in the sports pages for the first time was G. P. Putnam's Sons' ad for Mathewson's book, *Pitching in a Pinch*. It was ghostwritten by John Wheeler, but nonetheless was a popular book, especially with the youth. It sold at all bookstores for $1.00!

Two days later, Marquard beat Brooklyn 6–3 at Washington Park for his ninth consecutive victory.

May 28

Mathewson narrowly escaped a defeat, when the Giants scored a run in the eighth and two in the ninth to edge Brooklyn 5–4. Matty was tagged for ten hits and left after seven innings trailing 4–2. Crandall came on in relief to gain the victory as New York's first-place lead widened to five and a half games over Cincinnati. On May 30, Marquard's streak would reach ten straight.

June 1

Miffed over losing to St. Louis the day before, New York hammered two Cardinals pitchers for 16 hits and handed Mathewson an easy 13–4 victory, his sixth of the season. By the fourth inning the outcome of the game was no longer in doubt for the 25,000 fans at the Polo Grounds. Matty had a 9–2 lead and the rest of the game was simply exercise.

It was around this time (the exact date is unknown) that Mathewson received a letter from a young boy who lived in Little Mountain, South Carolina. The letter was dated May 27, 1912, and illustrates the widespread fame of Matty's fadeaway. It became one of his most cherished possessions.

> Dear Leaguer:
> Enclose will find fifty cents (.50) for which would you please tell and describe to me how to throw your fade-away and in and out-curves and write me at once please by mail if any more charges let me know and I will send the mony [sic]. I have heard of your famous fade-away and would like to know how to throw it. I thank you.
> Yours truly,
> Ernest Derrick[4]

Two days later Marquard ran his winning streak to 11 straight when he defeated St. Louis 8–3.

June 7

Mathewson gave up three runs in the first inning, six over the course of the game on 11 hits, but still managed to defeat Cincinnati 7–6. It was an exciting game for the Polo Grounds crowd as the Giants scored two runs in the eighth to gain the victory. Matty's record was now 7–3 while the Giants widened their lead over second-place Cincinnati to nine and a half games. Marquard made it 12 straight the next day.

June 11

After losing the opening game of the Chicago series, McGraw was taking no chances when the Giants entered the eighth inning holding on to a 4–3 lead; he replaced Ames with Mathewson. The strategy worked to perfection: Matty fanned three of the six batters he faced while his teammates scored four runs in the bottom of the eighth to seal the victory for Ames. The next day Marquard made it 13 straight.

June 13

Mathewson's brilliant clutch pitching in the ninth inning gave New York a 3–2 victory over the Chicago Cubs at the Polo Grounds before

15,000 spectators. Matty entered the last inning with a slim 3–2 lead. Up to this point he had scattered five hits, fanned seven and was in control of the game. Tommy Leach led off the inning and flied to Beals Becker but the center fielder lost the ball in the sun and Leach scampered all the way to third with a gift triple. With the tying run on third, nobody out, Matty reached back for something extra and retired the next three batters, stranding Leach at third. The inning went like this: Ward Miller grounded weakly back to Matty, Vic Saier whiffed on three pitches and Matty made a marvelous leap and stab to get Johnny Evers' bounder that was headed through the box and into center field. It was a masterful job of clutch pitching.

June 18

New York lost to Pittsburgh 7–2 as Mathewson was roughed up for seven hits and five runs in eight innings. It was not a good day for Matty or the Giants as his teammates chipped in with five errors. The defeat marked the first time all season the Giants lost a series.

The following day Marquard, in a relief role, defeated Boston 6–5 to register his fifteenth straight victory. On June 21 he made it 16 in a row with another victory against Boston.

June 22

New York made it five in a row over Boston when they won both ends of a doubleheader, 17–5 and 14–12, on a day when the hitters fattened up their batting averages. Matty was the benefactor of the first game slugfest in which the Giants scored ten runs in the seventh inning to seal his ninth victory of the season against four losses.

On June 25 Marquard upped his winning streak to 17 with a nifty 2–1 victory in Philadelphia.

June 28

The New York Giants were feasting on the Boston Braves and it would take more than a name change (they were the Rustlers in 1911) to transform this woeful bunch into a respectable club. No doubt McGraw was thoroughly enjoying his club's dominance as the Giants steamrolled to another twin killing, 10–3 and 12–3, making it ten straight over the last-place Braves. By the time the current series ended, the streak would reach 13 with Boston's only victory at the hands of Mathewson in his first game of the season, back on April 15.

Matty won the first game of the doubleheader, scattering nine hits to record his tenth victory against four losses. When the Giants scored runs by the bushel there was little challenge for Matty. His role was simply tossing the ball over the plate and letting his fielders do the work. The following day Marquard's record went to an incredible 18-0 and the team winning streak to 12 straight. One can imagine, with some degree of accuracy, that McGraw must have been overjoyed at the way the season was progressing.

July 3

It was a marvelous day of baseball for the more than 20,000 spectators, many from Brooklyn, who tramped into the Polo Grounds to witness an exciting and historic doubleheader. The two victories by the Giants, 2–1 and 10–9, ran their streak to 16 in a row. In the first game, Marquard, who was in trouble most of the time but managed to escape serious damage, eked out a narrow 2–1 victory for a record-setting 19 straight.

In his autobiography, McGraw claimed, "When right Marquard's fast ball had a peculiar jump to it that was a complete baffler to opponents. It was in the use of this ball at the right moment that he won his nineteen straight games."[5]

Marquard's phenomenal winning streak equaled the record set by another Giants player, Tim Keefe, back in 1888. According to Marquard, however, his streak should have been 20 straight. "Actually, I won 20 straight, not 19," claimed Marquard, "but because of the way they scored then I didn't get credit for one of them. I relieved Jeff Tesreau in the eighth inning of a game one day, with the Giants behind, 3–2. In the ninth inning Heinie Groh singled and Art Wilson homered, and we won, 4–3. But they gave Tesreau credit for the victory instead of me."[6] The game Marquard so accurately recalled occurred on April 20 against Brooklyn at the Polo Grounds.

During the second game Marquard, basking in his newly found glory, sat with New York treasurer John Whalen in his field box puffing on a cigar while observing a parade of Giants pitchers to and from the mound. First Ames, then Tesreau, then Wiltse before McGraw stopped the nonsense and called on Mathewson to put a halt to the Brooklyn attack. Big Six nailed down the victory for the Giants as their record went to 54-11, an incredible .830 winning percentage!

July 4

New York couldn't stand prosperity for long. They lost the holiday doubleheader to Brooklyn 10–3 and 5–2, ending the winning streak at 16. In the morning Mathewson was hammered for five hits and five runs in three innings. It was his fifth loss and earliest departure of the season. Wiltse lost the afternoon game but the Giants still led Chicago by 14½ games.

July 5

After pitching only three innings the day before, Mathewson returned to the mound determined to beat Brooklyn. It was a question of pride. Unlike the previous day, Matty had his full repertoire going and had the Dodgers completely baffled. He allowed five hits and walked only one batter while registering his eleventh win of the season. The final score was 6-1. It was also an historic moment for this victory represented Mathewson's three hundredth of his career, a milestone reserved for the greats of the game. It went unnoticed in the press.

July 9

The day before, kicking off the Giants' second western road trip, Marquard lost the first game of the Chicago Cubs' series, 7-2, at West Side Park. It stopped his winning streak at 19!

Mathewson hurled game two in the series against Three Finger Brown. Neither pitcher was extraordinary; in fact, both were hit quite freely. New York, however, was more adept at bunching its hits and won the game 5-2. Regardless of the actual performance, these two great pitchers had large followings, which always resulted in huge crowds. One of Brown's biggest fans was Kenesaw Mountain Landis, the future baseball commissioner. Claimed J. G. Taylor Spink, longtime publisher of *The Sporting News*, "Landis' favorite pitcher was Three Finger Brown. He loved to watch Matty and Brown duel at West Side Park. In fact, on one occasion as a young attorney, he asked the opposing counsel, 'Can't we get a postponement of this case until tomorrow? Brownie is pitching against Matty, and I just can't miss that.'"[7]

July 13

Mathewson opened the St. Louis series at Robison Field with an easy 7-2 victory. He was far from puzzling, giving up 13 hits but, as usual, pitched superbly with runners on base. His record was now 13-5.

July 17

This date marked Mathewson's twelfth anniversary with the New York Giants. He pitched his first game in a Giants uniform way back on July 17, 1900. Matty celebrated the event with a splendid pitching performance, defeating Pittsburgh 10-2 at Forbes Field. Big Six was stingy with hits, giving up only seven and not walking a batter until the eighth inning.

It was his third victory of the western trip which surprisingly was turning into a disaster. The Giants' record at this point was 3-7, with Matty accounting for all the victories. The rest of the staff, including Marquard, was pitching erratically. Mathewson's solid road performance also served to dispel talk that was circulating (for the umpteenth time) that he had outgrown his usefulness.

July 20

Rookie Jeff Tesreau held the hard-hitting Pittsburgh Pirates to three singles and one run over eight innings, but had the misfortune of opposing left-hander Hank Robinson, who had the Giants blanked entering the ninth. Singles by Art Fletcher, Art Shafer, Doyle and Crandall, however, netted the Giants two runs and brought on Mathewson in the bottom of the ninth. Matty retired the side with ease—pop foul, strikeout, ground out—and preserved a well-earned victory for Tesreau. The Giants' first-place lead over Chicago widened to 11½ games.

July 22

"Mathewson is still the king of all pitchers," wrote *The New York Times* after he defeated Cincinnati 4–1 at Redland Field. "He is far above all of the other pitchers in the game today, and this afternoon he gave further evidence of his great ability when he annexed another victory for the New York Giants...."[8] It was Matty's fifteenth win and one of his best performances of the season. Every one of his pitches was working to perfection and his change of pace had Cincinnati bewildered. With men on base he was resolute. For example, in the third inning with runners on first and third and no outs, Matty retired the top of the order without a ball leaving the infield nor a runner scoring. It was Mathewson at his best.

Several days later, New York ended its western swing, managing to salvage a 9-8 mark (Matty won four), the result of winning the last six of seven games. Regardless, the Giants were still 12 games ahead of Chicago.

July 26

Prior to the first game of the home stand against Chicago, Brush agreed to a new starting time of 3:45, an accommodation to the Wall Street patrons who wanted a 4:00 start. Brush's original plan for 3:30 met with a protest from Wall Street. Also, during the Cubs' series the railroad agreed to run a train from Wall Street to the Polo Grounds called the Broker's Special. Yes, they were the good old days.

More than 17,000 spectators came to celebrate the opening of the Giants' home stand against second place Chicago, but they went away with mixed emotions. The crowd was thrilled by the exciting play and the pitching of Mathewson, but was disappointed in the outcome—Chicago won 4–3. Matty led 2–1 after seven innings, but weakened in the eighth and ninth when the Cubs scored three runs to lead 4–2. The Giants fought back in the bottom of the ninth, scoring a run but the rally fell short. It was a tough loss for Matty and the Giants as his record went to 15-6.

July 30

The Giants scored five runs off Chicago rookie Jimmy Lavender in the first two innings, highlighted by Murray's home run, to give Mathewson a comfortable lead and an ultimate 10–4 victory. In a loosely played game (each team made four errors), Matty checked the Cubs with nine hits and continued his masterful pitching with men on base. The victory upped his record to 16-6 and the Giants' first-place lead to ten games.

August 3

Mathewson notched his seventeenth victory of the season when he defeated Cincinnati 3–2 before 15,000 fans at the Polo Grounds. All the Giants' runs were the result of the long ball, two by Merkle and the other by Becker. As was often the case Matty gave up a lot of hits but few runs. He was near unhittable with men on base and rarely walked a batter which aided his cause immensely.

By Matty's own admission Joe Tinker, Hans Wagner, Sherwood Magee and Fred Clarke were among the most dangerous batters he ever faced. Missing from that quartet was little known Armando Marsans, a Cuban with a lifetime batting average of .269. On this day, however, Marsans owned Matty, collecting four hits in four trips to the plate.

August 7

The Giants lost their third straight game to Pittsburgh as Mathewson was hit hard and often. He was tagged for an unbelievable 15 hits and six runs in eight innings. While Matty was getting shellacked, the Pirates' Marty O'Toole, who was purchased from St. Paul in 1911 for a then-exorbitant $22,500, had his elusive spitball working beautifully. O'Toole scattered eight hits (only one for extra bases, a double by Matty) and won easily, 7–2.

One can imagine how much more effective Mathewson would have been if on occasion he would have employed a spitter, which was a legal pitch then. In fact, prior to the 1912 World Series, it was rumored Matty had been practicing throwing a "moist ball." There was no evidence of his throwing it, however. Years later McGraw offered these observations: "Mathewson could pitch the spitter, but rarely used it in a game. He never considered it part of his equipment."[9]

August 12

For the second consecutive game Mathewson was hit hard, this time by St. Louis, in an 8–6 loss. Matty entered the game in the third inning after Ames was blasted, trailing 6–3. When the Giants scored three runs in the fourth, it was a brand new ball game. But Matty couldn't hold the lead, one of the few times in his career, giving up single runs in the fifth and eighth innings to take the loss. His record now stood at 17-8.

Prior to the game, the Polo Grounds had been the setting for a festive and gala event—the unfurling of the National League Pennant. A crowd of 10,000 anxiously watched as the huge flag was hauled to the top of the flagpole. The three-line inscription, which could be easily seen from a distance, read:

GIANTS
WORLD'S Champions 1905
NATIONAL LEAGUE CHAMPIONS 1904–1905–1911

And then the game began and ruined the afternoon.

August 17

New York's once-invincible lead was cut to five games when the Chicago Cubs scored a run off Mathewson in the eleventh inning to win a hard-fought contest, 6–5. It was Matty's third straight loss and brought his record to 17-9. Fully 30,000, the largest crowd to ever squeeze in West Side Park, witnessed the exciting finish. With one out in the eleventh, Jimmy Archer singled to center, sending Vic Saier home with the winning run, to the joy of thousands. No doubt, McGraw was eager to move on to St. Louis as the Giants had lost two of three to the Cubs and their final western trip was off to a poor start.

August 22

Five days later New York's lead was cut to four games when McGraw's men split a doubleheader with Pittsburgh at Forbes Field before another large crowd of 27,000. Mathewson lost the first game 3–2 and Marquard won the nightcap 8–6. It was Matty's fourth straight loss and another squeaker as he was out-pitched by Howie Camnitz. In seven innings Big Six gave up eight hits and all three runs.

Wagner had a marvelous day, going three for four off Matty and four for five (he hit for the cycle) off Marquard. His seven hits included two doubles, a triple and home run for 14 total bases. He scored five runs, drove in four, stole two bases and accepted 14 chances. Oh yes, he committed one error.

Long after the Flying Dutchman's career ended, McGraw claimed,

"So uniformly good was Wagner as a player that it is almost impossible to determine whether his highest point of superiority was in his fielding, in his batting or in his running. He was a topnotcher in all."[10]

August 24

In the fifth and last game of the Pittsburgh series Wiltse and Babe Adams were locked in a tense pitcher's duel. Both clubs had split the previous four games and it appeared Adams, with a 2–0 lead, and a no-hitter through six innings, was on his way to victory. But in the seventh lightning struck! The inning began innocently enough with Fred Snodgrass making out, but after that Adams never knew what hit him. Doyle singled for the Giants' first hit. Becker fouled out but Murray kept the rally going with a Texas Leaguer. Merkle came to the plate and promptly smacked one over the left-field fence, 360 feet from home plate. The Giants led 3–2; the crowd was stunned; McGraw was ecstatic and when the inning ended Mathewson entered the game. Matty pitched sparkling relief, blanking the Pirates over the last three innings on three hits to save the victory for Wiltse. In the meantime Chicago lost, increasing the Giants' lead to six full games.

August 27

Mathewson lost his fifth straight game, this time a victim of a brilliant pitching performance by Art Fromme. The Cincinnati hurler blanked the Giants on one hit, a single by Fletcher in the third inning. Matty pitched a steady game but could not match Fromme who hurled his best game of the season. Mathewson's record was now 17-11. He was 0-5 in August and probably welcomed September with open arms.

September 2

It was a great deay for Christy Mathewson. The veteran pitching marvel won both ends of a doubleheader with Boston at South End Grounds, 5–2 and 6–1. In the first game Matty relieved Marquard in the ninth inning with the score tied 2–2. He threw shutout ball for four innings and notched his eighteenth victory when Doyle slammed a three-run homer in the twelfth. Matty started the nightcap and after the Giants chased Braves' pitcher Ed Donnelly with five runs in the third inning, he coasted to his nineteenth win. The game was called in the seventh due to darkness. A crowd of more than 15,000 attended the doubleheader and, according to the press, it was the largest gathering since the Braves won the pennant in 1897.

September 5

New York won both tends of the doubleheader against Philadelphia at Baker Bowl, 8–1 and 4–2. In the first game Mathewson and rookie Tom Seaton dueled for seven innings, with the youngster holding onto a slim 1–0 lead. In the top of the eighth the Giants erupted for six runs and chased the kid from the mound. They added two more in the ninth as Matty recorded his twentieth victory of the season, the tenth consecutive year he reached this illustrious plateau! It was a marvelous achievement, which he would repeat for another two years.

September 6

The Giants played their third consecutive doubleheader against the Philadelphia Phillies and, like the previous day, won both games, 3–0 and 9–8. It would not have been at all surprising if McGraw's pitching staff had collapsed in the face of this demanding schedule, but that was not the case. In fact, Tesreau hurled a no-hitter in the first game, the only one in the National League in 1912.

But in the second game McGraw had to use three pitchers — Marquard, Crandall and finally Mathewson — to beat the Phillies. Matty was shaky in his two innings, giving up two runs and barely holding on to the 9–8 win. His record was now 21-11 and the Giants had widened their lead to eight games.

Off the diamond baseball history was made when David Lewis Fultz, a New York attorney and former major league center fielder announced the formation of the Player's Fraternity. Fultz was its president but prior to the formation, Mathewson was one of the players under consideration for the position. He "declined the office because he lacked the time and independence to do a thorough job. Mathewson and Cobb, however, pledged themselves to serve any new group as vice-presidents."[11] Within two months the Fraternity claimed nearly 300 members and at its peak more than 1,200, which included minor leaguers. It had several noteworthy goals, all aimed at benefiting the players and the game. Although the Fraternity was recognized by the National Commission in 1914 and achieved some benefits for players, in the long run it failed and eventually folded in 1918.

September 9

Doubleheaders continued to mount and the Giants kept right on winning them. They beat Brooklyn 2–1 and 7–2 at the Polo Grounds before 18,000 fans. Tesreau won the first game, his spitter dancing and darting and frustrating the Dodger hitters all afternoon. In the second game, the Giants scored five runs off Pat Ragan in the first inning and Mathewson registered another easy victory. In fact, Matty was working on a shutout until the ninth when Brooklyn nicked him for two runs. Mathewson improved his record to 22-11 and the Giants continued to increase their lead, which now reached nine and a half games.

September 12

New York gained another game on Chicago as it split a doubleheader with St. Louis while the Cubs lost twice to Boston. With a 10½-game lead it was now simply a matter of time. The Giants lost the first game 4–2 when Crandall, in relief of Mathewson with the score tied 2–2, was rocked for two runs in the ninth by the Cardinals. Matty pitched a fine game, five hits and two runs in eight innings, but came away with a no decision. Tesreau won the nightcap 4–1, his sixth consecutive victory, and was now an important member of the pitching rotation.

September 16

In a meaningless game New York lost to the Chicago Cubs 4–3 behind the less than impressive pitching of Mathewson. Matty scattered ten hits, which in itself was not unusual, but when he was tagged for a home run by Jim Archer, the crowd of 12,000 was stunned. It was one of the few times in his career he lost a tight game solely to the roundtripper. Matty's record was now 22-12 and when the Giants lost to the Cubs the next day their lead dropped to nine and a half games, nothing to fret about with less than three weeks to play.

Two days later, the Boston Red Sox clinched the American League pennant. They would turn out to be more than a worthy foe for McGraw and his band of thieves.

September 19

Cincinnati won its first game of the season at the Polo Grounds when it defeated Tesreau 3–1, ending his winning streak at seven straight. In the second game of the twin bill, Mathewson hooked up with Art Fromme, in a seesaw pitcher's duel. The Giants scored in the bottom of the eighth to lead 1–0. Matty, in a rare moment, faltered and relinquished the lead when he allowed Cincinnati to score two runs. But the Giants came right back and tied the game in their half of the ninth when Herzog singled home Merkle, who had singled and stolen second. The game ended in a 2–2 tie when darkness arrived.

The following Sunday (September 22) five New York Giants players attended the annual baseball sermon preached by The Rev. Dr. Christian A. Reisner of the Grace Methodist Episcopal Church on West 104th Street. The church was packed with kids (some who had not seen the inside of a church in a long time) eager to see their heroes. Art Wilson, Herzog, Fletcher, Snodgrass and Becker attended but Mathewson was absent. Half-tone portraits of Matty, however, were presented to every member of the congregation. Throughout his sermon The Rev. Reisner frequently quoted Cubs' stars Johnny Evers, Joe Tinker and others. He praised the game, the importance of players setting examples for the youth and the benefits of church attendance and clean living. He concluded: "Play the game of life with the same thought of doing your best and no matter what the score is at the end the Great Umpire will pronounce you 'safe.'"[12]

September 26

The Giants won a doubleheader from Boston, 8–3 and 4–0, to clinch the National League pennant! It was their eighth doubleheader in September. Before 10,000 jubilant fans in the first game Mathewson assured the Giants of a tie by spreading ten hits to notch his twenty-third, and last, victory of the season. Matty, never one to overwork himself needlessly, took advantage of the early 8–0 lead and slowed his pace over the last four innings.

McGraw called on Al Demaree, recently obtained from the Mobile club of the Southern League, to nail down the 1912 pennant. The rookie answered the call with a magnificent pitching performance, blanking the Braves on seven hits while fanning nine. The highly touted side-armer came to the Giants with a 25-10 record at Mobile. He would pitch eight years in the National League and finish with a lifetime record of 80-72. After baseball he became a nationally syndicated cartoonist and his work appeared in *The Sporting News* for over 30 years.

With the pennant now clinched, McGraw gave Mathewson a well-deserved rest; Matty would not pitch again until the World Series. Meanwhile the Giants played out the remaining games and finished the season with a 103-48 mark, 11½ games ahead of the Cubs. During this lame-duck period two interesting events took place. First, Mathewson and Marquard took time off to attend a game at Philadelphia to look over the Boston Red Sox hitters in preparation for the World Series. Boston pounded out 17 hits and demolished Philadelphia 17–5. With that display of awesome hitting, one can only imagine the discussion that took place between these two great pitchers. The other noteworthy occurrence came on October 5 when the Giants beat Brooklyn 1–0. It was the last game Brooklyn played at Washington Park. The Dodgers would open the 1913 season at their new home—Ebbets Field.

Prior to the beginning of the World Series, *The New York Times* sportswriter, Hugh Fullerton, created a brouhaha among avid Giants fans with his series of nine articles comparing the Giants and Boston players, position by position. It was a worthy endeavor and one of the best pieces of sportswriting at the time. What the Giants objected to was Fullerton's conclusion: Boston was a better club and would win the World Series. Letters from fans poured into the *Times,* many angrily denouncing Fullerton, claiming he had his facts wrong and as a Chicagoan couldn't view the series objectively. Fullerton had his supporters, though, who claimed his careful analysis was sound and blamed the New York newspapers for exaggerating the abilities of the Giants' players throughout the season.

Fullerton did nothing to ingratiate himself to New York fans when he compared the two pitching staffs and flatly stated the only way the Giants could win the series was if Tesreau developed into a one-man hero. He further incensed the locals and fans throughout the country when he lashed out at baseball's idol Christy Mathewson. "You may think it odd that I figure Mathewson as having a very small chance to beat the Red Sox," he wrote. "In fact, I am led to think that his style of pitching is just the kind the best hitters on the Boston team like to hit." Added Fullerton, "As to whether Matty can get away with his cunning and clever use of slow faders and floaters, the proof is that Boston hit him terrific when the two teams met before and Matty is not as good now as he was then." And now the coup de grace, "In fact the great Matty has had a bad year. He has pitched very few good games and many pretty bad ones. Against a team that can hit like Boston one needs more than brains."[13] If nothing else, Fullerton heightened the interest and emotions surrounding the World Series.

Although Fullerton, to some extent, was guilty of overstating the situation to grab headlines and thus sell papers, there was considerable evidence Boston was more than a formidable opponent. They won the American League pennant by 14 games with a 105-47 record. Their pitching staff was led by Smokey Joe Wood, who won 34 games, tops in the league against a mere five losses, plus two 20-game winners: Hugh Bedient (20-9) and Buck O'Brien (20-13). Moreover, their outfield trio was claimed by many baseball historians as the best ever, consisted of George "Duffy" Lewis, Tris Speaker and Harry Hooper.

Although McGraw realized he would have his hands full, it did not dampen his optimism. On the eve of the series' opener, as expected, he predicted the New York Giants would win it all. The experience his club gained playing Philadelphia in 1911, he believed, would make a significant difference in the confidence and knowledge the players would bring to the series. He also made it a point to praise Mathewson (whether this had anything to do with Fullerton's comments is unclear) as a proven veteran who can be counted on to pitch brilliantly at all times. It appeared all the elements were in place for a remarkable World Series.

October 9

When the Giants reached Fenway Park to start game two of the series, with Mathewson on the mound, McGraw's strategy in game one had already backfired. He chose Tesreau to face Joe Wood in the opener (October 8) at the Polo Grounds reasoning that the veteran Mathewson would be able to handle the emotional aspect of the game at Fenway better than the rookie. It was a logical move that proved inconsequential when Wood hurled a magnificent game, fanning 11 Giants. Fred Lieb, dean of baseball writers, held a different opinion as to why McGraw did not pitch Matty in the first game. Lieb claimed McGraw wanted his star pitcher to face a lesser opponent than Wood.

Now it was Matty's job to even the series before more than 30,000 noisy Boston fans. Mathewson pitched well, but received little support from his teammates, who committed five errors, accounting for four unearned runs. After 11 innings and a 6–6 tie, home-plate umpire Silk O'Laughlin, to whom Matty referred as an autocrat, called the game on account of darkness.

The next day Marquard evened the series. He hurled an outstanding game, defeating Boston 2–1, but it took a sensational running catch by Josh Devore (in fog, no less) in the bottom of the ninth with two men on to save the game. On October 11 Boston moved ahead again when Wood outpitched Tesreau for the second time, 3–1 at the Polo Grounds.

October 12

With the Giants trailing in the series two games to one and moving back to Fenway, Mathewson went to the mound to face Boston's Bedient and came up a hard-luck loser. Twenty-game winner Bedient pitched a masterful three-hitter, while Matty was victimized by Doyle's error in the third inning which allowed the winning run to score. Mathewson retired the last 17 Red Sox in a row but it was too late as Bedient continued to baffle the Giants. The final score was Boston 2, New York 1.

The Giants were now down in the series three games to one; they were seriously wounded but not yet dead. The Giants did not win 103 games over a six-month season on luck; nor was John J. McGraw considered the best manager in baseball for nothing. So the Giants fought back with Marquard winning his second series game 5–2 (October 14) when his teammates scored all five runs in the first inning. Tesreau coasted the next day at Fenway when the Giants finally caught up with Wood and blasted him for six runs in the first inning to tie the series at 3–3 and set the stage for the deciding seventh game. New York had climbed back from the brink of elimination and now had the momentum on its side.

October 16

A disappointing crowd of 17,000 turned out at Fenway Park to greet starting pitchers Mathewson and Bedient. The small crowd, compared to the 30,000-plus that viewed the previous games, was the result of a boycott

Left-hander Rube Marquard, after shaking the "$11,000 lemon" tag, teamed up with Mathewson to pitch the Giants to pennants in 1911, 1912 and 1913 (photo courtesy National Baseball Library, Cooperstown, N.Y.).

by the well organized Royal Rooters (the name of the Red Sox booster fan club), who were enraged when they were denied their seats in left field the game before. Apparently there was a mixup in ticket allocations.

The game began with Mathewson and Bedient pitching splendid baseball. Bedient gave up a run in the third and Boston nicked Matty for a run in the seventh. At the end of nine, the game was knotted at 1–1. In the top of the tenth with Wood pitching (he relieved Bedient in the eighth), Murray doubled and Merkle singled to give the Giants a 2–1 lead. All Matty needed was three outs to give the Giants the series.

The first batter, pinch hitter Clyde Engle, lofted a routine fly ball to center field which Snodgrass camped under and then dropped for a two-base error. "In Los Angeles, Fred Snodgrass's mother is in a movie theater, following the game on an electronic scoreboard. When the muff is shown, she faints and is carried out of the theater,"[14] claimed author Bill Chuck. Moments later Snodgrass redeemed himself when he made a fine running catch of Harry Hooper's long fly. Engle held second. Matty walked Steve Yerkes. Next, the dangerous Tris Speaker popped up between first and home. Matty, Merkle and Meyers converged. As Hooper claimed later, Matty yelled for Meyers to catch the ball even though Merkle had an easier play. When Merkle backed off, Meyers lunged for the ball and it rolled off his glove. Speaker returned to the batter's box and yelled to Mathewson, "Well, you just called for the wrong man. It's gonna cost you this ball game."[15] Sure enough, Speaker ripped a single to right, scoring Engle with the tying run and sending Yerkes to third. After Matty intentionally walked Duffy Lewis to set up a force at any base, Larry Garner drove a long fly to Devore in right field and Yerkes galloped home with the winning tally. It was a heart-rending loss for Mathewson and thousands of Giants fans.

Of course, the Snodgrass muff would go down in baseball infamy alongside the Merkle boner. Matty, however, would have little to do with exploiting either mistake. In fact, many years after the Snodgrass error he blamed the World Series loss on himself. "Any player is likely to make an error," commented Matty referring to Snodgrass. "What really lost the game is that I pitched wrong to Henriksen in the seventh. I gave him a ball on the outside, thinking he would hit it, if at all, to Red Murray in left field. Murray has a great throwing arm and could have easily caught Jake Stahl, who was on second, at the plate. But Henriksen cut the ball over third for a double and the run which cost us the game."[16]

It was a subdued and downtrodden bunch of ball players who arrived in New York on their return from Boston. For the second straight year the Giants failed to win the World Series, and even the loser's share of the gate receipts was little satisfaction. In reality, the Giants of 1912 had little to be ashamed of. As a club they led the league in runs scored (823), home runs (47), batting average (.286), stolen bases (319) and had a pitching staff with a 2.58 earned run average, the lowest in the league. Individually, there were many standouts: Meyers was second in the league with a .358 batting average; Merkle batted .309 with 11 home runs and 84 RBIs; Doyle hit .330 with 10 homers and 90 RBIs; while Murray drove in 92 runs batting .277. In addition, New York could boast of having four of the top six base stealers—Snodgrass (43), Murray (38), Merkle (37) and Herzog (37). In the pitching department Mathewson, Marquard and Tesreau were the mainstays. Marquard led the league with 26 wins and Tesreau with a minuscule 1.96 ERA. Fullerton notwithstanding, Matty had a wonderful season: fourth in the league with 23 wins, second with a 2.12

Outfielder Fred Snodgrass, a solid performer for the Giants for eight seasons, like Fred Merkle, will always be remembered for one mistake. He dropped a routine fly ball in the final game of the 1912 World Series to help the Red Sox win 3–2 (photo courtesy National Baseball Library, Cooperstown, N.Y.).

ERA and tops with less than one walk per nine innings. In spite of two World Series losses, his earned run average of 1.57 is probably a better measurement of his effectiveness.

At the disappointing conclusion of the World Series and with the long winter ahead of them, few people realized that the New York Giants and their devoted fans would have to suffer yet one more fall classic defeat.

Chapter 15
Masterful Control, 1913

W	L	Pct	ERA
25	11	.694	2.06

It was less than a month after the World Series had ended, on November 25, when New York baseball fans, Giants players and manager McGraw, in particular, were deeply saddened at the death of owner John T. Brush. He had been en route to southern California in his private railroad car. For years Brush had been in poor health, often watching games at the Polo Grounds in his automobile, parked in deep center field. At the funeral McGraw served as an honorary pallbearer and gave one of the eulogies. The beloved owner was looked upon by fans as the savior of the franchise when he rescued it from certain disaster at the hands of the despised Andrew Freedman. Brush and McGraw were good friends but more importantly, the owner supported the manager's efforts through the years and often gave him a free hand in his baseball dealings.

Commented author Graham, "Brush was his friend and his unquestioning supporter in all matters, from the making of deals and the salaries of players to the frequent jangles in which McGraw was involved with umpires, rival club owners, and league officials. Not again in his lifetime was he to have such a man at his side."[1]

The new president was Harry N. Hempstead, a son-in-law of Mrs. Brush by a previous marriage. With little baseball knowledge (he had been managing Brush's department stores in Indianapolis), Hempstead sought guidance from the club's secretary, John B. Foster, not McGraw. As the season progressed, McGraw felt he was being stripped of power to run the club except on the field. This did not, however, prevent Hempstead, in February 1913, from signing McGraw to a new five-year contract for $30,000 a year.

There was another signing in February, this one more for show than to improve the club. Jim Thorpe, the All-American football player from Carlisle Indian School and winner of the pentathlon and decathlon at the 1912 Olympics, signed a New York Giants contract. (Later he would have to return the Olympic medals when it was discovered he had played professional baseball in the minors in 1909.) The great athlete, whom Chief

Meyers described as having the build of a Greek god, did little to distinguish himself in the major leagues. In 1913 Thorpe played in only 19 games for the Giants and batted a paltry .229.

"McGraw didn't know how well Thorpe could play ball," claimed author Graham. "The chances are he didn't care particularly. He had all the good ball players he needed, and a few to spare. But Thorpe ... was a hero to the public; and McGraw, always a showman, knew that if Jim only hit in batting practice he would be a drawing card wherever the Giants played."[2]

Showmanship aside, there were several important changes made to the Giants' roster in 1913. George Burns, a young outfielder picked up from the Utica club in the New York State League in 1911, finally got his big chance. For two years the lad was McGraw's prize student. He sat on the bench, next to the manager, soaking up all the baseball knowledge he could, until 1913 when his patience was rewarded and he was inserted into the starting outfield, joining Red Murray and Fred Snodgrass. Always a big favorite, Burns would remain in the starting lineup until 1922, further evidence of McGraw's sharp eye for talent.

Al Demaree, the rookie right-hander who won the game that clinched the National League pennant for the Giants in 1912, would have a fine year, posting a 13-4 mark. However, when the Giants' pitching struggled early in the season, McGraw decided to bolster his staff. On May 22 he traded Red Ames, Josh Devore and Heinie Groh to Cincinnati for the veteran right-hander Art Fromme. Demaree and Fromme added 24 victories to the established pitching rotation of the big three: Mathewson, Rube Marquard and Jeff Tesreau.

The Giants won 101 games in 1913 and finished 12½ in front of the Philadelphia Phillies. Mathewson, with a 25-11 mark and a league-leading 2.06 ERA, put to rest, once again, rumors that he was slipping. It was another wonderful baseball season in New York City ... that is until the Giants faced Connie Mack's Philadelphia Athletics in the World Series.

The Season

April 17

After two Giants losses, four rainouts and a Sunday, Mathewson made it to the mound on opening day in Boston. More than 7,000 persons braved the cold east wind at South End Grounds to watch Matty register his and New York's first victory of the new season. Big Six went the distance, scattering nine hits and winning the ten-inning game 3–2, but the hero's mantle went to Larry Doyle. The fiery second baseman collected four of the Giants' five hits, scored twice and drove in two runs, including the game-winner in the tenth.

15 • Masterful Control, 1913

While the Giants were winning in Boston, the New York Yankees were losing their opening day game before 25,000 at the Polo Grounds, their new temporary home. Washington trounced the Yankees 9–3, spoiling the managerial debut of Frank Chance, who had been so successful leading the Chicago Cubs to four pennants and two World Championships. With Hilltop Park completely inadequate to play games, the Yankees signed a lease renting the Polo Grounds from the Giants. The Yankees continued playing at the Polo Grounds until 1923, when Yankee Stadium, a three-decker ballpark with a seating capacity of 65,000, was completed in time for opening day.

The next day Brooklyn played its first game of the season at new Ebbets Field and lost to Philadelphia 1–0. Actually, it was their second game at the new $750,000 stadium; the first was an exhibition game against the Yankees on April 5 before 25,000 screaming fans. The Dodgers won 3–2, with the help of an inside-the-park home run by a brash rookie named Casey Stengel. Although the Dodgers fared well in their new home early in the season, eventually it became clear that the new park had little to do with their ability to play winning baseball. The Dodgers finished sixth in 1913, one rung better than in 1912.

April 23

It took Mathewson one hour and twenty-five minutes to defeat Philadelphia 3–1 at the Polo Grounds. Matty's fadeaway was working like a charm as he gave up five hits, none after the fourth inning. His control was perfect and he wasted very few pitches; in the sixth inning it took Matty only six pitches to retire the side, and in the ninth he was even stingier, delivering five pitches. It was another Mathewson gem and it appeared the veteran hurler was at the top of his game early in the season.

April 29

Mathewson and Brooklyn's Nap Rucker hooked up in a magnificent pitcher's duel before 7,000 fans at Ebbets Field. For 12 innings the 29-year-old southpaw matched the veteran right-hander pitch for pitch while the game remained scoreless. In the top of the thirteenth, like a bolt of lightning, the Giants struck, driving a weakened and disheartened Rucker from the mound. When the inning was over the Giants had scored six runs and when Matty retired the Dodgers in their half of the thirteenth, the game ended 6–0.

To this point Mathewson's control was phenomenal. In 32 innings he had walked only two batters and, over the last 22, none! This was a mere preview of his uncanny control. In June he began a stretch of walkless innings that established a record at the time and stood for almost a half century until shattered by Kansas City's Bill Fisher in 1962.

When commenting on Mathewson's control, Chief Meyers who caught Matty for seven years, said it best. "I don't think he ever walked a man in his life because of wildness. The only time he might walk a man was because he was pitching too fine to him, not letting him get a good ball to hit. But there was never a time he couldn't throw the ball over the plate if he wanted to."[3]

May 3

Before 18,000 emotionally spent fans at Baker Bowl, the Philadelphia Phillies defeated the New York Giants 3–2 for the third straight game. The loss dropped the struggling Giants to fifth place. After the first two losses, McGraw chose Matty to put an end to the Phillies' dominance. For seven innings it appeared Matty would do just that, as he entered the eighth sporting a 2–0 lead. With one out and Mike Doolan on first, manager Red Dooin sent up pinch hitter Gavvy Cravath, who smacked Matty's first pitch over the left field fence to tie the score at 2–2. Matty, who prided himself on knowing the weakness of batters, apparently had a memory lapse when Cravath came to the plate. The husky Cravath, called "Cactus" for his prickly personality, was the home-run king of the dead ball era. From 1913 until 1919, a span of seven years, he led the league in the long ball. It was a faux pas Matty would rarely make during his long career.

The excitement was far from over, however. In the ninth, with the score still 2–2, Matty retired the first two batters but then weakened. He allowed two singles, sandwiched between a stolen base and the Phillies won 3–2 before a jubilant hometown crowd.

May 7

With a 3–1 lead in the second inning, a nervous John McGraw rushed Mathewson to the mound to stop the Cincinnati Reds at the Polo Grounds. Matty's early arrival in the game was the result of Ames' poor pitching; he allowed one run, had the bases loaded and, in McGraw's eyes, was clearly on the brink of blowing it all. Matty ended the inning with no further scoring by inducing Beals Becker to ground out. In hindsight, that was the game as the Giants scored three more runs in the third inning and Mathewson coasted to a 6–4 win, his fourth of the season against one loss. Also, Matty did not issue a walk.

May 12

While the Giants continued to languish in fifth place, with a 10–11 record, Mathewson was pitching with the grace and élan of a true master. He notched his fifth victory of the season by baffling the Cubs 5–1 on three hits. For the fifth consecutive game Matty did not issue a walk, a span of 47 innings. It was an incredible display of pinpoint control by a man who, at the time, was the closest thing to a pitching machine.

May 16

New York Giants fans got the scare of their lives in the eighth inning at the Polo Grounds when Pittsburgh erupted for three runs off Mathewson and nearly won the game. It all started so innocently; in fact, many of the 7,000 spectators were beginning to leave, figuring the game was won, when Matty strolled to the mound in the eighth with a 7–1 lead. The first batter, pinch hitter Ham Hyatt, homered into the upper tier of the right field stands making the score 7–2. Stunned by the blast, the Polo Grounds faithful were still optimistic with Matty on the mound and a comfortable five-run lead. Complacency quickly turned to panic, however, when their idol was tagged for five straight singles and two more runs while Tesreau was frantically warming up. All ended well when Matty rediscovered his poise and retired the side without further scoring. The Giants won 7–4 but not before proving to the fans that Big Six was indeed human.

May 20

Mathewson lost his second game of the season when the St. Louis Cardinals defeated New York 8–0 behind the splendid pitching of Bob Harmon. The Cardinals right-hander gave up only two hits, one a scratch single, and did not permit a Giants player to reach second base. Matty was far from effective, allowing 11 hits, four runs in six innings, but it didn't matter the way Harmon baffled the Giants all afternoon. It was one of the few times Matty failed to keep his club in the ball game. His record was now 6-2 as the Giants continued to struggle to keep from falling into the second division.

May 27

The Giants lost a doubleheader 1–0 and 5–2 at South End Grounds when they failed to hit Boston pitching all afternoon. Although outpitched in the first game by George Tyler and his side-arm delivery, Matty still had a chance to win the scoreless duel if not for a fluke play in the ninth. It happened this way: with two out and Joe Connolly on second, Bill Sweeney singled to right. Burns fielded the ball cleanly in right and fired home where his throw had Connolly beaten by yards, that is until the ball accidentally hit Sweeney's discarded bat. The run scored, Matty lost and by late afternoon the Giants had dropped all the way to fifth place. Clearly, New York was struggling.

May 31

The Giants ended their home stand with a flourish, defeating first-place Philadelphia 3–2 before 35,000 delighted patrons to complete a four-game sweep. The popular series drew over 100,000 spectators. Mathewson pitched a fine game, scattering six hits and not walking a batter. Eppa Jephtha Rixey, the 6' 5" left-hander from Culpepper, Virginia, was the loser. At the time, Rixey was the tallest hurler in the National League and, prior to Warren Spahn, the winningest left-hander with a 266-251 record over 21 years. According to the book *The Ballplayers*, "Eppa also acquired a middle name: Jephtha. It was invented by a sportswriter inspired by the resonance it had when spoken between 'Eppa' and 'Rixey.' In time the pitcher accepted it as his own."[4]

With the sweep of Philadelphia the Giants reclaimed third place (percentage points behind second place Brooklyn) and trailed the Phillies by only three and a half games as they headed west for their first road trip of the season.

June 4

The St. Louis Cardinals chased Mathewson after six innings of ineffective pitching for the second time this season. The final score was St. Louis 6, New York 4, with Matty giving up all six runs on 11 hits. It was not one of his better days and snapped the Giants' modest six-game winning streak. Matty's record was 7-4.

June 7

New York defeated St. Louis 9–8 in a wild slugfest as the two clubs collected 26 hits and 43 total bases. The Giants used five pitchers; Matty was the last and most effective, blanking the Cardinals on one hit in two innings of relief. He notched his eighth victory as the Giants remained in second place still trailing the surprising Phillies by four games.

June 9

The Giants routed the Cubs 11–3 at West Side Park as Mathewson coasted to an easy victory. New York put the game out of reach in the third inning when it scored six runs on six hits, chasing both Lew Richie and Al Leifield from the mound. With a comfortable 7–1 lead, Matty had things pretty much his own way throughout the game. When the score reached 11–1 after eight innings, McGraw sent in Thorpe to pinch-hit for Mathewson. Thorpe singled and caught the only ball to center field after he replaced Snodgrass. The American Indian made a big impression with the local fans in his first appearance in Chicago.

June 14

New York beat Pittsburgh 6–5, at Forbes Field, behind the erratic pitching of Mathewson, to sweep the three-game series. The Pirates scored a single run in the first and three more in the third (two singles, two triples) to take a 4–2 lead. Matty finally settled down and from the fourth inning through the eighth not a Pirate reached first. In the ninth Owen Wilson homered, but Matty regained his composure and closed out the game with no further damage. It was his tenth win against only four losses but the Giants still trailed Philadelphia by five games.

After watching their club lose all three games to the Giants, it would not have been surprising to see Pirates fans rooting for the Pittsburgh Fillipinos, the local entry in the new Federal League. The unusual name was in honor of their manager Deacon Phillippe, the former National Leaguer, who won 168 games for the Pirates over 12 years. The Federal League would also place teams in Chicago, St. Louis, Indianapolis, Cleveland and Covington–Kansas City (the Covington franchise moved to Kansas City in late June due to poor attendance), but would not seek major-league status until 1914.

It's unlikely the Fillipinos, in spite of playing in Exposition Park, significantly hurt the Pirates' attendance at Forbes Field. Even though the Pirates finished in fourth place, 21½ games in back of the Giants, the Fillipinos were considerably worse. The club finished dead last with a miserable 49-71 record. Not surprisingly, the rosters of the clubs in the Federal League were not impressive. "It was a mixture of highly touted semi-pros from local trolley leagues, marginal minor leaguers and a few over-the-hill major league players."[5] Lack of talent notwithstanding, the Federal League survived the season to the glee of owners.

June 19

New York defeated Cincinnati 8–7 at Redland Field to sweep the four-game series and move to within two games of league-leading Philadelphia. Mathewson picked up the victory with a subpar performance. The usual steady hurler allowed 12 hits and, if not for his teammates scoring four runs in each of the second and eighth innings, Matty could easily have sustained a loss. His record was now 11-4.

Victory aside, this game was important to Mathewson for another reason. The sixth inning marked the beginning of an amazing span of 68 consecutive innings in which Matty would not issue a base on balls.

June 23

The Giants split a doubleheader at the Polo Grounds before a huge Monday crowd of 25,000, losing to Brooklyn 4–2 in ten innings of the first game and winning the second 5–1 behind the almost flawless hurling of Mathewson. True or not, it was reported Matty threw 70 pitches in the game and only 11 were called balls by umpire Klem; two in the first, second and fourth and five in the eighth. It was an incredible display of control and an overall marvelous pitching performance. Matty's streak of innings without issuing a walk now reached 13.

June 26

Once again New York moved to within two and a half games of the Phillies when it twice defeated Boston at the Polo Grounds; a come-from-behind 5–4 victory in the first game and a runaway 11–3 win in the nightcap. In the opener, after the Giants scored four runs in the seventh to forge ahead of the Braves, McGraw called on Mathewson to close out the game. Matty retired all six batters to preserve the victory.

Following this two-inning warmup, Mathewson started the second game and pitched splendid baseball. After six innings Matty had given up two hits, one a scratch single and with the Giants leading 9–0, mainly on the strength of Doyle's grand slam, McGraw gave his star the rest of the afternoon off. Matty upped his record to 13-4 and his walkless streak to 21 innings.

The Giants won the next two games from Boston while the Phillies were losing two and moved to within half a game of the league leaders. The stage was now set for the most important series of the season so far, as the Giants traveled to Philadelphia to meet the Phillies in a four-game set.

June 30

And what a series it was! The Giants won all four games to move into first place with a solid three and one-half–game lead. The first game of the series was so exciting and volatile that the remaining contests, although critical, paled in comparison. And, as was so often the case, McGraw figured prominently in the outcome. It was a seesaw battle which saw the lead change several times and stir up the crowd of 15,000 into a nervous frenzy. Add to this McGraw's continued agitating of the Philadelphia players and you have the seeds for a hotly contested game. At the end of nine innings, with Mathewson now on the mound replacing Wiltse, who had relieved starter Tesreau, the score was deadlocked at 10–10! The end came quickly, however. In the tenth Snodgrass singled, advanced to second on a fielder's choice and scored on Buck Herzog's single over short. Matty shut the door in the bottom half of the tenth and New York moved into first by half a game. Matty's record went to 14-4 and his walkless streak to 25 innings.

It was a thrilling game but now time to focus on the next contest. Right? Wrong! The fireworks were just beginning and, of course, McGraw

15 • Masterful Control, 1913

was smack in the middle. The Giants manager was walking across the field on his way to the clubhouse with several Philadelphia players talking about the game when a mob of fans swarmed onto the field. Suddenly McGraw was attacked. "He received a blow from behind and was knocked down. While he was lying on the ground the crowd surged about him, and he received several blows and kicks in the face. A deep gash was cut in his chin and another painful wound was made on his right cheek close to his ear."[6] It occurred so quickly McGraw did not know who started the fight. Later, two Giants players claimed Phillies pitcher Addie Brennan struck McGraw. Eventually Brennan admitted it, but said it was in self-defense. There were other versions of the attack which were all conflicting. The next day National League president Thomas Lynch began his investigation of the brutal attack on McGraw. Later in the week, at the conclusion of his investigation, Lynch suspended both McGraw and Brennan for five days and additionally fined the pitcher $100, which closed the book on this ugly episode.

July 2

After embarrassing the Phillies 10–0 in game two of the series, Mathewson made it three straight, this time by a score of 8–4. Hit freely, Matty reserved his most effective pitching for the tight spots. With men on base throughout the game, as a result of 13 hits, Big Six managed to finesse his way out of jam after jam. It was his fifteenth victory; his last loss had been on June 4. Matty also ran his walkless streak to 34 innings.

July 5

Spectator McGraw, sitting out his suspension in a box seat, must have been quite proud of his club as they squeezed out a 3–2 victory over the Brooklyn Dodgers at Ebbets Field. It was the Giants' eleventh straight win and increased their first-place lead to four games. Mathewson pitched steady ball up until the seventh when he almost blew the 3–0 lead. In that inning the Dodgers nicked him for four hits and two runs on a rain-soaked, muddy field. As usual, Matty was puzzling in clutch situations and won his sixteenth game of the season. He also increased his walkless streak to 43 innings.

July 10

It's inevitable, all good things must come to an end. The Giants lost to the Cubs 3–2, halting their winning streak at 14 straight. It also put an end to Mathewson's personal winning streak at nine straight. Matty, however, added nine more innings to his walkless streak, which now totaled an amazing 52 — and would go on.

Actually, Mathewson pitched a fine game and might have been a winner except for one bad pitch in the sixth. It came with two Cubs on base and an 0-2 count on left-handed swinger Ward Miller. Matty's next delivery, a pitch he should have wasted, was smacked for a two-run triple. Every so often the celebrated pitcher would make a silly mistake, proving to his fans and peers he was mortal. This was one of those occasions.

July 15

It was a grand and festive day at the Polo Grounds with the ceremonial hoisting of the 1912 National League pennant and another classic matchup between two future Hall of Famers—Mathewson and Three Finger Brown, now decked out in a Cincinnati uniform. The Giants won 4–2. Both hurlers turned in solid outings but Matty was a mite better and coupled with Snodgrass' hitting was enough to register his seventeenth win. He also increased his consecutive walkless innings to 61.

Over the years Mathewson developed great respect for Brown and considered him a complete pitcher in all aspects of the game. For example, Matty claimed, "He [Brown] spends weeks in the spring preparing himself to field short hits in the infield, and it is fatal to try to bunt against him." Continued Matty, "It is Brown's perfect control that has permitted catchers like Kling and Archer to make such great records as throwers." And with regard to holding men on base Matty added, "Brown helps a catcher by the way in which he watches the bases, not permitting the runners to take any lead on him. All around, I think he is one of the most finished pitchers of the game."[7]

July 18

The Giants, before 12,000 fans at the Polo Grounds, turned in an afternoon of schizophrenic baseball. They lost the first game to St. Louis 4–3 on errors and sloppy defensive play but looked like an entirely different club in the nightcap when Mathewson tossed a nifty five-hit 5–0 shutout. The victory brought Matty's record to 18-5 and increased the Giants' first-place lead to eight games. With a 56-26 record, McGraw had the team playing excellent baseball and building momentum.

The day, however, was not without its disappointment. Sadly, in the eighth inning Matty issued a base on balls to first baseman Ed Kovetchy. It came after Matty had recorded a record 68 consecutive innings without walking a batter, a phenomenal achievement which stood until 1962.

July 22

Over 35,000 enthusiastic Giants fans, who jammed into the Polo Grounds with the temperature exceeding 100 degrees, were richly rewarded when their club defeated Pittsburgh 8–3 and 2–1 in 11 innings. After the first-game rout, when Demaree tamed the Pirates, the sweltering crowd sat back and enjoyed a pitcher's duel between Mathewson and Babe Adams. Matty hurled excellent baseball for eight innings. He allowed five hits, walked one and fanned five. He was replaced by Fromme, the former Pirates pitcher, with the score knotted at 1–1. When Fred Merkle drove in Burns in the eleventh, Fromme picked up the victory and the Giants maintained their eight-game lead.

July 28

Mathewson tossed his second consecutive shutout against the hapless St. Louis Cardinals, this time beating Bob Harmon 4–0 at Robison Field. It brought Matty's record to a splendid 19-5 as the Giants continued to steamroll over the opposition. Although Matty was clearly the leader of the pitching staff, Marquard, Tesreau, Demaree and Fromme were all making significant contributions. In fact, the day before, Marquard had registered his ninth consecutive victory when he defeated the Cardinals 2–1. McGraw had the Giants' locomotive headed for the pennant and there was no stopping it.

August 1

Mathewson, who was clearly in a pitching groove, continued his mastery by baffling the Chicago Cubs 5–2 for his twentieth victory of the season. It was the eleventh consecutive season in which this pitching marvel had won 20 or more games, an incredible feat. Matty gave up five hits and didn't walk a batter. The Giants' lead went to eight and a half games. Although Mathewson pitched well, it was by no means a cinch victory. In fact, the game was tied 2–2 entering the top of the eighth when the Giants scored the tie-breaker on a controversial call by umpire Bill Byron. There was a near riot when Byron called Art Fletcher safe on his steal of second base; he scored later on Meyers' triple. Stones were thrown at Byron, who was not struck, but when the uproar continued until the end of the game he had to be escorted from the field by policemen. Known as the "Singing Umpire," he once heaved McGraw from a game accompanied by this little ditty:

> To the clubhouse you must go
> You must go
> You must go
> To the clubhouse you must go
> My fair manager.[8]

His most famous verse, however, was rendered to a rookie: "You'll have to learn before you're older, you can't get a hit with the bat on your shoulder."[9]

Although Byron's comments might have been amusing at times, apparently he opened his mouth once too often. It happened in 1917 in a tumultuous game between the Giants and Cincinnati, in which both sides argued vehemently with Byron. When the contest ended, McGraw and Byron were still snarling at each other, that is until Byron hit his hot button and claimed McGraw was kicked out of Baltimore. Without hesitating McGraw belted Byron, splitting his lip, and continued to punch him until players and police intervened. It touched off a row that involved the National League president, the league's board of directors, special counsels, the Baseball Writers' Assocation and finally ended with McGraw receiving a heavy fine and suspension.

August 6

In his worst game of the season, Mathewson was pounded by Pittsburgh for ten hits and nine runs in five innings. In the fifth inning alone, the Pirates scored seven runs off Matty, putting the game out of reach. It was his first loss in nearly a month and brought his record to 20-6. The Giants' juggernaut was stalled for a moment as their lead dropped to six games.

August 9

Three days later, Mathewson, in the broiling August sun in Cincinnati, bounced back from his drubbing at the hands of Pittsburgh, to easily defeat the Reds 11-2. Wiltse relieved Matty after seven innings with New York commanding a comfortable 9-1 lead. Matty was nicked for five hits and one run while registering his twenty-first victory against six losses. The Giants' lead was now seven games.

August 12

Mathewson, celebrating his thirty-third birthday at Ebbets Field, gave Giants fans a scare in the eleventh inning when he relieved Fromme. The score was 6-4, New York had scored twice against Brooklyn in its half of the eleventh, when Matty gave up a lead-off triple to Zack Wheat, who eventually scored before McGraw's ace settled down and retired the side to preserve the 6-5 victory for Fromme. The Giants' lead was back to eight games.

August 16

The Pittsburgh Pirates, before 28,000 paying customers at the Polo Grounds, blasted Mathewson for eight hits and eight runs in three innings. Honus Wagner, recuperating from a variety of ailments earlier in the season, was particularly troublesome for Matty. The Flying Dutchman had four hits for the afternoon; two off Mathewson, one a two-run homer in the first and a single in the third. The great Hall of Famer would end his illustrious career with a .327 average and eight batting titles. Wagner took the mystery out of hitting when in 1908 he summed up his philosophy for *The New York Times*: "The only way I have ever been able to bat is to study the ball. There is no use trying to make a study of pitchers ... A batsman should simply watch the ball, and if he sees it coming within easy reach he should step out and meet it. Most any batter ... can tell which way the ball is going to curve the moment he sees it leave the hands of the pitcher."[10] The great ones have a knack for stripping away impediments and getting to the core of the problem. Execution, however, is another matter.

Although the Giants gallantly fought back, the 8–0 deficit was too much to overcome and they lost 8–6. Matty's record was now 21-7.

August 21

The Giants' first-place lead widened to ten games over the Phillies when Mathewson scattered eight hits to defeat the Chicago Cubs 8–2. With a 6–1 lead after four innings, Matty eased to his twenty-second victory. Johnny Evers, of the famous Tinker to Evers to Chance double play combination, quite often would give Matty fits on the mound. This game was no different; the Cubs second baseman went three for four, including a home run in the fifth inning.

August 26

Mathewson pitched a sparkling 1–0 shutout over the Cincinnati Reds at the Polo Grounds. He gave up eight hits and whenever he found himself in trouble reverted to his outpitch, the fadeaway. In this game, the famous pitch did not fail him and he recorded his twenty-third win. The hard-luck loser, who hurled a splendid game, was the Winnebago Indian, Chief Johnson. The Chief limited the Giants to three hits; the big blow was Merkle's triple in the seventh inning, in which he eventually scored the only run of the game.

August 30

All hell broke loose in Philadelphia when umpire Bill Brennan forfeited the game to the Giants 9–0 after the Phillies were leading 8–6 (and had already won the first two games of the series) with one out in the ninth. The inning began innocently enough with Moose McCormick, batting for Merkle, grounding out to second. At this point McGraw, the master psychologist who was always looking for the edge, complained to Brennan that the sun's rays, reflecting off the spectators' straw hats in the center field bleachers, were interfering with the vision of his batters. Brennan asked Philadelphia manager Red Dooin to have the fans move from the center field bleachers. When the fans refused to budge, Brennan forfeited the game to the Giants. The Phillies' fans went wild. Seat cushions were hurled at the umpires and those Giants players not quick enough to get to the clubhouse.

That was only the beginning. It really turned ugly when the two umpires and the New York players tried to get to the North Philadelphia station of the Pennsylvania Railroad. McGraw and Brennan were attacked and it took one of the policemen drawing his revolver to keep the crowd back. With the help of other police the umpires and players made it safely inside the station where they left for New York.

Matty pitched a fine game until the sixth inning, when he gave up five hits and five runs, aided by three errors. He allowed two more runs in the seventh and another in the eighth but escaped the loss; at least that's what everyone believed. Three days later National League president Thomas Lynch reversed Brennan's decision claiming "That the umpire plainly went beyond his authority in declaring a forfeiture, for which action he had neither the protection of the regular playing rules nor of any special ground rule."[11] Lynch awarded the victory to Philadelphia 8–6 and the next day in the press the league standings carried an asterisk explaining Lynch's decision. The bizarre game was finally over ... or was it? On September 15, in a precedent-setting decision, the Board of Directors of the National League overruled Lynch and ordered the game to be completed on October 2. Stay tuned.

September 3

The Giants and Mathewson ran smack into the middle of a buzzsaw by the name of George Watt Tyler. The Boston southpaw, who the previous year lost a league-leading 22 games, spun a masterful one-hitter to defeat the Giants 2–1. Matty hurled his typical game, eight hits and two runs, certainly good enough to win on most days. The loss brought Matty's record to 23-8, but more importantly it narrowed the slumping Giants' lead to seven and a half games. The week before the lead stood at 12. Clearly, McGraw would have to reignite his charges prior to the upcoming western trip.

A few days earlier Giants fans were privy to happier news when Jim Thorpe announced his intentions to marry Margaret Miller, a beautiful Cherokee Indian woman, sometime in October. Mrs. McGraw, in her book, relates a comic scene that involved Thorpe, Miss Miller and Giants' catcher Meyers. Apparently in those days it was the accepted practice to appoint a team member as a "protector" to supervise an Indian with the purpose of keeping him out of trouble. Meyers was named as Thorpe's guardian but failed to tell him of the fact. Furthermore, the Chief made the mistake of carrying his new duties too far when he began opening Thorpe's mail, some of which was letters from Miss Miller, who was then residing in California. All went well until Thorpe discovered Meyers was opening his mail. "Thorpe simply exploded when he actually found one of his precious letters in the Chief's locker," claimed Mrs. McGraw. "Clad only in Turkish bath towels, which each carried in his hand, the two Indians were racing up and down the aisles, around the big grandstand. Meyers was screaming protests of innocence. Thorpe shouted threats at the culprit who had tampered with his mail."[12]

September 6

New York's dismal batting slump continued when Ed Reulbach flipped a two-hit shutout and the Giants lost to Brooklyn 2–0 at the Polo Grounds. Once again, Mathewson was the victim of the anemic offense, suffering his ninth loss of the season. McGraw's frustration with his forces reached the boiling point in the last inning when he engaged in a meaningless argument with umpire Mal Eason and was ejected. The Giants still maintained an eight-game lead over the Phillies.

In the American League, a 26-year-old pitcher by the name of Walter Johnson was having the greatest season of his fabulous 21-year career. The Big Train would end the season with a 36-7 mark, a 1.09 ERA, 29 complete games, 243 strikeouts and 11 shutouts pitching in 346 innings, all league-leading totals. Often compared with Mathewson, it was evident the mantle of greatness was passing from one right-hander to another. In fact, *The New York Times*, without the least bit of equivocation, claimed Johnson was "the greatest pitcher of modern days." No doubt a strong argument could be made for both pitchers. However, the title of idol of America would always remain with Matty, at least during his lifetime.

September 13

After three consecutive losses, Mathewson bounced back and defeated Pittsburgh 4–2 in the first game of a doubleheader at Forbes Field. It was the Giants' third straight win over the Pirates and, even though they would lose the nightcap 8–0, it still represented a positive beginning to their last western trip of the season. Matty issued his usual seven hits, two runs and since his mates grabbed an early lead, had little trouble controlling the Pittsburgh bats. He upped his mark to 24-9, while the Giants maintained their eight-game lead.

September 19

New York, expecting to feast on the last-place St. Louis Cardinals, ran into excellent pitching and barely managed to split a doubleheader, losing the first 1–0 and winning the second 2–0. Mathewson lost the 1–0 heartbreaker on a questionable triple in the tenth inning, which was poorly played by Snodgrass. It was Matty's tenth loss and, in all likelihood, not his last since the Giants had to complete the August 30 game. Interestingly, in Matty's ten losses the Giants scored an average of 1.6 runs per game and were blanked four times.

Three days later, on September 22, what everyone anticipated was finally made official—the Philadelphia Athletes clinched the American League pennant when they defeated Detroit twice, 4–0 and 1–0. It was Connie Mack's fourth pennant in 13 years and third in the last four. The baseball community now waited for the Giants to do the same.

September 24

A mere 8,000 fans turned out at the Polo Grounds to welcome the Giants back from their short western swing where they won six and lost four. Mathewson didn't disappoint his loyal followers, spacing 11 Brooklyn hits, walking none and dominating the game with men on base. The final score was New York 2, Brooklyn 1. The victory brought Matty's won-loss mark to 25-10. Three days later the Giants backed into the pennant when they lost to Brooklyn and Boston defeated Philadelphia 9–3. It was McGraw's fifth flag since becoming manager of the Giants and third in a row.

October 2

The August 30 New York–Philadelphia fiasco was finally played out at the Polo Grounds before more than 16,000 curious spectators who came to see the doubleheader that followed. As instructed by the National League Board of Directors both clubs lined up as they were when umpire Brennan put a halt to the activity—score 8–6 Philadelphia, the Giants at bat with one out and the bases empty. Murray picked up the action by grounding out. Meyers rapped a single to right (Eddie Grant ran for Meyers) and Larry McLean, batting for Snodgrass, forced Grant at second. Yes, it finally ended. Matty took the loss which brought his record to 25-11.

The Giants split the doubleheader that followed, winning the first game 8–3 and losing the second 4–3. Mathewson and Marquard, in a World Series tune-up, shared the pitching duties in the 8–3 game with the latter picking up the victory. Matty pitched four innings and gave up three hits and one run.

The season ended October 4, on a meaningless but high note, when the Giants won both ends of a doubleheader against Philadelphia. It brought their record to 101-51, 12½ games ahead of the ornery Phillies. All eyes now focused on the World Series.

15 • Masterful Control, 1913

Shortly before the New York Giants clinched the National League pennant, the National Baseball Commission issued a highly controversial ruling prohibiting ball players involved in the World Series from writing accounts of the games or using their names. Behind the edict, of course, was the Baseball Writers Association of America which believed it was "a growing evil that threatens baseball reporting in a pecuniary way. It also is making the reports of world series ridiculous, and must, in a way, hurt the series itself eventually. And it further belittles in the minds of the public, the trained baseball writers who labor all the year around as a competent critic, to be subordinated to a novice in one of the biggest weeks of the baseball year."[13]

If that gross exaggeration by the BBWAA wasn't enough, a few days later August Hermann, chairman of the National Commission, really went overboard when he threatened to call off the World Series if the players did not comply. Mack and Ban Johnson, who was a member of the commission, traded salvos. Mack stated he would not interfere with Frank Baker and Eddie Collins from writing for newspapers in which they were under contract. Johnson claimed Mack's players would be punished.

The coolest head of all was David Fultz, president of the Player's Fraternity, who lit out after the National Commission with a vengeance and a little hyperbole of his own. Fultz, an attorney, claimed if the National Commission called off the World Series because players insist on writing articles for newspapers, in which they were under contract, the individual members of the commission would be liable for hefty damage suits. The liability number that was tossed around was nearly $150,000, the amount the players received in the 1912 World Series. Fultz, who said the Player's Fraternity backed writing players fully, criticized Johnson for advocating the disregard of a contractual agreement and summed up the entire episode as absurd.

In reality, it turned out to be much to-do about nothing. When the series ended the National Commission, in a last-minute decision, forgave the people involved, namely: McGraw, Mathewson, Merkle, Marquard, cartoonist Demaree, Collins and Baker for their extracurricular activities. The commission, in a final show of authority, chastised the players and basically said don't do it again.

During the last two weeks of the season, Hugh Fullerton, *The New York Times* sportswriter, compared Philadelphia and New York position by position as he had in 1912. After 12 articles of exhausting analysis his conclusion was the same as the previous year: the Giants would lose the World Series. He did add one biting remark! If the Athletics won the series it would mean American League supremacy. Surprisingly, Fullerton's prediction solicited virtually no criticism or rebuttal, as his 1912 prediction did. Either the fans were over the shock of a local sportswriter favoring the opposition or they agreed with his conclusion.

Again, Mack had a strong club which featured the famed "$100,000 infield" of Home Run Baker, Jack Barry, Eddie Collins and "Stuffy" McInnis. His pitching wasn't too shabby either: Eddie Plank, Chief Bender, "Bullet Joe" Bush, "Boardwalk" (who obtained his nickname when he was discovered on the sandlots in Atlantic City) Brown and Byron Houck.

The Giants had a solid club, too, and McGraw was never known to back away from a battle. Writing for *The New York Times,* he once again predicted a New York victory in the World Series. "Taking the two contenders, team for team and man for man, I believe that my club is the better one . . . I consider my club to be 20 percent stronger than it was in 1911. . . . The question is whether this added 20 percent of strength is enough to overcome the edge that the Athletics had on us in 1911. . . . I believe it is." McGraw took the opportunity, as he did with other players, to praise his celebrated pitcher. "Mathewson of course, will be working with his head. He should be as effective as he was in 1911, or even more so. He has had a better season, and he knows this bunch of Athletics well."[14]

October 8

McGraw's optimism notwithstanding, the New York Giants found themselves in Philadelphia before more than 20,000 roaring spectators trying to even the series at one apiece. The day before the Athletics beat the Giants 6–4 behind the strong pitching of Bender and the hitting of Baker, who drove in three runs and collected three hits, including a home run in the fifth inning.

With Matty on the mound, even in hostile country, the hopes of Giants fans were high. Like a true icon Mathewson was predictable and pitched brilliantly. He blanked Philadelphia on eight hits, walking only one batter and tossing a mere 104 pitches.

Prior to the first pitch, however, it was a gloomy scene that McGraw and the Giants faced. For Philadelphia, the great veteran left-hander, Eddie Plank, was on the mound and New York found itself riddled with injuries. Meyers and Merkle were out of the lineup while the hobbling Snodgrass gamely tried to play but was replaced in the third inning by pitcher Wiltse.

Both Mathewson and Plank fought doggedly for nine innings and all they had to show for it was a 0–0 tie. In the top of the tenth, however, Plank faltered and the Giants trotted eight men to the plate, scoring three times with Matty driving in the first run and Fletcher two more insurance runs. In the Athletics' half of the tenth, Matty retired the side in order to record the 3–0 victory and even the series.

McGraw summed up Mathewson's performance and career in glowing prose, claiming his pitching was outstanding in this game and in his 13 years in the big leagues he was the greatest that ever lived.

With the series tied and play resuming at the Polo Grounds, Giants fans were confident their club could beat the Athletics and cop another World Championship as they did in 1905. But as the song goes: what a difference a day makes—or in this case two days. Philadelphia took the next two games: 20-year-old Bush beat Tesreau 8–2 at the Polo Grounds; Bender notched his second win, defeating Demaree 6–5 at Shibe Park. The Giants limped back to the Polo Grounds for game five in a do-or-die situation. All hopes rested on the right arm of Christy Mathewson.

October 11

Before a crowd of 38,000, many of them women, the Philadelphia Athletics behind the marvelous pitching of aging veteran Plank defeated the New York Giants 3–1 to record their third World Championship. The 38-year-old Plank, bouncing back from his loss in game two, tossed a magnificent two-hitter. His gutsy performance, facing only 29 batters, ranked as one of his best games in a 17-year Hall-of-Fame career. In a spirit of true sportsmanship, New York fans swarmed onto the field, at the conclusion of the game, cheering Plank and his teammates in a wild celebration.

Lost for the moment, however, was the outstanding pitching of Mathewson who allowed six hits, one walk and three questionable runs, which were directly attributed to faulty defense. McGraw was magnanimous in his praise for Mack and his players. In particular he singled out Collins for his marvelous play and unselfish attitude and boldly said, "I want to go on record as saying that Collins is the greatest ball player in the world." McGraw also heaped praise on his star pitcher. "I cannot say enough in praise of Mathewson. He has the greatest heart of any ball player I ever knew, and by heart I mean courage. He never quits, and he always uses his head. To show that he is a great money player, he not only supplied all the good pitching that I got in the series, but he also led the club in batting, banging the ball for an average of .600. I regret to see him growing old, I don't believe that there ever will be another like him for ability, brains and courage."[15]

The Giants were clearly outclassed by the Athletics. Overall, their pitching was stronger, their hitting superior and their defense airtight. The Philadelphia Athletics were an outstanding club, with much of the credit going to Mack for his assembly, nurturing and steady guidance, and they deserved to win the 1913 World Series.

The World Series defeat made it three in a row for McGraw and his Giants, a disappointing and frustrating experience. One other sad note further marred the Fall Classic and that was the firing of Wilbert Robinson, McGraw's first base coach and close friend from the Baltimore days. Robertson, in his three years with the Giants, was credited with developing Marquard and Tesreau, among others. But Robinson's teaching talent and baseball savvy, not to mention the long friendship, meant little to McGraw, who accused his coach of missing a sign during one of the games! This oversight resulted in Snodgrass being tossed out on the bases, hardly a reason for such a severe penalty. The two parted bitter enemies and did not speak to each other again for 17 years.

Amid the gloom and sadness, there were some bright moments, however. Each Giants player received over $2,100 as the losers share of the World Series while the winning Philadelphia players received more than $3,200 each. It was a lucrative five games.

In addition to the money, many of the Giants players were looking forward to the upcoming world tour. The plan was to play the White Sox in a series of games in the United States before heading overseas. They started on October 18 in Cincinnati and played their way west to Vancouver where, more than a month later, they boarded the *Empress of Japan* to begin a 23-day journey at sea. The tour took them to Yokohama, Kobe, Nagasaki, Shanghai, Hong Kong, Manila, and they reached Brisbane, Australia, on New Year's Day. In January they played at Brisbane, Sydney, Adelaide, Freemantle and Colombo, then journeyed through the Suez Canal with games at Cairo, Alexandria, Naples, Florence, Monte Carlo, Nice, Marseilles and Paris. In Rome they had an audience with His Holiness, Pope Pius X, before their final stop in London to meet King George V and then home aboard the liner *Lusitania*. It was a marvelous goodwill tour and, as McGraw described it, a "monument" to baseball.

Mathewson, for personal reasons, did not make the trip, at least not beyond the first stop in Cincinnati, where he pitched and won the game. Afterwards he headed back East as the tour entourage moved on. Matty's refusal to go was always a mystery, that is until October 1949 when Mrs. Mathewson revealed the reasons. "My husband was indifferent to fame," she said. "A trip of that sort—exhibitions and dinners and handshaking—didn't appeal to him. But he might have gone, just to please John McGraw, and his other friends, if it had not been for his fear of seasickness. It was a great fear," she said. "We took a boat trip on our honeymoon, a trip to Savannah where the Giants were training. He was terribly ill all the way down and nobody ever got him on a boat again."[16]

Whether Mathewson made the trip or not was an interesting topic of conversation. More importantly to baseball fans was that their idol had played in his final World Series, though no one knew it at the time. Big Six played in 11 World Series games finishing with a 5-5 record, which hardly tells the true story of his pitching skills. In $101\frac{2}{3}$ innings he allowed 76 hits, walked 10, fanned 48 and turned in a phenomenal earned run average of 1.15. Of his five victories, four were shutouts.

Even though Matty would not appear in another Fall Classic, and he was growing old as McGraw had recently reminded fans, there were still many more victories left in that magnificent right arm. Clearly though, the end of a legendary career was drawing near.

Chapter 16
Last Great Season, 1914

W	L	Pct	ERA
24	13	.649	3.00

The 1914 season turned out to be a major disappointment for New York Giants fans and a bitter and frustrating second-place finish for manager John McGraw and his players. From the outset, their quest for an unprecedented fourth straight pennant was fraught with problems. For openers, after returning in March from the hectic 1913 World Tour, McGraw unhappily discovered that club president Harry Hempstead and secretary John Foster had traded third baseman Buck Herzog and Grover Hartley, a young catcher, to Cincinnati for Bob Bescher. "This was quite a surprise to me," explained McGraw. "It resulted in my having to make several trades to strengthen up my club again. The need of a third baseman, following the accident to Hans Lobert [the Giants acquired him after the season] later on, eventually brought about my trading Larry Doyle, Baby Doll Jacobson and Herbert Hunter for Heinie Zimmerman."[1] Actually, the deal wasn't all that bad and McGraw admittedly liked Bescher as a ball player. What really miffed McGraw was that the trade was made without consulting him beforehand. Under Brush this would never have happened.

There were other annoyances too. The Federal League, with one year of experience, claimed major-league status and was vigorously signing players. Fortunately for the Giants, they weren't badly hurt. Management had the foresight at the end of the 1913 season to sign most of their players to two- or three-year contracts with pay boosts. It was reported Mathewson was receiving $12,000 a year under his new contract. The three consecutive World Series checks also contributed to the players' satisfaction and lack of desire to jump to the new league. In his autobiography McGraw admitted he was offered $100,000 simply to join the Federal League and could name his salary. Overall, the raiding of players by the Federal League had little impact on either National or American League clubs. Their success was limited to luring younger players, substitutes and several aging stars.

It wasn't the Herzog trade or the Federal League that resulted in the

Giants' second-place finish in 1914. It was their own poor play, in particular after July 4, that did them in. Before the holiday, the Giants' record was 40-24 (.625) but after the Fourth, they posted a poor 44-46 (.488). McGraw blamed it on overconfidence and, no doubt, that was a factor. However, the rigors of three hard-fought pennants and the pressured defeats in the World Series could have sapped the energy and drive of some players, while others may have been feeling their age. Newly acquired Bescher, noted for his speed, slowed down considerably. Neither Milton Stock nor Fred Snodgrass could play third as well as Herzog. Rube Marquard was erratic and Mathewson, from July 30 on, had a record of 6-9.

Just as important as the Giants' flop, however, was the surprising play of manager George Stallings' Boston Braves. Finishing sixth in 1913, few if any baseball experts considered the Braves serious contenders, and certainly none picked them to win the pennant. Buried in the cellar on July 18, the Braves began their incredible climb to the top of the league, winning their last 34 of 44 games. Not only did the Braves overtake the Giants but finished the season 10½ games ahead of them! Later dubbed the "Miracle Braves," the club was led by the sharp-tongued, foul-mouthed Stallings, who described his team as "one .300 hitter, the worst outfield that ever flirted with sudden death, three pitchers and a good working combination around second base."[2]

An accurate description or not, the Braves weren't satisfied with a mere pennant. They topped their miraculous season by zapping Connie Mack's World Champion Philadelphia Athletics four straight! The Braves wouldn't win another pennant until 1948.

One other event took place in 1914 that was more important than any baseball season, club or league. On August 4, England declared war on Germany, which further heated up the European conflict that the United States would eventually enter three years later. Little did anyone realize that this raging war in Europe, a distant 3,000 miles away, would one day shorten the life of the great Christy Mathewson. That's getting ahead of the story, however. Matty still had one more oustanding year before the end of his career, which came swiftly.

The Season

April 18

After losing the first two games of the new season to Philadelphia in the City of Brotherly Love, McGraw brought his Giants into Ebbets Field to face the Brooklyn Dodgers, now managed by Wilbert Robinson, the man he had summarily fired six months before. Now bitter enemies, it was their first confrontation as opposing managers. Robbie won handily as Brooklyn pounded Mathewson for ten hits and nine runs in seven innings.

16 • Last Great Season, 1914

Giants second baseman Larry Doyle, a lifetime .290 hitter, played behind Mathewson for many years and claimed the star pitcher was at his most "glorious" in a tight ball game (photo courtesy National Baseball Library, Cooperstown, N.Y.).

Zack Wheat, a graceful, left-handed line-drive hitter, was Matty's main nemesis. The Hall of Famer drove in five runs, including a three-run homer in the seventh that sent Big Six to the clubhouse.

New York was 0-3 and, coupled with several rainouts, this accounted for McGraw's early frustration and disappointment. He frankly admitted the club was not playing well and needed to have a game every day in order to find its stride.

April 27

It was nine days before Mathewson pitched again. Rainouts and Sundays accounted for the long delay. The layoff had little effect on his performance. Matty handcuffed the Phillies on six hits and won the game 4–3. Both clubs made numerous errors and on several occasions Mathewson displayed uncharacteristic annoyance at his teammates' sloppy play.

Actually, there seemed to be more fan interest off the field. For the first time, hot dogs were offered for sale at the Polo Grounds. It was the entrepreneurial genius of Harry Stevens at work again.

The previous week there had been another first at the Polo Grounds, one that would have a more significant impact on the Giants players than the sale of hot dogs. Harry E. Aitken, president of Mutual Film Corporation, approached McGraw with a new method of teaching baseball: to film the Giants players in action. At the time it was a unique idea and McGraw snapped at it. Arrangements were quickly made to install the equipment in the clubhouse so that film from the previous day's game could be shown. Clearly, it was an innovative idea that McGraw immediately recognized would help his club. Today, video filming is commonplace and an integral part of a team's teaching technique and game preparation.

May 4

Mathewson won his second game of the season, defeating Brooklyn 4–3 at the Polo Grounds. It was a lucky victory for Matty, who had given up three runs in the fourth inning when the Dodgers hit for the cycle, capped by Casey Stengel's run-scoring double. At that point the score was 3–0, but thanks to catcher Lew McCarty, who heaved a ball into left field that accounted for two runs, the Giants tied the game in the fifth. They went on to win with another run the next inning as Matty blanked the Dodgers over the last five.

After the game McGraw met McCarty and in his most gracious manner said, "In behalf of myself, Mr. Mathewson and the other Giants, we thank you."[3]

May 7

In a hard-fought, come-from-behind battle at the Polo Grounds the Giants defeated the last-place Boston Braves 7–6. Trailing 6–3 going into the bottom of the eighth, New York scored four runs on four hits and questionable fielding by the Braves to take a 7–6 lead. McGraw immediately lifted Art Fromme and called on Mathewson to close out the game, which he did, retiring the Braves in order in the ninth. Fromme picked up the victory as the Giants' record went to 7–6.

May 9

Before a Saturday crowd of 18,000, Mathewson tossed his first shutout of the season, defeating Boston 2–0, when Chief Meyers doubled home both runs in the seventh inning. Matty was steady all afternoon, never permitting the Braves to bunch their ten hits. Boston's record was now 3-11 and after less than a month of baseball they were already ten games behind first-place Pittsburgh. Matty's mark was 3-1.

May 15

New York made it two in a row over Pittsburgh on their first western swing of the season. The score was 5–3 and a total team effort. The Giants featured timely hitting (Stock, Merkle, and Snodgrass), outstanding fielding (Eddie Grant and Art Fletcher) and splendid pitching by Mathewson (referred to in the press as the "grand old man of baseball"). Matty gave up single runs in the second, fifth and sixth innings but managed to control the tempo of the game to record his fourth victory. It also upped the Giants record to 11-6, good enough for second place where they would settle in for the next two weeks.

May 19

After moving on to Cincinnati, the Giants lost two straight to the Reds before McGraw called on Mathewson to put a stop to the slide. Matty responded, limiting Cincinnati to seven hits (three of which came in the fourth) and winning the game 5–2. The victory kept the Giants in second place, one and a half games behind Pittsburgh.

The day before, in New Jersey, a new mechanical device was unveiled at Princeton University that automatically pitched a baseball to a batter. Netting encased the pitching device and was angled so that batted balls returned to a chute beneath the machine. The invention was the brainchild of Alexander MacMillan, son of a professor on the Princeton faculty. Called "Bat-Ball," the machine delivered a ball over the plate every eight seconds at the same height and speed, which could be regulated. At the public viewing, a participant was charged one cent for each ball thrown. Another giant step on the road to modern baseball.

May 23

Bad breaks and a poor start by Mathewson resulted in the Giants losing to St. Louis 4–3 at Robison Field. Matty gave up four runs in the first three innings, but then settled down to blank the Cardinals the rest of the way. But it was too late as Cardinals southpaw Slim Sallee checked the Giants over the last three innings to win the game 4–3. Sallee was the beneficiary of some fine fielding by his teammates, particularly in the eighth when first baseman Johnny Miller leaped high in the air to spear Snodgrass' liner (a sure double) and turn it into a double play. Matty's record was now 5-2.

May 26

The Giants won a seesaw slugfest at West Side Park, defeating the Cubs 10-7 on key pinch hits and solid relief pitching by Mathewson. Down 5-1 entering the sixth inning, New York scored four runs to tie the game, spearheaded by Jim Thorpe's two-run pinch-hit double and Red Murray's pinch-hit sacrifice fly. McGraw made it three for three in the eighth inning when he called on Turkey Mike Donlin to pinch hit. McGraw had signed Donlin for exactly this type of situation. With two men on Donlin put the game on ice for New York when he blasted a home run. Matty relieved Fromme (who relieved Jeff Tesreau) in the eighth to nail down the victory. The final score was New York 10, Chicago 7.

McGraw's selection of pinch hitters was uncanny, especially Thorpe, who struck the key blow that shifted momentum from the Cubs to the Giants. Thorpe, who was a marvelous athlete, was known to have an unusually large appetite. One can only imagine what the big Indian ate on this day but Chief Meyers, his roommate, described a typical breakfast to author Lawrence Ritter. "Boy, could that guy eat! For breakfast he'd order a beefsteak smothered in pork chops. And corned beef and cabbage, that was his favorite. He could down four servings in one sitting."[4]

May 27

The Giants took the series from Chicago two games out of three when Mathewson tossed a solid six-hitter to beat the Cubs 3-1. Matty did not allow more than one hit in any inning and walked only one batter. His won-lost mark was now 6-2 and the victory concluded a successful western trip which saw the Giants post a 9-5 record. In the process they picked up half a game on the front-running Pirates and would soon begin a lengthy home stand.

June 1

The New York Giants and the Philadelphia Phillies beat up on each other for two hours and ten minutes, and when the game ended Mathewson had his seventh win of the season. The final score was 11-7. In spite of the victory, Matty had a miserable time of it. He allowed 16 hits, including four doubles, a triple and a home run. No doubt, it was a performance of which Matty was not particularly proud. Nonetheless, the win kept the Giants in first place where they had landed two days earlier by beating Brooklyn twice at Ebbets Field, while Pittsburgh was dropping two games. Hardly anyone noticed the Boston Braves, who were solidly entrenched in the basement with a 10-24 record, 12½ games behind the Giants.

June 6

For the second straight game Mathewson was hit hard but still managed to win, defeating St. Louis 6–4 at the Polo Grounds. Matty was nailed for ten hits and in the third inning when he was tagged for two home runs, one by Chief Wilson with a man on and another by Ivy Wingo with the bases empty, the crowd of 25,000 clamored for McGraw to yank him. In spite of the cat calls from the stands, McGraw stuck with his superstar and was rewarded handsomely. Over the last seven innings Matty gave up only one more run while the Giants reached Sallee for three runs in the eighth to wrap up the victory. Matty upped his record to 8-2, although the last two wins had been a bit tarnished.

June 11

Mathewson was hit hard once again, this time by the Chicago Cubs, as the Giants lost 7–4. It was a tight game until the sixth when Matty's pitches deserted him and he lost his composure. During that miserable inning he allowed four singles, walked a batter and uncorked a wild pitch. In addition, Meyers committed an error and the Cubs wound up with five runs. Matty was relieved by Fromme after seven innings.

A few days earlier, on June 9, the great Honus Wagner ripped a double off Philadelphia's Erskine Mayer in the ninth and later scored as the Pittsburgh Pirates won 1–0. According to *The New York Times* it was Wagner's 3,000th career hit. Some sources claim the date was June 30 and others July 4.

June 17

After three consecutive bad starts, Mathewson returned to form, blanking the sinking (fourth place) Pittsburgh Pirates 5–0 on five hits. Matty was at the top of his game and in complete control. In only two innings, the third and fourth, did he face more than three batters. It was a quality outing and increased Matty's mark to 9-3. The Giants' lead over second-place Cincinnati was two games and ten over last-place Boston.

Three days later, the National Commission, feeling the pressure from the upstart Federal League, announced a wacky scheme to form a third major league (the commission did not recognize the Federal League). It would be composed of four clubs from each of two minor leagues — the International and American Association. The clubs selected would be placed in cities where they would give the strongest opposition to the Federal League clubs. The idea had very little merit and clearly was not given much thought. A few days later Ban Johnson ate crow when he announced there would be no third league. "The third league idea was merely suggested to the National Commission," explained an embarrassed Johnson, "and it is merely a possibility. No definite action was taken at our meeting in New York."[5]

June 22

New York defeated second-place Cincinnati 3–2 behind the steady pitching of Mathewson. The victory was the Giants' third straight over the Reds and increased their first-place lead to four games. Matty turned in a vintage performance, scattering seven hits and using fancy footwork in the sixth inning to save a run. With the score tied 2–2, the Reds had a runner on second with two out when third baseman Bert Niehoff lined a pitch headed up the middle, but on the way the ball caromed off Matty's foot and into the hands of third baseman Stock, who tossed it to Merkle for the third out. After that bit of chicanery, the Giants pushed a run across in the bottom of the ninth to win the game. Matty's record was now 10-3 and McGraw had the Giants playing exciting baseball.

June 26

The Giants traveled to Boston and, after losing two of three to the hapless Braves, regained their hitting stroke and punched out 27 hits, winning a doubleheader, 8–4 and 10–4. Mathewson won the first and Fromme the nightcap. Matty scattered six hits while posting his eleventh win against three losses. The double victory brought the Giants' record to 35-21, a full six-game lead over Cincinnati. The Braves, still buried in last place, with a pathetic 24-34 mark, were 12 games behind New York.

June 29

Before 16,000 spectators at the Polo Grounds, the Giants and Dodgers squared off in a doubleheader during which, at times, it appeared that neither team wanted to win or, better still, that neither team deserved to win. Brooklyn won the first 8–7, and New York the second 8–6. Mathewson was rushed into the nightcap in the third inning after Tesreau was ejected by umpire Harry Johnson for disputing his call at first base. At the time the game was tied 1–1. Matty retired Brooklyn in the third; the Giants scored four runs in their half and went on to win 8–6. It brought Mathewson's record to 12-3.

Over in the Federal League it appeared attendance was hurting. President Robert B. Ward of the Brooklyn Tiptops, owner of the baking company that produced Tip Top bread, announced that baseball prices were too high and beginning the following day, at Washington Park, prices would be reduced. Except for the two front rows, all seats would be either 50 or 25 cents. Shortly after, the Pittsburgh Filipinos followed suit and adopted the same admissions. Competition among the three leagues was beginning to intensify.

July 4

The Giants and Mathewson celebrated the holiday at the Polo Grounds in grand style. New York won both games from Philadelphia 5–4 in the morning before 10,000 fans and 3–0 in the afternoon when Matty pitched and drew another 20,000 spectators. Mathewson was at his best, spreading eight hits and was in danger only twice. It was Matty's three hundred fiftieth career win, a marvelous pitching achievement. Like a giant magnet, the celebrated pitcher continued to draw fans to the Polo Grounds and around the league. Never a colorful personality like Babe Ruth, Casey Stengel or McGraw, Matty's hold on the public was expressed by sportswriter Jack Sher in these words: "Although the fans never got close to Mathewson, the way they later did to Ruth, they showered on him the same sort of affection. They respected his shy dignity. They seemed content to worship him from a distance. They seemed to know, instinctively, that here was a fine, gentle, decent man. Why they did is a mystery, because he had none of the expansive, colorful characteristics usually found in those who grab and hold public attention."[6] His popularity with the public was more closely aligned with the type of adoration given the great Joe DiMaggio.

The next day, in Boston, when Braves fans read their morning paper it would be hard to imagine anyone smiling. The Braves were in last place with a record of 26-40, 15 games behind the Cubs. But that would soon change with all of Boston getting caught up in the frenzy of the baseball miracle.

July 8

The Giants lost to the Cardinals 4–3 in the opener of a four-game set in St. Louis. Mathewson was the loser, but he had plenty of help from Fletcher and Meyers. Matty allowed two runs in the eighth and lost a game he should have won. In fact, with the Giants ahead 3–2 going into the eighth and Matty on the mound, some of the Cardinals fans thought the game hopeless and were making an early exit. However, two singles, an error by Fletcher and poor judgment by Meyers in a rundown situation gave the Cardinals a lead and eventual victory. Matty's record was now 13-4.

July 11

For the second time during the season, Mathewson was tagged for 16 hits, but still managed to win, defeating St. Louis 13–9 at Robison Field. One newspaper described the game as "a long series of innings full of continuous hitting." And that it was with the Giants collecting 18 hits for a game total of 34. Seven of the hits Matty gave up were for extra bases, including three home runs! It was not a good day for baseball's premier pitcher, but thanks to his mates he still was credited with the victory, his fourteenth against four losses. New York now headed for Chicago and an important four-game series with the second-place club.

July 14

After splittng the first two games in Chicago, the Giants took game three in a wild slugfest, defeating the Cubs 12–8 at West Side Park. Mathewson relieved Al Demaree, who experienced a shaky three innings, in the fourth and was treated unkindly by the Cubs. He was tagged for two runs in that inning, another in the sixth and three more in the eighth. But in the battle of base hits, the Giants were the victors, roughing up Larry Cheney and Jimmy Lavender for 12 runs and handing Matty his fifteenth victory. The Giants extended their lead to four and a half games.

Three days later, Marquard and Pittsburgh's Babe Adams dueled each other for 21 innings with the Giants' left-hander emerging the winner. Doyle's two-run homer in the top of the twenty-first inning broke the 1–1 tie and gave the well-deserved 3–1 victory to Marquard. He also drove in the Giants' first run. Both untiring hurlers displayed excellent control: Marquard walked two and Adams amazingly did not issue a free pass the entire game. It was a remarkable contest and at the time set a National League record for the longest game ever.

July 18

The Giants moved on to Pittsburgh and, after winning the opening game of the series, split a doubleheader losing the first game 3–0, but winning the second in ten innings 6–5, behind the erratic pitching of Mathewson. The Giants scored three runs in the top of the tenth to snap the tie and take a safe 6–3 lead, at least it seemed so at the time. Matty faltered and gave up two runs and had the tying run at third before he induced Max Carey to pop up to Doyle. It was a close call for the Giants that kept the 21,000 fans riveted to their seats to the bitter end.

Interestingly, the next day the Boston Braves climbed out of the basement into seventh place. Two days later they jumped to fourth where they settled in for the next three weeks.

July 21

In Cincinnati, Mathewson was clearly the hero of the afternoon. Called into the game in the ninth inning with the score 4–4, Matty blanked the Reds, without a hit or walk, for the next five innings to win the game 6–5. If that wasn't enough of a contribution, Matty iced his claim to star of the day when he singled in the winning run with two out in the top of the thirteenth. It was a marvelous performance from the old master and proved to those claiming his skills were eroding that the veteran still could pitch with the best of them. Matty upped his record to 17-4 while the Giants, heading home, clung to a two and one-half–game lead over Chicago.

July 25

On the eve of the Giants' opening their long home stand, McGraw voiced strong optimism that his club could win its fourth-straight pennant, an unprecedented feat in major league baseball. Commenting on the recent road trip and the immediate future he said, "We did better than break even [9-7] and if we keep up that stride we can hold our lead. We are glad to get back, and I think that on our home grounds the club will get under way against Pittsburgh and increase their lead to a substantial margin before we have that hard series with the Cubs beginning August 4.

"I'll admit we have played some pretty bad ball since going away, but some of the teams we have been up against have been playing worse. The boys, however, are hitting again, and I have no fear that we will more than hold our own."[7]

Mathewson began the home stand in fine fashion when he spun a six-hitter and defeated the Pirates 4–2, a team that led the league almost until June, then collapsed, and was now an eyelash out of the cellar. Matty pitched a remarkable game which delighted the crowd of 18,000. The victory advanced his record to 18-4. The batting heroes of the day were Bob Bescher and Burns; each collected two hits and scored two runs to contribute to the win and maintain the two and one-half–game spread over the Cubs. The Braves, although entrenched in fourth place, were still 12 back of McGraw's men.

July 30

The Giants lost to Cincinnati 2–0 with the defeat officially credited to Mathewson's record, which was now 18-5. However, if it were at all possible to change the record books, the loss clearly should have gone to Meyers. The Giants catcher had one of the most miserable days of his career and was the cause of the heart-breaking loss. Meyers' troubles began in the fifth inning when, after smacking a double, he was declared out for not touching first base. Right then McGraw should have sensed this was an omen and pulled his catcher out of the game. In fairness to McGraw, he may have been a managerial genius, but he was not clairvoyant. Meyers stayed behind the plate and in the ninth literally threw the game away. First, he threw over Stock's head at third allowing the Reds' first run; next he set up run two when he bounced the ball to second trying to prevent a steal; finally, when Herzog singled and Dave Robertson, the Giants' right fielder, attempted to nail the runner at home, Meyers was nowhere near the plate. When he retrieved the ball he threw it into center field trying to nail Herzog going to second. When the inning ended, Cincinnati had two runs and Meyers three errors.

After a game like this, it was amusing to read Meyers' praise of Mathewson, years later. "How we loved to play for him!" said the catcher. "We'd break our necks for that guy. If you made an error behind him, or anything of that sort, he'd never get mad or sulk. He'd come over and pat you on the back."[8] No doubt, compassion was one of Matty's strong personality traits, which several players had observed along with Meyers. In this game, however, it's difficult to imagine Matty not feeling some anger towards his catcher.

August 3

New York split a doubleheader with Cincinnati, winning the first 7–2 behind Mathewson and dropping the second 5–4 after blowing a 4–0 lead. Matty had little trouble containing the Cincinnati hitters after his teammates spotted him three runs. In the eighth the Giants scored four more, the big blow Snodgrass' two-run triple, to seal the victory for Mathewson, his nineteenth of the season. The Giants' lead was now three and a half games.

While most fans focused on the hot pennant race between New York and Chicago, the Boston Braves quietly put together a nine-game winning streak. Still mired in fourth place, they were now only seven and a half games behind the Giants.

August 6

The Giants took the first two games of the long-awaited series with the Cubs and with Mathewson on the mound and a five and one-half–game lead, it appeared McGraw was poised to crush the challenge from the Windy City. Not so. Chicago, in a nail biter, fought back gallantly to beat Matty 4–3. Vic Saier's home run in the eighth ignited the Cubs and when the inning ended they led 2–1. The Giants tied the game in their half of the eighth on Fletcher's RBI single to give Matty another chance at his twentieth victory. It was not to be. Big Six gave up two more runs in the top of the ninth and Chicago regained the lead, 4–2. The Giants gave it a valiant effort in the last of the ninth but fell a run short. The Giants' lead was now reduced to four and a half over Chicago and six and a half over Boston.

16 • Last Great Season, 1914

August 11

The Giants and Mathewson lost a hard-luck game to St. Louis with a huge assist from Mother Nature. Trailing 3–2 after five innings, Matty returned to the mound to begin the sixth when the rain, which had begun in the third inning, suddenly came down in a torrent. The umpires had no choice but to call the game, which was now official. It was a tough way to lose, especially in a tight pennant race.

While the Giants continued to struggle, especially the pitching staff, the Boston Braves were now being taken seriously and the miracle was a genuine possibility. In fact, the day before, the Braves had moved into second place in their remarkable quest for the pennant and were anxious to meet the Giants in the upcoming three-game series.

August 15

An overflow crowd of 32,000 jammed into the Polo Grounds to witness the final game of the series against the Boston Braves, the hottest club in the National League. Already winners of the first two games, which cut the Giants' lead to four and a half, manager Stallings sent southpaw George Tyler to the mound to complete the sweep. McGraw countered with Mathewson. There wasn't a disappointed fan in the huge crowd as Matty and Tyler battled each other for nine exhausting innings, only to wind up in a scoreless tie. Boston was not to be denied. Hank Gowdy, who the Giants traded to the Braves in 1911, dealt a crippling blow to Matty when he tripled in the tenth, driving in Red Smith who had previously singled. Moments later, a shaken Mathewson tossed a wild pitch and Gowdy trotted home with the second run.

The Giants, however, did not give up easily. In the bottom of the tenth they loaded the bases with no outs ... but failed to score, sending thousands of fans home for dinner, emotionally drained and disappointed. Swept by the relentless Braves (now trailing by only three and a half), the future looked bleak for the Giants as they headed west for their final road trip of the season.

August 21

After losing two of three games to Pittsburgh, the Giants traveled to Cincinnati, where Mathewson lost the opener of the series, 3–2. In a game not at all characteristic of Matty, he allowed the Reds to score three runs in the first inning on four hits, including a triple, and a double steal. New York got back two runs in the second and that's where the scoring ended. Demaree relieved Mathewson after six innings as his record went to 19-9. It was Matty's fourth loss in a row and fifth loss in the last six decisions. A month earlier it appeared Big Six was headed for one of his greatest seasons, then the flop. Author Tom Meany explains the reason: "Matty started great but soon petered out. He began to complain of pains in his left side after he had pitched, and no reasonable explanation ever was found for these complaints on the side opposite his pitching arm."[9]

The next morning when McGraw was eating breakfast and reading the local newspaper, what he already knew appeared in bold black and white. The Boston Braves were now only one game behind the Giants!

August 26

The Giants were still clinging to first place, even though Cincinnati won all three games at Redland Field, when the pullman, carrying a tired bunch of players, rolled into hot and humid St. Louis to face the Cardinals in a doubleheader. When the Giants lost the first game 1–0 on a magnificent three-hitter by Bill Doak, McGraw seized the moment. The angered manager laced into his faltering players with a tirade that only McGraw could deliver. The players reacted favorably and won the second game, behind the brilliant two-hit pitching of Mathewson. Matty had a good fast ball, his fadeaway was puzzling and his control perfect. He was characterized by one newspaper as "monotonously good" as he retired the opposition with "machine-like regularity." It was Matty's twentieth victory, the twelfth consecutive time he accomplished the feat and snapped the Giants' six-game losing streak. It was an important victory at the time, but, in hindsight, it meant little to the eventual outcome of the pennant race.

August 29

In Chicago, before an overflow crowd of more than 20,000, the Giants split a doubleheader, Marquard losing the first game 1–0 and Mathewson winning the second 7–5. Staked to a 6–1 lead, Matty had one bad inning, the seventh. The Cubs scored four times on four hits, but fell short as the veteran held on to bring his record to 21-9. The Giants' lead over Boston was now a mere half game with only a month of baseball remaining.

New York fans were saddened to learn that the Giants asked for waivers on Hooks Wiltse, the popular left-hander. When no club picked him up he ended an 11-year Giants career with an excellent 136-85 mark. In 1915 he pitched, without distinction, for Brooklyn in the Federal League.

September 3

On September 1, the Giants announced the purchase of Pittsburgh pitcher Marty O'Toole, for the waiver price of $2,500. The move was an obvious attempt by McGraw to bolster his tired and inconsistent pitching staff with a veteran performer. O'Toole, who was purchased by Pittsburgh in 1911 for the enormous sum of $22,500, never lived up to expectations, the chief reason being his lack of control. McGraw had believed he could change that.

On September 2, the Giants dropped out of first place for the first time since May 30. It was a brief appearance by the Braves, however. The next day the Giants swept both ends of the doubleheader against Brooklyn, while Boston lost. The Giants were back in first by a mere half game. Mathewson won the first game 6-3 and Tesreau the second 7-2, aided by Burns' grand slam. Matty was touched for 13 hits but always managed to escape a big inning by the Dodgers. His record was now 22-9 and over the last three games appeared back in form in spite of the pain in his left side.

September 7

Before 73,000 fans, the largest one-day crowd ever to witness baseball in the National League, the Giants split a doubleheader with the Boston Braves. The games were played at Fenway Park, home of the American League Red Sox, because the paint was still drying at South End Grounds. About 34,000 filed into Fenway for the morning contest, which the Giants lost 5-4 with Mathewson on the mound, and 39,000 jammed the park in the afternoon, a game the Giants won by the lopsided score of 10-1.

Matty took a 4-3 Giants lead in the bottom of the ninth and, in a rare collapse, allowed the Braves to score two runs on two singles and a double. It was a bitter and shocking loss and put Boston in first place by one game, although for several hours only.

It was a riotous day at Fenway which involved several on-field incidences with McGraw, as was often the case, in the middle of it all. In the morning the Giants' manager was tossed out of the game, and midway through the afternoon, pop bottles began to fly because of gestures made by Snodgrass at pitcher George Tyler.

Years earlier, Matty described McGraw in colorful language as a fearless leader. "I have seen McGraw go onto ball fields where he is as welcome as a man with the black smallpox and face the crowd alone that, in the heat of its excitement, would like to tear him apart. I have seen him take all sorts of personal chances. He doesn't know what fear is..."[10] The next day when Boston whipped New York 8-2, the Giants tumbled out of first place for good.

September 11

Mathewson pitched a gem, at the Polo Grounds, blanking Brooklyn 3-0 on seven hits. The victory kept the fading Giants two and a half back of Boston and renewed the hope of New York fans that maybe somehow, somewhere McGraw and the great Mathewson could team up to find a way, as they had done the previous three years, to win another pennant. It was not to be, however. In fact, as the season drew to a close, the red-hot Braves increased their lead, eventually winning the pennant by ten and a half games.

September 14

The Giants split a doubleheader at Philadelphia, winning the first 3–2 and losing the second 10–6 in a game which saw Mathewson clobbered for seven hits and seven runs in three innings. O'Toole relieved in the fourth and did a decent job but the deficit was too much for McGraw's men to overcome. The loss, one of the worst in Matty's career, brought his record to 23-11.

September 17

The Giants took advantage of the wildness of Cincinnati pitcher Phil Douglas to hand Mathewson an easy 10–1 victory. Douglas walked eight, gave up seven hits and ten runs in seven innings as Matty coasted to his twenty-fourth and last win of the season. The Giants were only three and a half back, but regardless of how often they won the Braves were impossible to catch as they lost infrequently down the stretch.

September 22

More than 10,000 loyal Giants fans trudged out to the Polo Grounds to give support to their idol, Mathewson, and the club they loved so dearly. Sadly, their hopes for a fourth straight pennant were dashed. Matty was pounded by Chicago for five hits and as many runs in the first inning! Matty regained his composure and pitching skill and blanked the Cubs over the next six innings, but it was too late. Larry Cheney tossed a three-hitter and the Cubs had an easy 5–0 win. The Giants were now five games back of the "unbeatable" Braves.

September 24

The St. Louis Cardinals made it three in a row at the Polo Grounds when they defeated the Giants 4–3 and dropped them seven games out of first place. It was another bitter loss for the Giants. Mathewson relieved Demaree in the ninth with the score 3–3 and let in the winning run on a Cozy Dolan double to deep left center. The official scorer, in an unusual judgment call, awarded the loss to Demaree. Matty's record remained at 24-12.

September 26

While the Giants were splitting a doubleheader with the lowly Pirates, winning the first 4–2 and losing the second by the identical score, Boston took two from Chicago and increased its lead to eight and a half games. Mathewson pitched a steady game in the nightcap, before 15,000, giving up 11 hits and four runs. But it was not good enough on this day which saw Babe Adams, after allowing the Giants two runs in the first inning, blank them on four hits the rest of the way. It was Matty's thirteenth and final loss of the season.

Three days later, on September 29, the "Miracle Braves" clinched the pennant. McGraw's dream of four pennants in a row remained just that, a dream.

September 30

With the pennant race decided, only a handful of fans turned out to watch the Giants play the Braves in a doubleheader at the Polo Grounds. Proving that winning the pennant was no fluke, Boston whipped the Giants 7–1 in the first game and battled them to a 7–7 tie in the second. Mathewson started the tie game, his final appearance of the season, and left after three innings, losing 6–0. Fortunately for Matty, the Giants still had enough spunk and pride to fight back to tie the game with three runs in the fifth and four in the sixth. The game was called due to darkness after eight innings.

The next day Boston edged the Giants 7–6, but the victory was incidental. More interesting was the action of umpire Bill Klem. The Old Arbitrator, a nickname he adored, conducted a thorough and dramatic housecleaning of the Giants bench. It happened in the seventh inning when some Giants players began calling Klem names after he had made two close calls against them. The one remark that hit Klem's hot button was that he had eyes like a fish. Upon hearing this jibe, Klem sent everyone not in the game to the Giants clubhouse, a total of 24 players, many of them rookies called up from the minors. Amusingly, the banished 24 mobilized in parade formation, led by a jaunty Mathewson, and marched in step across the Polo Grounds to the clubhouse.

On the surface, Klem's bench clearing appeared to be an overreaction to the situation. On closer examination, however, his action was understandable. Klem, for unexplained reasons, hated the name Catfish and maybe, just maybe, he felt the remarks by the Giants' players were a wee bit too close to the despised nickname. Chief Meyers, in *The Glory of Their Times* relates Klem's sensitivity to the magical word: "If Klem was umpiring behind the plate, all you had to do was call him 'Catfish' and out of the game you'd go. That's all. Just that one word and you were out. I'm not quite sure why."[11]

While the Boston Braves continued their miracle by sweeping Connie Mack's mighty Athletics in the World Series, the Giants played the seventh-place New York Yankees in an uninspired city series. The Giants, while going through the motions, won four of five games with Mathewson taking the opener, the only game he pitched, 6–5. Total attendance for the five games was slightly more than 40,000, a poor showing by the local fans, no doubt disappointed with both clubs' regular season performance.

Aside from the Braves playing excellent baseball in the second half of the season and almost unbeatable ball down the stretch, the Giants were inconsistent most of the year. Doyle dropped from a .280 batting average to .260; Snodgrass from .291 to .263; Meyers from .312 to .286. Their most glaring weakness, however, was the pitching staff. In 1913 the Giants' rotation led the National League with a 2.43 ERA; in 1914 it was 2.94, topped only by Philadelphia. Tesreau and Mathewson were the mainstays, winning 50 of the 84 games, while Marquard and Demaree were major disappointments. Marquard finished with a miserable 12-22 record and Demaree 10-17. Marquard, at one point, lost 12 straight.

Overall, Matty turned in a fine season, 24-13 with a 3.00 earned run average. It was also the second year in a row in which he won more games than he walked batters. In 1913 he won 25 games and walked 21; in 1914 he won 24 and walked 23. The only other twentieth century pitcher to accomplish this feat was Cincinnati's Slim Sallee, when he won 21 games and gave up only 20 walks in 1919. Clearly, Mathewson was the premier control pitcher in the National League.

For the first time, however, there were signs that age and pitching in over 4,500 innings were beginning to take their toll. Down the stretch, from July 30 through September 26, Matty's record was a poor 6–9, and during the second half of the season he had frequent periods of inconsistency. Most glaring though, were several occasions when he was severely pounded by the opposition: in two games (he won both) he was raked for 16 hits and in other games he failed to make it past the third inning. These were new experiences for Matty and difficult for his legion of loyal fans to accept.

Few people, if any, knew it at the time, but 1914 was Christy Mathewson's last great season. The end of his fabulous baseball career would come swiftly, as would his premature and tragic death.

Chapter 17
The End Is Near, 1915

W	L	Pct	ERA
8	14	.364	3.58

The 1915 season was an unusual one for many reasons, not the least of which was the collapse of two great baseball teams—the New York Giants and the Philadelphia Athletics. Pennant winners in 1913 (Philadelphia again in 1914), both tumbled to last place in 1915. In the case of the Athletics, Connie Mack refused to pay the salaries required to compete with the Federal League. He released pitchers Chief Bender, Eddie Plank and Jack Coombs and peddled off most of his other stars. Conversely, McGraw had little control over his demise; several key players were fading a great deal faster than anyone expected. Rube Marquard, coming off a miserable 12-22 season, continued to pitch lousy baseball. By late August, McGraw was fed up with Marquard and threatened to unload him if he could only find a taker. Author Noel Hynd in *The Giants of the Polo Grounds* relates the terse conversation between the two:

> "Okay," Marquard answered. "Can I use your phone?"
> "Sure," said McGraw.
> "Marquard telephoned Wilbert Robinson and traded himself to Brooklyn ... within a few minutes."[1]

Fred Snodgrass, in less dramatic fashion, was also sold in August. One of the mainstays of the Giants outfield since 1910, Snodgrass was unceremoniously shipped to the Boston Braves.

The rigors of catching finally took their toll on Chief Meyers, who was nearing the age of 35. He finished the season batting .232 with 26 RBIs, both the lowest numbers since joining New York in 1909.

The saddest and most difficult decline in player skills for the Giants' fans to accept was that of idol Christy Mathewson. After throwing more than 4,500 innings, Matty's arm could no longer do the job. He finished the season 8-14 and was bothered throughout the campaign with back and shoulder pain.

McGraw, sensing a difficult season ahead, made changes early in the year, but they turned out to be of little consequence. In January, he traded Al Demaree, Milt Stock and Bert Adams to the Phillies for veteran third-baseman Hans Lobert. Shortly after, McGraw worked a deal with St. Louis manager Miller Huggins, sending Bob Bescher to the Cardinals for lanky right-hander Bill Perritt. Both acquisitions were a disappointment; Lobert batted .251 and drove in only 38 runs, while Perritt won 12 and lost 18. Even a great season by Larry Doyle, who led the league in batting average (.320), hits (189) and doubles (40) could not help the fading Giants. It was the worst team McGraw ever managed and the only one to finish in last place, excluding the 1902 club, which he had taken over late in the season.

Prior to beginning the new season, the Federal League in January filed an antitrust suit against organized baseball and chose to submit their case to Judge Kenesaw Mountain Landis, a man with a reputation for fighting monopolies. But Landis was also an avid baseball fan and, shrewdly, put off a decision.

The Federal League opened on April 10 to much fanfare, but the initial enthusiasm faded as ticket office results proved disappointing. As the season continued, the legal battles began to take their toll and Federal League backers began to doubt the viability of a third major league. When the season ended, rumors of a peace settlement were being mentioned more frequently.

Late in the year, the war among the three leagues came to a screeching halt. "That winter, the 'peace treaty' was announced. The majors partially compensated the debt-ridden Federal League owners; the FL withdrew its lawsuit, still being sat on by Judge Landis; and FL owners Phil Ball and Charles Weeghman bought, respectively, the Browns and the Cubs. The grateful major leagues appointed Judge Landis to the new office of Commissioner five years later."[2]

The Season

April 17

Mathewson went to the mound, at the Polo Grounds, to begin his fifteenth full season as a major league pitcher with the same confidence he had always displayed in previous campaigns. The results, however, were atypical and, more importantly, a harbinger of future games. Matty lasted only three innings against the Philadelphia Phillies, giving up four runs on three hits and, at one point, walking two consecutive batters, a rare occurrence indeed. The final score was Philadelphia 7, New York 1. Grover Cleveland Alexander was the winning pitcher.

Three days earlier, the Giants opened the season by mauling Brooklyn 16–3. The next day Marquard flipped a no-hitter against the same

Dodgers, facing only 30 batters, three over the minimum. (Casey Stengel and Zack Wheat walked and George Cutshaw was safe on an error.) It was a marvelous game by the left-hander, and it appeared the Giants were off to a fast start. But the fortunes of baseball can turn on a dime. Brooklyn bounced back to take the third game of the series 5–3, and Matty's loss evened the Giants' record at 2-2.

April 24

Mathewson lost his second game of the season, this time to Brooklyn, at Ebbets Field, by the score of 7–5. It was the Giants' seventh consecutive loss and, after winning the first two games of the season in convincing fashion, they now found themselves buried in last place. Matty twice blew leads; in the first inning he was spotted three runs but gave back two in the third and another pair in the fourth; the Giants regained the lead in the fifth, 5–4, but Matty let it slip away again, this time for good. Although still early in the season, it appeared Mathewson was not the pitcher of old.

Off the diamond, organized baseball and the Federal League continued their bitter battle. Moreover, Judge Landis was being pressured to make a decision regarding the Federal League's antitrust suit. Landis, a true fan of the game, wanted both parties to reach an agreement on their own. In all probability he was guilty of a touch of hyperbole when he said, "Do you realize a decision in this case may tear down the very foundations of this game, so loved by thousands, and do you realize that the decision might also seriously affect both parties?"[3]

May 1

For the second time in two weeks, the great Alexander beat the Giants and Mathewson. The score was Philadelphia 4, New York 2. It was Matty's third loss. Of the three appearances so far, this was Matty's best performance. He showed a lot of his old form and had the fadeaway working to perfection. Matty gave up four runs on six hits and was relieved after seven innings. The Giants remained in the basement with a 3-10 record.

The superb pitching of Alexander, a well-known alcoholic, was really the difference. The ungainly 28-year-old right-hander was in the prime of his career and led the Phillies to a pennant in 1915 with an outstanding season. The man with the graceful pitching motion and checkered lifestyle led the league in the following categories: wins (31-10), winning percentage (.756), ERA (1.22), complete games (36), innings pitched (376.1), strikeouts (241) and shutouts (12). Alexander was elected to the Hall of Fame in 1938.

The biggest commotion of the season occurred a few days earlier when Benny Kauff appeared in a Giants uniform ready to play against the Boston Braves. The star outfielder had jumped from the Federal League.

Over the winter Kauff had gone to the Brooklyn Tip Tops from Indianapolis where he led the league with a .366 batting average and 75 stolen bases.

So when Braves president James E. Gaffney, who happened to be at the game, spotted Kauff in a Giants uniform he ordered his club off the field. Umpire Ernie Quigley, in response, forfeited the game to New York 9-0. In the meantime, while all this was happening on the field, the other umpire, Mal Eason, was in contact with National League president John Tener who ruled Kauff was ineligible to play because he was still under a three-year contract with Indianapolis.

McGraw, still believing he had won the forfeit, agreed to an exhibition game, which Boston won 13-6. The next day all hell broke loose when Tener overruled Quigley's forfeit and the so-called exhibition game was awarded to Boston as an official victory! After the smoke cleared, Kauff ended back with the Tip Tops, where he once again led the league in hitting (.344) and thefts (54). Not surprisingly he was called the Ty Cobb of the Federal League.

May 12

After a month of baseball, Mathewson finally won his first game, defeating Cincinnati 6-5 at the Polo Grounds. It was the Matty of old, scattering 11 hits and bearing down in the clutch. It wasn't an easy victory, however. In the ninth, Big Six almost lost it when he entered the frame with what seemed like a comfortable 6-3 lead. With two out the Reds scored two runs before Matty got the final out to record the victory. The Giants were still mired in last place with a 7-14 record. Matty wouldn't pitch again for another 15 days and during that period several interesting developments happened off the field as well as on.

The continued legal battles between organized baseball and the Federal League, verbal fights between magnates, broken contracts, player squabbles over money were all seriously affecting attendance at most ballparks in all leagues. Because of these machinations, an adoring public was witnessing the changing of the game from a sport to a crass commercial enterprise. And the fans' attitude was changing right along with it. Fans were disgusted with the commercialism, the bickering, the squabbles, the greed and were rapidly losing interest in a game they grew up with and loved so dearly. It's an old refrain, still heard today, but over 75 years ago it was a bitter revelation to a naive public.

On May 18 nearly 4,100 women bought tickets to see the Giants play the Chicago Cubs at the Polo Grounds. They were there in support of Suffrage Day. Suffragettes swarmed all over the place handing out literature, trying to influence the male population to cast a ballot for suffrage on November 2. One of the flyers, in typical baseball jargon, read: "Line out a Votes-For-Women homer on Nov. 2." Prior to the game, the suffragettes announced they would give five dollars to each player who scored a run. As it turned out the "Suffs" only had to fork up five bucks and that went to Frank Schulte, who stole home to beat the Giants and Jeff Tesreau 1–0. It was later reported Mrs. Schulte wound up with the five dollars. Although the "Suffs" fought hard and made their point, women would not be granted the right to vote until August 1920.

On the field, McGraw's frustration continued to build, as it became a rare occurrence when he received a solid performance from his bedraggled pitching staff. Injuries were also mounting, the latest occurring on May 23, as luck would have it, in an exhibition game at Perth Amboy, New Jersey. Fred Merkle's nose was broken when he was hit by an errant throw in a rundown between first and second. To the astute baseball fan, it was evident that the season was going to be a long and painful one.

May 27

After being idle for 15 days Mathewson took the mound against St. Louis at the Polo Grounds and immediately gave up four runs in the first inning. From that point on the Giants played catch-up and were successful taking the game into extra innings before Ralph Stroud gave up the winning run in the tenth. The final score was St. Louis 6, New York 5. Mathewson escaped the loss, being relieved after seven innings. He gave up five runs on 13 hits and was in trouble all afternoon.

Baseball's now fading idol, however, was still worshipped by fans, especially by youths. Prior to the game Matty was given a wonderful reception by a brass band composed of young men, adorned in blue uniforms, from the Catholic Protectory while hundreds of school boys and girls cheered.

Mathewson always attracted fans, throughout his career, in spite of his quiet dignity. Doyle recalled that Matty did not particularly enjoy the attention but put up with it gracefully. "I remember how baseball bugs would rush up to him and pester him with questions. Matty hated it. But he was always courteous. I never saw a man who could shake off those bugs so slick, without hurting their feelings."[4]

June 1

Once again Mathewson was hit hard and failed to go beyond seven innings as the Giants lost to Boston 7–0. Matty escaped a big Boston first inning when a line drive to Art Fletcher resulted in a double play. He settled down until the seventh when he was roughed up for four runs on three doubles and a single. In the meantime, Pat Ragan was tossing a two-hit gem for the Braves. Mathewson's record was now 1-4 and the Giants had now been stuck in last place (except for one day) since May 7.

A few days later, McGraw's frustration at his club's poor play came to a head when he "told his players to leave their wives at home and forbade them to drink even one glass of beer on the trip. Neither prescription made much difference in the team's lackluster play...."[5]

June 11

Mathewson finally got on track (*The Sporting News* claimed he had been suffering from a rheumatic cold all season) and pitched his best game of the year, whipping St. Louis 3-2 at Robison Field. He did it in grand fashion on a muddy field, the result of an all-night rain. Matty's guile and experience served him well as the veteran dazzled the Cardinals batters with an assortment of off-speed deliveries that nibbled at the corners.

In spite of Mathewson's fine win, McGraw's troubles continued to mount. His latest problem was catcher Larry McLean who was playing for the injured Meyers. Suspended earlier for ten days because of drinking, McLean went on a rampage at the Buckingham Hotel, picking a fight with his manager and scout Dick Kinsella. His actions infuriated McGraw to such an extent that he banished the catcher from ever playing with the New York Giants again. Yes, it was shaping up to be a long, long season.

June 16

The day before the Giants had blanked Cincinnati 8-0 to even their road record at 4-4. McGraw, in desperate need to get a winning streak going, trotted out Mathewson to face Cincinnati with the hope of getting another fine performance from his star. Matty pitched well but not great. He held the Reds scoreless until the sixth when he tired and gave up two runs. At that point, McGraw yanked him in favor of Rube Schauer, who lasted one inning before Stroud entered the game. Stroud eventually got credit for the victory when the Giants scored twice in the twelfth inning after two were out.

Matty's record remained at 2-4. He wouldn't get to pitch for another 12 days, at least in an official major league game. On the way back to New York from their western swing, the Giants played an exhibition contest against the Detroit Tigers in Toledo, Ohio. The Tigers won 4-3, but it was an historic moment—two giants of the game, Mathewson and Cobb faced each other for the first time. On Matty's first pitch, the incomparable Cobb singled, then immediately stole second. Standing on the mound, looking towards second, Mathewson flashed Cobb a broad smile, perhaps a gesture acknowledging his greatness.

June 28

The Giants won their first doubleheader of the season, beating Boston at the Polo Grounds 3-2 and 5-3. Just when everyone began counting

Mathewson down and out, the wily veteran tossed a gem that had fans recalling fond memories of earlier times. It was vintage Mathewson, scattering six hits over 11 innings and faltering only once, in the fourth, when Sherwood Magee lofted a two-run homer into the right field grandstand. The Giants tied the game in their half of the fourth and it remained 2-2 until the eleventh inning, when Fletcher scored the winning run on an error by second baseman Ed Fitzpatrick. Tesreau won the second game as the Giants now hovered in sixth place with little hope of ever catching Chicago or Philadelphia.

July 2

Not since October 17, 1911, in the third game of the World Series, had Mathewson and Jack Coombs (then pitching for the Athletics, now Brooklyn) opposed each other. In spite of the intervening years both aging veterans pitched marvelous baseball, with the younger Brooklyn hurler besting Matty 3-0. For seven innings these two greats matched each other in both brains and brawn with Coombs holding on to a narrow 1-0 lead. In the eighth Matty was the first to crack, giving up two runs on two singles sandwiched between a booming triple by Wheat, to put the game out of reach. Matty's record was now 3-5.

July 7

Mathewson, fighting age and shoulder pain, bounced back from the loss to Brooklyn to defeat the Phillies 5-4 in the first game of a doubleheader at Baker Bowl. Matty was far from puzzling. The Phillies tagged him for 12 hits and tied the game in the sixth when Bert Niehoff homered into the left field bleachers. That was the end of the Phillies scoring. Mathewson reached back for that indefinable something extra, blanking the Phillies the rest of the way and registering his fourth victory when the Giants scored in the eighth.

The meager Philadelphia crowd of 8,000, including hundreds of suffragettes, were back cheering their club during the second game and were delighted at the outcome. The Phillies won 1-0 with former Giants player, Demaree, picking up the victory.

July 12

New York lost to Cincinnati 6-0 at the Polo Grounds in a lopsided game that saw Mathewson get slapped for nine hits and five runs in eight innings. While Matty was being hit freely, Cincinnati hurler, Gene Dale, scattered eight hits on the way to an easy victory. Although McGraw needed little encouragement to argue with an umpire, the frustrating season was having its effect. His beefing in this game got him ejected for the umpteenth time in his career. Matty, on the other hand, had a great deal of respect for umpires—both their ability and honesty. "Many times have I, in the excitement of the moment," remarked Matty, "protested against the decision of an umpire, but fundamentally I know that the umpires are honest and are doing their best, as all ball players are. The future of the game," continued Matty, "depends on the umpire, for his honesty must not be questioned."[6]

Off the field, the National League found a way to skirt the 21-player limit rule (down from 25) which was installed at the start of the season due to competition from the Federal League. They created the DL (Disabled List) which allowed a player to be kept out of a game at least ten days and an extra player substituted for him. Over the years the DL has been updated and refined but is still used today.

July 16

Pitching as if he was in the prime of his career, Matty dominated the Chicago Cubs for nine innings, blanking them on five hits, 2–0. He did not walk a batter and his elusive, tantalizing fadeaway was working to perfection. Matty's splendid performance even ignited his teammates, who played superbly. The Giants remained in sixth place, five and a half games in back of league-leading Philadelphia.

July 23

The Giants lost both ends of a doubleheader against Pittsburgh at the Polo Grounds, 6–1 and 4–3, before a crowd of 12,000. Mathewson lost the first game and if one word could describe his season up to this point, it would be inconsistent. Fresh from hurling a 2–0 gem over the Cubs, Matty never got past the third against the Pirates, when Doc Johnston blasted a three-run homer. Matty's record was now an unimpressive 5-7. Clearly, baseball's once-premier pitcher was struggling. When the Giants dropped the second game, they tumbled from fourth to seventh place.

July 26

Three days later McGraw, realizing Mathewson had only worked three innings in his previous start against Pittsburgh, called on his ace to invoke a measure of revenge against the Pirates. Matty pitched well, allowing six hits and two runs in eight innings, but had trouble with Honus Wagner. The Flying Dutchman was responsible for the Pirates' two runs—driving in one and scoring the other to tag Matty with the 2–1 loss. New York salvaged the second game 3–0, thanks to a five-hitter by Tesreau and were back in fourth place as the club began making preparations for its second western swing.

July 31

The Giants played their second twin bill in a row with Chicago and for the second time they split the games at West Side Park. Chicago won the first 7-3, chasing Mathewson from the mound after four innings. The big blow was a three-run homer by Cy Williams in the fourth. It was Matty's ninth loss against five victories. The Giants ran away with the second game 9-2, when they scored five times in the first inning, but they continued to bounce up and down in the standings between fourth and sixth place.

August 4

On an unusual cold and raw day in St. Louis the Giants won a doubleheader from the Cardinals by the scores of 11-9 and 7-0. In the first game slugfest, Mathewson coasted for six innings, and when he entered the seventh was sporting a 10-0 lead! St. Louis picked up two runs in the seventh but McGraw wasn't worried; he still had a big lead and his star (albeit fading) was on the mound. The Giants added another run in the eighth, making the score 11-2. But fortunes can change quickly. Before McGraw could say fadeaway, St. Louis had reached Mathewson for seven more runs and McGraw had to rush Tesreau to the rescue. Matty's mark was now 6-9.

August 7

New York closed out the Cincinnati series, defeating the Reds 5-4 behind a fine pitching performance by Mathewson after a shaky first inning when he gave up three runs. Like a battered and groggy prizefighter who somehow regains his strength and composure, Matty settled down and, after the first inning, allowed only one run, to notch his seventh win of the season. The victory moved the Giants into fourth place, three games back of the front-running Phillies.

The war between organized baseball and the Federal League continued to take its toll at the gate. In fact, attendance at Washington Park, where the Brooklyn Tip Tops played, dropped to a daily average of 250 customers! This poor showing coupled with Newark's (another Federal League club) increase in attendance when they dropped ticket prices, prompted Brooklyn president Robert B. Ward to announce ten cent bleacher seats. It worked, at least temporarily. Attendance at the next Brooklyn game was 2,500, of which 984 were bleacher patrons at ten cents a head. Cutting prices, however, was not the answer, as all three leagues would readily discover.

August 12

The Giants lost to Pittsburgh 4-0 at Forbes Field, ending their western road trip on a negative note, but overall posting an 8-6 mark—not a bad showing for a club with a mediocre pitching staff and a bunch of injured players. Tesreau started the game and left after five innings, trailing 3–0. Mathewson pitched the sixth and seventh, giving up three hits and one run. Hank Ritter blanked the Pirates in the eighth. Al Mamaux, the 21-year-old Pirates sensation handcuffed the Giants on three hits and was on his way to a marvelous 21-8 season. He would have another fine year in 1916 (21-15), but then faded into oblivion, finishing a 12-year career with a mark of 76-67. In 1915 he was called "the new Christy Mathewson."

August 17

Two wily veterans—Mathewson and Coombs—squared off again at the Polo Grounds with the Brooklyn right-hander coming out on top 3–2. Matty threw a fine game, allowing seven hits and three runs in seven innings. Actually, Big Six had only two shaky frames, the second and fourth. It was his teammates inability to get the key hit, during the many opportunities they had to score, that lost the game. Matty's record was now 7-10 as the Giants remained in fourth place with a 50-52 record.

McGraw, realizing time was running out, began making personnel changes. Earlier he had acquired southpaw Rube Benton from Cincinnati, where he posted a 9-13 record in 35 games. Benton would win only four games while losing five, but would have several good seasons with the Giants before rejoining Cincinnati in 1923.

A more significant move was made the day after Matty lost to Coombs. McGraw gave Snodgrass, the young lad he brought to the Giants in 1908, his unconditional release. Snodgrass immediately hooked up with the Boston Braves, where he batted .278 in 23 games. No doubt it was an emotional move by McGraw, but at the time Snodgrass was batting a feeble .194. Years later Snodgrass had only fond memories of his days with McGraw and the Giants: "It was an education to play under John J. McGraw. He was a great man, really a wonderful fellow, and a great manager to play for."[7] Added Snodgrass, "The years I look back on most fondly, and those I'd like most to live over, are the years when I was playing center field for the New York Giants."[8]

August 23

The Giants lost a doubleheader to the St. Louis Cardinals, at the Polo Grounds, 5–4 and 4–3. Mathewson pitched the second game and with a mite more offensive support could have come away a winner. After setting down the Cardinals in order in the first three innings, Matty ran into trouble in the fourth. St. Louis scored three runs on three hits and a walk to tie the game at 3–3. They scored another run the next inning and that's the way the game ended. Matty's record was now 7-11 and the Giants were resting in seventh place, eight and a half games back of the league-leading Phillies.

Two days later, McGraw released Marquard to the Toronto club in the International League. Marquard refused to go to the minors and, as mentioned earlier, worked out his own deal with Brooklyn manager Wilbert Robinson. In fact, the first time he appeared for the Dodgers, in relief, he beat Pittsburgh 3–2. Although he finished with a 2-2 mark for Brooklyn, McGraw might have been hasty in dumping Marquard. In 1916 he helped lead Brooklyn to a pennant with a 13-6 record and a 1.58 ERA. The following year he was 19-12 before he started to fade, ending his career in 1925 with a 201-177 mark. He was elected to the Hall of Fame in 1971.

August 27

In one hour and ten minutes, Mathewson disposed of the Pittsburgh Pirates, defeating them 2–1, as he dominated the contest from start to finish. It was one of his best pitched games of the disappointing season. He allowed seven hits, walked one and fanned six. The excellent performance brought back memories of his glory years. Commented *The New York Times*, "By some magic he [Mathewson] had brought to his command all the cunning that was his before they began to talk about the decline of Big Six. There was no decline yesterday; the Pirates can attest to that fact. Matty had the Pittsburgh sluggers waving circles around the ball."[9] It was Matty's eighth victory and last of the season.

September 2

The league-leading Philadelphia Phillies trimmed the Giants in a doubleheader at the Polo Grounds, 3–1 and 2–0. Tesreau lost the first game and Mathewson the second, having the poor luck of drawing Alexander as his opponent. Matty hurled a fine game, allowing only one run on seven hits in eight innings. But the Giants could do nothing with Alexander, who was having a sensational season, and now replaced the aging Mathewson as the premier pitcher in the National League. Matty's record slipped to 8-12 as the Giants struggled to keep out of the cellar.

September 7

The Giants continued to play listless baseball, losing to Boston 7–2 at the Polo Grounds. Perritt started but was relieved by Mathewson after seven innings with Boston leading 3–2. McGraw's plan was for Mathewson to hold Boston in check while the Giants caught up. But nothing was going as planned this season. Matty was clobbered. He gave up four runs and seven hits in two innings and dashed any hopes of a Giants come-from-behind victory.

September 11

In an effort to duplicate the glory years of the past, McGraw called on Mathewson to start the first game against Cincinnati on the Giants' last visit of the season to western cities. But a washed-up Mathewson and a spiritless club were not equal to the task. Cincinnati won 4-0 behind the superb pitching of Thomas Edward George, a virtual unknown. His peers called him Lefty George. Matty's downfall was that he allowed the Reds to bunch their ten hits for single runs in the first, third, fifth and seventh innings, something he had rarely done in his prime.

Meanwhile the Giants managed only seven hits (one for extra bases) off the deliveries of George, who had been pitching without distinction for four years in the major leagues. Clearly, this was George's greatest moment in the big time. In the minor leagues, however, George had been a sensation. In the New York–Pennsylvania League (now the Eastern League) he holds the record for most lifetime victories, 165, which he accomplished from 1923 through 1933, at an advanced age. Author Gerald Tomlinson, in an article that appeared in *The Baseball Research Journal,* points out that "Lefty George was one of the all-time greats" of the minor leagues. "His record in the minors," commented Tomlinson, "specifically for teams in York, Pennsylvania, attracted a lot of attention in the 1920s. ... The amazing part is Lefty's durability; he was still playing in the 1940s. Any man who can pitch and win professional baseball games at the age of 57 has to be rated a phenomenon."[10]

Mathewson's record was now 8-13 and the Giants, once again, were planted in last place, 14½ back of Philadelphia with 25 games left to play.

September 14

The Giants lost the final game of the Cincinnati series, which the Reds captured four games to one, by a score of 9-2. Mathewson pitched the middle innings in relief of Al Schauer, who was racked for six runs in two and one-third innings. Matty was a small improvement, giving up six hits and three runs in three and two-thirds innings before Ritter took over. The next stop was Pittsburgh, and the Giants were now simply going through the motions, playing out the schedule.

September 18

The New York Giants split a doubleheader with the Pittsburgh Pirates, losing the first game 8-2 and winning the nightcap 7-2, in their final appearance of the season at Forbes Field. In the first game, Mathewson was battered for seven runs on 11 hits in five innings. It was a frustrating afternoon for the fading veteran who was one of the most popular players ever to visit Pittsburgh. The fans, sensing this might be the last opportunity they would have to see the great star, were pulling for him to do well. All their wishing was in vain. In fact, the fans were witness to a rare display of emotion by Matty in the very first inning. After the Giants scored two runs, Mathewson gave them right back when Bill Hinchman tripled with two on. In disgust and utter hopelessness, Matty tossed his glove high in the air. When the inning ended and Matty walked off the playing field, the fans cheered him in a spontaneous display of love and affection for the excitement he had provided for so many years.

In spite of winning the second game, the Giants remained in last place and were officially eliminated from the pennant race the following day in Chicago.

The 1915 season was now complete for Mathewson and his final mark of 8-14 with a 3.58 ERA was the worst of his career, not counting 1900. It was also Matty's first experience playing for a last-place club, which was something he had dreaded doing. "Traveling with a tail-end ball club," he said, "is the poorest pastime in the world. I would rather ride in the first coach of a funeral procession."[11]

The New York Giants, now eliminated from the pennant race, completed the rest of the season in lackluster fashion, losing four of five and finishing last with a 69-83 mark, 21 games out of first place.

While the Giants were completing their season, the Phillies clinched the National League pennant on September 29 by defeating Boston 5-0. They immediately began preparing for the World Series against Bill Carrigan's Red Sox, which Boston won in five games.

An incident on October 4, however, proved more interesting to Giants fans. The feisty McGraw, frustrated over the miserable last-place finish, erupted after a doubleheader loss to Boston. As McGraw was leaving the field a rowdy fan, who had been taunting Giants' pitcher Benton, claimed that McGraw tripped him and when he asked for an apology, the manager called him "a yellow cur." The fan went on to claim that McGraw drew a knife but was prevented from opening it by other spectators. The incident ended with no one harmed but you could always count on McGraw to keep things lively.

The Giants' glory days, led by two great pitching stars—Mathewson and Marquard—were over. Marquard was now with Brooklyn and, for all practical purposes, Matty's career was finished. Mrs. McGraw said it best, "More important than the [last-place] finish was that Christy Mathewson had reached the end of the pitching trail. There would be other Giant greats on that rubber, but none could possibly compare with him. John's biggest job from then on was to keep Christy set apart as something special in his mind. As a result, John never compared his later pitchers with the immortal Matty."[12]

Last place was intolerable to the likes of McGraw. He knew his club needed a major overhaul and the peace settlement with the Federal League might offer an enterprising manager a rare opportunity to pick up good ball players and help rebuild a club. It wouldn't be long, therefore, before McGraw began making his moves, including trading his long-time friend and pitching immortal—Christy Mathewson.

Chapter 18
Farewell Matty, 1916

W	L	Pct	ERA
4	4	.500	3.01

With the Federal League now defunct, club owners, after two years of financial losses, were ready and eager to sell ball players to both National and American League teams. And McGraw, never a man to waste time, was ready to buy. He quickly purchased the contracts of catcher Bill Rariden, infielder Bill McKechnie, outfielder Edd Roush, pitcher Fred Anderson and the plum of the group, outfielder Benny Kauff. In February, McGraw completed his maneuvering by shipping Chief Meyers to Brooklyn where he was reunited with manager Wilbert Robinson and his old battery mate Rube Marquard. McGraw had great plans for the colorful and talented Kauff, who he was counting on to be a big drawing card at the Polo Grounds and throughout the rest of the National League. He intended to build up Kauff as one of the league's top stars. There was one minor hitch; Kauff wanted $10,000 or he would hold out. At first McGraw would have none of that, but after several failed attempts to convince the brash outfielder to forget the money, he finally had to relinquish. So he and former Newark owner, Harry Sinclair (who had obtained the rights to Kauff from Brooklyn), chipped in $5,000 each to settle the matter for good. Satisfied with the money, Kauff reported to Marlin, Texas, for spring training where he made another big splash.

"Benny's arrival in the camp excited even the ball players," wrote author Frank Graham. "He wore a loudly striped silk shirt, an expensive suit, patent leather shoes, a fur-collared overcoat and a derby hat. He had a huge diamond stickpin, an equally huge diamond ring and a watch encrusted with diamonds. His luggage consisted of three bags and four trunks—and he had $7,500 in cash in his pockets."[1]

The real gem of the Giants' acquisitions, however, was Roush. Few people knew of his potential, including McGraw. In fact, McGraw bought the outfielder for $6,000 because nobody else wanted him. According to McGraw, the only man that told him Roush was a better ball player than Kauff was his friend, Herman "Germany" Schaefer, one of the zaniest characters in baseball history.

"There was one of the most delightful and whimsical of personalities," recalled McGraw in his autobiography. "To this day I smile when I think of his very serious announcement to the newspaper men, during the war, that he had changed his name to 'Liberty' Schaefer. He got this witty notion from a sign he saw where the word 'sauerkraut' had been changed to 'liberty cabbage.'"[2]

In spite of basically the same pitching staff he had the previous year, which landed him a last-place berth, McGraw was still hopeful for the new season. His judgment that the "Miracle Braves" were a one-year team was born out; he also believed the Phillies were just an ordinary club and the Dodgers did not impress him at all. He was optimistic that his club would be right back on top. McGraw's feelings were ill founded as the Giants finished fourth with an 86-66 record, a significant improvement over 1915 but not near the caliber of the great teams of the past. In fact, the three clubs—Brooklyn, Philadelphia and Boston—that he didn't think much of, all finished ahead of the Giants.

It was still a remarkable season for several reasons. After a poor start, the team went on the road in May and won 17 straight games. It was a wonderful accomplishment, especially away from home, but in retrospect it proved to be merely a tune-up for their next winning streak. On September 7, in a game against Brooklyn, the Giants began the greatest winning streak in the history of the major leagues—26 games in a row!

The incredible streak brought great joy to Giants fans, but could hardly make up for the loss of Christy Mathewson. It was his last season in a Giants uniform. In July he was traded to Cincinnati to launch a new career as manager of the Reds.

The Season

May 4

It was more than three weeks into the new season before Mathewson went to the mound to pitch his first game. The constant pain in the back of his left shoulder, which bothered him throughout the 1915 campaign (when innings pitched dropped from 312 to 186), lingered at the start of the new season and prevented him from pitching. During this span he was relegated to the third-base coaching box while he was undergoing treatment, apparently with favorable results.

While Mathewson was idle, the rest of the club was off to a horrible start with a 2-10 record, including eight losses in a row. Matty added little encouragement to the woebegone last-place club as he was trounced by the Boston Braves 7–6 in ten innings. But he did go the distance, giving up 15 hits, one of which was a home run by Braves pitcher Lefty Tyler. Matty struggled in the first inning, his worst, when he was clobbered for four runs on five hits, but settled down after that. Trailing 4-0, the Giants fought back to tie the game in the ninth on a home run by Fred Merkle. The Braves won out in the tenth on a single by Hank Gowdy after Matty walked Red Smith and Kauff dropped a fly ball. Ironically, it was Matty's only pass of the game.

Although Mathewson's marvelous pitching skills were clearly a thing of the past, his popularity continued, especially with young boys. The May issue of *The American Boy* featured Matty on the cover with ads appealing to youth claiming: "'Matty' shows you how. Be the 'Matty' of your team. Get 'em 'swinging like a gate' at the famous 'fadeaway.' Make 'em bite on deceptive curves. Develop speed and control. The great Christy Mathewson tells the secret of how he does it, and shows you how you can become a star pitcher."[3] All this for the bargain price of ten cents.

May 9

The New York Giants began their first western road trip, opening at Forbes Field in Pittsburgh with a decisive 13-5 victory. It was the first of 17 consecutive wins on the road, a new major league record. The Giants' offense was impressive. They clobbered three Pirates hurlers for 16 hits, scoring in five of the nine innings. McGraw used three also, starting with Jeff Tesreau followed by Rube Benton and then Mathewson in a mop-up role. In three and two-thirds innings Matty allowed one hit and a run, a much improved outing compared to his previous appearance.

May 12

The Giants edged the Pirates 3-2, making it a clean sweep of the four-game series. Mathewson started for the Giants before a slim crowd of 2,000, who gave the one-time premier pitcher of the National League a warm and enthusiastic welcome. Matty responded by hurling shutout ball for five innings. But in the sixth the Pirates got to Matty, scoring two runs, the key blow a triple by Doc Johnston. Benton relieved Mathewson in the seventh as the Giants went on to win the game with single runs in each of the last three innings. It was another strong performance by Matty amidst reports that his arm was feeling fine.

May 20

The red-hot Giants moved on to Chicago and won both games, then headed to St. Louis where they took three more before McGraw called on Mathewson to pitch the final game of the series against the Cardinals. Matty responded brilliantly, handcuffing St. Louis 4-1. As if magically transported back in time, Mathewson dominated the opposition inning after inning. Through eight only one Cardinal had reached as far as second base. In spite of the run in the ninth, Matty hurled magnificently, which prompted the press to praise the wily veteran in glowing terms, even claiming he would lead the Giants in their quest for the 1916 pennant. Clearly, the acclaim was more the result of emotion than logic. It was only Matty's first win of the season, but the Giants' tenth straight on the road.

May 23

The Giants won their twelfth consecutive game, defeating Cincinnati 4–3, when Mathewson came to the rescue with a sparkling relief performance. Entering the ninth Benton had a 4–1 lead, but when Cincinnati scored a run with only one out, McGraw called on Tesreau to put out the fire. Tesreau proved ineffective, pitching to one batter who singled in another run, making the score 4–3. McGraw wasted no time and rushed Mathewson into the game. When Matty took his place on the mound, he had runners on first and third with one out. Big Six induced Heinie Groh to ground to Art Fletcher at short who nailed the runner from third trying to score. Moments later the game ended when Clarence Mitchell popped out. Trivia buffs will remember Mitchell, then playing for the Dodgers, as the man who hit into the famous unassisted triple play pulled off by Bill Wambsganss in the 1920 World Series. The Giants had now climbed into second.

May 29

"It remained for the favorite Christy Mathewson to pitch the Giants to their seventeenth consecutive victory today," reported *The New York Times*. "Big Six bowling out the desperate Braves for a 3-to-0 score, allowing them four scattered singles, and setting them back without even a momentary glimpse of second base." Continued the *Times*, "McGraw's veteran surely came back to his own today. He did not try to speed them up, but depended on the good old gray matter of which he is possessed in such abundance. Sometimes he seemed simply to lob the ball over, but with a curve that at all times was working and breaking well. With here and there a flash of a moist ball or a fadeaway, he stood the Stallings tribesmen on their heads."[4]

It was a marvelous performance by the celebrated pitcher while the record-setting victory was a fitting tribute to a great player. In fact, Matty was a key figure during the entire streak; he won two games and pitched excellent relief in three others. The Giants were now only one and a half in back of front-running Brooklyn.

Fame is often fleeting, as the Giants learned the next day when they lost to Philadelphia to end the streak. The 17-game streak would remain unchallenged until 1984 when the Detroit Tigers ran off 17 straight from April 3 to May 01.

June 2

The Giants were greeted by an enthusiastic crowd of 18,000 at the Polo Grounds, eager to see the club that racked up 17 straight and climbed from last to second while on the road. McGraw selected Mathewson, fresh from his shutout over the Braves, to show the fans that this was a new and inspired club from the one they had seen in early May. Sadly, Mathewson lasted only three innings as Cincinnati roughed him up for eight hits and four runs. The Giants fought back and tied the game, but lost in the thirteenth inning when the Reds scored two runs off Bill Perritt. The final score was Cincinnati 6, New York 4. Matty's record remained at 2-1, with the Giants clinging to second place.

June 14

It was almost two weeks before Mathewson pitched again, mainly due to rainouts and Sundays, and during this time the Giants had slipped to third place. Matty tried to halt the slide, but encountered nothing but bad luck. First, Cubs spitballer Jimmy Lavender hurled a magnificent 4–0 one-hitter, narrowly missing a no-hitter when Kauff beat out an infield hit. Second, the Giants' support of Mathewson was horrible. All four runs were unearned, thanks to Kauff, Fletcher, Merkle and Rariden. Matty's record dropped to 2-2 as the Giants trailed first-place Brooklyn by four and a half games.

June 21

Before 8,000 fans the Giants lost to Boston 5–4 in extra innings. It began drizzling early, then it rained and later it poured. By the time Mathewson relieved Perritt in the ninth inning, with the score tied 4–4, the rain was coming down in buckets. Matty made it through the ninth untouched, but in the tenth Boston snapped the tie on two singles and a sacrifice fly. It was a hard-luck loss for Mathewson in a game that should have been called after regulation play.

June 24

Over 25,000 fans jammed into Ebbets Field, which Brooklyn owner Charlie Ebbets claimed was the largest crowd ever, to watch their beloved Dodgers take a doubleheader from the Giants, 6–4 and 5–4. Mathewson entered the first game in the fifth inning in relief of Anderson, who took the loss. Matty gave up a run on two hits in one and two-thirds innings and was relieved by Ferdie Schupp in the seventh. A bow-legged right fielder by the name of Casey Stengel was the batting hero, going three for four while driving in a run and scoring another. The Giants dropped to fourth place.

June 26

After being idle on Sunday, the Giants and Dodgers were back for another doubleheader battle at Ebbets Field, this time before 18,000, the largest Monday crowd of the year. Owner Ebbets was seen chuckling to himself as he surveyed the packed house with dollar signs dancing in front of his eyes while his club occupied first place.

The Giants fared better in this doubleheader, winning the first game in a slugfest 11–8, but losing the nightcap in a squeaker 2–1. The first game looked like a snap for the Giants. They were leading 6–0 and had two out in the bottom of the fifth when all hell broke loose. Four runs later Perritt, who started, was relieved by Rube Schauer. After Zack Wheat singled scoring Stengel, Mike Mowrey beat out an infield hit, took second on Schauer's wild throw while Wheat scampered to third. The Giants were clinging to a 6–5 lead with runners on second and third and still two out. McGraw had seen enough bleeding and quickly called for Mathewson to stop the hemorrhaging. George Cutshaw greeted Matty with a tremendous home run to deep center field and Brooklyn led 8–6.

It was only a momentary scare, however, as Matty blanked the Dodgers the rest of the game, while his teammates scored five more runs. The win evened his record at 3-3. This was Christy Mathewson's last victory in a New York Giants uniform.

July 4

On this holiday, in yet another doubleheader against Brooklyn, Mathewson pitched his last game for the New York Giants. He lost 7–6 in relief. Perritt started the game and, after the Dodgers scored two runs in the first inning, McGraw sent for Matty who slammed the door shut. The Giants came back and scored five runs in their half of the first. The Dodgers countered with a single run in the third and broke the game wide open in the fifth when Mathewson weakened, giving up four hits and four runs. It wasn't entirely his fault: Fletcher committed two key errors and Rariden a wild throw in the inning. The doubleheader loss dropped the Giants all the way down to sixth place with a 30–33 record. Matty's mark was 3-4.

On July 20, with New York still hovering in fourth place with a 38-40 record, Giants president Harry Hempstead made a startling announcement to the press: Christy Mathewson was traded to the Cincinnati Reds. In addition to Matty, Cincinnati received Roush and McKechnie. The Giants got Charlie Herzog, a former Giants player and the current Reds' manager, plus outfielder Wade Killifer. The acquisition of Herzog cleared the way for Mathewson to manage, a desire he had expressed to McGraw for several years.

18 • Farewell Matty, 1916

"It wasn't easy for me to part with Matty," said McGraw to the press. "He not only was the greatest pitcher I ever saw but he is my friend. However, I'm convinced that his pitching days are over—and he agrees with me. He could stay with the Giants as long as he wanted to, of course. But he is ambitious to become a manager—and I have helped him to gratify that ambition."[5]

On the train to Cincinnati with Roush and McKechnie, Mathewson was equally laudatory about his 16 years with the Giants and his high regard for McGraw. Matty's comments were instigated by Roush when he recalled how he and McKechnie were happy to be getting away from McGraw and asked Mathewson if he wasn't glad too. "I'll tell you something, Roush," he said. "You and Mac have only been on the Giants a couple of months. It's just another ball club to you fellows. But I was with that team for 16 years. That's a mighty long time. To me, the Giants are 'home.' And leaving them like this, I feel the same as when I leave home in the spring of the year.

"Of course, I realize I'm through as a pitcher. But I appreciate McGraw making a place for me in baseball and getting me this managing job. He's doing me a favor, and I thanked him for it. And by the way, the last thing he said to me was that if I put you in center field I'd have a great ball player. So starting tomorrow you're my center fielder."[6]

True to his word, the next day in his first game as the Reds' manager Matty put Roush in center field and batted him second. The future Hall of Famer responded with a three for five day, including a two-run triple, but the Reds still lost to Philadelphia 6–4 to spoil Mathewson's debut. In spite of the loss it was a joyous day. Earlier, Matty had signed a contract binding him through the 1918 season. Of more immediate concern, 2,500 cheerful fans showed up, the number held down somewhat by rain, but still the best weekday attendance in a long time. Matty received a tremendous ovation when he took the batting order to home plate. Clearly, the charisma was still evident.

With Mathewson, Roush and McKechnie gone and the Giants drifting between fourth and sixth place, McGraw knew he had to make additional changes to improve his club. So he purchased the veteran left-hander, Slim Sallee, from the St. Louis Cardinals for $10,000. Then in August he dumped two veterans from the glory years: Merkle went to Brooklyn for catcher Lew McCarty; Larry Doyle went to Chicago in a five-player deal that included infielder Henry "Heinie" Zimmerman or, as he liked to be called, "The Great Zim."

On September 7, McGraw's new-look club, which was in fourth place, gave the fans a preview of what they could expect in 1917. They beat Brooklyn 4–1 at the Polo Grounds and began the longest winning streak in baseball history, 26 consecutive games—a record which still stands today. The streak ended on September 30 when they lost the second game of a doubleheader to Boston, 8–3. It was a marvelous streak but unfortunately did nothing to change the Giants' position in the standings. When the streak ended the Giants were still in fourth place, exactly where they were when it began. The Giants, however, did help Brooklyn win the pennant when they took four games in a row from the Phillies, which permitted the Dodgers to slip back into first where they held on until the end. More importantly, the streak brought the club together, gave the ball players confidence and the fans renewed hope, which was realized in 1917 when McGraw and the Giants were once again back on top of the National League.

The Cincinnati Reds' season, under new manager Mathewson, was hardly as interesting as that of the Giants. Actually, it turned out to be a boring and lackluster summer. Even with the support and adoration of the fans, Matty could do little to turn the Reds' season around. Herzog had the Reds playing at a .410 clip (34-49); Matty at .368 (25-43). Cincinnati finished the season in seventh, 33½ games behind pennant-winning Brooklyn. It was going to take more than Mathewson's baseball knowledge, savvy and charisma to make the Reds a winning club. Major changes were needed and Matty had a lot of work to do.

One of the more memorable moments for Cincinnati fans came in early September when the Reds were in Chicago for a series. It began innocently enough when the great veteran Three Finger Brown announced he was going to pitch his final game as a Cub in the nightcap of the doubleheader on September 4. Mathewson decided that game would also be a good opportunity to test his sore arm one more time. It was a matchup made in heaven.

As September 4 drew near, fan interest mounted and the doubleheader was quickly sold out. One poster advertised the game as the "Greatest Treat of the Year for Baseball Fans." It also featured action photos of both pitchers and a blowup of Brown's mangled right hand.

Adding to the hoopla and excitement, both veterans announced they intended to pitch complete games, much to the fans' delight. After Chicago won the morning contest 3–0, the long-anticipated clash was soon to be a reality as both stars received great ovations when they stepped on the field. After a short ceremony celebrating Brown's retirement, the game began.

At the end of five innings, with the Reds leading 6–5, it was evident these two great pitchers were fighting their last battle. Neither had much on the ball as hits were flying all over the field. In fact, when the game ended Matty had given up 15 hits, Brown 19. Gamely they fought on. The Reds pounded Brown for two more runs in the sixth and single tallies in the eighth and ninth for a 10–5 lead. True to his word Brown completed the game and as he walked off the field the crowd gave him a standing ovation.

Mathewson entered the bottom of the ninth with a comfortable lead, needing only three outs for the victory. It turned out to be the most agonizing

18 • Farewell Matty, 1916

From 1903 until 1916 Three Finger Brown (note his pitching hand) and Christy Mathewson hooked up 24 times with each hurler winning 12 games, many of them classic duels (photo courtesy National Baseball Library, Cooperstown, N.Y.).

three outs of his career. Matty, shaky from the start of the inning, managed to get two outs, but not before the Cubs added three more runs making the score 10–8. He now had the tying run at the plate, represented by pinch hitter Fritz Mollwitz. Mathewson, pitching solely on guts and guile, induced Mollwitz to pop up on a pitch some claim was, rather appropriately, the fadeaway. Christy Mathewson had won the game, his three hundred seventy-third and final major league victory!

After the game, in the Reds' clubhouse, Mathewson told the players, "Boys, I thought I could pitch a few more games, but I find I haven't got the stuff anymore. If I ever go into the box again, I'll buy every one of you a suit of clothes."[7]

So ended Mathewson's career as an active player. His managerial reign, front-office experience and private life were still ahead of him but would end, all too early, on a tragic note.

Unlike McGraw, his long-time mentor, Mathewson made few changes or adjustments to his 1917 Cincinnati club. In spite of this, the Reds finished fourth with a 78-76 record, a major improvement over the seventh-place club Matty inherited the previous year. Roush led the league in batting with a .341 average, and along with Hal Chase, Heinie Groh and Earle Neale had solid seasons. The pitching staff improved significantly, possibly the result of Matty's knowledge and teaching skill. Fred Toney and Pete Schneider won 44 games between them, almost twice as many as the year before, while rookies Mike Regan and Horace Eller added another 21 wins.

The fine season was marred, however, by the first in a series of tragedies that would follow Mathewson through the coming years like an ominous dark cloud. Matty's younger brother, Henry, who earlier had a short undistinguished career with the Giants, committed suicide during the summer.

Mathewson returned to manage the Reds in 1918, the final year of his contract, as the United States' involvement in World War I intensified. It was basically the same club as the previous year, adequate, but never a serious pennant contender. After struggling through an up and down season and watching ball players joining up in droves, Matty finally called it quits in late August, with a record of 61-57, ten games before the war-shortened season officially ended.

Matty accepted a commission as a captain in the Army's Chemical Warfare Division. On the voyage to France, he caught the flu and had trouble shaking the illness in the cold, damp autumn of Chaumont. It was Mathewson's job to instruct recruits on the proper use of gas masks. During training sessions real gas was used in an enclosed building and Matty's accidental breathing of the dangerous fumes into his lungs, which were already weakened by the lingering influenza, made him highly susceptible to the dreaded disease tuberculosis. Other accounts claim that while touring empty trenches, Matty inhaled deadly gas that had not been purged from the area.

With the war ending on November 11, 1918, Matty returned home in the spring of 1919 without a job. Pat Moran had been hired as manager of the Reds. McGraw wasted little time and quickly signed Matty to a contract as a coach with the title of "assistant manager." Once again, McGraw and Mathewson were reunited.

18 • Farewell Matty, 1916

Earlier, in a strange twist of events, McGraw had obtained controversial first baseman Hal Chase from Cincinnati for catcher Rariden. McGraw always liked Chase as a ball player despite his checkered background. He had been accused of throwing games and Mathewson had suspended him in August 1918, prior to joining the service. Actually, according to sportswriter Fred Lieb, Mathewson suspected Chase's loyalty as early as 1916. Matty did nothing, however, until late August 1918 when he finally suspended Chase and filed an affidavit with National League president, John Heydler, charging that the first baseman had thrown some games. Shortly after, Matty sailed for France.

Heydler launched a full-scale investigation into the matter and in late January held a hearing in his New York office. Heydler listened for five hours to testimony from Chase (accompanied by three lawyers), Reds players Earle Neale, Jimmy Ring and Mike Regan and McGraw, who admitted Bill Perritt, his own pitcher, told him he had been propositioned by Chase the previous August. With Mathewson overseas and unable to testify and Heydler not able to communicate with him, the president had little hope of building a case and, thus, cleared Chase. Privately he had come to an entirely different conclusion. According to Lieb, "In off-the-record talks Heydler told me that he felt Hal was guilty. 'But I have no proof that will stand up in a court of law.' In the end, just before the teams left for 1919 spring training, Heydler acquitted the great first baseman. He said in his statement that with Mathewson unavailable, he could not make Matty's charges stand up."[8]

Throughout the 1919 season Mathewson was hampered by a chronic cough which was diagnosed later as much more serious. The Mathewson-Chase affair now entered a new phase; they were both members of the same club, which did little to heal their strained relations. During the season neither would comment on the other's presence on the team nor would they speak to each other. Chase continued his shenanigans, unhampered by McGraw, apparently the result of the manager's long-time friendship with the first baseman. McGraw's lack of action was even more surprising when he later admitted he strongly suspected Chase of laying down during the crucial Cincinnati series, which ostensibly decided the pennant. It was, however, Chase's last season in a major-league uniform.

In the spring of 1920 Mathewson, not feeling well, was examined by physicians and diagnosed as having contracted bronchitis. By the end of June, as Matty's condition persisted, it was discovered not to be bronchitis but tuberculosis. Matty and Jane began packing for a stay at Lake Saranac, the well-known treatment center for tuberculosis in the Adirondack Mountains of New York. Matty had been given six months to live.

At Saranac one of Matty's lungs collapsed, further adding to his discomfort and depression. Mathewson's body was slowly losing the battle, but his mind was still alert and active. He said of his uncomfortable situation, "When a fellow cannot reach, or write or talk, and can only move his fingers and forearms, it requires some resourcefulness to keep his mind off his troubles." Added Matty, "I started working out a baseball game, figuring every chance and studying how it should be played mechanically so as to offer the same chances as are offered on a ball field. It interested me and kept my mind engaged."[9]

Even though he was suffering physically, baseball was not far from Matty's mind. In 1921, when the Giants won the pennant, McGraw called from his hotel in Pittsburgh to tell him the good news. The room was jammed with reporters and Matty spoke to each of them. It was an emotional scene during which few could hold back the tears.

Not long after the phone call, on September 30, Mathewson was given a testimonial by his friends and admirers in conjunction with the Giants-Braves game. Fred Lieb, head of the New York Baseball Writers at the time, was tapped as chairman of the testimonial committee. A crowd of 20,000 showed up on a warm and sunny day. Prior to the regularly scheduled game the Giants Old Timers whipped McGraw's current club 2–0 in a five-inning contest. A gala of past Giants stars were enthusiastically welcomed, especially favorites Roger Bresnahan, George Wiltse, Larry Doyle, Jack Murray, Art Devlin and Fred Tenney.

By the time the Giants-Braves contest started, clouds had gathered and, after one scoreless inning, the rain came down in buckets and the game was called. Only 4,000 fans asked for a refund, a tribute to Mathewson's popularity and when the shrewd Lieb collected a $25,000 rain insurance check, the result of a policy he had taken out weeks earlier, a grand total for Matty was in the neighborhood of $45,000, a substantial sum in those days.

Besides gate receipts, some money came from the sale of souvenir score books, autographed baseballs and personal checks. According to Lieb, the prize of the day was the ball autographed by Mathewson, President Warren Harding, Vice President Calvin Coolidge, Governor Nathan Miller, Babe Ruth, Walter Johnson, Ty Cobb, George M. Cohan and several other actors, athletes and politicians. It was the most autographed ball Lieb had ever seen and was auctioned for $450 (some accounts went as high as $750), which sadly was never collected from the purchaser.

From Saranac Lake Mathewson sent a message of appreciation to the team and fans for their thoughtfulness in giving him a day and their support during his battle with tuberculosis.

The pure air and rest at Saranac proved helpful to Mathewson's condition. By 1923 Matty had recovered sufficiently to return to baseball and become the president of the Boston Braves. Mathewson was more a figurehead than an active executive. Judge Emil Fuchs, owner of the Braves, told Matty he need only come to Boston when his health permitted. Fuchs, however, would seek his advice on player salaries, trades and acquisitions. In spite of this light schedule, Mrs. McGraw believed Mathewson worked too hard and worried too much.

18 • Farewell Matty, 1916

By the spring of 1925 Mathewson's condition took a turn for the worse and he suffered a relapse. He and Jane returned to Saranac Lake. Through the summer and early fall, the once great physical specimen and idol of America began to wither away from the debilitating illness. His last days were spent reading about baseball in the newspapers, playing checkers and taking quiet rides in the mountains.

On the morning of October 7, 1925, Christy Mathewson, knowing the end was near, said to his wife, "Now, Jane, I suppose you will have to go out and have a good cry. Don't make it a long one. This cannot be helped."[10] Matty quietly slipped away that afternoon.

News of Matty's death reached Forbes Field in Pittsburgh in the fifth inning of the first game of the World Series, which the Washington Senators won 4–1. It is said that when winning pitcher Walter Johnson, who was often compared to Matty, heard of Matty's death he turned pale and silent. For the remaining World Series games all players wore black armbands in memory of a true gentleman and one of the greatest pitchers in National League history.

McGraw, attending the World Series at the time, immediately left Pittsburgh for New York, picked up his wife, Blanche, and then headed for the Adirondacks. Three days later, the McGraws and Jane Mathewson, close friends since 1902, accompanied the body to Lewisburg, Pennsylvania, where Matty was buried near the campus of Bucknell University. McGraw and Doyle were pallbearers.

The following summer, the Christy Mathewson Memorial Foundation was established. The goal of the foundation was to erect two memorials to perpetuate Matty's name: one at Bucknell, the other at Saranac Lake. Throughout the summer, many games were played by professional, industrial, amateur and semiprofessional teams, with the proceeds going to the foundation in a marvelous national tribute to the memory of Matty.

Eleven years after his death, in 1936, Christy Mathewson was honored with baseball's greatest tribute. The Baseball Writers of America chose five immortals as the first inductees to the Hall of Fame in Cooperstown, New York. The five, in order of the votes received, were: Ty Cobb, Babe Ruth, Honus Wagner, Christy Mathewson and Walter Johnson.

It was a well-deserved honor, but to the millions of people throughout the country, Matty represented more than merely the best in his profession. His persona, like Ruth after him, transcended the game and reached heights of public adoration never attained before. In spite of the idolatry, Matty never forgot his humble roots.

These words, taken from *A History of Keystone College*, where Mathewson received his early education while living in Factoryville, simply but poignantly describe what Matty meant to this country during the early 1900s.

Plaque in Honesdale, Pennsylvania, honoring Mathewson, who played for the Honesdale Eagles in 1898 and 1899 (photo by Arlene C. Mayer).

18 • Farewell Matty, 1916

Christy Mathewson was an American hero during his lifetime. His life, on and off the field, epitomized America. He was a farm boy who became one of the greatest to ever play America's game, a hero figure to the nation's youth, and a courageous soldier. Mathewson was cheered in every city he played. Following the baseball season, he would bring home bats, balls and uniforms and distribute them to the children of Factoryville; he did not forget his roots.[11]

Christy Mathewson will never be forgotten either.

Appendix A: Milestones in the Career of Mathewson

First Victory	April 26, 1901	New York 5, Brooklyn 3
No-Hitter	July 15, 1901	New York 5, St. Louis 0
One-Hitter	June 13, 1903	New York 4, Cincinnati 0
One-Hitter	June 10, 1904	New York 5, Chicago 0
Struck Out 16 (Career High)	October 3, 1904	New York 3, St. Louis 1
Victory 100	May 1, 1905	New York 8, Boston 2
No-Hitter	June 13, 1905	New York 1, Chicago 0
First World Series Victory	October 9, 1905	New York 3, Philadelphia 0
Second World Series Victory	October 12, 1905	New York 9, Philadelphia 0
Third World Series Victory	October 14, 1905	New York 2, Philadelphia 0
Victory 150	October 4, 1906	New York 7, Philadelphia 6
One-Hitter	April 27, 1908	New York 2, Boston 0
Victory 200	August 24, 1908	New York 5, Pittsburgh 1
24 Consecutive-Game Winning Streak Versus St. Louis	June 16, 1904 to September 15, 1908	
37th Victory (Season High)	October 1, 1908	New York 4, Philadelphia 3
One-Hitter	May 2, 1910	New York 6, Brooklyn 0
Victory 250	July 4, 1910	New York 6, Brooklyn 5
22 Consecutive-Game Winning Streak Versus Cincinnati	June 17, 1908 to August 16, 1911	

Fourth World Series Victory	October 14, 1911	New York 2, Philadelphia 1
Victory 300	July 5, 1912	New York 6, Brooklyn 1
68 Consecutive Innings Without Issuing a Walk	June 19 to July 18, 1913	
Fifth World Series Victory	October 8, 1913	New York 3, Philadelphia 0
Victory 350	July 4, 1914	New York 3, Philadelphia 0
Last Victory (373)	September 4, 1916	Cincinnati 10, Chicago 8

Appendix B: Mathewson's Lifetime Pitching Record

	W	L	Pct.	ERA	G	GS	CG	IP	H	BB	SO	SHO
1900 NY N	0	3	.000	5.08	6	1	1	33.2	37	20	15	0
1901	20	17	.540	2.41	40	38	36	336	288	97	221	5
1902	14	17	.452	2.11	34	32	29	276.2	241	73	159	8
1903	30	13	.698	2.26	45	42	37	366.1	321	100	267	3
1904	33	12	.733	2.03	48	46	33	367.2	306	78	212	4
1905	31	9	.775	1.27	43	37	32	339	252	64	206	8
1906	22	12	.647	2.97	38	35	22	266.2	262	77	128	6
1907	24	12	.667	2.00	41	36	31	315	250	53	178	8
1908	37	11	.771	1.43	56	44	34	390.2	285	42	259	11
1909	25	6	.806	1.14	37	33	26	275.1	192	36	149	8
1910	27	9	.750	1.89	38	35	27	318.1	292	60	184	2
1911	26	13	.667	1.99	45	37	29	307	303	38	141	5
1912	23	12	.657	2.12	43	34	27	310	311	34	134	0
1913	25	11	.694	2.06	40	35	25	306	291	21	93	4
1914	24	13	.649	3.00	41	35	29	312	314	23	80	5
1915	8	14	.364	3.58	27	24	11	186	199	20	57	1
1916 NY N	3	4	.429	2.33	12	6	4	65.2	59	7	16	1
CIN N	1	0	1.000	8.00	1	1	1	9	15	1	3	0
17 yrs.	373	188	.628	2.65	635	551	434	4777.5	4218	844	2502	79

World Series

	W	L	Pct.	ERA	G	GS	CG	IP	H	BB	SO	SHO
1905 NY N	3	0	1.000	0.00	3	3	3	27	14	1	18	3
1911	1	2	.333	2.00	3	3	2	27	25	2	13	0
1912	0	2	.000	1.57	3	3	3	28.2	23	5	10	0
1913	1	1	.500	0.95	2	2	2	19	14	2	7	1
4 yrs.	5	5	.500	1.13	11	11	10	101.2	76	10	48	4

Appendix C: Mathewson's 373 Career Victories

Christy Mathewson's 373 lifetime victories, including innings pitched, hits, walks and strikeouts, were compiled by the author using three sources: game accounts by *The New York Times;* Mathewson's official game-by-game pitching records of Information Concepts Incorporated for the years 1900–02; and those kept by the National League statisticians for the years 1903–16. Credit for the remaining statistics quoted in this book must be given to *Total Baseball* (second edition) and the *Baseball Encyclopedia* (eighth edition).

1901

# 1	April 26	New York 5, Brooklyn 3 at Polo Grounds. Allowed 4 hits, walked 2, struck out 8. Losing pitcher: Wild Bill Donovan.
# 2	April 30	New York 3, Philadelphia 2 at Baker Bowl. Allowed 3 hits, walked 3, struck out 4. Losing pitcher: Al Orth.
# 3	May 3	New York 2, Boston 1 at South End Grounds. Allowed 3 hits, walked 0, struck out 3. Losing pitcher: Kid Nichols.
# 4	May 6	New York 4, Philadelphia 0 at Polo Grounds. Allowed 5 hits, walked 2, struck out 7. Losing pitcher: Red Donahue.
# 5	May 11	New York 7, Brooklyn 0 at Washington Park. Allowed 2 hits, walked 1, struck out 4. Losing pitcher: William Kennedy.
#6	May 15	New York 4, Chicago 0 at Polo Grounds. Allowed 9 hits, walked 2, struck out 2. Losing pitcher: Jack Taylor.
# 7	May 21	New York 2, Pittsburgh 1 at Polo Grounds. Allowed 6 hits, walked 2, struck out 3. Losing pitcher: Deacon Phillippe.

Appendix C: 373 Career Victories 315

# 8	May 24	New York 1, Cincinnati 0 at Polo Grounds. Allowed 3 hits, walked 1, struck out 4. Losing pitcher: Bill Phillips.
# 9	June 1	New York 2, Boston 1 at Polo Grounds. Allowed 5 hits, walked 3, struck out 10. Losing pitcher: Kid Nichols.
#10	June 24	New York 3, St. Louis 2 at Polo Grounds. Allowed 6 hits, walked 1, struck out 7. Losing pitcher: Willie Sudhoff.
#11	June 26	New York 6, Cincinnati 2 at Polo Grounds. Allowed 9 hits, walked 1, struck out 6. Losing pitcher: Dick Scott.
#12	June 29	New York 14, Chicago 1 at Polo Grounds. Allowed 4 hits, walked 1, struck out 5. Losing pitcher: Rube Waddell.
#13	July 4	New York 5, Pittsburgh 3 at Exposition Park. Allowed 11 hits in 12 innings, walked 6, struck out 10. Losing pitcher: Jack Chesbro.
#14	July 8	New York 9, Cincinnati 3 at League Park. Allowed 6 hits, walked 4, struck out 5. Losing pitcher: Dick Scott.
#15	July 15	*New York 5, St. Louis 0 at Robison Field. Allowed no hits, walked 4, struck out 4. Losing pitcher: Willie Sudhoff.*
#16	August 1	New York 9, Boston 8 at South End Grounds. Allowed 12 hits, walked 4, struck out 5. Losing pitcher: Kid Nichols.
#17	August 8	New York 4, Brooklyn 1 at Polo Grounds. Allowed 9 hits, walked 1, struck out 9. Losing pitcher: Jim Hughes.
#18	August 26	New York 3, Philadelphia 1 at Baker Bowl. Allowed 3 hits, walked 5, struck out 7. Losing pitcher: Red Donahue.
#19	September 9	New York 5, St. Louis 1 at Polo Grounds. Allowed 5 hits, walked 4, struck out 8. Losing pitcher: Ed Murphy.
#20	September 21	New York 5, Cincinnati 1 at League Park. Allowed 3 hits, walked 5, struck out 7. Losing pitcher: Bill Phillips.

1902

| #21 | April 17 | New York 7, Philadelphia 0 at Polo Grounds. Allowed 4 hits, walked 4, struck out 6. Losing pitcher: Harry Felix. |
| #22 | April 21 | New York 6, Boston 3 at Polo Grounds, Allowed 4 hits, walked 3, struck out 7. Losing pitcher: Ray Hale. |

APPENDIX C: 373 CAREER VICTORIES

#23	May 1	New York 3, Philadelphia 0 at Polo Grounds. Allowed 2 hits, walked 3, struck out 9. Losing pitcher: Henry Vorhees.
#24	May 14	New York 10, St. Louis 7 at Robison Field. Allowed 9 hits, walked 3, struck out 4. Losing pitcher: Mike Joyce.
#25	May 21	New York 4, Pittsburgh 3 at Exposition Park. Allowed 0 hits in 2⅔ innings of relief, walked 1, struck out 1. Losing pitcher: Jesse Tannehill.
#26	July 8	New York 1, Chicago 0 at West Side Park. Allowed 6 hits, walked 1, struck out 5. Losing pitcher: Bob Rhodes.
#27	July 17	New York 6, Cincinnati 3 at League Park. Allowed 8 hits, walked 2, struck out 5. Losing pitcher: Henry Thielman.
#28	July 24	New York 2, Brooklyn 0 at Washington Park. Allowed 5 hits, walked 1, struck out 11. Losing pitcher: Doc Newton.
#29	July 28	New York 2, Brooklyn 0 at Polo Grounds. Allowed 2 hits in 5 innings, walked 3, struck out 5. Losing pitcher: Roy Evans.
#30	August 1	New York 4, St. Louis 2 at Polo Grounds. Allowed 11 hits, walked 1, struck out 2. Losing pitcher: Alex Pearson.
#31	August 13	New York 4, Cincinnati 2 at Polo Grounds. Allowed 6 hits, walked 3, struck out 4. Losing pitcher: Henry Thielman.
#32	August 18	New York 5, Chicago 0 at West Side Park. Allowed 4 hits, walked 0, struck out 1. Losing pitcher: Jack Taylor.
#33	August 26	New York 6, Cincinnati 0 at League Park. Allowed 8 hits, walked 3, struck out 6. Losing pitcher: Henry Thielman.
#34	September 10	New York 6, Chicago 0 at Polo Grounds. Allowed 7 hits, walked 0, struck out 7. Losing pitcher: Bob Rhodes.

1903

#35	April 21	New York 2, Brooklyn 1 at Washington Park. Allowed 3 hits, walked 2, struck out 5. Losing pitcher: Henry Schmidt.
#36	April 27	New York 10, Boston 7 at South End Grounds. Allowed 6 hits, walked 4, struck out 9. Losing pitcher: John Malarkey.
#37	May 1	New York 11, Philadelphia 3 at Baker Bowl. Allowed 8 hits, walked 0, struck out 5. Losing pitcher: Chick Fraser.

Appendix C: 373 Career Victories

#38 May 7   New York 8, Philadelphia 4 at Polo Grounds. Allowed 9 hits, walked 1, struck out 4. Losing pitcher: Fred Mitchell.

#39 May 16   New York 7, Pittsburgh 3 at Polo Grounds. Allowed 8 hits, walked 0, struck out 7. Losing pitcher: William Kennedy.

#40 May 19   New York 4, Pittsburgh 3 at Polo Grounds. Allowed 1 hit in 2 innings of relief, walked 1, struck out 4. Losing pitcher: Deacon Phillippe.

#41 May 20   New York 2, Pittsburgh 0 at Polo Grounds. Allowed 6 hits, walked 1, struck out 5. Losing pitcher: Sam Leever.

#42 May 26   New York 4, Chicago 3 at Polo Grounds. Allowed 5 hits, walked 3, struck out 6. Losing pitcher: Jack Taylor.

#43 May 29   New York 3, Boston 0 at Polo Grounds. Allowed 5 hits, walked 3, struck out 5. Losing pitcher: Charles Pittinger.

#44 June 1   New York 10, Pittsburgh 2 at Exposition Park. Allowed 10 hits, walked 2, struck out 2. Losing pitcher: Ed Doheny.

#45 June 4   New York 9, Chicago 1 at West Side Park. Allowed 4 hits, walked 1, struck out 5. Losing pitcher: Carl Lundgren.

#46 June 9   New York 11, St. Louis 2 at Robison Field. Allowed 6 hits in 6 innings, walked 1, struck out 6. Losing pitcher: Warren Sanders.

#47 June 13   New York 4, Cincinnati 0 at League Park. Allowed 1 hit, walked 2, struck out 5. Losing pitcher: Frank Hahn.

#48 June 26   New York 8, Pittsburgh 2 at Polo Grounds. Allowed 8 hits, walked 2, struck out 7. Losing pitcher: Sam Leever.

#49 July 6   New York 5, Chicago 1 at West Side Park. Allowed 7 hits, walked 7, struck out 7. Losing pitcher: John Menefee.

#50 July 9   New York 4, St. Louis 2 at Robison Field. Allowed 9 hits in 8 innings, walked 0, struck out 0. Losing pitcher: Three Finger Brown.

#51 July 15   New York 6, Pittsburgh 3 at Exposition Park. Allowed 10 hits in 14 innings, walked 4, struck out 11. Losing pitcher: Ed Doheny.

#52 August 3   New York 4, Boston 1 at South End Grounds. Allowed 9 hits in 11 innings, walked 2, struck out 11. Losing pitcher: Vic Willis.

#53 August 7   New York 7, Philadelphia 5 at Polo Grounds. Allowed 9 hits, walked 5, struck out 10. Losing pitcher: Bill Duggleby.

#54	August 10	New York 3, Brooklyn 1 at Washington Park. Allowed 5 hits, walked 2, struck out 8. Losing pitcher: Henry Schmidt.
#55	August 13	New York 6, St. Louis 2 at Polo Grounds. Allowed 7 hits, walked 1, struck out 10. Losing pitcher: Three Finger Brown.
#56	August 17	New York 7, Cincinnati 4 at Polo Grounds. Allowed 7 hits, walked 1, struck out 5. Losing pitcher: Jack Sutthoff.
#57	August 20	New York 13, Pittsburgh 7 at Polo Grounds. Allowed 10 hits in 6 innings, walked 2, struck out 1. Losing pitcher: Ed Doheny.
#58	August 21	New York 9, Pittsburgh 5 at Polo Grounds. Allowed 11 hits, walked 0, struck out 9. Losing pitcher: Bucky Veil.
#59	August 24	New York 8, Chicago 1 at Polo Grounds. Allowed 6 hits in 7 innings, walked 1, struck out 4. Losing pitcher: John Menefee.
#60	August 28	New York 12, Boston 6 at South End Grounds. Allowed 10 hits, walked 4, struck out 11. Losing pitcher: John Malarkey.
#61	September 5	New York 3, Brooklyn 1 at Washington Park. Allowed 1 hit in 5⅓ innings, walked 1, struck out 5. Losing pitcher: Bill Reidy.
#62	September 12	New York 4, St. Louis 3 at Robison Field. Allowed 12 hits in 10 innings, walked 3, struck out 5. Losing pitcher: Jim Hackett.
#63	September 18	New York 7, Cincinnati 5 at League Park. Allowed 2 hits in 2 innings of relief, walked 1, struck out 0. Losing pitcher: Jack Sutthoff.
#64	September 21	New York 8, Chicago 3 at West Side Park. Allowed 11 hits, walked 4, struck out 6. Losing pitcher: Clarence Currie.

1904

#65	April 14	New York 7, Brooklyn 1 at Washington Park. Allowed 3 hits, walked 2, struck out 3. Losing pitcher: Oscar Jones.
#66	April 25	New York 9, Brooklyn 2 at Polo Grounds. Allowed 6 hits in 7 innings, walked 2, struck out 3. Losing pitcher: Ed Poole.
#67	April 30	New York 10, Boston 1 at Polo Grounds. Allowed 3 hits in 6 innings, walked 3, struck out 4. Losing pitcher: Pat Carney.
#68	May 5	New York 10, Boston 5 at South End Grounds. Allowed 11 hits, walked 1, struck out 3. Losing pitcher: Togie Pittinger.

Appendix C: 373 Career Victories

#69	May 27	New York 3, Brooklyn 1 at Polo Grounds. Allowed 6 hits, walked 4, struck out 6. Losing pitcher: Ned Garvin.
#70	May 30	New York 15, Philadelphia 4 at Baker Bowl. Allowed 3 hits in 5 innings, walked 1, struck out 0. Losing pitcher: Johnny Lush.
#71	June 2	New York 2, Cincinnati 1 at Polo Grounds. Allowed 4 hits, walked 1, struck out 6. Losing pitcher: Jack Sutthoff.
#72	June 6	New York 15, Pittsburgh 2 at Polo Grounds. Allowed 3 hits in 5 innings, walked 0, struck out 4. Losing pitcher: Roscoe Miller.
#73	June 10	New York 5, Chicago 0 at Polo Grounds. Allowed 1 hit, walked 4, struck out 5. Losing pitcher: Jake Weimer.
#74	June 16	New York 4, St. Louis 3 at Polo Grounds. Allowed 7 hits, walked 1, struck out 4. Losing pitcher: Mike O'Neill.
#75	June 20	New York 12, Brooklyn 4 at Polo Grounds. Allowed 10 hits, walked 1, struck out 6. Losing pitcher: Bill Reidy.
#76	June 23	New York 6, Boston 2 at South End Grounds. Allowed 9 hits, walked 3, struck out 9. Losing pitcher: Togie Pittinger.
#77	June 30	New York 3, Boston 0 at Polo Grounds. Allowed 8 hits, walked 2, struck out 3. Losing pitcher: Togie Pittinger.
#78	July 4	New York 11, Philadelphia 3 at Polo Grounds. Allowed 4 hits in 7 innings, walked 1, struck out 4. Losing pitcher: Fred Mitchell.
#79	July 6	New York 12, Philadelphia 3 at Baker Bowl. Allowed 5 hits in 6 innings, walked 2, struck out 4. Losing pitcher: Chick Fraser.
#80	July 12	New York 7, Cincinnati 4 at League Park. Allowed 6 hits in 10 innings, walked 2, struck out 4. Losing pitcher: Noodles Hahn.
#81	July 15	New York 5, Cincinnati 2 at League Park. Allowed 7 hits, walked 2, struck out 5. Losing pitcher: Bob Ewing.
#82	July 21	New York 4, Chicago 3 at West Side Park. Allowed 1 hit in $3^{2}/_{3}$ innings of relief, walked 0, struck out 1. Losing pitcher: Jake Weimer.
#83	July 23	New York 5, Chicago 1 at West Side Park. Allowed 6 hits, walked 0, struck out 6. Losing pitcher: Three Finger Brown.
#84	August 3	New York 4, Chicago 3 at Polo Grounds. Allowed 8 hits, walked 0, struck out 2. Losing pitcher: Bob Wicker.

#85	August 6	New York 8, St. Louis 1 at Polo Grounds. Allowed 5 hits in 6 innings, walked 1, struck out 3. Losing pitcher: Mike O'Neill.
#86	August 8	New York 4, St. Louis 3 at Polo Grounds. Allowed 0 hits in 1 inning of relief, walked 0, struck out 2. Losing pitcher: Charles McFarland.
#87	August 11	New York 5, Cincinnati 2 at Polo Grounds. Allowed 6 hits, walked 2, struck out 11. Losing pitcher: Bob Ewing.
#88	August 17	New York 9, Pittsburgh 6 at Polo Grounds. Allowed 13 hits, walked 3, struck out 8. Losing pitcher: Charlie Case.
#89	August 20	New York 5, Pittsburgh 0 at Exposition Park. Allowed 3 hits in 6 innings, walked 1, struck out 2. Losing pitcher: Sam Leever.
#90	August 24	New York 3, Chicago 0 at West Side Park. Allowed 3 hits, walked 1, struck out 3. Losing pitcher: Herb Briggs.
#91	August 27	New York 9, St. Louis 3 at Robison Field. Allowed 5 hits, walked 2, struck out 2. Losing pitcher: Jack Taylor.
#92	August 30	New York 3, Cincinnati 1 at League Park. Allowed 8 hits, walked 2, struck out 5. Losing pitcher: Noodles Hahn.
#93	September 5	New York 6, Boston 1 at Polo Grounds. Allowed 8 hits, walked 0, struck out 5. Losing pitcher: Irvin Wilhelm.
#94	September 8	New York 4, Philadelphia 1 at Polo Grounds. Allowed 7 hits in 7 innings, walked 3, struck out 3. Losing pitcher: Thomas Sparks.
#95	September 16	New York 2, Brooklyn 1 at Polo Grounds. Allowed 4 hits, walked 2, struck out 5. Losing pitcher: Oscar Jones.
#96	September 24	New York 3, Pittsburgh 1 at Polo Grounds. Allowed 4 hits, walked 1, struck out 6. Losing pitcher: Joe Robitaille.
#97	October 3	New York 3, St. Louis 1 at Polo Grounds. Allowed 6 hits, walked 3, struck out 16. Losing pitcher: Kid Nichols.

1905

#98	April 15	New York 15, Boston 0 at Polo Grounds. Allowed 2 hits in 6 innings, walked 0, struck out 3. Losing pitcher: Dick Harley.
#99	April 24	New York 5, Philadelphia 4 at Baker Bowl. Allowed 7 hits, walked 2, struck out 8. Losing pitcher: Bill Duggleby.

Appendix C: 373 Career Victories 321

#100	May 1	New York 8, Boston 2 at South End Grounds. Allowed 8 hits, walked 3, struck out 4. Losing pitcher: Chick Fraser.
#101	May 11	New York 4, St. Louis 0 at Polo Grounds. Allowed 5 hits, walked 4, struck out 3. Losing pitcher: Jack Taylor.
#102	May 23	New York 7, Cincinnati 0 at Polo Grounds. Allowed 3 hits, walked 1, struck out 8. Losing pitcher: Orval Overall.
#103	May 27	New York 4, Brooklyn 1 at Polo Grounds. Allowed 6 hits, walked 2, struck out 3. Losing pitcher: Oscar Jones.
#104	June 1	New York 8, Boston 2 at South End Grounds. Allowed 11 hits, walked 4, struck out 1. Losing pitcher: Irvin Wilhelm.
#105	June 7	New York 5, Pittsburgh 3 at Exposition Park. Allowed 5 hits, walked 1, struck out 10. Losing pitcher: Patsy Flaherty.
#106	June 13	*New York 1, Chicago 0 at West Side Park. Allowed no hits, walked 0, struck out 2. Losing pitcher: Three Finger Brown.*
#107	June 17	New York 7, St. Louis 2 at Robison Field. Allowed 10 hits in 6 innings, walked 1, struck out 3. Losing pitcher: Charlie McFarland.
#108	June 21	New York 6, Cincinnati 3 at League Park. Allowed 7 hits, walked 2, struck out 4. Losing pitcher: Tom Walker.
#109	June 24	New York 2, Boston 1 at Polo Grounds. Allowed 1 hit in 3 innings of relief, walked 1, struck out 1. Losing pitcher: Irv Young.
#110	June 29	New York 11, Brooklyn 1 at Washington Park. Allowed 2 hits in 5 innings, walked 2, struck out 7. Losing pitcher: Mal Eason.
#111	July 15	New York 8, Pittsburgh 7 at Polo Grounds. Allowed 0 hits in 2⅔ innings of relief, walked 0, struck out 2. Losing pitcher: Mike Lynch.
#112	July 21	New York 14, St. Louis 2 at Polo Grounds. Allowed 5 hits in 5 innings, walked 0, struck out 3. Losing pitcher: Jack Taylor.
#113	July 25	New York 7, Cincinnati 2 at Polo Grounds. Allowed 9 hits, walked 5, struck out 8. Losing pitcher: Jack Harper.
#114	July 29	New York 3, Cincinnati 0 at League Park. Allowed 6 hits, walked 1, struck out 6. Losing pitcher: Orval Overall.
#115	August 2	New York 3, Pittsburgh 1 at Exposition Park. Allowed 7 hits, walked 1, struck out 5. Losing pitcher: Deacon Phillippe.

APPENDIX C: 373 CAREER VICTORIES

#116	August 10	New York 1, Chicago 0 at West Side Park. Allowed 3 hits, walked 1, struck out 6. Losing pitcher: Ed Reulbach.
#117	August 17	New York 3, Chicago 0 at Polo Grounds. Allowed 3 hits, walked 0, struck out 6. Losing pitcher: Bob Wicker.
#118	August 21	New York 10, Pittsburgh 2 at Polo Grounds. Allowed 7 hits, walked 4, struck out 5. Losing pitcher: Deacon Phillippe.
#119	August 24	New York 8, Cincinnati 0 at Polo Grounds. Allowed 2 hits, walked 1, struck out 2. Losing pitcher: Charlie Chech.
#120	August 28	New York 8, St. Louis 1 at Polo Grounds. Allowed 9 hits, walked 2, struck out 3. Losing pitcher: Jake Thielman.
#121	September 1	New York 4, Philadelphia 1 at Polo Grounds. Allowed 3 hits, walked 1, struck out 9. Losing pitcher: Togie Pittinger.
#122	September 4	New York 11, Philadelphia 6 at Polo Grounds. Allowed 8 hits, in 8 innings, walked 1, struck out 3. Losing pitcher: Togie Pittinger.
#123	September 7	New York 3, Boston 0 at Polo Grounds. Allowed 3 hits, walked 2, struck out 9. Losing pitcher: Vic Willis.
#124	September 12	New York 3, Brooklyn 2 at Polo Grounds. Allowed 7 hits, walked 2, struck out 7. Losing pitcher: Harry McIntire.
#125	September 16	New York 3, Boston 1 at South End Grounds. Allowed 8 hits, walked 1, struck out 8. Losing pitcher: Irv Young.
#126	September 19	New York 2, Philadelphia 1 at Baker Bowl. Allowed 2 hits, walked 0, struck out 6. Losing pitcher: Bill Duggleby.
#127	September 25	New York 10, Pittsburgh 4 at Exposition Park. Allowed 6 hits, walked 1, struck out 7. Losing pitcher: Deacon Phillippe.
#128	September 29	New York 6, St. Louis 5 at Robison Field. Allowed 12 hits in 11 innings, walked 4, struck out 7. Losing pitcher: Jake Thielman.

1906

#129	May 14	New York 6, Cincinnati 3 at League Park. Allowed 9 hits, walked 7, struck out 6. Losing pitcher: Orval Overall.
#130	May 24	New York 6, Chicago 5 at West Side Park. Allowed 3 hits in 2⅓ innings, walked 2, struck out 1. Losing pitcher: Carl Lundgren.

Appendix C: 373 Career Victories

#131	May 26	New York 5, St. Louis 4 at Robison Field. Allowed 10 hits in 8 innings, walked 2, struck out 3. Losing pitcher: Jack Taylor.
#132	May 30	New York 5, Brooklyn 2 at Washington Park. Allowed 8 hits, walked 2, struck out 6. Losing pitcher: Bill Scanlan.
#133	June 15	New York 2, St. Louis 1 at Polo Grounds. Allowed 8 hits, walked 4, struck out 3. Losing pitcher: Jack Taylor.
#134	June 21	New York 5, Pittsburgh 4 at Polo Grounds. Allowed 7 hits in 5 innings of relief, walked 2, struck out 1. Losing pitcher: Sam Leever.
#135	June 23	New York 5, Philadelphia 0 at Polo Grounds. Allowed 6 hits, walked 2, struck out 3. Losing pitcher: Lew Richie.
#136	June 27	New York 6, Boston 4 at South End Grounds. Allowed 6 hits, walked 3, struck out 5. Losing pitcher: Jeff Pfeffer.
#137	July 5	New York 1, Boston 0 at Polo Grounds. Allowed 5 hits, walked 2, struck out 6. Losing pitcher: Jeff Pfeffer.
#138	July 14	New York 4, St. Louis 0 at Robison Field. Allowed 6 hits, walked 2, struck out 4. Losing pitcher: Buster Brown.
#139	July 25	New York 3, Pittsburgh 0 at Exposition Park. Allowed 8 hits, walked 2, struck out 6. Losing pitcher: Deacon Philippe.
#140	July 30	New York 9, Cincinnati 1 at Polo Grounds. Allowed 4 hits in 6 innings, walked 0, struck out 2. Losing pitcher: Bob Wicker.
#141	August 4	New York 7, Chicago 4 at Polo Grounds. Allowed 8 hits in 6 innings, walked 1, struck out 2. Losing pitcher: Jack Taylor.
#142	August 9	New York 6, Pittsburgh 0 at Polo Grounds. Allowed 5 hits in 7 innings, walked 0, struck out 4. Losing pitcher: Al Leifield.
#143	August 13	New York 2, Pittsburgh 1 at Polo Grounds. Allowed 6 hits, walked 0, struck out 6. Losing pitcher: Al Leifield.
#144	August 25	New York 8, Cincinnati 3 at League Park. Allowed 9 hits in 8 innings, walked 1, struck out 2. Losing pitcher: Bob Wicker.
#145	September 3	New York 4, Boston 0 at Polo Grounds. Allowed 3 hits, walked 2, struck out 2. Losing pitcher: Jeff Pfeffer.
#146	September 6	New York 6, Brooklyn 2 at Polo Grounds. Allowed 7 hits, walked 2, struck out 14. Losing pitcher: Harry McIntire.

APPENDIX C: 373 CAREER VICTORIES

#147	September 11	New York 3, Boston 0 at South End Grounds. Allowed 6 hits, walked 3, struck out 9. Losing pitcher: Irv Young.
#148	September 17	New York 13, Philadelphia 2 at Polo Grounds. Allowed 8 hits in 7 innings, walked 2, struck out 2. Losing pitcher: Walter Moser.
#149	September 28	New York 8, St. Louis 2 at Polo Grounds. Allowed 6 hits in 8 innings, walked 0, struck out 4. Losing pitcher: Fred Beebe.
#150	October 4	New York 7, Philadelphia 6 at Polo Grounds. Allowed 11 hits, walked 1, struck out 1. Losing pitcher: Tully Sparks.

1907

#151	April 22	New York 1, Boston 0 at South End Grounds. Allowed 8 hits, walked 1, struck out 7. Losing pitcher: Patsy Flaherty.
#152	April 26	New York 5, Philadelphia 4 at Baker Bowl. Allowed 9 hits in 8 innings, walked 3, struck out 6. Losing pitcher: Tully Sparks.
#153	May 3	New York 1, Brooklyn 0 at Polo Grounds. Allowed 2 hits, walked 1, struck out 8. Losing pitcher: Elmer Stricklett.
#154	May 8	New York 4, Pittsburgh 0 at Polo Grounds. Allowed 4 hits, walked 1, struck out 6. Losing pitcher: Al Leifield.
#155	May 11	New York 9, Pittsburgh 6 at Polo Grounds. Allowed 2 hits in 3 innings of relief, walked 1, struck out 2. Losing pitcher: Mike Lynch.
#156	May 17	New York 2, St. Louis 1 at Polo Grounds. Allowed 3 hits in 12 innings, walked 1, struck out 11. Losing pitcher: Fred Beebe.
#157	May 25	New York 9, Boston 1 at Polo Grounds. Allowed 7 hits in 6 innings, walked 1, struck out 0. Losing pitcher: Irv Young.
#158	May 30	New York 6, Philadelphia 1 at Polo Grounds. Allowed 8 hits, walked 2, struck out 7. Losing pitcher: Lew Richie.
#159	June 11	New York 8, St. Louis 7 at Robison Field. Allowed 0 hits in 2⅔ innings of relief, walked 1, struck out 0. Losing pitcher: Stoney McGlynn.
#160	June 27	New York 2, Philadelphia 0 at Baker Bowl. Allowed 4 hits in 5⅔ innings, walked 3, struck out 5. Losing pitcher: Lew Moren.
#161	July 9	New York 5, St. Louis 3 at Polo Grounds. Allowed 6 hits, walked 1, struck out 4. Losing pitcher: Johnny Lush.

Appendix C: 373 Career Victories

#162	July 13	New York 4, Cincinnati 0 at Polo Grounds. Allowed 11 hits, walked 1, struck out 7. Losing pitcher: Roy Hitt.
#163	July 20	New York 1, Chicago 0 at Polo Grounds. Allowed 3 hits, walked 0, struck out 7. Losing pitcher: Carl Lundgren.
#164	July 25	New York 4, Cincinnati 3 at League Park. Allowed 5 hits, walked 1, struck out 2. Losing pitcher: Bob Ewing.
#165	July 29	New York 4, St. Louis 3 at Robison Field. Allowed 8 hits in 11 innings, walked 2, struck out 4. Losing pitcher: Ed Karger.
#166	August 8	New York 4, Pittsburgh 3 at Exposition Park. Allowed 9 hits in 8 innings, walked 1, struck out 5. Losing pitcher: Al Leifield.
#167	August 12	New York 5, Pittsburgh 3 at Exposition Park. Allowed 8 hits, walked 2, struck out 5. Losing pitcher: Al Leifield.
#168	August 24	New York 7, Pittsburgh 4 at Polo Grounds. Allowed 8 hits, walked 2, struck out 0. Losing pitcher: Deacon Phillippe.
#169	August 27	New York 1, St. Louis 0 at Polo Grounds. Allowed 3 hits, walked 1, struck out 5. Losing pitcher: Ed Karger.
#170	August 31	New York 3, Boston 2 at South End Grounds. Allowed 10 hits in 12 innings, walked 1, struck out 5. Losing pitcher: Gus Dorner.
#171	September 6	New York 2, Philadelphia 0 at Polo Grounds. Allowed 3 hits in 7 innings, walked 2, struck out 2. Losing pitcher: Lew Moren.
#172	September 13	New York 2, Brooklyn 1 at Washington Park. Allowed 5 hits, walked 2, struck out 11. Losing pitcher: Jim Pastorius.
#173	September 21	New York 6, Cincinnati 2 at League Park. Allowed 6 hits, walked 2, struck out 5. Losing pitcher: Charlie Smith.
#174	September 24	New York 2, Pittsburgh 0 at Exposition Park. Allowed 8 hits, walked 1, struck out 4. Losing pitcher: Al Leifield.

1908

#175	April 14	New York 3, Philadelphia 1 at Baker Bowl. Allowed 4 hits, walked 1, struck out 7. Losing pitcher: George McQuillan.
#176	April 18	New York 4, Brooklyn 0 at Washington Park. Allowed 6 hits, walked 1, struck out 12. Losing pitcher: Jim Pastorius.

APPENDIX C: 373 CAREER VICTORIES

#177 April 22   New York 3, Brooklyn 2 at Polo Grounds. Allowed 7 hits, walked 0, struck out 11. Losing pitcher: Harry McIntire.

#178 April 27   New York 2, Boston 0 at South End Grounds. Allowed 1 hit, walked 0, struck out 4. Losing pitcher: Irv Young.

#179 May 4   New York 12, Philadelphia 2 at Polo Grounds. Allowed 3 hits in 6 innings, walked 1, struck out 1. Losing pitcher: Tully Sparks.

#180 May 9   New York 7, Boston 3 at Polo Grounds. Allowed 10 hits, walked 2, struck out 2. Losing pitcher: Irv Young.

#181 May 29   New York 1, Brooklyn 0 at Washington Park. Allowed 4 hits, walked 1, struck out 8. Losing pitcher: Nap Rucker.

#182 June 3   New York 3, Boston 0 at South End Grounds. Allowed 3 hits, walked 1, struck out 11. Losing pitcher: Irv Young.

#183 June 6   New York 3, St. Louis 2 at Polo Grounds. Allowed 4 hits, walked 2, struck out 8. Losing pitcher: Art Fromme.

#184 June 17   New York 2, Cincinnati 1 at Polo Grounds. Allowed 7 hits, walked 0, struck out 7. Losing pitcher: Andy Coakley.

#185 June 20   New York 4, Chicago 0 at Polo Grounds. Allowed 3 hits, walked 1, struck out 6. Losing pitcher: Chick Fraser.

#186 June 24   New York 7, Boston 1 at Polo Grounds. Allowed 5 hits in 7 innings, walked 1, struck out 4. Losing pitcher: Irv Young.

#187 June 27   New York 5, Brooklyn 2 at Washington Park. Allowed 9 hits, walked 0, struck out 8. Losing pitcher: Irvin Wilhelm.

#188 July 2   New York 4, Philadelphia 3 at Polo Grounds. Allowed 7 hits, walked 4, struck out 7. Losing pitcher: Bill Foxen.

#189 July 6   New York 2, Cincinnati 1 at League Park. Allowed 4 hits, walked 0, struck out 6. Losing pitcher: Bob Ewing.

#190 July 9   New York 2, Cincinnati 1 at League Park. Allowed 4 hits, walked 0, struck out 5. Losing pitcher: Andy Coakley.

#191 July 13   New York 7, Pittsburgh 0 at Exposition Park. Allowed 3 hits, walked 0, struck out 2. Losing pitcher: Al Leifield.

#192 July 21   New York 4, St. Louis 2 at Robison Field. Allowed 11 hits in 12 innings, walked 2, struck out 10. Losing pitcher: Harry Sallee.

Appendix C: 373 Career Victories

#193	July 29	New York 1, St. Louis 0 at Polo Grounds. Allowed 3 hits, walked 1, struck out 3. Losing pitcher: Harry Sallee.
#194	August 4	New York 4, Cincinnati 3 at Polo Grounds. Allowed 0 hits in 3⅔ innings of relief, walked 0, struck out 0. Losing pitcher: Andy Coakley.
#195	August 4	New York 4, Cincinnati 1 at Polo Grounds. Allowed 4 hits in 8 innings, walked 1, struck out 7. Losing pitcher: Andy Coakley.
#196	August 10	New York 3, Chicago 2 at Polo Grounds. Allowed 7 hits, walked 0, struck out 6. Losing pitcher: Orval Overall.
#197	August 13	New York 5, Brooklyn 3 at Polo Grounds. Allowed 4 hits in 7 innings of relief, walked 0, struck out 4. Losing pitcher: George Bell.
#198	August 17	New York 3, St. Louis 0 at Robison Field. Allowed 4 hits in 6 innings, walked 0, struck out 4. Losing pitcher: Harry Sallee.
#199	August 20	New York 2, Cincinnati 0 at League Park. Allowed 8 hits, walked 2, struck out 4. Losing pitcher: Andy Coakley.
#200	August 24	New York 5, Pittsburgh 1 at Exposition Park. Allowed 6 hits, walked 0, struck out 7. Losing pitcher: Al Leifield.
#201	August 26	New York 4, Pittsburgh 3 at Exposition Park. Allowed 0 hits in 1 inning of relief, walked 0, struck out 0. Losing pitcher: Irv Young.
#202	September 1	New York 8, Boston 0 at South End Grounds. Allowed 3 hits in 8 innings, walked 1, struck out 7. Losing pitcher: Patsy Flaherty.
#203	September 5	New York 5, Philadelphia 1 at Baker Bowl. Allowed 6 hits, walked 0, struck out 5. Losing pitcher: George McQuillan.
#204	September 8	New York 1, Brooklyn 0 at Polo Grounds. Allowed 5 hits in 11 innings, walked 1, struck out 7. Losing pitcher: Nap Rucker.
#205	September 12	New York 6, Brooklyn 3 at Polo Grounds. Allowed 10 hits, walked 1, struck out 5. Losing pitcher: Harry McIntire.
#206	September 15	New York 5, St. Louis 4 at Polo Grounds. Allowed 0 hits in 1⅔ innings of relief, walked 1, struck out 3. Losing pitcher: Irv Higginbotham.
#207	September 18	New York 7, Pittsburgh 0 at Polo Grounds. Allowed 5 hits, walked 0, struck out 3. Losing pitcher: Nick Maddox.
#208	September 24	New York 5, Chicago 4 at Polo Grounds. Allowed 2 hits in 3 innings of relief, walked 0, struck out 3. Losing pitcher: Three Finger Brown.

#209	September 26	New York 6, Cincinnati 2 at Polo Grounds. Allowed 6 hits, walked 0, struck out 3. Losing pitcher: Bob Ewing.
#210	September 29	New York 6, Philadelphia 2 at Polo Grounds. Allowed 9 hits, walked 1, struck out 8. Losing pitcher: George McQuillan.
#211	October 1	New York 4, Philadelphia 3 at Baker Bowl. Allowed 10 hits, walked 0, struck out 5. Losing pitcher: Frank Corridon.

1909

#212	May 13	New York 4, Chicago 1 at Polo Grounds. Allowed 4 hits, walked 1, struck out 3. Losing pitcher: Floyd Kroh.
#213	May 17	New York 6, Cincinnati 0 at Polo Grounds. Allowed 6 hits, walked 0, struck out 5. Losing pitcher: Jack Rowan.
#214	May 28	New York 3, Philadelphia 0 at Polo Grounds. Allowed 2 hits in 6 innings, walked 0, struck out 4. Losing pitcher: Harry Coveleski.
#215	May 31	New York 5, Philadelphia 4 at Polo Grounds. Allowed 6 hits, walked 2, struck out 6. Losing pitcher: Lew Moren.
#216	June 8	New York 3, Chicago 2 at West Side Park. Allowed 2 hits, walked 2, struck out 4. Losing pitcher: Three Finger Brown.
#217	June 12	New York 2, Cincinnati 0 at League Park. Allowed 4 hits, walked 1, struck out 7. Losing pitcher: Bob Ewing.
#218	June 16	New York 8, Pittsburgh 2 at Exposition Park. Allowed 10 hits, walked 0, struck out 3. Losing pitcher: Al Leifield.
#219	June 23	New York 5, Boston 4 at Polo Grounds. Allowed 0 hits in 1 inning of relief, walked 0, struck out 2. Losing pitcher: Al Mattern.
#220	June 23	New York 11, Boston 1 at Polo Grounds. Allowed 1 hit in 2 innings, walked 0, struck out 3. Losing pitcher: Kirby White.
#221	June 25	New York 9, Brooklyn 1 at Polo Grounds. Allowed 3 hits in 5 innings, walked 1, struck out 0. Losing pitcher: Harry McIntire.
#222	June 30	New York 3, Brooklyn 0 at Washington Park. Allowed 4 hits, walked 0, struck out 9. Losing pitcher: Irvin Wilhelm.
#223	July 3	New York 5, Brooklyn 3 at Washington Park. Allowed 2 hits in 6 innings of relief, walked 0, struck out 5. Losing pitcher: Harry McIntire.

Appendix C: 373 Career Victories

#224	July 12	New York 3, Pittsburgh 2 at Polo Grounds. Allowed 4 hits, walked 1, struck out 3. Losing pitcher: Vic Willis.
#225	July 16	New York 2, Cincinnati 1 at Polo Grounds. Allowed 5 hits, walked 2, struck out 2. Losing pitcher: Jack Rowan.
#226	July 27	New York 6, Boston 2 at South End Grounds. Allowed 7 hits, walked 2, struck out 7. Losing pitcher: Forrest More.
#227	August 3	New York 7, Cincinnati 6 at League Park. Allowed 15 hits in 10 innings, walked 3, struck out 3. Losing pitcher: Billy Campbell.
#228	August 7	New York 7, St. Louis 1 at Robison Field. Allowed 6 hits, walked 2, struck out 7. Losing pitcher: Fred Beebe.
#229	August 12	New York 3, Chicago 0 at West Side Park. Allowed 4 hits, walked 0, struck out 5. Losing pitcher: Jack Pfiester.
#230	August 21	New York 1, Cincinnati 0 at Polo Grounds. Allowed 5 hits, walked 0, struck out 9. Losing pitcher: Jack Rowan.
#231	August 25	New York 3, Pittsburgh 2 at Polo Grounds. Allowed 5 hits, walked 0, struck out 2. Losing pitcher: Nick Maddox.
#232	August 30	New York 5, Chicago 0 at Polo Grounds. Allowed 5 hits, walked 0, struck out 2. Losing pitcher: Ed Reulbach.
#233	September 6	New York 5, Boston 4 at Polo Grounds. Allowed 6 hits in 10 innings, walked 0, struck out 5. Losing pitcher: Al Mattern.
#234	September 11	New York 4, Brooklyn 0 at Polo Grounds. Allowed 3 hits, walked 1, struck out 6. Losing pitcher: Elmer Knetzer.
#235	September 16	New York 2, Chicago 1 at West Side Park. Allowed 7 hits, walked 0, struck out 4. Losing pitcher: Three Finger Brown.
#236	September 22	New York 4, St. Louis 3 at Robison Field. Allowed 12 hits, walked 1, struck out 7. Losing pitcher: Fred Beebe.

1910

#237	April 16	New York 3, Boston 1 at South End Grounds. Allowed 6 hits, walked 2, struck out 9. Losing pitcher: Kirby White.
#238	April 27	New York 3, Philadelphia 2 at Baker Bowl. Allowed 7 hits, walked 5, struck out 2. Losing pitcher: George McQuillan.

#239	May 2	New York 6, Brooklyn 0 at Washington Park. Allowed 1 hit, walked 0, struck out 8. Losing pitcher: Doc Scanlon.
#240	May 6	New York 3, Philadelphia 2 at Polo Grounds. Allowed 9 hits, walked 2, struck out 3. Losing pitcher: Bill Foxen.
#241	May 18	New York 10, Cincinnati 6 at League Park. Allowed 11 hits, walked 1, struck out 6. Losing pitcher: George Suggs.
#242	May 23	New York 7, Pittsburgh 1 at Forbes Field. Allowed 6 hits in 6 innings of relief, walked 0, struck out 0. Losing pitcher: Deacon Phillippe.
#243	May 28	New York 3, Philadelphia 2 at Baker Bowl. Allowed 10 hits, walked 1, struck out 5. Losing pitcher: Jim Moroney.
#244	June 1	New York 5, Cincinnati 2 at Polo Grounds. Allowed 4 hits, walked 0, struck out 4. Losing pitcher: Jack Rowan.
#245	June 6	New York 5, St. Louis 1 at Polo Grounds. Allowed 3 hits, walked 2, struck out 5. Losing pitcher: Harry Sallee.
#246	June 15	New York 5, Pittsburgh 1 at Polo Grounds. Allowed 6 hits, walked 0, struck out 3. Losing pitcher: Al Leifield.
#247	June 21	New York 12, Brooklyn 1 at Washington Park. Allowed 7 hits in 8 innings, walked 3, struck out 3. Losing pitcher: Nap Rucker.
#248	June 25	New York 4, Philadelphia 1 at Polo Grounds. Allowed 5 hits, walked 2, struck out 5. Losing pitcher: Bill Foxen.
#249	June 29	New York 3, Philadelphia 2 at Polo Grounds. Allowed 9 hits in 10 innings, walked 1, struck out 3. Losing pitcher: Lou Schettler.
#250	July 4	New York 6, Brooklyn 5 at Polo Grounds. Allowed 3 hits in 5 innings of relief, walked 1, struck out 5. Losing pitcher: Nap Rucker.
#251	July 6	New York 8, Boston 3 at South End Grounds. Allowed 10 hits in 14 innings, walked 2, struck out 9. Losing pitcher: Buster Brown.
#252	July 19	New York 6, Cincinnati 4 at League Park. Allowed 14 hits in 11 innings, walked 3, struck out 9. Losing pitcher: Art Fromme.
#253	July 23	New York 9, St. Louis 2 at Robison Field. Allowed 10 hits, walked 3, struck out 2. Losing pitcher: Ed Zmich.
#254	August 5	New York 10, Chicago 1 at Polo Grounds. Allowed 7 hits, walked 1, struck out 7. Losing pitcher: Floyd Kroh.

Appendix C: 373 Career Victories 331

#255	August 11	New York 5, Cincinnati 4 at Polo Grounds. Allowed 11 hits, walked 4, struck out 6. Losing pitcher: Jack Rowan.
#256	August 19	New York 9, Cincinnati 3 at League Park. Allowed 9 hits, walked 3, struck out 2. Losing pitcher: Jack Rowan.
#257	August 27	New York 18, Chicago 9 at West Side Park. Allowed 10 hits in 6 innings, walked 1, struck out 1. Losing pitcher: Ed Reulbach.
#258	August 30	New York 5, Pittsburgh 2 at Forbes Field. Allowed 12 hits, walked 1, struck out 6. Losing pitcher: Babe Adams.
#259	September 7	New York 2, Boston 0 at Polo Grounds. Allowed 7 hits, walked 3, struck out 5. Losing pitcher: Sam Frock.
#260	September 10	New York 3, Boston 1 at Polo Grounds. Allowed 5 hits, walked 1, struck out 6. Losing pitcher: Cliff Curtis.
#261	September 16	New York 3, Pittsburgh 1 at Polo Grounds. Allowed 5 hits, walked 0, struck out 3. Losing pitcher: Al Leifield.
#262	September 20	New York 3, St. Louis 2 at Polo Grounds. Allowed 10 hits, walked 1, struck out 10. Losing pitcher: Ed Zmich.
#263	September 24	New York 6, Chicago 5 at Polo Grounds. Allowed 11 hits, walked 0, struck out 4. Losing pitcher: Three Finger Brown.

1911

#264	April 25	New York 3, Boston 1 at Hilltop Park. Allowed 7 hits, walked 2, struck out 7. Losing pitcher: Patsy Flaherty.
#265	April 29	New York 7, Brooklyn 3 at Washington Park. Allowed 10 hits, walked 1, struck out 7. Losing pitcher: Cy Barger.
#266	May 4	New York 7, Boston 2 at South End Grounds. Allowed 9 hits, walked 5, struck out 3. Losing pitcher: Buster Brown.
#267	May 9	New York 5, Chicago 3 at Hilltop Park. Allowed 8 hits, walked 0, struck out 4. Losing pitcher: Three Finger Brown.
#268	May 13	New York 19, St. Louis 5 at Hilltop Park. Allowed 1 hit in 1 inning, walked 0, struck out 1. Losing pitcher: Harry Sallee.
#269	May 23	New York 7, Cincinnati 2 at Hilltop Park. Allowed 7 hits, walked 2, struck out 5. Losing pitcher: Frank Smith.

APPENDIX C: 373 CAREER VICTORIES

#270 May 26   New York 5, Philadelphia 3 at Hilltop Park. Allowed 0 hits in 1⅔ innings of relief, walked 0, struck out 0. Losing pitcher: Bill Burns.

#271 May 27   New York 2, Philadelphia 0 at Hilltop Park. Allowed 8 hits, walked 0, struck out 6. Losing pitcher: Earl Moore.

#272 June 5   New York 7, Chicago 1 at West Side Park. Allowed 5 hits, walked 0, struck out 2. Losing pitcher: Harry McIntire.

#273 June 9   New York 6, Pittsburgh 3 at Forbes Field. Allowed 8 hits, walked 3, struck out 6. Losing pitcher: Al Leifield.

#274 June 13   New York 5, Cincinnati 2 at League Park. Allowed 11 hits, walked 3, struck out 2. Losing pitcher: Art Fromme.

#275 June 21   New York 4, Boston 0 at South End Grounds. Allowed 7 hits, walked 1, struck out 3. Losing pitcher: Orlie Weaver.

#276 June 24   New York 7, Brooklyn 4 at Washington Park. Allowed 8 hits, walked 2, struck out 7. Losing pitcher: Elmer Knetzer.

#277 June 28   New York 3, Boston 0 at Polo Grounds. Allowed 9 hits, walked 0, struck out 3. Losing pitcher: Al Mattern.

#278 July 15   New York 4, Cincinnati 3 at Polo Grounds. Allowed 10 hits, walked 1, struck out 4. Losing pitcher: Harry Gaspar.

#279 July 22   New York 10, St. Louis 2 at Polo Grounds. Allowed 4 hits in 7 innings, walked 1, struck out 2. Losing pitcher: Bill Steele.

#280 July 26   New York 5, Cincinnati 3 at League Park. Allowed 2 hits in 1⅔ innings of relief, walked 0, struck out 0. Losing pitcher: Harry Gaspar.

#281 August 2   New York 8, Pittsburgh 4 at Forbes Field. Allowed 15 hits, walked 0, struck out 1. Losing pitcher: Babe Adams.

#282 August 11   New York 6, Philadelphia 0 at Polo Grounds. Allowed 11 hits, walked 1, struck out 9. Losing pitcher: Bill Burns.

#283 August 16   New York 6, Cincinnati 1 at Polo Grounds. Allowed 2 hits, walked 0, struck out 5. Losing pitcher: George Suggs.

#284 August 26   New York 6, Pittsburgh 2 at Polo Grounds. Allowed 9 hits, walked 0, struck out 4. Losing pitcher: Howie Camnitz.

#285 September 1 New York 3, Philadelphia 2 at Baker Bowl. Allowed 10 hits, walked 0, struck out 5. Losing pitcher: Earl Moore.

Appendix C: 373 Career Victories

#286	September 12	New York 11, Boston 2 at South End Grounds. Allowed 1 hit in 2 innings, walked 0, struck out 0. Losing pitcher: Cy Young.
#287	September 18	New York 7, Pittsburgh 2 at Forbes Field. Allowed 4 hits, walked 1, struck out 3. Losing pitcher: Howie Camnitz.
#288	September 23	New York 6, Cincinnati 2 at League Park. Allowed 10 hits, walked 3, struck out 4. Losing pitcher: Harry Gaspar.
#289	October 4	New York 2, Brooklyn 0 at Washington Park. Allowed 7 hits, walked 0, struck out 5. Losing pitcher: Nap Rucker.

1912

#290	April 19	New York 6, Brooklyn 2 at Polo Grounds. Allowed 12 hits, walked 1, struck out 4. Losing pitcher: Nap Rucker.
#291	April 25	New York 3, Philadelphia 1 at Baker Bowl. Allowed 7 hits, walked 1, struck out 6. Losing pitcher: Tom Seaton.
#292	May 4	New York 4, Philadelphia 3 at Polo Grounds. Allowed 5 hits, walked 2, struck out 3. Losing pitcher: Cliff Curtis.
#293	May 9	New York 8, St. Louis 3 at Robison Field. Allowed 8 hits, walked 1, struck out 5. Losing pitcher: Gene Woodburn.
#294	May 22	New York 6, Cincinnati 1 at Redland Field. Allowed 3 hits, walked 0, struck out 2. Losing pitcher: Rube Benton.
#295	June 1	New York 13, St. Louis 4 at Polo Grounds. Allowed 13 hits, walked 3, struck out 7. Losing pitcher: Bill Steele.
#296	June 7	New York 7, Cincinnati 6 at Polo Grounds. Allowed 11 hits, walked 0, struck out 2. Losing pitcher: George Suggs.
#297	June 13	New York 3, Chicago 2 at Polo Grounds. Allowed 6 hits, walked 1, struck out 8. Losing pitcher: Larry Cheney.
#298	June 22	New York 17, Boston 5 at South End Grounds. Allowed 12 hits, walked 2, struck out 7. Losing pitcher: Walt Dickson.
#299	June 28	New York 10, Boston 3 at Polo Grounds. Allowed 9 hits, walked 2, struck out 5. Losing pitcher: Ed Donnelly.
#300	July 5	New York 6, Brooklyn 1 at Polo Grounds. Allowed 5 hits, walked 1, struck out 0. Losing pitcher: Cy Barger.

#301	July 9	New York 5, Chicago 2 at West Side Park. Allowed 11 hits, walked 0, struck out 4. Losing pitcher: Three Finger Brown.
#302	July 13	New York 7, St. Louis 2 at Robison Field. Allowed 13 hits, walked 0, struck out 0. Losing pitcher: Joe Willis.
#303	July 17	New York 10, Pittsburgh 2 at Forbes Field. Allowed 7 hits, walked 1, struck out 0. Losing pitcher: Howie Camnitz.
#304	July 22	New York 4, Cincinnati 1 at Redland Field. Allowed 8 hits, walked 0, struck out 4. Losing pitcher: George Suggs.
#305	July 30	New York 10, Chicago 4 at Polo Grounds. Allowed 9 hits, walked 1, struck out 4. Losing pitcher: Jimmy Lavender.
#306	August 3	New York 3, Cincinnati 2 at Polo Grounds. Allowed 10 hits, walked 0, struck out 4. Losing pitcher: Art Fromme.
#307	September 2	New York 5, Boston 2 at South End Grounds. Allowed 1 hit in 4 innings of relief, walked 0, struck out 2. Losing pitcher: Hub Perdue.
#308	September 2	New York 6, Boston 1 at South End Grounds. Allowed 7 hits in 7 innings, walked 0, struck out 6. Losing pitcher: Ed Donnelly.
#309	September 5	New York 8, Philadelphia 1 at Baker Bowl. Allowed 8 hits, walked 1, struck out 5. Losing pitcher: Tom Seaton.
#310	September 6	New York 9, Philadelphia 8 at Baker Bowl. Allowed 1 hit in 2 innings of relief, walked 1, struck out 0. Losing pitcher: George Chalmers.
#311	September 9	New York 7, Brooklyn 2 at Polo Grounds. Allowed 6 hits, walked 0, struck out 5. Losing pitcher: Pat Ragan.
#312	September 26	New York 8, Boston 3 at Polo Grounds. Allowed 10 hits, walked 3, struck out 4. Losing pitcher: Hub Perdue.

1913

#313	April 17	New York 3, Boston 2 at South End Grounds. Allowed 9 hits, walked 2, struck out 3. Losing pitcher: Bill James.
#314	April 23	New York 3, Philadelphia 1 at Polo Grounds. Allowed 5 hits, walked 0, struck out 4. Losing pitcher: Ad Brennan.
#315	April 29	New York 6, Brooklyn 0 at Ebbets Field. Allowed 8 hits, walked 0, struck out 1. Losing pitcher: Nap Rucker.

Appendix C: 373 Career Victories

#316	May 7	New York 6, Cincinnati 4 at Polo Grounds. Allowed 8 hits in 7⅓ innings of relief, walked 0, struck out 6. Losing pitcher: Rube Benton.
#317	May 12	New York 5, Chicago 1 at Polo Grounds. Allowed 3 hits, walked 0, struck out 2. Losing pitcher: Lou Richie.
#318	May 16	New York 7, Pittsburgh 4 at Polo Grounds. Allowed 12 hits, walked 1, struck out 6. Losing pitcher: Marty O'Toole.
#319	May 31	New York 3, Philadelphia 2 at Polo Grounds. Allowed 6 hits, walked 0, struck out 3. Losing pitcher: Eppa Rixey.
#320	June 7	New York 9, St. Louis 8 at Robison Field. Allowed 1 hit in 2 innings of relief, walked 0, struck out 2. Losing pitcher: Sandy Burk.
#321	June 9	New York 11, Chicago 3 at West Side Park. Allowed 7 hits in 8 innings, walked 1, struck out 5. Losing pitcher: Lou Richie.
#322	June 14	New York 6, Pittsburgh 5 at Forbes Field. Allowed 7 hits, walked 0, struck out 3. Losing pitcher: Hank Robinson.
#323	June 19	New York 8, Cincinnati 7 at Redland Field. Allowed 12 hits, walked 2, struck out 1. Losing pitcher: Rube Benton.
#324	June 23	New York 5, Brooklyn 1 at Polo Grounds. Allowed 8 hits, walked 0, struck out 1. Losing pitcher: Cliff Curtis.
#325	June 26	New York 11, Boston 3 at Polo Grounds. Allowed 2 hits in 6 innings, walked 0, struck out 3. Losing pitcher: Otto Hess.
#326	June 30	New York 11, Philadelphia 10 at Baker Bowl. Allowed 1 hit in 4 innings of relief, walked 0, struck out 2. Losing pitcher: Grover Alexander.
#327	July 2	New York 8, Philadelphia 4 at Baker Bowl. Allowed 13 hits, walked 0, struck out 0. Losing pitcher: George Chalmers.
#328	July 5	New York 3, Brooklyn 2 at Ebbets Field. Allowed 12 hits, walked 0, struck out 4. Losing pitcher: Pat Ragan.
#329	July 15	New York 4, Cincinnati 2 at Polo Grounds. Allowed 11 hits, walked 0, struck out 0. Losing pitcher: Three Finger Brown.
#330	July 18	New York 5, St. Louis 0 at Polo Grounds. Allowed 5 hits, walked 1, struck out 5. Losing pitcher: Bill Perritt.
#331	July 28	New York 4, St. Louis 0 at Robison Field. Allowed 4 hits, walked 2, struck out 5. Losing pitcher: Bob Harmon.

#332	August 1	New York 5, Chicago 2 at West Side Park. Allowed 5 hits, walked 0, struck out 1. Losing pitcher: Bert Humphries.
#333	August 9	New York 11, Cincinnati 2 at Redland Field. Allowed 5 hits in 7 innings, walked 2, struck out 1. Losing pitcher: Gene Packard.
#334	August 21	New York 8, Chicago 2 at Polo Grounds. Allowed 8 hits, walked 0, struck out 0. Losing pitcher: Eddie Stack.
#335	August 26	New York 1, Cincinnati 0 at Polo Grounds. Allowed 8 hits, walked 0, struck out 2. Losing pitcher: Chief Johnson.
#336	September 13	New York 4, Pittsburgh 2 at Forbes Field. Allowed 7 hits, walked 1, struck out 1. Losing pitcher: Bill Luhrsen.
#337	September 24	New York 2, Brooklyn 1 at Polo Grounds. Allowed 11 hits, walked 0, struck out 2. Losing pitcher: Ed Reulbach.

1914

#338	April 27	New York 4, Philadelphia 3 at Polo Grounds. Allowed 6 hits, walked 2, struck out 1. Losing pitcher: George Chalmers.
#339	May 4	New York 4, Brooklyn 3 at Polo Grounds. Allowed 7 hits, walked 2, struck out 2. Losing pitcher: Ed Reulbach.
#340	May 9	New York 2, Boston 0 at Polo Grounds. Allowed 10 hits, walked 0, struck out 1. Losing pitcher: George Tyler.
#341	May 15	New York 5, Pittsburgh 3 at Forbes Field. Allowed 9 hits, walked 1, struck out 0. Losing pitcher: George McQuillan.
#342	May 19	New York 5, Cincinnati 2 at Redland Field. Allowed 7 hits, walked 0, struck out 2. Losing pitcher: Dave Davenport.
#343	May 27	New York 3, Chicago 1 at West Side Park. Allowed 6 hits, walked 1, struck out 2. Losing pitcher: George Zabel.
#344	June 1	New York 11, Philadelphia 7 at Baker Bowl. Allowed 16 hits, walked 2, struck out 2. Losing pitcher: Erskine Mayer.
#345	June 6	New York 6, St. Louis 4 at Polo Grounds. Allowed 10 hits, walked 0, struck out 4. Losing pitcher: Harry Sallee.
#346	June 17	New York 5, Pittsburgh 0 at Polo Grounds. Allowed 5 hits, walked 0, struck out 4. Losing pitcher: George McQuillan.

Appendix C: 373 Career Victories

#347	June 22	New York 3, Cincinnati 2 at Polo Grounds. Allowed 7 hits, walked 0, struck out 0. Losing pitcher: Red Ames.
#348	June 26	New York 8, Boston 4 at South End Grounds. Allowed 6 hits, walked 1, struck out 2. Losing pitcher: George Tyler.
#349	June 29	New York 8, Brooklyn 6 at Polo Grounds. Allowed 11 hits in 7 innings of relief, walked 0, struck out 2. Losing pitcher: Frank Allen.
#350	July 4	New York 3, Philadelphia 0 at Polo Grounds. Allowed 8 hits, walked 2, struck out 1. Losing pitcher: Erskine Mayer.
#351	July 11	New York 13, St. Louis 9 at Robison Field. Allowed 16 hits, walked 0, struck out 1. Losing pitcher: Bill Steele.
#352	July 14	New York 12, Chicago 8 at West Side Park. Allowed 10 hits in 6 innings of relief, walked 0, struck out 5. Losing pitcher: Larry Cheney.
#353	July 18	New York 6, Pittsburgh 5 at Forbes Field. Allowed 10 hits in 10 innings, walked 0, struck out 4. Losing pitcher: George McQuillan.
#354	July 21	New York 6, Cincinnati 5 at Redland Field. Allowed 0 hits in 5 innings of relief, walked 0, struck out 0. Losing pitcher: Red Ames.
#355	July 25	New York 4, Pittsburgh 2 at Polo Grounds. Allowed 6 hits, walked 2, struck out 3. Losing pitcher: Babe Adams.
#356	August 3	New York 7, Cincinnati 2 at Polo Grounds. Allowed 11 hits, walked 0, struck out 4. Losing pitcher: Rube Benton.
#357	August 26	New York 4, St. Louis 0 at Robison Field. Allowed 2 hits, walked 0, struck out 0. Losing pitcher: Slim Sallee.
#358	August 29	New York 7, Chicago 5 at West Side Park. Allowed 8 hits, walked 1, struck out 4. Losing pitcher: Bert Humphries.
#359	September 3	New York 6, Brooklyn 3 at Ebbets Field. Allowed 13 hits, walked 0, struck out 2. Losing pitcher: Pat Ragan.
#360	September 11	New York 3, Brooklyn 0 at Polo Grounds. Allowed 7 hits, walked 0, struck out 1. Losing pitcher: Charlie Schmutz.
#361	September 17	New York 10, Cincinnati 1 at Polo Grounds. Allowed 6 hits in 7 innings, walked 0, struck out 1. Losing pitcher: Phil Douglas.

1915

#362	May 12	New York 6, Cincinnati 5 at Polo Grounds. Allowed 11 hits, walked 1, struck out 2. Losing pitcher: Gene Dale.
#363	June 11	New York 3, St. Louis 2 at Robison Field. Allowed 7 hits, walked 2, struck out 0. Losing pitcher: Dan Griner.
#364	June 28	New York 3, Boston 2 at Polo Grounds. Allowed 6 hits in 11 innings, walked 3, struck out 6. Losing pitcher: Pat Ragan.
#365	July 7	New York 5, Philadelphia 4 at Baker Bowl. Allowed 12 hits, walked 2, struck out 2. Losing pitcher: Erskine Mayer.
#366	July 16	New York 2, Chicago 0 at Polo Grounds. Allowed 5 hits, walked 0, struck out 4. Losing pitcher: George Zabel.
#367	August 4	New York 11, St. Louis 9 at Robison Field. Allowed 10 hits in 7⅓ innings, walked 2, struck out 0. Losing pitcher: Leon Ames.
#368	August 7	New York 5, Cincinnati 4 at Redland Field. Allowed 5 hits, walked 1, struck out 3. Losing pitcher: Pete Schneider.
#369	August 27	New York 2, Pittsburgh 1 at Polo Grounds. Allowed 7 hits, walked 1, struck out 6. Losing pitcher: Babe Adams.

1916

#370	May 20	New York 4, St. Louis 1 at Polo Grounds. Allowed 6 hits, walked 2, struck out 1. Losing pitcher: Henry Jasper.
#371	May 29	New York 3, Boston 0 at Braves Field. Allowed 4 hits, walked 0, struck out 2. Losing pitcher: Dick Rudolph.
#372	June 26	New York 11, Brooklyn 8 at Ebbets Field. Allowed 2 hits in 4⅓ innings of relief, walked 0, struck out 1. Losing pitcher: John Mails.
#373	September 4	Cincinnati 10, Chicago 8 at Weegham Park. Alowed 15 hits, walked 1, struck out 3. Losing pitcher: Three Finger Brown.

Appendix D: Classic Matchups Mathewson vs. Brown

Date	Score	Park	Winner
July 9, 1903	New York 4, St. Louis 2	Robison Field	Mathewson
August 13, 1903	New York 6, St. Louis 2	Polo Grounds	Mathewson
June 13, 1904	Chicago 3, New York 2	Polo Grounds	Brown
July 23, 1904	New York 5, Chicago 1	West Side Park	Mathewson
June 13, 1905	New York 1, Chicago 0	West Side Park	Mathewson
July 12, 1905	Chicago 8, New York 1	Polo Grounds	Brown
July 17, 1906	Chicago 6, New York 2	West Side Park	Brown
August 18, 1906	Chicago 6, New York 2	West Side Park	Brown
May 21, 1907	Chicago 3, New York 2	Polo Grounds	Brown
June 5, 1907	Chicago 8, New York 2	West Side Park	Brown
August 2, 1907	Chicago 5, New York 0	West Side Park	Brown
July 17, 1908	Chicago 1, New York 0	West Side Park	Brown
August 29, 1908	Chicago 3, New York 2	West Side Park	Brown
September 24, 1908	New York 5, Chicago 4	Polo Grounds	*Mathewson
October 8, 1908	Chicago 4, New York 2	Polo Grounds	*Brown
June 8, 1909	New York 3, Chicago 2	West Side Park	Mathewson
August 28, 1909	Chicago 6, New York 1	Polo Grounds	Brown
September 16, 1909	New York 2, Chicago 1	West Side Park	Mathewson
September 24, 1910	New York 6, Chicago 5	Polo Grounds	Mathewson
May 9, 1911	New York 5, Chicago 3	Hilltop Park	Mathewson
August 7, 1911	Chicago 8, New York 6	West Side Park	Brown
July 9, 1912	New York 5, Chicago 2	West Side Park	Mathewson
July 15, 1913	New York 4, Cincinnati 2	Polo Grounds	Mathewson
September 4, 1916	Cincinnati 10, Chicago 8	Weeghman Park	Mathewson

*In relief

Appendix E: Mathewson's Career Victories vs. Opposing Teams

In compiling his 373 victories Christy Mathewson had no particular favorites or patsies; he whipped all teams—and often. Although Matty beat Cincinnati 19 more times than Chicago, over a 17-year career it amounts to a little more than one game per season. There were stretches, however, in which Matty dominated certain clubs, for example, St. Louis and Cincinnati (see Appendices F and G).

Opposing Team	*Number of Victories*
Cincinnati	65
Boston	55
Pittsburgh	54
Philadelphia	52
St. Louis	52
Brooklyn	49
Chicago	46
TOTAL	373

Appendix F: Mathewson's 24-Game Winning Streak vs. St. Louis

Game	Date	Score	Park
1	June 16, 1904	New York 4, St. Louis 3	Polo Grounds
2	August 6, 1904	New York 8, St. Louis 1	Polo Grounds
3	August 8, 1904	New York 4, St. Louis 3	Polo Grounds
4	August 27, 1904	New York 9, St. Louis 3	Robison Field
5	October 3, 1904	New York 3, St. Louis 1	Polo Grounds
6	May 11, 1905	New York 4, St. Louis 0	Polo Grounds
7	June 17, 1905	New York 7, St. Louis 2	Robison Field
8	July 21, 1905	New York 14, St. Louis 2	Polo Grounds
9	August 28, 1905	New York 8, St. Louis 1	Polo Grounds
10	September 29, 1905	New York 6, St. Louis 5	Robison Field
11	May 26, 1906	New York 5, St. Louis 4	Robison Field
12	June 15, 1906	New York 2, St. Louis 1	Polo Grounds
13	July 14, 1906	New York 4, St. Louis 0	Robison Field
14	September 28, 1906	New York 8, St. Louis 2	Polo Grounds
15	May 17, 1907	New York 2, St. Louis 1	Polo Grounds
16	June 11, 1907	New York 8, St. Louis 7	Robison Field
17	July 9, 1907	New York 5, St. Louis 3	Polo Grounds
18	July 29, 1907	New York 4, St. Louis 3	Robison Field
19	August 27, 1907	New York 1, St. Louis 0	Polo Grounds
20	June 6, 1908	New York 3, St. Louis 2	Polo Grounds
21	July 21, 1908	New York 4, St. Louis 2	Robison Field
22	July 29, 1908	New York 1, St. Louis 0	Polo Grounds
23	August 17, 1908	New York 3, St. Louis 0	Robison Field
24	September 15, 1908	New York 5, St. Louis 4	Polo Grounds

Appendix G: Mathewson's 22-Game Winning Streak vs. Cincinnati

Game	Date	Score	Park
1	June 17, 1908	New York 2, Cincinnati 1	Polo Grounds
2	July 6, 1908	New York 2, Cincinnati 1	League Park
3	July 9, 1908	New York 2, Cincinnati 1	League Park
4	August 4, 1908	New York 4, Cincinnati 3	Polo Grounds
5	August 4, 1908	New York 4, Cincinnati 1	Polo Grounds
6	August 20, 1908	New York 2, Cincinnati 0	League Park
7	September 26, 1908	New York 6, Cincinnati 2	Polo Grounds
8	May 17, 1909	New York 6, Cincinnati 0	Polo Grounds
9	June 12, 1909	New York 2, Cincinnati 0	League Park
10	July 16, 1909	New York 2, Cincinnati 1	Polo Grounds
11	August 3, 1909	New York 7, Cincinnati 6	League Park
12	August 21, 1909	New York 1, Cincinnati 0	Polo Grounds
13	May 18, 1910	New York 10, Cincinnati 6	League Park
14	June 1, 1910	New York 5, Cincinnati 2	Polo Grounds
15	July 19, 1910	New York 6, Cincinnati 4	League Park
16	August 11, 1910	New York 5, Cincinnati 4	Polo Grounds
17	August 19, 1910	New York 9, Cincinnati 3	League Park
18	May 23, 1911	New York 7, Cincinnati 2	Hilltop Park
19	June 13, 1911	New York 5, Cincinnati 2	League Park
20	July 15, 1911	New York 4, Cincinnati 3	Polo Grounds
21	July 26, 1911	New York 5, Cincinnati 3	League Park
22	August 16, 1911	New York 6, Cincinnati 1	Polo Grounds

Notes

Preface

1. Kevin Kerrane, *The Hurlers* (Virginia: Redefinition, 1989), p. 122.
2. Donald Honig, *The Greatest Pitchers of All Time* (New York: Crown Publishers, Inc., 1988), p. 13.

Chapter 1: Factoryville to New York

1. Lawrence S. Ritter, *The Glory of Their Times* (New York: The Macmillan Company, 1966), p. 88.
2. Ibid., p. 168.
3. Kevin Kerrane, *The Hurlers* (Virginia: Redefinition, 1989), p. 124.
4. Charles Einstein, *The Fireside Book of Baseball* (New York: Simon and Schuster, 1956), p. 194.
5. Daniel Okrent and Harris Lewine, eds., *The Ultimate Baseball Book* (Boston: Houghton Mifflin Company, 1979), p. 69.
6. Ritter, *The Glory of Their Times*, p. 38.
7. Ibid., p. 51.
8. Kevin Nelson, *Baseball's Greatest Quotes* (New York: Simon and Schuster, 1982), p. 23.
9. Ritter, *The Glory of Their Times*, p. 2.
10. Ibid., p. 168.
11. Douglass Wallop, *Baseball: An Informal History* (New York: W.W. Norton & Company, Inc., 1969), p. 115.
12. Noel Hynd, *The Giants of the Polo Grounds* (New York: Doubleday, 1988), p. 117.
13. Donald Honig, *The National League* (New York: Crown Publishers, Inc., 1983), p. 6.
14. Donald Honig, *The Greatest Pitchers of All Time* (New York: Crown Publishers, Inc., 1988, p. 14.
15. Gene Schoor with Henry Gilfond, *Christy Mathewson: Baseball's Greatest Pitcher* (New York: Julian Messner, 1953), p. 59.
16. Christy Mathewson, *How I Came to Be a Big Leaguer*, Mathewson Collection at Keystone Junior College, LaPlume, Pennsylvania.

Chapter 2: Inauspicious Start, 1900

1. Lawrence S. Ritter, *The Glory of Their Times* (New York: The Macmillan Company, 1966), p. 55.

2. Christy Mathewson, *Pitching in a Pinch* (New York: Grosset & Dunlap, 1912), p. 11.
3. Steven A. Riess, *Touching Base* (Connecticut: Greenwood Press, 1980), p. 68.
4. Noel Hynd, *The Giants of the Polo Grounds* (New York: Doubleday, 1988), p. 88.
5. *The Sporting News*, December 28, 1939, p. 5.
6. Hynd, *The Giants of the Polo Grounds*, p. 94.
7. *The New York Times*, July 18, 1900, p. 5.
8. *Sporting Life*, July 28, 1900, p. 4.
9. *Sporting Life*, September 22, 1900, p. 10.

Chapter 3: Rookie Season, 1901

1. *The New York Times*, May 1, 1901, p. 7.
2. *The New York Times*, May 7, 1901, p. 7.
3. *The Sporting News*, May 18, 1901, p. 4.
4. Lawrence S. Ritter, *The Story of Baseball* (New York: William Morrow and Company, 1983), p. 5.
5. *The New York Times*, May 14, 1901, p. 7.
6. *The New York Times*, May 16, 1901, p. 7.
7. *The Sporting News*, June 1, 1901, p. 1.
8. *The New York Times*, June 12, 1901, p. 7.
9. Kevin Kerrane, *The Hurlers* (Virginia: Redefinition, 1989), p. 82.
10. Lawrence S. Ritter, *The Glory of Their Times* (New York: The Macmillan Company, 1966), p. 168.
11. Daniel Okrent and Harris Lewine, eds., *The Ultimate Baseball Book* (Boston: Houghton Mifflin Company, 1979), p. 70.
12. James Kahn, *The Umpire Story* (New York: G.P. Putnam's Sons, 1953), p. 50.
13. Eugene Murdock, *Ban Johnson: Czar of Baseball* (Connecticut: Greenwood Press, 1982), p. 98.
14. *The New York Times*, August 8, 1901, p. 5.
15. Margaret Leech, *In the Days of McKinley* (New York: Harper & Brothers, 1959), p. 601.
16. *The New York Times*, September 20, 1901, p. 1.

Chapter 4: Saved by McGraw, 1902

1. Noel Hynd, *The Giants of the Polo Grounds* (New York: Doubleday, 1988), p. 96.
2. *The New York Times*, January 9, 1902, p. 10.
3. Ibid.
4. Hynd, *The Giants of the Polo Grounds*, p. 98.
5. *The New York Times*, September 30, 1902, p. 10.
6. *The New York Times*, April 18, 1902, p. 6.
7. *The New York Times*, May 22, 1902, p. 10.
8. *Sporting Life*, June 21, 1902, p. 2.
9. *The New York Times*, July 1, 1902, p. 6.

10. Charles C. Alexander, *John McGraw* (New York: Viking, 1988), p. 90.
11. Ibid., p. 91.
12. *The New York Times*, July 10, 1902, p. 3.
13. *The New York Times*, July 9, 1902, p. 6.
14. Frank Graham, *The New York Giants* (New York: G.P. Putnam's Sons, 1952), p. 40.
15. Mrs. John J. McGraw, *The Real McGraw* (New York: David McKay Co., 1953), p. 166.
16. Graham, *The New York Giants*, p. 41.
17. Joseph Durso, *Casey & Mr. McGraw* (St. Louis: The Sporting News, 1989), p. 41.
18. *The New York Times*, September 16, 1902, p. 6.

Chapter 5: First 30-Game Season, 1903

1. Joseph Durso, *The Days of Mr. McGraw* (New Jersey: Prentice-Hall, 1969), p. 50.
2. Mrs. John J. McGraw, *The Real McGraw* (New York: David McKay Co., 1953), p. 187.
3. Ibid., p. 190.
4. Charles C. Alexander, *John McGraw* (New York: Viking, 1988), p. 101.
5. *The New York Times*, April 13, 1903, p. 7.
6. Christy Mathewson, *Pitching in a Pinch* (New York: Grosset & Dunlap, 1912), p. 64.
7. Ibid.
8. Ibid., p. 54.
9. *The New York Times*, June 19, 1903, p. 10.
10. Alexander, *John McGraw*, p. 103.
11. *The New York Times*, July 8, 1903, p. 10.
12. James Kahn, *The Umpire Story* (New York: G.P. Putnam's Sons, 1953), p. 41.
13. Lyall Smith, "Matty Just a 'Cousin' to Brownie," *Baseball Digest*, July 1949, p. 52.
14. *New York Daily Tribune*, August 4, 1903, p. 5.
15. *New York Daily Tribune*, August 9, 1903, p. 5.
16. Kahn, *The Umpire Story*, p. 42.
17. Mrs. John J. McGraw, *The Real McGraw*, p. 196.

Chapter 6: First Pennant!, 1904

1. Frank Graham, *McGraw of the Giants* (New York: G.P. Putnam's Sons, 1944), p. 26.
2. *Sporting LIfe*, April 16, 1904, p. 2.
3. *The New York Times*, April 18, 1904, p. 10.
4. Mike Shatzkin, ed., *The Ballplayers* (New York: Arbor House, 1990), p. 311.
5. Joseph Durso, *The Days of Mr. McGraw* (New Jersey: Prentice-Hall, 1969), p. 53.
6. Charles Einstein, *The Second Fireside Book of Baseball* (New York: Simon and Schuster, 1958), p. 257.

7. Benton Stark, *The Year They Called Off the World Series* (New York: Avery Publishing Group, 1991), pp. 122–123.
8. Frank Graham, *The New York Giants* (New York: G.P. Putnam's Sons, 1952), p. 47.
9. *The New York Times*, August 12, 1904, p. 5.
10. Christy Mathewson, *Pitching in a Pinch* (New York: Grosset & Dunlap, 1912), pp. 8–9.
11. *The New York Times*, October 7, 1904, p. 7.
12. Charles C. Alexander, *John McGraw* (New York: Viking, 1988), p. 109.

Chapter 7: World Series Hero, 1905

1. Charles C. Alexander, *John McGraw* (New York: Viking: 1988), pp. 111–12.
2. Joseph Durso, *Casey & Mr. McGraw* (St. Louis: The Sporting News, 1989), pp. 55–56.
3. *The New York Times*, April 15, 1905, p. 13.
4. *The Sporting News*, April 29, 1905, p. 1.
5. Frank Graham, *The New York Giants* (New York: G.P. Putnam's Sons, 1952), p. 51.
6. Alexander, *John McGraw*, p. 115.
7. Ibid., p. 106.
8. Joseph Durso, *The Days of Mr. McGraw* (New Jersey: Prentice-Hall, 1969), p. 64.
9. James Kahn, *The Umpire Story* (New York: G.P. Putnam's Sons, 1953), p. 79.
10. *The New York Times*, July 20, 1905, p. 5.
11. Lawrence S. Ritter, *The Glory of Their Times* (New York: The Macmillan Company, 1966), p. 120.
12. John J. McGraw, *My Thirty Years in Baseball* (New York: Arno Press Reprint, 1974), p. 164.
13. *The New York Times*, October 8, 1905, p. 11.
14. Mrs. John J. McGraw, *The Real McGraw* (New York: David McKay Co., 1953), p. 211.

Chapter 8: A Bout with Diphtheria, 1906

1. Harvey Frommer, *Primitive Baseball* (New York: Atheneum, 1988), p. 53.
2. John J. McGraw, *My Thirty Years in Baseball* (New York: Arno Press Reprint, 1974), p. 185.
3. Frank Graham, *The New York Giants* (New York: G.P. Putnam's Sons, 1952), p. 58.
4. *The New York Times*, April 15, 1906, p. 10.
5. Christy Mathewson, *Pitching in a Pinch* (New York: Grosset & Dunlap, 1912), p. 172.
6. McGraw, *My Thirty Years in Baseball*, p. 221.
7. Mathewson, *Pitching in a Pinch*, p. 4.

8. *The New York Times*, August 9, 1906, p. 4.
9. Charles C. Alexander, *John McGraw* (New York: Viking, 1988), p. 36.
10. Jack Sher, "The Immortal Big Six," *Sport*, October 1949, p. 60.

Chapter 9: Most Victories in National League, 1907

1. Noel Hynd, *The Giants of the Polo Grounds* (New York: Doubleday, 1988), p. 142.
2. *The New York Times*, April 12, 1907, p. 10.
3. Charles Einstein, *The Fireside Book of Baseball* (New York: Simon and Schuster, 1956), p. 248.
4. John J. McGraw, *My Thirty Years in Baseball* (New York: Arno Press Reprint, 1974), p. 159.
5. *The New York Times*, June 23, 1907, p. 2.
6. Correspondence with Christopher D. Green, September 15, 1991, Author's Collection, East Hanover, New Jersey.
7. Frank Graham, *The New York Giants* (New York: G.P. Putnam's Sons, 1952), p. 59.
8. Lawrence S. Ritter, *The Glory of Their Times* (New York: The Macmillan Company, 1966), p. 123.
9. Hynd, *The Giants of the Polo Grounds*, p. 143.
10. Frank Graham, *McGraw of the Giants* (New York: G.P. Putnam's Sons, 1944), p. 35.

Chapter 10: Most Career Victories, 1908

1. John J. McGraw, *My Thirty Years in Baseball* (New York: Arno Press Reprint, 1974), p. 187.
2. Mrs. John J. McGraw, *The Real McGraw* (New York: David McKay Co., 1953), p. 215.
3. *The New York Times*, April 23, 1908, p. 7.
4. Lawrence S. Ritter, *The Glory of Their Times* (New York: The Macmillan Company, 1966), pp. 83–87.
5. Christy Mathewson, *Pitching in a Pinch* (New York: Grosset & Dunlap, 1912), p. 58.
6. Ibid., pp. 83–84.
7. *The New York Times*, August 6, 1908, p. 6.
8. McGraw, *My Thirty Years in Baseball*, p. 143.
9. Noel Hynd, *The Giants of the Polo Grounds* (New York: Doubleday, 1988), pp. 147–48.
10. McGraw, *My Thirty Years in Baseball*, p. 180.
11. Joseph Durso, *The Days of Mr. McGraw* (New Jersey: Prentice-Hall, 1969), p. 75.
12. Ray Robinson, "Yesterday's Heroes," *Boy's Life*, March 1984, p. 30.
13. Mathewson, *Pitching in a Pinch*, p. 27.
14. Jack Sher, "The Immortal Big Six," *Sport*, October 1949, p. 62.
15. Mathewson, *Pitching in a Pinch*, p. 185–86.

Chapter 11: Lowest Career ERA, 1909

1. *The New York Times*, May 10, 1909, p. 7.
2. Christy Mathewson, *Pitching in a Pinch* (New York: Grosset & Dunlap, 1912), pp. 220-21.
3. Philip J. Lowry, *Green Cathedrals* (Cooperstown: Society for American Baseball Research, 1986), p. 72.
4. Jack Sher, "The Immortal Big Six," *Sport*, October 1949, p. 60.
5. James Kahn, *The Umpire Story* (New York: G.P. Putnam's Sons, 1953), p. 42.
6. Sher, "The Immortal Big Six," p. 60.
7. Frank Graham, *The New York Giants* (New York: G.P. Putnam's Sons, 1952), p. 65.
8. John J. McGraw, *My Thirty Years in Baseball* (New York: Arno Press Reprint, 1974), p. 103.

Chapter 12: Most Victories in National League, Again, 1910

1. Mrs. John J. McGraw, *The Real McGraw* (New York: David McKay Co., 1953), p. 233.
2. Christy Mathewson, *Pitching in a Pinch* (New York: Grosset & Dunlap, 1912), p. 18.
3. *The New York Times*, May 5, 1910, p. 12.
4. Ray Robinson, "Yesterday's Heroes," *Boy's Life*, March 1984, p. 30.
5. Jack Sher, "The Immortal Big Six," *Sport*, October 1949, p. 65.
6. John J. McGraw, *My Thirty Years in Baseball* (New York: Arno Press Reprint, 1974), p. 19.
7. Ibid., p. 106.
8. Charles C. Alexander, *John McGraw* (New York: Viking, 1988), p. 149.
9. *The Sporting News*, July 28, 1910, p. 1.
10. *The New York Times*, August 19, 1910, p. 8.
11. *The New York Times*, August 28, 1910, p. 5.
12. Donald Honig, *The Greatest Pitchers of All Time* (New York: Crown Publishers, Inc., 1988), p. 14.
13. Noel Hynd, *The Giants of the Polo Grounds* (New York: Doubleday, 1988), p. 159.

Chapter 13: M and M Boys, 1911

1. John J. McGraw, *My Thirty Years in Baseball* (New York: Arno Press Reprint, 1974), p. 197.
2. Christy Mathewson, *Pitching in a Pinch* (New York: Grosset & Dunlap, 1912), p. 252.
3. Steven A. Riess, *Touching Base: Professional Baseball and American Culture in the Progressive Era* (Connecticut: Greenwood Press, 1980), p. 100.
4. McGraw, *My Thirty Years in Baseball*, p. 141.
5. Lawrence S. Ritter, *The Glory of Their Times* (New York: The Macmillan Company, 1966), p. 15.
6. *The New York Times*, July 27, 1911, p. 9.

7. Mathewson, *Pitching in a Pinch*, p. 83.
8. Ibid., p. 51.
9. Jack Sher, "The Immortal Big Six," *Sport*, October 1949, p. 62.
10. Ibid., p. 61.
11. *The New York Times*, October 17, 1911, p. 1.
12. Ibid., p. 2.

Chapter 14: Tough World Series Loss, 1912

1. Charles C. Alexander, *John McGraw* (New York: Viking, 1988), p. 162.
2. Frank Graham, *McGraw of the Giants* (New York: G.P. Putnam's Sons, 1944), p. 45.
3. *The New York Times*, May 19, 1912, p. 2.
4. Mathewson Collection, Keystone Junior College, LaPlume, Pennsylvania.
5. John J. McGraw, *My Thirty Years in Baseball* (New York: Arno Press Reprint, 1974), p. 104.
6. Lawrence S. Ritter, *The Glory of Their Times* (New York: The Macmillan Company, 1966), p. 14.
7. J. G. Taylor Spink, *Judge Landis and Twenty-five Years of Baseball* (St. Louis: The Sporting News, 1974), p. 27.
8. *The New York Times*, July 23, 1912, p. 10.
9. McGraw, *My Thirty Years in Baseball*, p. 106.
10. Ibid., p. 202.
11. Lee Lowenfish and Tony Lupien, *The Imperfect Diamond* (New York: Stein and Day, 1980), p. 78.
12. *The New York Times*, September 23, 1912, p. 9.
13. *The New York Times*, October 6, 1912, p. 2.
14. Bill Chuck, "Boston–New York: The Really Exciting World Series," *Baseball Research Journal* 16, 1987, p. 6.
15. Ritter, *The Glory of Their Times*, p. 142.
16. Jack Sher, "The Immortal Big Six," *Sport*, October 1949, p. 65.

Chapter 15: Masterful Control, 1913

1. Frank Graham, *The New York Giants*, (New York: G.P. Putnam's Sons, 1952), p. 73.
2. Frank Graham, *McGraw of the Giants* (New York: G.P Putnams's Sons, 1944), p. 65.
3. Lawrence S. Ritter, *The Glory of Their Times* (New York: The Macmillan Company, 1966), p. 168.
4. Mike Shatzkin, ed., *The Ballplayers* (New York: Arbor House, 1990), p. 919.
5. Marc Okkonen, *The Federal League of 1914–1915: Baseball's Third Major League* (Maryland: Society of American Baseball Research, 1989), p. 4.
6. *The New York Times*, July 1, 1913, p. 10.
7. Christy Mathewson, *Pitching in a Pinch* (New York: Grosset & Dunlap, 1912), pp. 84–86.
8. James Kahn, *The Umpire Story* (New York: G.P. Putnam's Sons, 1953), p. 11.

9. Shatzkin, *The Ballplayers*, p. 144.
10. *The New York Times*, August 23, 1908, Sports Section, p. 1.
11. *The New York Times*, September 3, 1913, p. 10.
12. Mrs. John J. McGraw, *The Real McGraw* (New York: David McKay Co., 1953), p. 241.
13. *The New York Times*, September 25, 1913, p. 11.
14. *The New York Times*, October 6, 1913, p. 8.
15. *The New York Times*, October 12, 1913, Sports Section, p. 1.
16. Jack Sher, "The Immortal Big Six," *Sport*, October 1949, p. 61.

Chapter 16: Last Great Season, 1914

1. John J. McGraw, *My Thirty Years in Baseball* (New York: Arno Press Reprint, 1974), pp. 249–50.
2. Mike Shatzkin, ed., *The Ballplayers* (New York: Arbor House, 1990), p. 1034.
3. *The New York Times*, May 5, 1914, p. 9.
4. Lawrence S. Ritter, *The Glory of Their Times* (New York: The Macmillan Company, 1966), p. 175.
5. *The New York Times*, June 23, 1914, p. 9.
6. Jack Sher, "The Immortal Big Six," *Sport*, October 1949, p. 60.
7. *The New York Times*, July 25, 1914, p. 5.
8. Ritter, *The Glory of Their Times*, p. 168.
9. Tom Meany, *Baseball's Greatest Players* (New York: Grosset & Dunlap, 1953), p. 179.
10. Christy Mathewson, *Pitching in a Pinch* (New York: Grosset & Dunlap, 1912), pp. 98–99.
11. Ritter, *The Glory of Their Times*, p. 167.

Chapter 17: The End Is Near, 1915

1. Noel Hynd, *The Giants of the Polo Grounds* (New York: Doubleday, 1988), pp. 191–92.
2. Mike Shatzkin, ed., *The Ballplayers* (New York: Arbor House, 1990), p. 326.
3. *The New York Times*, April 27, 1915, p. 10.
4. Jack Sher, "The Immortal Big Six," *Sport*, October 1949, p. 60.
5. Charles C. Alexander, *John McGraw* (New York: Viking, 1988), p. 186.
6. Christy Mathewson, *Pitching in a Pinch* (New York: Grosset & Dunlap, 1912), pp. 165–66.
7. Lawrence S. Ritter, *The Glory of Their Times* (New York: The Macmillan Company, 1966), p. 83.
8. Ibid., p. 108.
9. *The New York Times*, August 28, 1915, p. 5.
10. Gerald Tomlinson, "Lefty George: The Durable Duke of York," *The Baseball Research Journal*, 1983, p. 39.
11. Mathewson, *Pitching in a Pinch*, p. 52.
12. Mrs. John J. McGraw, *The Real McGraw* (New York: David McKay Co., 1953), p. 256.

Chapter 18: Farewell Matty, 1916

1. Frank Graham, *McGraw of the Giants* (New York: G.P. Putnam's Sons, 1944), p. 82.
2. John J. McGraw, *My Thirty Years in Baseball* (New York: Arno Press Reprint, 1974), p. 250.
3. *The New York Times*, April 25, 1916, p. 12.
4. *The New York Times*, May 30, 1916, p. 10.
5. Graham, *McGraw of the Giants*, p. 89.
6. Lawrence S. Ritter, *The Glory of Their Times* (New York: The Macmillan Company, 1966), pp. 209–10.
7. Lee Alen and Tom Meany, *Kings of the Diamond* (New York: G.P. Putnam's Sons, 1965), p. 47.
8. Fred Lieb, *Baseball As I Have Known It* (New York: Coward, McCann & Geohegan, Inc., 1977), p. 101.
9. Jack Sher, "The Immortal Big Six," *Sport*, October 1949, p. 66.
10. Donald Honig, *Baseball America* (New York: The Macmillan Company, 1985), p. 153.
11. Glenn D. Adams, *A History of Keystone College* (Boston: Camera & Press, 1990), p. 36.

Bibliography

For the benefit of future Mathewson scholars and researchers, the book portion of this bibliography is divided into three parts. The first lists books which are entirely about Mathewson or a substantial portion about him; these have been annotated. The second part lists books that contain only a brief mention of the great pitcher. The third part is composed of books on baseball in general, which do not mention Mathewson at all.

Books

Alexander, Charles C. *John McGraw.* New York: Viking, 1988.
    In spite of this being a biography of John McGraw, the information on certain segments of Mathewson's career is detailed and, equally important, documented. The discussion of Mathewson's feud with Hal Chase and his newspaper and magazine writings are revealing. The short profile of Matty is balanced and insightful. In many instances the author gives reasons why things happened the way they did.

Honig, Donald. *Baseball America.* New York: Macmillan Publishing Company, 1985.
    The author devotes most of chapter four in this baseball history to a profile of Mathewson. It is detailed and focuses on Matty's personality and his influence on players, fans and the game. Except for one instance, sources of quotations are not cited.

Honig, Donald. *The Greatest Pitchers of All Time.* New York: Crown Publishers, Inc., 1988.
    The short profile of Mathewson, one of 22 in the book, covers seven pages. It scans the highlights of Matty's career but adds little new information. The author devotes a good portion of the profile to making the point that Mathewson was the first national sports idol. He quotes Mathewson and others freely but fails to provide the sources.

Lieb, Fred. *Baseball As I Have Known It.* New York: Coward, McCann & Geoghegan, Inc., 1977.
    This is a valuable, but unfortunately limited source of information about Mathewson. Lieb, the well known sportswriter, was on the scene so the writing is first-hand. His account of the Hal Chase–Mathewson feud and the testimonial he ran for the pitcher are especially enlightening.

Macht, Norman L. *Christy Mathewson: Baseball Legends.* New York: Chelsea House Publishers, 1991.

This book is one of 33 biographies in a series about baseball legends written for young readers. The players range from Cy Young to Carl Yastrzemski. The book is well written and contains many interesting photos. Since it is aimed at young readers, highlighting Mathewson's career in 64 pages, it is of limited use to the serious researcher.

Mathewson, Christy. *Pitching in a Pinch.* New York: Grosset & Dunlap, 1912.

The fact that the book was ghostwritten by sportswriter John Wheeler does nothing to diminish its stature. The book is a gem because it offers the reader a rare glimpse inside baseball in the early 1900s. It also reveals Matty's pitching techniques, baseball philosophy and opinions of several players and umpires. Clearly, it supports the image of Mathewson as a knowledgable and shrewd baseball man.

Meany, Tom. *Baseball's Greatest Players.* New York: Grosset & Dunlap, 1953.

Most of this short profile of Mathewson covers well known events of his career, for example, the 1908 season and Fred Merkle's boner, the Fred Snodgrass muff in the 1912 World Series and highlights from other postseason play. It contains interesting notes and anecdotes, but sources are incomplete. There is no mention of Matty's minor league career or events in his life after he left baseball as an active player.

Okrent, Daniel and Harris Lewine, eds. *The Ultimate Baseball Book.* Boston: Houghton Mifflin Company, 1979.

Chapter two is devoted to Mathewson. It is a short but complete profile that brings balance to the Mathewson legend, making him indeed human. Check the statistics carefully. The book credits Mathewson with 367 victories, not the correct 373. There is no bibliography or chapter notes.

Salant, Nathan. *Superstars, Stars, and Just Plain Heroes.* New York: Stein and Day, 1982.

This book contains one of the most complete, although brief, profiles of Mathewson. It covers his early years through his untimely death in 1925 from tuberculosis at Saranac Lake, New York. Unfortunately for future researchers the authors did not choose to include a bibliography or chapter notes.

Schoor, Gene with Henry Gilfond. *Christy Mathewson: Baseball's Greatest Pitcher.* New York: Julian Messner, Inc., 1953.

This book is one in a series of sport biographies for young readers. It is an unrealistic portrait of Mathewson which appeals to kids. The dialogue between Matty and his managers during games plus that with his future wife, Jane Stoughton, appear to be pure fiction. This makes one question the believability of the rest of the book. It's a biased and unbalanced account that should be used with caution.

Sutton, Keith. *Wayne County Sports History, 1871–1972.* Pennsylvania: The Wayne Independent, 1972.

Although this book is about Wayne County sports, the first 12 pages are devoted to Mathewson's baseball career. Written by Honesdale resident and

Mathewson scholar, Keith Sutton, it provides detailed and little-known information about Matty's semiprofessional and minor league career. It also contains first-hand insights of the pitcher by former Honesdale players.

Books that Briefly Mention Mathewson

Alexander, Charles C. *Ty Cobb.* New York: Oxford University Press, 1984.
Allen, Lee and Tom Meany. *Kings of the Diamond.* New York: G.P. Putnam's Sons, 1965.
Chadwick, Alex. *Illustrated History of Baseball.* New York: Portland House, 1988.
Creamer, Robert C. *Stengel: His Life and Times.* New York: Simon and Schuster, 1984.
Davids, Robert L. *Insider's Baseball.* New York: Charles Scribner's Sons, 1983.
Durso, Joseph. *Baseball and the American Dream.* New York: Missouri: The Sporting News, 1986.
———. *Casey & Mr. McGraw.* St. Louis: The Sporting News, 1989.
———. *The Days of Mr. McGraw.* New Jersey: Prentice-Hall, Inc., 1969.
Einstein, Charles. *The Fireside Book of Baseball.* New York: Simon and Schuster, 1956.
Fleming, G. H. *The Unforgettable Season.* New York: Holt, Rinehart and Winston: 1981.
Graham, Frank. *McGraw of the Giants.* New York: G.P. Putnam's Sons, 1944.
———. *The New York Giants.* New York: G.P. Putnam's Sons, 1952.
Honig, Donald. *The American League.* New York: Crown Publishers, Inc., 1983.
———. *The National League.* New York: Crown Publishers, Inc., 1983.
Hynd, Noel. *The Giants of the Polo Grounds.* New York: Doubleday, 1988.
Kahn, James M. *The Umpire Story.* New York: G.P. Putnam's Sons, 1953.
Karst, Gene and Martin J. Jones, Jr. *Who's Who in Professional Baseball.* New York: Arlington House, 1973.
Kerrane, Kevin. *The Hurlers.* Virginia: Redefinition, 1989.
Levine, Peter, ed. *Baseball History #2.* Connecticut: Meckler Books, 1989.
Lowenfish, Lee and Tony Lupien. *The Imperfect Diamond.* New York: Stein and Day, 1980.
McGraw, John J. *My Thirty Years in Baseball.* New York: Arno Press Reprint Edition, 1974.
McGraw, Mrs. John J. *The Real McGraw.* New York: David McKay Company, Inc., 1953.
Meany, Tom and Tommy Holmes. *Baseball's Best.* New York: Franklin Watts, Inc., 1964.
Murdock, Eugene C. *Ban Johnson: Czar of Baseball.* Connecticut: Greenwood Press, 1982.
Nelson, Kevin. *Baseball's Greatest Quotes.* New York: Simon and Schuster, 1982.
Porter, David L., ed. *Biographical Dictionary of American Sports: Baseball.* Connecticut: Greenwood Press, 1987.
Rickey, Branch and Robert Riger. *The American Diamond.* New York: Simon and Schuster, 1965.
Riess, Steven A. *Touching Base: Professional Baseball and American Culture in the Progressive Era.* Connecticut: Greenwood Press, 1980.
Ritter, Lawrence. *The Story of Baseball.* New York: William Morrow and Company, 1983.
———. *The Glory of Their Times.* New York: The Macmillan Company, 1966.

Seymour, Harold. *Baseball: The Early Years.* New York: Oxford University Press, 1960.
_____. *The Golden Age.* New York: Oxford University Press, 1971.
Shatzkin, Mike, ed. *The Ballplayers.* New York: Arbor House, 1990.
Smith, Robert. *Baseball.* New York: Simon and Schuster, 1947.
_____. *Baseball in America.* New York: Holt, Rinehart and Winston, 1961.
Spink, J. G. Taylor. *Judge Landis and Twenty-five Years of Baseball.* St. Louis: The Sporting News, 1974.
Thorn, John. *A Century of Baseball Lore.* New York: Hart Publishing Company, Inc., 1974.
_____ and Pete Palmer, eds. *Total Baseball.* New York: Warner Books, 1989.
Wolff, Rick, ed. *The Baseball Encyclopedia.* New York: Macmillan Publishing Company, 1990.

Other Books

Frommer, Harvey. *Primitive Baseball.* New York: Atheneum, 1988.
Leech, Margaret. *In the Days of McKinley.* New York: Harper & Brothers, 1959.
Levine, Peter. *A. G. Spalding and the Rise of Baseball.* New York: Oxford University Press, 1985.
Lord, Walter. *A Night to Remember.* New York: Holt, Rinehart and Winston, 1976.
Lowry, Philip J. *Green Cathedrals.* Cooperstown: Society for American Baseball Research, 1986.
Okkonen, Marc. *The Federal League of 1914–1915: Baseball's Third Major League.* Maryland: Society of American Baseball Research, 1989.

Articles and Periodicals

Adams, Glenn D. "A History of Keystone College," Boston Camera & Press (1990), p. 36.
Adams, Joe. "Christy Mathewson's Greatest Fight," *Baseball Magazine* (October 1960), pp. 32–33.
"Baseball Nicknames 1870–1946," Gates-Vincent Publications (1946), pp. 1–24.
Buckly, James, Jr. "World Series Kings of the Hill," *Sports Illustrated* (October 7, 1991), pp. 45–58.
Buege, Bob. "You Shoulda Been There!—The Real McGraw," *Oldtyme Baseball News* (Volume III, No. 5 1991), pp. 16–17.
Carmichael, John P. "You Could Catch Mathewson Sitting in a Chair," *Baseball Digest* (August 1982), pp. 79–81.
"Christy Mathewson Testimonial," Mathewson collection at Keystone Junior College, LaPlume, Pennsylvania (September 30, 1921), pp. 1–15.
"Christy Mathewson Memorial Stadium Rededication—Bucknell vs. Dartmouth," Department of Athletics, Bucknell University (September 30, 1989), pages unnumbered.
Chuck, Bill. "The 1912 World Series," *The Baseball Research Journal* (1987), pp. 2–5.
Donovan, Dan. "Christy Mathewson: He Was Someone Special," *Baseball Digest* (December 1981), pp. 82–84.
Hannan, William M. "Christy Mathewson's First Baseball Contract," *The Baseball Magazine* (December 1914), pp. 33–40.

Harris, John M. "'Pinhead' Christy Mathewson," *The National Pastime* 10 (1990), pp. 17–20.
Karnofsky, Louis. "Fireball Rusie, Now 68, Who Fanned 345 in 1890, Tells How He Held Out Full Year—and Received Pay," *The Sporting News* (December 28, 1939).
"McGraw Could Count on Matty," *Sport* (October 1960), pp. 32–33.
Mathewson, Christy. "How I Came to Be a Big Leaguer," Mathewson collection at Keystone Junior College, LaPlume, Pennsylvania.
———. "Outguessing the Batter," *Parson's Magazine* (May 1911), pp. 568–75.
Molen, Sam. "Two Field Goals Kept Matty in Baseball," *Baseball Digest* (April 1943), pp. 55–56.
Robinson, Ray. "Yesterday's Heroes," *Boy's Life* (March 1984), pp. 28–59.
Sher, Jack. "The Immortal Big Six," *Sport* (October 1949), pp. 56–66.
Smith, Lyall. "Matty Just a 'Cousin' to Brownie," *Baseball Digest* (July 1949), pp. 51–52.
Tomlinson, Gerald. "Lefty George: The Durable Duke of York," *The Baseball Research Journal* (1983), pp. 39–44.
Ward, John J. "Christy Mathewson Stages a Come Back," *Baseball Magazine* (May 1923), pp. 561–72.
Williams, Frank J. "All the Record Books Are Wrong," *The National Pastime* (Fall 1982), pp. 50–62.

Newspapers

Boston Sunday Globe, January 24, 1926.
Bucknell Alumni Monthly (Mathewson Memoria Issue), November 1925, Vol. X, No. 2.
Bucknellian, October 7, 1925; November 18, 1983; Apiril 21, 1989.
Chicago Daily News, August 19, 1902.
Chicago Inter-Ocean, August 19, 1902.
Chicago Tribune, August 19, 1902.
Harrisburgh Evening News, April 4, 1952.
New York Herald, April 18, 1902; August 19, 1902.
New York Sun, April 18, 1902; August 19, 1902.
New York Times, 1900–1916; May 5, 1919; October 21, 1921; July 8, 1926; August 28, 1926.
New York Tribune, April 18, 1902; August 19, 1902; August 4, 9, 1903; January 22, 1930.
New York World, August 19, 1902.
Philadelphia Inquirer, April 18, 1902.
Philadelphia Press, April 18, 1902.
Philadelphia Public Ledger, April 18, 1902.
St. Louis Post-Dispatch, August 5, 1900; July 10, 1903.
Sporting Life, June 21, 1902; March 24, 1900–March 16, 1901; April 16, 1904.
The Sporting News, May 18, 1901; June 1, 1901; April 29, 1905; July 28, 1910; December 28, 1939; May 29, 1989.
Toronto Daily Star, June 26, 27, 28, 1907; July 2, 4, 5, 6, 8, 1907.
Toronto Evening Telegram, June 26, 1907.

Other

Christy Mathewson game-by-game stat sheets from 1900 to 1902 compiled by Information Concepts, Inc. On file at National Baseball Library, Cooperstown, New York.

Christy Mathewson game-by-game stat sheets from 1903 to 1916 maintained by the National League Statisticians. On file at National Baseball Library, Cooperstown, New York.

Index

Abbaticchio, Ed 94
Abbott, Fred 89
Adams, Babe 206, 234, 253, 272, 279, 282
Aitken, Harry 266
Alexander, Grover Cleveland 1, 180, 282, 283, 291
Altizer, David 206
American League: founding of 17, 18, 31
Ames, Leon 67, 76, 79, 81, 90–92, 103–104, 111, 118, 123–124, 126, 133, 152, 159, 161–162, 171, 178, 184, 189, 194, 199, 217, 220–221, 227, 229, 233, 244, 246
Anderson, Fred 295, 299
Anson, Adrian 13, 88
Archer, Jimmy 233, 236, 252

Babb, Charlie 63, 67, 75
Baker, Frank 218–220, 259–260
Baker Bowl, collapse of 62
Ball, Phil 282
Barry, Jack 260
Bartley, Bill 65
Bary, Shad 78, 100
baseball: early years 3, 9, 163, 195; betting on 158; filming of 266
"Bat-Ball" 267
Batch, Emil 82
Bates, Johnny 150
Bausewine, George 97–98, 100
Beaumont, Ginger 25, 40, 43, 63, 82, 90
Beck, Fred 206
Becker, Beals 193, 228, 234, 237, 246

Beckley, Jake 27–28, 53
Bedient, Hugh 238–240
Beebe, Fred 132, 179
Beecher, Roy 150
Bender, Chief 105–106, 196, 218, 220, 260–261, 281
Bennett, Pug 115
Benton, Rube 290, 293, 297–298
Bernard, Curt 21
Berra, Yogi 80
Bescher, Bob 263, 273, 282
Bingham, Theodore H. 114, 116, 128, 162
Bonner, Frank 52
Bowerman, Frank 24, 41, 45, 59, 67, 69, 76, 77, 89, 94, 113, 115, 117, 123, 133, 138, 140–141, 147
Brain, Dave 75
Bransfield, Kitty 54
Brennan, Addie 251
Brennan, Bill 220, 255–256, 258
Bresnahan, Roger 26, 43, 46, 54, 56, 60–61, 63, 65–67, 73, 75–77, 80–81, 84, 86, 91–93, 95, 108, 115, 117, 119, 127–128, 131–133, 135, 137, 140, 142, 144–145, 147, 150, 169, 172, 208, 306
Bridwell, Al 100, 139, 147, 153, 161–162, 164, 187, 193, 209–210
Brodie, Steve 41, 46
Brown, Charles 118
Brown, Three Finger 1, 23, 58, 62, 74, 77, 92–93, 95, 109, 118, 122, 132, 134, 139–140, 156–157, 160, 164–165, 167–168, 174, 181, 183, 199, 205, 211–212, 230, 252, 302–303
Brown, William 260

INDEX

Browne, George 46–47, 56, 61, 64–67, 69, 73, 80, 84, 92, 95, 112, 128, 147
Brush, John T. 16, 36–37, 50, 57, 69–70, 82, 84, 90–91, 104, 118, 120, 155, 168, 170, 199, 201–202, 204, 205, 231, 243
Buelow, Charlie 27
Burch, Al 155
Burkett, Jesse 18
Burns, George 244, 247, 253, 273, 277
Bush, Joe 260–261
Byron, Bill 253–254

Camnitz, Jack 141, 151, 233
Camp, Walter 6, 148
Campbell, Billy 179
Cannell, Rip 94
Casey, Max 272
Carrick, Bill 14, 18
Carrigan, Bill 293
Casey, Doc 102
Chadwick, Henry 12, 149
Chance, Frank 74, 77–78, 109, 138, 167, 192, 245, 255
Charles, Raymond 158
Chase, Hal 304–305
Cheney, Larry 272, 278
Chesbro, Jack 18, 27, 40, 43, 46, 51, 76, 83, 179
Clade, Fred 83
Clarke, Fred 43, 59, 90, 115, 196, 232
Clymer, Otis 96
Coakley, Andy 105–106, 135, 137–138, 151, 159
Cobb, Ty 214, 218, 226, 233, 284, 286, 306–307
Colgan, Harry 27
Collins, Eddie 72, 179, 218, 259–261
Collins, Jimmy 18
Comiskey, Charles 225
Conlon, Jocko 143
Connolly, Joe 247
Conway, John 136
Coogan, Mrs. Harriet G. 205
Coombs, Jack 196, 217–218, 281, 287, 290

Corcoran, Tommy 41, 97, 100, 127, 132, 137
Corridon, Frank 197
Covelesky, Harry 167
Crandall, Otis 148, 151, 154, 156, 158, 166, 173–175, 177, 180, 184, 187, 194, 198, 210, 214–216, 220–221, 226, 231, 235–236
Cravath, Gavvy 246
Crawford, Sam 3, 9, 18
Creamer, Dr. Joseph 178
Criger, Lou 83
Cronin, Jack 43, 67, 78
Cross, Lave 14, 106
Cusack, Steve 172
Cutshaw, George 283, 300

Dahlen, Bill 14, 21, 30, 67, 70, 75–76, 80, 84, 88, 91–92, 95, 101–102, 105, 109, 112, 115, 127, 131, 139, 147
Dale, Gene 287
Daly, Tom 14, 30
Daubert, Jake 214
Davis, George 11–13, 15–16, 21, 27–29, 33, 57
Davis, Harry 218
Davis, Lefty 135
Day, John 13
Delahanty, Ed 18, 57
Delahanty, Jim 39, 81
Delahanty, Joe 153, 177
Demaree, Al 237, 244, 253, 259, 261, 272, 275, 278, 280, 282, 287
Denzer, Roger 24, 29
Derrick, Ernest 227
Devlin, Art 67, 69–70, 73–74, 88, 92, 98, 100, 113, 115, 117, 120, 138, 144–145, 150–151, 153, 187, 189, 306
Devore, Josh 186, 201, 206, 210, 218, 239, 241, 244
Dexter, Charlie 21
Dieu, Blanche 200
DiMaggio, Joe 271
Dineen, Bill 30, 34, 83
Disabled List (DL) 288
Doak, Bill 276
Doheny, Ed 13, 15, 59

Index   361

Dolan, Cozy 30, 117, 278
Donlin, Mike 73, 79–80, 84, 86, 92,
   95, 101, 104–105, 108, 113, 124,
   126–127, 148, 150, 159–160, 163,
   170, 268
Donnelly, Ed 234
Donovan, Patsy 114, 149
Donovan, Wild Bill 18, 35
Dooin, Red 246, 256
Doolan, Mickey 206, 246
Dougherty, Patsy 83
Douglas, Phil 278
Dovey, George 175
Downey, Tom 174, 225
Doyle, Jack 12, 15–16, 18, 26–27,
   40–41
Doyle, Larry 125, 127, 138, 141, 144,
   150, 153, 157, 174, 177, 180,
   183–184, 187, 190, 193, 199, 201,
   209–210, 213–214, 216, 221, 225,
   231, 234, 239, 241, 244, 250, 263,
   265, 272, 280, 282, 285, 301,
   306–307
Dreyfuss, Barney 36, 59, 90–91, 98,
   169, 201
Drucke, Louis 187, 192–193, 200
Duffy, Hugh 31
Duggleby, Bill 60, 101, 123
Dunleavy, Jack 65
Dunn, Jack 61, 75
Durocher, Leo 143
Dwyer, John 30

Eason, Mal 95, 114, 257, 283
Ebbets, Charlie 16, 36, 111, 114, 155,
   299–300
Ebbets, Mrs. Charles H. 52
Egan, Dick 172, 196
Elberfeld, Norman 57, 155
Eller, Horace 304
Elliot, Claude 95–96
Emslie, Bob 71–72, 98, 102, 115,
   120, 163–164
Engle, Clyde 240
Evans, Billy 143
Evans, Roy 40
Evers, Johnny 74, 102, 109, 163–164,
   228, 237, 255
Ewing, Buck 13

Factoryville, Pa. 2, 4–6, 25, 35, 110,
   307, 309
Farrell, Duke 14
Farrell, Frank 202, 204
Farrell, John 65
Faust, Charles "Victory" 203, 213,
   215, 217–218, 221
Federal League 249, 263, 269–270,
   276, 281–284, 288–289, 293, 295
Ferguson, George 114, 121, 124, 133,
   140, 145, 147
Fisher, Bill 245
Fitzpatrick, Ed 287
Flaherty, Patsy 92
Fletcher, Art 189, 200, 209, 219,
   231, 234, 237, 253, 260, 266, 271,
   274, 285, 287, 398–300
Flick, Elmer 18
Flood, Timothy 136
Fogel, Horace 37, 41, 46
Forbes, John 175–176
Foster, John B. 243, 263
Foxen, Bill 155
Fraser, Chick 53, 114, 145
Freedman, Andrew 11–13, 16–17, 22,
   26, 33, 36–37, 41–43, 88, 243
Fromme, Art 169, 234, 236, 244,
   253–254, 266, 268–270
Fuchs, Emil 306
Fullerton, Hugh 237–238, 242,
   259–260
Fultz, David 235, 259

Gaffney, James E. 284
Ganzel, John 18, 135
Garner, Larry 241
Garvin, Ned 11, 59
Gaynor, William J. 75, 89
George, Thomas Edward 292
Gibson, George 98, 181
Gilbert, Billy 51, 54, 61, 63, 67, 73,
   76, 78, 88–89, 92, 95, 115, 117
Gleason, Kid 18
Gordon, Joseph 51, 58
Gowdy, Henry 210, 275, 297
Grady, Mike 118
Graham, George 225
Grant, Eddie 258, 266
Gremminger, Ed 60

362   INDEX

Griffith, Clark 51, 155
Groh, Heinie 229, 244, 298, 304
Gwynn, Tony 72

Hahn, Frank 56
Hanlon, Ned 20, 36–37, 114
Hannifin, Jack 143
Harley, Dick 88
Harmon, Bob 208, 247, 253
Harper, Jack 24, 73, 82
Hart, Burt 31
Hart, Jim 36, 90–91
Hartley, Grover 263
Haskell, John 31–32
Hawley, Pink 18
Hempstead, Harry N. 243, 263, 300
Hermann, August 259
Herrmann, Garry 50
Herzog, Charles 148, 201, 210, 213, 219, 236–237, 241, 250, 263–264, 274, 300, 302
Heydler, John 172–173, 178, 305
Hickman, Piano Legs 26, 33
Hinchman, Bill 293
Hite, Mabel 127, 170
Hoey, Fred 13
Hofman, Solly 163–164
Holliday, James 56
Honesdale 7, 308
Hooper, Harry 238, 241
Houck, Byron 260
Howard, Del 133
Huggins, Miller 135, 282
Hughes, Tom 34
Hulbert, William A. 31
Humphries, Joe 120, 157
Hunter, Herbert 263
Hurst, Tim 64, 179–180
Hyatt, Ham 181, 247

Irwin, Arthur 12

Jackitsch, Frank 75
Jackson, Jim 38
Jacobson, Baby Doll 263

Johnson, Ban 17–18, 31–32, 42, 50, 52, 58, 72, 84, 96, 158, 179–180, 191, 225–226, 259, 270
Johnson, Chief 255
Johnson, Harry 270
Johnson, Walter 1, 10, 257, 306–307
Johnston, Doc 288, 297
Johnstone, Jim 56, 80, 90, 94, 96, 100, 120, 140, 214
Jones, Davy 3
Jones, Oscar 69, 75
Jordan, Dutch 61
Joyce, Bill 13
Joyce, Mike 39

Karger, Ed 141, 169
Katoll, John 32
Kauff, Benny 283–284, 295, 297, 299
Keefe, Tim 229
Keeler, Wee Willie 18, 30, 51, 189
Kelley, Joe 14, 30, 43, 53, 56, 79, 97, 118
Kellog, Nathaniel 7
Keystone Academy (Junior College) 4, 19, 23, 38
Killifer, Wade 300
Kinsella, Dick 144, 286
Kitson, Frank 29
Kleinow, Red 83
Klem, Bill 96, 98–99, 128, 139, 144, 178, 208, 224, 250, 279
Kling, Johnny 140, 252
Knowles, Fred 42, 83, 137, 157
Kovetchy, Ed 252

Lajoie, Nap 18
Landis, Kenesaw 99, 139, 230, 282–283
Latham, Arlie 181
Lauder, Bill 40, 47–48, 54
Lavender, Jimmy 232, 272, 299
Leach, Tommy 40, 63, 77, 82, 90, 194, 196, 213, 228
Leever, Sam 46, 63, 92, 115
Leifield, Al 112, 134, 196, 248
Lewis, George "Duffy" 238, 241

Lief, Fred 239, 305–306
Lobert, Hans 263, 282
Lopes, Dave 72
Lowe, Bobby 20
Lundgren, Carl 55, 102, 137, 145
Lush, John 113, 172
Lynch, Mike 90, 103, 141
Lynch, Thomas J. 205, 208, 251, 256

McBride, Algie 18, 28
McCarty, Lew 266, 301
McCormick, Harry 67, 70, 79, 148, 156, 163, 171, 186, 155
McElveen, Pryor 189
McFarland, Chappie 115
McGann, Dan 43, 56, 63, 67, 69–70, 72, 81, 84, 88–89, 91, 95, 99, 101, 113, 115, 127, 131, 133, 135, 138–139, 143–145, 147
McGinnity, Joe 14, 18, 43–45, 49, 53, 57–64, 66–67, 69, 71–74, 76–79, 82, 84, 88, 90–93, 95, 100–101, 104, 106, 110, 112, 114–115, 123, 125, 127, 132–133, 136, 139, 142, 145, 149, 152, 154, 156, 158, 160–161, 163–164, 170, 174, 177
McGlynn, Ulysses 134
McGraw, Blanche 44, 51, 66, 107, 147, 186, 220, 257, 293, 306–307
McGraw, John 10, 13, 15, 18–20, 33, 37, 42–43, 45–47, 50–51, 54–55, 59–63, 65–67, 69–71, 73–75, 78, 80–82, 84–86, 88–93, 95–96, 98, 100, 103–122, 126–128, 132–135, 137–139, 144–145, 147–149, 151–158, 161–162, 164, 166, 168–171, 173–175, 177, 181–182, 184, 186, 188–195, 201, 203, 205, 207, 208, 210, 212, 214–222, 224–225, 227–229, 232–239, 243–244, 246, 248, 250–266, 268–271, 273–279, 281–282, 284–302, 304–307
McInnis, John "Stuffy" 260
McIntire, Harry 113, 124, 150
Mack, Connie 3, 25, 104–106, 113, 139, 183, 196, 217–218, 220, 244, 258–259, 261, 264, 280–281

McKechnie, Bill 295, 300–301
McLean, Larry 135, 258, 286
MacMillan, Alexander 267
McQuillan, George 155, 184, 195
Magee, Sherwood 180, 188, 195, 232, 287
Mahon, John K. 42
Malarkey, Bill 150, 154
Maloney, Billy 95, 155
Mamaux, Al 290
Mannassau, Al 31
Mantle, Mickey 203
Maris, Roger 203
Marquard, Rube 3, 155, 165–166, 173, 175, 184–185, 198, 201, 203, 205, 207–209, 211–221, 223, 225–230, 233–235, 237, 239–241, 244, 253, 258–259, 261, 264, 272, 276, 280–282, 291, 293, 295
Marsans, Armendo 210, 232
Marshall, Doc 109, 115, 118
Mathewson, Christy: Bucknell 3, 4, 6, 7, 13, 20, 23, 87, 99, 109, 129, 148, 170, 175, 307; childhood of 2, 4, 5; death of 307; family of 4, 6, 10, 87, 125–126, 131, 216, 219–220, 262, 304, 307; Hall of Fame 8, 16, 307; health of 35, 108–114, 116, 119, 124, 126, 128, 134, 166, 177, 187, 198, 276, 281, 296, 304–307; as idol 2, 3, 10, 35, 37–38, 48, 51, 53, 107, 110, 126, 170, 185, 200, 257, 285, 294, 307; lifestyle of 3, 4, 107, 215–216, 262, 271; as manager 301–304; in military 187, 304–305; nickname of 6; in praise of 1, 3, 4, 6, 14, 20–22, 25–26, 37–38, 60–61, 79, 93–94, 100, 106, 109, 116, 125, 128, 152, 161, 177, 180, 182, 190–191, 197–198, 207, 211–212, 230–232, 246, 260, 271, 274, 276, 285, 291, 293, 297–298, 301, 309; quitting baseball 183; quotes by 119, 154, 157, 164, 167–168, 173, 188, 203, 215, 226, 241, 252, 277, 288, 293, 301, 304, 306–307; salary of 7, 48, 263; semiprofessional career 6, 7, 9; testimonial for 306; trade of 296, 300–301; on umpires 113, 239, 288; World Series 2, 84–85

(1904), 104–107 (1905), 218–220 (1911), 237–242 (1912), 259–262 (1913); as writer 11, 80, 218–219, 226, 259
Mathewson, Henry 125–126, 131, 304
Maul, Al 33
Mayer, Erskine 269
Mercer, George 14, 16, 18
Merkle, Fred 127, 144, 148, 163–165, 178–179, 186, 189, 193, 196, 201, 206–207, 210, 214, 220, 222, 232, 234, 236, 240–242, 253, 255, 259–260, 266, 270, 285, 297, 299, 301
Mertes, Sam 57, 66–67, 73, 77, 79–80, 84, 88, 92, 95–97, 104, 109, 115, 118
Meyers, Chief 1, 3, 26, 169, 173, 182, 187, 190, 194, 202, 206, 218–219, 222–223, 241, 244, 246, 253, 256–258, 260, 266, 268–269, 271, 273–274, 279–281, 286, 295
Miller, John 180, 268
Miller, Margaret 256–257
Miller, Roscoe 56, 62, 73
Miller, Ward 228, 252
Milligan, Billy 70–71
Mitchell, Clarence 298
Mollwitz, Fritz 303
Moore, Earl 180
Moran, August 53, 56, 63
Moran, Pat 304
Moren, Lew 133, 142
Morgan, Harry 196
Moser, Walter 124
Mowrey, Mike 300
Murphy, Danny 106
Murphy, Frank 33
Murphy, Thomas J. 51
Murray, Red 132, 169, 180, 184, 187, 192, 201, 210, 222, 232, 234, 240–241, 244, 258, 268, 306

Nash, Billy 22
National Agreement 50–51
Neale, Earle 304–305
Nealon, Jim 115
Needham, Tom 81, 147, 150

Niagara Movement 122
Nichols, Kid 29–32
Niehoff, Bert 270, 287
Norfolk Club 7, 9, 16

O'Brien, Buck 238
O'Connor, Jack 27
O'Day, Hank 20–21, 28, 37, 63, 102, 106, 113, 115, 163–164
Odwell, Fred 100
O'Hagen, Hal 43
O'Hara, Bill 170
O'Keefe, Arthur J. 111, 113
O'Laughlin, Silk 239
O'Rourke, Jim 82
O'Toole, Marty 232, 276–278
Overall, Orval 91, 100, 111, 195

Padden, Dick 24
Parent, Fred 83
Paskert, George 209
Pastorius, Jim 142, 143
Pattee, Harry 155
Peitz, Heinie 73
Perdue, Hub 223
Perritt, Bill 282, 291, 299–300, 305
Pfeffer, Jeff 117, 123
Pfiester, Jack 109, 140, 163, 167
Phelps, Ed 97
Phillippe, Deacon 40, 46, 100, 103, 249
Phillips, Bill 40
Pittinger, Togie 101
Plank, Eddie 1, 6, 104–105, 131, 196, 218, 260–261, 281
Player's Fraternity 235, 259
Polo Grounds: fire at 201; man killed at 168; new construction at 205–206, 209; renovation of 159, 171
Powell, Jack 22
Pulliam, Harry 36, 50, 52–54, 57–58, 88–91, 96, 98, 120–121, 143–144, 164, 173, 175, 178

Quigley, Ernie 284

Ragan, Pat 235, 285
Rariden, Bill 295, 299–300, 305
Raymond, Arthur "Bugs" 169, 174–177, 181, 184, 186, 188, 191–195, 202–203, 206–208
Reach, Alfred J. 36
Regan, Mike 304–305
Reidy, Bill 64
Reisner, The Rev. Christian 236–237
Reulbach, Ed 99, 109, 138, 179, 182, 257
Richie, Lew 248
Rigler, Charlie 131, 155, 174
Ring, Jimmy 305
Ritchey, Claude 98
Ritter, Hank 290, 292
Rixey, Eppa 248
Robertson, Dave 274
Robinson, Hank 231
Robinson, Jack 47
Robinson, Wilbert 173, 201, 221, 261, 264, 281, 291, 295
Robison, Frank 36
Robison, Stanley 169, 197
Roth, Frank 172
Roush, Edd 295, 300–301, 304
Rowan, Jack 204
Rucker, Nap 10, 161, 245
Rusie, Amos 10, 12, 16, 37, 177
Ruth, Babe 2, 99, 271, 306–307

Saier, Vic 228, 233, 274
Sallee, Harry 157–158, 267, 269, 280, 301
San Francisco earthquake (1906) 110–111, 115
Schaefer, Herman "Germany" 295–296
Schauer, Rube 286, 292, 300
Schlei, George 169–170, 182–183
Schmidt, Henry 61
Schneider, Pete 304
Schulte, Frank 109, 285
Schupp, Ferdie 299
Scott, Dick 27

Seaton, Tom 235
Sebring, Harry 79
Selbach, Kip 21, 24, 30
Seymour, Cy 43, 97, 110, 118–120, 123, 134, 138, 149, 151, 159–161, 186
Shafer, Art 231
Shannon, Spike 109, 118, 121, 131, 134, 149, 152–153, 156
Shay, Danny 75, 103, 118, 139
Sheckard, Jimmy 14, 30, 48, 125, 133, 140
Sheridan, John F. 58, 106
Shugart, Frank 32
Sinclair, Harry 295
Slagle, Jimmy 56, 77, 102, 137
Smith, Aleck 20, 115
Smith, Charlie 143
Smith, George 41–43, 46, 48
Smith, Heinie 15
Smith, John "Phenomenal" 7
Smith, Lonnie 72
Smith, Red 275, 297
Smith, Wally 216
Snodgrass, Fred 1, 153, 160, 186, 191, 201, 210, 214, 234, 237, 241–242, 244, 248, 250, 252, 258, 260, 262, 264, 266, 268, 274, 277, 280–281, 290
Soden, Arthur H. 36, 90–91
Spade, Bob 178, 183
Spahn, Warren 248
Spalding, Albert 36
Sparks, Tom "Tully" 41, 76, 123, 150
Speaker, Tris 238, 241
Stahl, Jake 241
Stallings, George 264, 298
Steinbrenner, Gene 224
Steinbrenner, George 13, 16
Steinfeldt, Harry 53, 59, 100, 109, 119
Stengel, Casey 245, 266, 271, 283, 299–300
Stevens, Harry 82, 266
Stock, Milton 264, 266, 270, 274, 282
Strang, Sammy 18, 26, 28, 30, 86, 96, 99, 115, 117, 120–121, 131, 145
Stricklett, Elmer 131
Stroebel, Allie 117

Stroud, Ralph 285–286
suffragettes 284–285
Suggs, George 190
Sunday baseball 4, 69–70, 72–73, 75, 89, 91, 111, 113–114, 116–117
Sutthoff, Jack 95
Sweeney, Bill 247
syndicate baseball 36

Tannehill, Jesse 40, 45–46
Taunton Club 6–7, 11
Taylor, Jack 28, 39, 43, 46, 61, 67
Taylor, Luther "Dummy" 18–20, 26, 33, 40, 45, 54, 62–63, 65, 71–74, 76, 81, 84, 90–92, 94, 96, 100, 102, 104, 113, 116, 133–134, 140, 142, 154, 157, 160–161, 170, 174
Temple Cup 11
Tener, John K. 225, 284
Tenney, Fred 42, 52, 143, 147, 149–151, 162, 187, 306
Tesreau, Jeff 221, 225, 229, 231, 235–236, 239, 241, 244, 250, 253, 261, 268, 270, 277, 280, 285, 287–288, 290–291, 297–298
Thielman, Henry 47
Thomas, Roy 20
Thorpe, Jim 243–244, 248, 256–257, 268
Tinker, Joe 74, 109, 112, 119, 122, 157, 164, 217, 232, 237, 255
Titanic 224
Toney, Fred 304
Tooley, Bert 214
Twelve-Club League 96–97
Tyler, George 247, 256, 275, 277, 296

umpires 3, 21–22, 27–28, 31–32, 52, 56, 58, 79–80, 97–99, 120, 128, 134–136, 143, 163–164, 172, 179–180, 197, 205, 208, 253–256, 279, 284

Van Haltren, George 21, 24–25, 33, 53–54, 61

Van Zandt, Ike 30, 33
Von der Ahe, Chris 108

Wadell, Rube 1, 25–26, 105, 139
Wagner, Honus 14, 39, 59, 63, 82, 90, 97–98, 103, 112, 115, 121, 159, 181, 213, 215, 232–234, 254–255, 269, 288
Wallace, Bobby 18
Walsh, Ed 1
Wambsganss, Bill 298
Ward, John Montgomery 11–12, 88
Ward, Robert B. 270, 289
Warner, John 22, 52, 54, 59, 61, 65, 67, 82
Watkins, Henry 12
Weeghman, Charles 282
Weimer, Jake 56, 65, 72, 77
Western League 17, 31, 52
Whalen, John 229
Wheat, Zack 189, 254, 265, 283, 287, 300
Wheeler, John 226
Wicker, Bob 74, 118, 120, 122
Wiggins, Alan 72
Williams, Cy 289
Williams, Walt 60
Willis, Vic 60, 101, 153, 158, 163, 178
Wilson, Art 212, 229, 237
Wilson, Chief 269
Wilson, Owen 249
Wiltse, George "Hooks" 67, 70, 75–76, 79, 81, 84, 88, 90, 94, 104, 112–113, 117, 120–121, 123, 131–135, 139–140, 150, 152, 154–156, 158, 160–161, 163–164, 167, 173, 175, 181, 184, 188, 190, 211–216, 220–221, 229, 234, 250, 254, 260, 276, 306
Wingo, Ivy 269
Wood, Joe "Smokey" 238–240
world tour (1913) 262

Yeager, George 38
Yerkes, Steve 241

Young, Cy 1, 18, 89, 214
Young, Irv 89, 102, 133, 142, 150, 155
Young, Nick 27, 36

Zimmer, Charlie 73, 78
Zimmer, Chief 22
Zimmerman, Heine 262, 301
Zmich, Ed 194

www.ingramcontent.com/pod-product-compliance
Ingram Content Group UK Ltd.
Pitfield, Milton Keynes, MK11 3LW, UK
UKHW041921140426
5217IPUK00014B/262